Indigenous Knowledge and the Environment in Africa and North America

Ohio University Press Series in Ecology and History
James L. A. Webb, Jr., Series Editor

Conrad Totman
The Green Archipelago: Forestry in Preindustrial Japan

Timo Myllyntaus and Mikko Saikku, eds.
Encountering the Past in Nature: Essays in Environmental History

James L. A. Webb, Jr.
Tropical Pioneers: Human Agency and Ecological Change in the Highlands of Sri Lanka, 1800–1900

Stephen Dovers, Ruth Edgecombe, and Bill Guest, eds.
South Africa's Environmental History: Cases and Comparisons

David M. Anderson
Eroding the Commons: The Politics of Ecology in Baringo, Kenya, 1890s–1963

William Beinart and JoAnn McGregor, eds.
Social History and African Environments

Michael L. Lewis
Inventing Global Ecology: Tracking the Biodiversity Ideal in India, 1947–1997

Christopher A. Conte
Highland Sanctuary: Environmental History in Tanzania's Usambara Mountains

Kate B. Showers
Imperial Gullies: Soil Erosion and Conservation in Lesotho

Franz-Josef Brüggemeier, Mark Cioc, and Thomas Zeller, eds.
How Green Were the Nazis? Nature, Environment, and Nation in the Third Reich

Peter Thorsheim
Inventing Pollution: Coal, Smoke, and Culture in Britain since 1800

Joseph Morgan Hodge
Triumph of the Expert:
Agrarian Doctrines of Development and the Legacies of British Colonialism

Diana K. Davis
Resurrecting the Granary of Rome:
Environmental History and French Colonial Expansion in North Africa

Thaddeus Sunseri
Wielding the Ax: State Forestry and Social Conflict in Tanzania, 1820–2000

Mark Cioc
The Game of Conservation:
International Treaties to Protect the World's Migratory Animals, 1900–1946

Karen Brown and Daniel Gilfoyle, eds.
Healing the Herds: Disease, Livestock Economies, and the Globalization of Veterinary Medicine

Marco Armiero and Marcus Hall, eds.
Nature and History in Modern Italy

Karen Brown
Mad Dogs and Meerkats: A History of Resurgent Rabies in Southern Africa

Diana K. Davis and Edmund Burke III, eds.
Environmental Imaginaries of the Middle East and North Africa

David Gordon and Shepard Krech III, eds.
Indigenous Knowledge and the Environment in Africa and North America

Indigenous Knowledge

*and the Environment in
Africa and North America*

Edited by
David Gordon and Shepard Krech III

OHIO UNIVERSITY PRESS
ATHENS

Ohio University Press, Athens, Ohio 45701
ohioswallow.com
© 2012 by Ohio University Press
All rights reserved

To obtain permission to quote, reprint, or otherwise reproduce or distribute material from
Ohio University Press publications, please contact our rights and permissions department
at (740) 593-1154 or (740) 593-4536 (fax).

Printed in the United States of America
Ohio University Press books are printed on acid-free paper.∞ ™

First paperback printing in 2014
ISBN 978-0-8214-2079-9

Library of Congress Cataloging-in-Publication Data

Indigenous knowledge and the environment in Africa and North America /
  edited by David M. Gordon and Shepard Krech III.
    p. cm.
  Includes bibliographical references and index.
  ISBN 978-0-8214-1996-0 (hc : alk. paper)—ISBN 978-0-8214-4411-5 (electronic)
  1. Indigenous peoples—Ecology—Africa. 2. Traditional ecological knowledge—
Africa. 3. Indigenous peoples—Ecology—North America. 4. Traditional ecological
knowledge—North America. I. Gordon, David M., 1970– II. Krech, Shepard, 1944–
GF701.I64 2012
304.2096—dc23   2011040641

Contents

Acknowledgments vii

Introduction
Indigenous Knowledge and the Environment
DAVID M. GORDON AND SHEPARD KRECH III 1

PART 1: MIDDLE GROUND

Chapter 1. Looking Like a White Man
Geopolitical Strategies of the Iowa Indians during American Incorporation
DAVID BERNSTEIN 27

Chapter 2. On Biomedicine, Transfers of Knowledge, and Malaria Treatments in Eastern North America and Tropical Africa
JAMES L. A. WEBB, JR. 53

Chapter 3. Indigenous Ethnoornithology in the American South
SHEPARD KRECH III 69

Chapter 4. Nation-Building Knowledge
Dutch Indigenous Knowledge and the Invention of White South Africanism, 1890–1909
LANCE VAN SITTERT 94

PART 2: CONFLICT

Chapter 5. Locust Invasions and Tensions over Environmental and Bodily Health in the Colonial Transkei
JACOB TROPP 113

Chapter 6. Navajos, New Dealers, and the Metaphysics of Nature
MARSHA WEISIGER 129

Chapter 7. Cherokee Medicine and the 1824 Smallpox Epidemic
PAUL KELTON 151

PART 3: ENVIRONMENTAL RELIGION

Chapter 8. Spirit of the Salmon
Native Religion, Rights, and Resource Use in the Columbia River Basin
ANDREW H. FISHER 173

Chapter 9. Indigenous Spirits: Ancestral Power in a South-Central African Kingdom
DAVID M. GORDON 196

Chapter 10. Recruiting Nature
Snakes, Serpents, and Social Movements in East Africa and North America
PARKER SHIPTON 216

PART 4: RESOURCE RIGHTS

Chapter 11. Marine Tenure of the Makahs
JOSHUA REID 243

Chapter 12. Reinventing "Traditional" Medicine in Postapartheid South Africa
KAREN FLINT 259

Chapter 13. Dilemmas of "Indigenous Tenure" in South Africa
Traditional Authorities and the Constitutional Challenge to the 2004 Communal Land Rights Act
DERICK FAY 287

Selected Bibliography 307
Contributors 317
Index 319

Acknowledgments

A SUGGESTION from Lance van Sittert inspired the conference "Indigenous Environments: African and North American Environmental Knowledge and Practices Compared," upon which this volume is based. During and after the conference, Lance contributed to the discussion evident in this volume. A grant from the Andrew W. Mellon Foundation made the conference possible, and DeWitt John, Rosemary Armstrong, and Eileen Johnson of the Environmental Studies Program at Bowdoin College helped to facilitate and organize it. Arun Agrawal set the stage for an invigorating exchange of ideas in his keynote address. Numerous scholars who do not appear in this volume presented papers or were discussants at the conference. Elizabeth Green Musselman, Helen Tilley, Scott MacEachern, Susan Tananbaum, William Parenteau, Darren J. Ranco, Brian Hosmer, Coll Thrush, Pekka Hämäläinen, Nancy Jacobs, Robert Gordon, Gwenn Miller, and Michael Sheridan inspired the authors. Matthew Klingle and Connie Chiang deserve special mention for their collegiality and their dedication to the conference and to this volume. As contributor and series editor, James L. A. Webb, Jr., provided valuable guidance and advice. Special thanks to Gill Berchowitz and Ohio University Press for their commitment to the publication of the volume.

Introduction

Indigenous Knowledge and the Environment

David M. Gordon and Shepard Krech III

"INDIGENOUS KNOWLEDGE" excites and infuriates. One of its leading academic proponents and critics, Michael Dove, argues that its conceptual space has evolved from "innovative tool to hackneyed dichotomy."[1] Historians and anthropologists are uncomfortable at its mention—increasingly so, we sense, at the very moment that others press its birth as a discipline. After all, is not the notion of an impenetrable body of knowledge that belongs to an unchanging group of indigenes a romantic projection of our modern imaginations into the past? As newcomers—transients and immigrants—arrive in any particular place, some conquering, some settling, some exchanging genes and culture, and so on, with people already present, might not the notion of "indigenous" lack historical nuance? At the same time, however, indigenous knowledge holds political appeal and moral valence. It offers an alternative to a Western teleology of civilization (or development), even if the notion is a creation of the encounter between the West and the rest. It offers an alternative to the power-knowledge nexus of Western thought, and yet it introduces its own modalities of power. It unsettles stable categories of knowledge and fields of human agency, such as science and religion, and then tends to confirm the very same epistemological oppositions. This conceptual and political slipperiness is what makes "indigenous knowledge" such an academic apostasy, so essential and so interesting to study.

This book investigates the historical constructions, the political uses, and the epistemological nuances of indigenous knowledges. Rather than claiming that indigenous knowledge stands in some kind of exterior relationship to Western conquest, colonialism, and science, we argue that the emergence of modern indigenous knowledges was intimately related to conquest and colonial rule. This is not to claim that people who are now termed indigenous—or who term themselves indigenous—did not have knowledge prior to contact with Europeans. Quite the opposite: the chapters in this volume detail such precolonial forms of knowledge. But they also show that during times of conquest and colonization, by Europeans and by others, attaching "indigenous" to "knowledge" often was, and often continues to be, a strategy entwined with acts of domination and resistance. Rather than an established body of knowledge that can be owned, written, and transmitted unchanged over time, we regard indigenous knowledges as claims, as strategic maneuvers that challenge the imposition of power and make claims to power. Most of all, we reveal modern indigenous knowledges as palimpsests upon which, if we look carefully and ask the right questions, we can detect the signs of past conflicts that scraped out notions of indigeneity.

We are not the first to notice the conceptual and political inconsistencies of indigenous knowledge. In a seminal article that appeared just as indigenous knowledge became the catchphrase of environmental and developmental policy-makers and activists, Arun Agrawal pointed to the fallacious oppositions that scholars and activists invoke between "Western science" and indigenous knowledge. Agrawal argued that the tendencies to try to "preserve" indigenous knowledges *ex situ* have not confronted the political and economic processes that marginalize people termed "indigenous."[2] Others, including Dove, Roy Ellen, and Paul Sillitoe, have followed Agrawal with significant contributions to the debate that we join in this collection.[3]

This book emerged from the conference "Indigenous Environments: African and North American Environmental Knowledge and Practices Compared," held at Bowdoin College on April 3–5, 2008, and supported by the Mellon Foundation. Both the conference and this volume were premised on the belief that in juxtaposing scholarship on two continents, a vision clarifying still-pressing predicaments of the concept of indigenous knowledge would emerge.[4] In its expansive and comparative scope, this work is related to several recent conferences and volumes focused on traditional environmental knowledge, indigenous knowledge, or natural knowledges.[5] To this literature, this volume adds a sustained historical focus that supports its contention and contribution: the notion and character of modern indigenous knowledges emerged from the contested terrains of conquest and colonialism. Since then, those on the periphery of postcolonial and neocolonial centers of power have resurrected and sustained indigenous knowledges in an effort to exert greater control over their lives and reverse ongoing processes of marginalization.

The cases in this volume make possible comparison of separate historical and colonial experiences on two continents; separate encounters and outcomes in meetings of indigenous and nonindigenous people and their environmental knowledges. The experiences in North America alone seem remarkably diverse, from the Southeast (a cluster of cases) and the Great Lakes to the Southwest and the Pacific Northwest. European settlers and, in the Southeast, African slaves colonized this vast territory over a period of several centuries. The majority of contributions from Africa come from southern Africa, an area in itself almost as diverse as North America, first settled by Khoe and San peoples, then colonized by various Bantu-speaking groups, and approximately one thousand years later by settlers from European nations.

In an effort to ensure that this volume provides a global perspective to ongoing discussions over indigenous knowledge in environmental history, the book is divided into four sections based on common themes. The remainder of this introduction considers some of the central debates concerning indigenous knowledge and the environment addressed by all the papers to varying degrees, from who counts as an indigenous person, and knowledge as local or global, to knowledge and power, and indigenous knowledge in environmental history. We then offer brief introductions to each of the four sections of the book, which include comparative insights drawn from the individual essays.

Who Is an Indigenous Person?

The term "indigenous" has evolved without much consideration of what it means.[6] As in biological description, it implies a timeless connection to the land, even though biologists prefer the term "endemic" over "indigenous." Yet if notions of endemicity and indigeneity are controversial in biological discourse, they are even more fraught in human history.[7] Societies and polities across Africa and North America have grown from waves of conquerors and settlers, with the arrival of Europeans and Asians in Africa and Europeans and Africans in the Americas over the last several centuries only the last of many, preceded and accompanied on each continent by expansions of people indigenous to the continent although foreign to territories into which they moved. Each new wave of immigration, each new conquest or settlement, produced notions of indigeneity that became more complicated through time.[8]

On the surface, these complications seem avoidable. Does *indigenous* not mean native to or born in a particular place, prior to the arrival of others whose ancestral native lands rest elsewhere (and whose indigeneity, therefore, resides in another place)?[9] Would definition and practice be so straightforward. In its use, the word *indigenous* (or *indigeneity*) reveals, as Roy Ellen and Holly Harris have suggested, a minefield.[10] First, *indigenous* is just one of a range of alternatives for what is at or near its heart—native to or born in—including native, autochthonous, and aboriginal. Each of these concepts and labels has specific derivation and precise if overlapping meanings. Furthermore, when it comes to a modifier for the knowledge of people who assert or are granted indigeneity, other terms rise as alternatives, including "tribal," "local," "traditional," and "folk."[11] None are ideal; indeed, all have strikes against them.[12] We write conscious of these debates and of the realization that for many, including people themselves to whom it is applied, "indigenous" is preferred over other alternatives—and that the term is not going to go away.

That "indigenous" is not simply going to vanish is surely due in large measure to the recent history of indigenous peoples in the political programs of the United Nations, the World Bank, nongovernmental organizations, and certain nation-states. Applying "indigenous" to a particular people arguably has as much to do with political relationships as with any inherent characteristics shared with other so-called indigenous peoples. It often depends on what the state defines as indigenous. African states vigorously contest the idea that any one ethnic group is more indigenous than another. In Africa, groups began to proclaim their indigenous status only after building alliances with an international community of indigenous peoples.[13] In the Russian Federation, the state recognizes as indigenous only one-third of arguably indigenous people—the groups with populations under fifty thousand.[14] In the United States, federal recognition of tribal status is critical to the formally sanctioned definition of indigeneity. Being indigenous thus depends on what the nation-state or the international community grants to those with that status. Indigeneity can also be an expression of opposition to the dominant political authority; a relational or structural claim of exploitation and domination rather than an essentialist claim of origins.[15] Globally, "indigenous" has a certain moral charge, a valiant effort to counter the hegemony of outsiders.[16] In this volume, such morality and political instrumentalities are everywhere evident.

Some newcomers—immigrants, colonizers, and settlers—also proclaim indigeneity, however. This is especially true in southern Africa, and several such cases are highlighted in this volume. Lance van Sittert, for instance, demonstrates how a folk system of water divining became a form of indigenous knowledge in early twentieth-century South Africa. David M. Gordon illustrates how Bemba proclamations of indigeneity in the south-central African highlands followed their conquest of the autochthonous Bisa. Sometimes political proclamations attempt to transcend the divide between colonizers and colonized and help in the construction of new nations. For example, in postapartheid South Africa, as Karen Flint points out, indigeneity is asserted as a national asset that can be improved by subjecting African traditional medicines to Western scientific methods and state bureaucracy.[17]

Similar processes unfold elsewhere: in western Japan the inheritors of the preagrarian Jomon period have had greater success in asserting and being seen as indigenous than the arguably autochthonous Ainu.[18] In the North American cases examined in this volume, the line between indigenous and nonindigenous seems more sharply drawn, perhaps because these particular cases focus on environmental knowledge and not, for example, on who gains (or loses, or is denied) formal affiliation with a particular Indian group—a process that would expose the contradictions inherent in "indigenous." These contradictions involve indigenous people attempting to hold the line on whether or not other people claiming indigeneity should gain it, especially where the stakes are high (as with casino revenues).

Despite the instrumental, moral, and ideological qualities of indigeneity, some still insist on viewing it in biological terms. Early twentieth-century racial theories remain inscribed in theories of indigenous belonging. This biological—or "blood"—understanding of indigeneity emerges from legal formulations that insist on proof of belonging. Blood seems to offer such convincing proof. In addition, outside of institutional, state, and legal arrangements, blood kinship models still inspire models of wider corporate group membership. For these reasons, even while this volume—along with a range of scholarship—emphasizes the historical model of the indigenous belonging, the biological blood model of indigenous belonging prevails in quotidian, and even some academic understandings. The notion of "indigenous people" may even "provide ideological ammunition to those who would reorder the world according to blood and soil," as André Béteille points out.[19] Yet, as analyses in this volume and elsewhere make clear, lurking beneath the surface of blood is always power: power, exercised by the state or by the people of indigenous status themselves, to determine that indigeneity depends on descent from an ancestor on a particular historical list; on descent from a man but not a woman or a woman but not a man; on descent from a person free but not from one enslaved; on comportment; on culture—the vexed tradition; on membership in a group of a certain size; or on myriad other historical and cultural factors.

In its emphasis on an unchanging body of knowledge and in its opposition to modernity, indigenous knowledges share a conceptual relationship with "tradition." Like "tradition," "indigenous" implies something ancient, even primordial. In their influential work *The Invention of Tradition*, Eric Hobsbawm and Terence Ranger argue that while tradition disguises itself as unchanging, it is dynamic and invented according to political and ideological exigencies.[20] In their view, tradition is often conservative, involving cultural artifacts that legitimize established elites—thus the need for historians to lay bare its invention. Tradition is also typically modern in its nostalgia for a lost past. The idea of indigenous knowledge has comparable qualities (indeed, indigenous knowledge is often referred to as "traditional environmental knowledge," or TEK). Indigenous knowledges conceal their dynamism under the appearance of a timeless body of knowledge. They share a nostalgia for a culturally particular form of knowledge and an imagined past, which makes them an adept tool to resist ostensibly scientific and universal discourses. (Unlike "traditions," however, indigenous knowledges are often thought to be a tool of the disempowered and dispossessed, rather than of the elite.) Indigenous knowledges invoke their conceptual power by claims of timelessness, even while their ability to respond to contemporary articulations of power demands flexibility. Like tradition, indigenous knowledges have hidden and often repressed histories.

Over time, cultural (including indigenous) knowledge is unevenly produced, unevenly shared, and unevenly distributed. And society is rarely, if ever, insular, tightly bounded, and exclusionary. It rarely remains homogeneous in its membership and composition. What this means is obvious: No assumption should be made that indigenous knowledges are closed to external influence or history, that they do not incorporate or reflect originally nonindigenous conception or perception, or that what one or several people might think or perceive is held universally in that society.

Local and Global Knowledges

The concept of indigenous knowledge applies in the first instance to particular sets of environmental resources that sustained particular peoples. For this reason, we prefer "indigenous knowledges" over "indigenous knowledge." Ongoing pressures—now, global—to standardize such systems of knowledge, during colonialism and currently as part of a worldwide indigenous peoples' rights movement, have attempted to reconcile the very particular forms of indigenous knowledges with universal (or Western) language and epistemologies.

Anthropologists first attempted to standardize indigenous knowledges before the label "indigenous knowledge" was fashionable in cross-cultural categories like primitive religion, animism, kinship terminology, and so on (although the analytical or "etic" source of the categories for knowledge was always recognized). Their goal was to develop an all-embracing, comparative, conceptual, and ostensibly scientific scheme. On their part, Africanist historians, joined by anthropologists, identified generic features of "oral knowledge," often termed "oral tradition," in an attempt to give value to the intellectual products of peoples without writing.[21] More recently, policy-oriented monographs that list features that characterize indigenous knowledges—many of them drawn in opposition to a universal, abstract, written, secular, and Western form of scientific knowledge—transparently view them as (paradoxically generically) local, practical, oral, communal, and spiritual.[22] Rather than providing a definition of indigenous knowledge, which tends to move us further away from the particular natures of indigenous knowledges, the authors in this volume historicize indigenous knowledges and locate their analyses in the contexts that shaped them.

The particular character of indigenous knowledges alongside the vagueness of the notion of indigeneity have led some scholars to call for the replacement of the notion of indigenous knowledge with "local" or "practical" knowledge.[23] The local features of indigenous knowledges are, however, Janus-faced, since indigenous knowledges rely on globalization and cosmopolitanism. The more we learn of the indigenous knowledges of others, the more our own indigenous knowledges are enriched. The discovery of the indigenous knowledge of others led early modern Europeans to appreciate their own indigenous knowledges.[24] Indigenous knowledges were hybrids, the product of many global exchanges. Moreover, the indigenous knowledges of people from one continent could become colonial knowledges on another, as in the case of the risicultural knowledge of enslaved West Africans that informed cultivation practices on South Carolina's and Georgia's lowland rice plantations.[25] In this volume James L. A. Webb, Jr., David Bernstein, and Shepard Krech demonstrate how indigenous knowledges were diffused and appropriated, making the knowledge of others into our knowledge. The local character of indigenous knowledges conceals their cosmopolitan sources and inspirations.

The practical nature of indigenous knowledges is also bedeviled with inconsistencies. James Scott has been the leading proponent of a situated "practical" or commonsense knowledge that he terms "mētis," in opposition to the high modernism of scientific discourse.[26] But identifying indigenous knowledges as practical in the way that "practical" is understood in the West is fallacious. Practical formulations are based within broader cosmologies that gauge their practicality. Surely, Scott is not suggesting that indigenous societies remain—and have always been—focused on fulfilling basic subsistence needs. Isn't knowledge "practical" for religious ends, for example? Scott claims that what matters in floral and faunal classification for indigenous peoples is their "local use and value. . . . The litmus test for mētis is practical success."[27] But what does "practical success" mean? The practical success of indigenous forms of classification was linked to broader theories of the world, sometimes to religious cosmologies, as Krech demonstrates for birds in Native American forms of classification, or Parker Shipton does for snakes and serpents in Africa and the Americas (this volume). If such a definition of practicality is set in the context of particular worldviews and abstractions, it is no more practical than scientific taxonomy.

Knowledge and Power

That knowledge is entwined with power is frequently discussed with reference to Western scientific discourses. Yet indigenous knowledges also have constituted modalities of power. As Bernstein points out in this volume, indigenous knowledges have rarely been scrutinized and deconstructed to reveal their architectures of power—and when taken apart they are sometimes found to embed (and reflect back) the nonindigenous.

In this volume, indigenous knowledges are viewed as both an intervention in power relations and a product of power relations. Revealing the power relationships in which indigenous knowledges are entwined does not necessarily disparage the political utility of indigenous knowledges. Indigenous knowledge–based claims are often oppositional to those in authority and made by those marginalized through the historical and contemporary operations of power in order to leverage their otherwise weak claims to resources. Conversely, however, such claims and their associated traditions can also be appropriated by those in power as a way of authenticating and legitimating themselves in the eyes of the conquered. In Africa, Indirect Rule during colonialism mobilized aspects of indigenous knowledge rather than marginalizing it, as assumed in the conventional academic wisdom.[28] As Derick Fay illustrates for South Africa (this volume), apartheid-era communal tenure arrangements claimed a relationship to indigenous forms of tenure. Indigenous knowledges in this case constituted colonial forms of authority. By contrast, the overtly aggressive and at times genocidal modernism of Euro-American policies toward Native Americans posed a more direct attack on tradition, making tradition itself a more convincing mode of resistance.

Those concerned with the politics of indigenous peoples today should take note of the operations of power in which indigenous knowledges are embedded. Over the last two decades, mechanisms of international intervention by the developed world have increasingly insisted on grassroots approaches to development, which co-opt local players, often representatives of indigenous people, and employ their indigenous knowledges. Conservation biologists have called on indigenous knowledges as a means to propose or mobilize local conservation interventions.[29] Identifying useful and appropriate forms of indigenous knowledge has become a rallying cry for the continued relevance of anthropology in the postcolonial age. Beginning in the 1990s, NGOs and government agencies concerned with economic development and environmental conservation began to publish monographs on indigenous knowledge.[30]

In the minds of well-meaning ecologists, the model of biological conservation became confused with a model of the cultural survival of indigenous peoples, as if they and their knowledge were connected ecological entities, a species threatened with extinction through the eradication of their habitat. Many conservationists then take the imaginative step of linking the degradation of the natural environment and the extinction of biological species to the supposed extinction of indigenous peoples. Such biological-cum-anthropological descriptions resemble anthropology at its early twentieth-century functionalist inception.[31] Ecological and anthropological interdisciplinarity has become a muddle of academic concepts and political agendas.

More insidious than this interdisciplinary muddle, however, is the architecture of power in which such appropriations of indigenous knowledge become entwined. Environmental and development projects that claim to "see like a local" may seem to be an improvement on self-confident, top-down, modernist projects that "see like a state," as Scott puts it.[32] And yet they represent similar dynamics that expose local players to powerful international networks, molding the shape of civil society and the state to international interests and agendas, even when concern for the marginalized through an appreciation of things indigenous is proclaimed. Anthropologists now accompany development economists and agrarian scientists.[33] For years they have been recruited to the ranks of the World Bank to propose and develop programs with aims that include the alleviation of poverty. But what is the real difference in terms of environmental, economic, and political outcomes? Sometimes none at all.[34] In general, strategies of poverty alleviation and conservation inspired by indigenous knowledges are more neoliberal than previous state-oriented strategies. Local economies are exposed to global markets in commodities, international ecotourism and cultural tourism established, and freehold rights in property encouraged. The impact on poverty alleviation has been uneven at best. One undeniable effect is that through greater exposure to market forces, the indigenous becomes commodified and ethnicities incorporated, as Jean and John Comaroff have recently pointed out.[35] In a self-referencing and reinforcing process, the neoliberal order proliferates indigenous knowledges.

Rather than rallying scholars to an appreciation of indigenous knowledges, as so much published scholarship has done, the essays in this book reveal the intricate and intimate ties between knowledge and power. Unlike countless development texts in the recent past, this book calls not to mobilize usable indigenous knowledges but to understand the conditions under which indigenous knowledges came to be identified as a usable category of knowledge that constructed and intervened in a spectrum of power relations.

The Environment

Indigenous knowledge has become a core concept in the environmental history of Africa and the Americas, even as its meaning has become more contested and less clear. In Africanist historiography, the most productive tradition of scholarship on environmental history considers the imposition of European forms of environmental control through forestry science, game management, soil conservation strategies, and hunting and fishing regulations. European environmental management techniques sought to intervene in a self-constructed reality, which environmental historians of Africa refer to as "degradation narratives."[36] Such degradation narratives blamed the alleged disappearance of wilderness, reduction in biodiversity, and depletion of natural resources on African "overexploitation" and "overpopulation." These degradation narratives understated European and colonial agency in environmental change, focusing instead on Malthusian crises inspired by Africans themselves. The major environmental narrative in North America was equally declensionist but in a different fashion: the intrusion of specifically European demands, values, economies, commodification, efficiencies, technologies, power, and insatiable desires set the continent on a course of destruction that veered sharply from a putatively Edenic pre-European arrival state.

Thus, on one continent, the agents of declension initially were seen as indigenous, and on the other, they were understood as exogenous. Yet on both continents the declensionist narratives would ultimately invoke Western science and resource management techniques to counteract environmental change. As many historians point out, such interventions became vehicles for more intrusive forms of colonial or state intervention.[37] In turn, scholars and activists in both Africa and North America would ultimately view indigenous knowledges as forms of resistance to these statist impositions. Nevertheless, scholars assumed that African and Native American indigenous knowledges had different relationships to the environment, in part due to the differing perceptions of environmental change. In North America, where dominant ideas held that Europeans were responsible for environmental degradation, scholars and activists posed Native American indigenous knowledges as ecologically innocent alternatives to European-inspired capitalist transformations. On the other hand, Africanist scholarship, which emphasized African agency in environmental change, focused on African efforts to harness and transform the environment. The differences in emphasis are subtle, not stark. Yet the seminal works of African and North American environmental history, such as William Cronon's *Changes in the Land*, in the North American case, and Robert Harms's *Games Against Nature*, in the African case, illuminate these different approaches.[38] Contributions to this volume also illustrate this historiographic divide.

Recent Africanist and Native Americanist scholarship attempts to move beyond the paradigm of ecological harmony versus ecological destruction by analyzing indigenous knowledges as "changing intellectual tools and knowledge about . . . the environment," as Tamara Giles-Vernick puts it.[39] Those who have taken the challenging and sometimes perilous step in taking seriously the local historical processes that shaped and were shaped by indigenous environmental knowledges have arrived at conclusions that strike some as revisionist and others as disturbing. For example, in North America, Krech's analysis in *The Ecological Indian*—which problematized and historicized the relationship between Indians and natural resources, and concluded that despite evidence being ample for ecological thought, it is scant until recent times for Western-style conservation—produced both robust debate but strong endorsement as "consistent with major reviews of the conservation literature in the ethnographic world."[40] And in the central African context, Giles-Vernick points out that although "some environmental practices . . . do make ecological sense, all of these practices are a porous changing body of knowledge that cannot be uncritically embraced as a fail-safe solution guaranteeing the success of environmental interventions."[41]

The implication is that indigenous knowledges encouraged the exploitation of environmental resources in some cases and were harnessed toward conservation strategies in others. For example, in the case of central African fisheries management, Gordon demonstrates that indigenous knowledges had deleterious ecological consequences.[42] By contrast, in a contribution to the conference upon which this volume was drawn, Michael Sheridan points to the possibilities of sacred groves, generally graveyards of important ancestors, as potential sites for conservation, since they have been free from agriculture, hunting, or the collection of wood fuel.[43] Even in single cases, as Joshua Reid illustrates for Makah marine tenure in this volume, indigenous knowledges developed elements of conservation while at the same time justifying local resource exploitation.

The remainder of this introduction highlights the contributions and the comparative insights of the essays found in each of the four sections of the book: Middle Ground, Conflict, Environmental Religion, and Resource Rights.

Part One: Middle Ground

Recent scholarship has pointed to the colonial origins of many scientific disciplines such as botany, geography, ecology, and zoology—in which collaborations between Europeans and native Africans and Americans, often in the form of informants and hired research associates, figured significantly. So also did a concern for environmental deterioration as well as for conservation arise in the context of the colonial enterprise, as Richard Grove has written. In similar fashion, indigenous knowledges were hybrid forms of knowledge concerned with environmental change. Like many natural sciences, they also emerged through exchanges made possible in what Mary Louise Pratt termed the "contact zones" and Richard White the "middle ground" of the colonial encounter.[44] In colonial Africa and North America, indigenous knowledges changed, adopted new forms, and appropriated other types of knowledge. They incorporated new ideas and adapted to explain and act on environmental changes.

While a number of papers in this book point to these qualities of indigenous knowledges, the papers in this section highlight the permeability of boundaries between indigenous and nonindigenous knowledges such that in time, the provenance of specific ideas becomes difficult to trace. European conquest and colonialism brought together people with distinct ideas of the world and different technical expertise to create new forms of knowledge. Even if the landscapes of power were highly uneven, exchanges between colonized and colonizers produced knowledge. These exchanges occurred not only at the level of culture and expertise, but also at the biological and ecological levels, which in turn inspired quests for knowledge.[45] People sought out ways to deal with new diseases and ways to harness the power of newly domesticated crops and plants.[46]

In this section, James L. A. Webb, Jr., points to the diverse borrowings that constituted malarial therapeutics for Europeans and Native Americans. At the same time, Webb suggests why the exchange of medical knowledge between Europeans and Africans did not occur. In a setting in which people of American Indian, African, and British and other European descent interacted, Shepard Krech explores the possibility of African and European influences on the making of Native American knowledge about birds. In a third contribution in this section, David Bernstein demonstrates with Notchininga's Map, the Iowan illustration that adapted European forms of spatial representation to the art of treaty negotiations, how the inscription and representation of knowledge changed to accommodate new struggles.

Europeans engaged in colonial pursuits also began to recognize their own indigenous knowledges.[47] The final essay in this section considers one case of colonial settlers' developing an indigenous knowledge in an effort to anchor themselves to the land and position themselves in relation to scientific and modernist interventions of a colonial state, a process that occurred in both southern Africa and North America. In southern Africa, such declarations of indigeneity were particularly fraught for Dutch and French settlers who were suspicious of —and sometimes rebelled against—British colonial interference, even while these settlers distinguished themselves from African indigenes (the resemblance to the historical experience of the European settlers of North America is striking). These settlers came to proclaim their indigeneity, calling themselves "Afrikaners," and developing appropriate indigenous knowledges. Lance van Sittert takes up in some detail one example of this settler-created indigenous knowledge, water divining.

Taken together, these four papers demonstrate that the rise of modern European empires led not merely to the spread of European forms of knowledge. Through the settlement of new lands, encounters with native peoples and knowledges, and the spread of diseases, fauna, and flora, there emerged new forms of knowledge that were simultaneously local and global, indigenous and cosmopolitan, and subaltern and elite. These processes also produced conflict, as seen in the next set of papers.

Part Two: Conflict

Whereas colonialism brought different people together, it also involved violent acts of domination, some of which were genocidal in intent, with concomitant acts of resistance and rebellion. The results included very uneven exchanges of knowledge. The colonial "middle ground" was indeed precarious, fomenting misunderstanding in its most benign form and a war zone in its most destructive. Yet conflict also produced new forms of knowledge among colonizers and colonized. Groups defined and redefined themselves in opposition to multiple others. Acts of domination and resistance not only drew upon existing reservoirs of local knowledge but also transformed and shaped them to the exigencies of local struggles.

In this section, the authors point out that opportunities for the appreciation of other forms of knowledge were often cut short due to colonial conflicts. In the case of medicine for the new disease of smallpox, as illustrated by Paul Kelton, the Cherokees innovated a dance but rejected vaccine due to its conflation with the Christian religion, which undermined Cherokee sovereignty. Marsha Weisiger and Jacob Tropp illustrate how scientific and colonial chauvinism inspired alternative worldviews that looked to restore past, harmonious relations with the natural world.

From a Native American perspective, the experience of colonialism was deeply felt and lengthy and involved immense consequences from population relocations, epidemiological catastrophe, violence, the extirpation of important animal resources, and environmental alterations. In Africa, by contrast, a more precarious colonial state spread in the twentieth century. Colonialism was often little more than a rudimentary state apparatus administered by far-flung district commissioners who were supported when necessary by mobile police units. In most places, the colonial period lasted about sixty years. Even in the European settler colonies of southern Africa, from which many examples in this volume are drawn, European-imposed state and legal institutions were weaker than in North America. Besides a brief period of colonial conquest, periods of warfare and violence against Africans were shorter than the sustained periods of violence against Native Americans. Disease had some impact, but far less than in North America. In no case did settlers come close to outnumbering native Africans, and their ability to monopolize violence and ensure continued colonial hegemony remained precarious.

In both cases, however, European colonialism radically disrupted old ways of being. Colonial politics bent preexisting forms of knowledge toward particular and strategic ends. Treaty negotiations between Native Americans and European Americans changed the focus of knowledge from kin and lineage to tribe. Indirect Rule in Africa inspired the codification of indigenous knowledges and generally strengthened the notion that indigenous knowledges belonged to tribes controlled by powerful men termed "chiefs."[48] The reorganization of power and transformation of livelihoods, disrupting old historical patterns, inspired new understandings of the world. This occurred at the same time as Christian missionary evangelism, which explained the world according to a new set of supernatural forces.

Even given its Christian influences, European colonialism claimed to be the harbinger of a progressive secularism rooted in a scientific understanding of the world (even though many would argue it did not live up to these claims). In contrast, indigenous knowledges justified and legitimized themselves as alternate ways of understanding the world. They questioned the modernist scientific thrust of human interventions in the natural world characteristic of colonial thought and practice. Weisiger, for example, demonstrates how Navajo concepts of order and disorder engaged with New Deal scientific regulations.[49] The mobilization of tradition was also evident in parts of Africa most affected by European settlers. In the Eastern Cape, an area that witnessed similar frontier violence to North America, Tropp describes African resistance to colonial environmental intrusions through ostensibly traditional practices that joined bodily health to environmental health. Africans and Native Americans developed indigenous knowledges to preserve access to resources and to defend cultural and religious identities when faced with colonial violence.

Part Three: Environmental Religion

Western assumptions have it that scientific thought was freed from its religious (often imagined to be "closed") moorings during the Enlightenment; in contrast, non-Western thought is still imagined to be mired in such religious understanding of the world. Such representations of the West's "other" pervade writings on the Middle East—and have been criticized there.[50] Globally modern forms of representation, such as museums, tend to construct differences between a scientific modernity and closed traditional indigenous knowledges.[51] They often elide that the secular has its own dogmas (often based in Christian belief) and power relations.[52] The flip side of this "Orientalist" discourse is an "Occidentalism," a criticism of Western science and rationalism and a celebration of its religious or spiritual "other."[53]

Such Occidentalist critiques of Western science have become a standard feature of indigenous knowledges. In the Native American context, activists and even scholars are prone to defend a sort of cultural difference between Western science and native religion. The reasons for the saliency of this romantic opposition in the Native American case probably lies in the experience of traumatic episodes of conquest and colonialism, which have left little option for a corporate sovereignty except through claims of an absolute cultural difference expressed in religious idioms. In North America, the position of the Native American in the American imagination further contributed to an emphasis on environmental religion. It also coincided with activist agendas. Some Western scientists and conservationists seem to be born-again into this spiritual way of appreciating and understanding the natural environment.[54]

The nature of environmental religion proved to be a controversial discussion among contributors to this volume, with lines often (but not exclusively) drawn between scholars of Africa and of Native America. This section on environmental religions represents some of these multiple perspectives. Andrew Fisher argues that Washat ideas of a spiritual figure, a "Creator" of people and nature, was a guiding principle in their negotiations over environmental regulations (similar to the argument presented by Weisiger in part 2 of this volume that Navajo metaphysical concepts contrasted with the scientific worldview of the New Dealers). In parallel fashion, David M. Gordon points to the spiritual dimensions of indigeneity in central Africa and Parker Shipton to prophetic movements in East Africa and Native America. In contrast to the claim of a consistent environmental religion, however, Gordon emphasizes that central African environmental religion reflected local political struggles over agricultural prosperity and human fertility. During European colonialism, administrators and anthropologists codified hegemonic claims by certain clan elites who had become colonial chiefs, making past conflicts appear to be timeless traditions. Shipton points out that many indigenous religious ideas were innovations in the face of colonial trauma and Christian dogma. Prophetic movements oriented around totemic animals emerged from a "shaken sense of position in the world." As with many other issues examined in this volume, historical and strategic interpretations contrast with cultural interpretations.

Part Four: Resource Rights

Debates over indigenous knowledge ramify into the present because they continue to provide ways of making claims to environmental resources. In the final section of the book, the implications of indigenous knowledge for recent and present-day resource claims are considered in three important arenas: Joshua Reid considers rights over marine resources; Karen Flint over medicinal plant products; and Derick Fay over land. Each of these resources presents distinctive challenges for those who wish to claim rights by employing indigenous knowledge. But several issues weigh heavily on all of these cases: claims for scientific conservation measures (or standardized testing in the case of medicine); the relative power of the individual, the lineage, ethnicity, and nation; and the general imperatives of a neoliberal modernity in which private property rights trump communal rights.

Part of the problem is that indigenous knowledges only rarely conform to modern legal arrangements that stress precedent, consistency, and individual or corporate patents and rights in resources. The dynamism and hybridity of indigenous knowledge makes it difficult to attribute legal ownership over indigenous knowledge and resources. To whom would such resources and knowledge belong? The tribe, lineage, family, or individual? Indeed, indigenous knowledges may emerge out of conflict within the group, rather than between the group and outsiders. In controversies over authorship, the language of communal knowledge confronts that of individual or subgroup agency, the consensus of the group versus conflict within the group, the right of individuals versus that of their communities. The challenge becomes even more vexing with the appreciation that the names and the boundaries of tribal groupings have also been dynamic— and were artificially fixed largely during the colonial encounter. Unlike modern corporations, it is often difficult to determine their membership.

In this section, Flint points to the ongoing contestation over who benefits from the bioprospecting of indigenous remedies, with pharmaceutical companies and national and even international states engaging with the most devastated and marginalized of South African indigenous communities, the San. Given that indigenous knowledges confound corporate unity and mire any intellectual rights in controversy, the ability of these communities to gain effectively from their ancient remedies by employing indigenous knowledge claims seems slight. Indigenous knowledge claims may be a weak substitute for other development agendas.[55]

These issues are not only limited to intellectual knowledge, but are manifest in land rights directly. In postcolonial contexts, indigenous knowledges continue to be deployed in the contestation of older claims to resources by those dispossessed during colonialism. Sometimes this process can be counterintuitive, especially when colonialism buttressed the power of certain traditional leaders. For example, Fay demonstrates how traditional leaders in South Africa had to redefine claims to communal land in postapartheid South Africa, as individuals dispossessed of their land in favor of chiefs during apartheid have sought legal redress by appealing to their private property rights.

By contrast, in the Native American cases in this volume, such inner-group contestations seem less evident and the unity of the corporate groups taken for granted—although there are exceptions, such as Reid's contribution to this section, which demonstrates contestation between individual, lineage, and tribe over fishing and whaling rights.[56] Here, cutting across inner-group contestations is the challenge of national and international fishing regulations that claim that the sustenance of fish stocks should be regulated by scientific principles for universal benefit instead of indigenous knowledge traditions for local communal benefit.

All of these cases demonstrate that indigenous knowledges provide marginalized communities with alternative ways of claiming rights in resources. Thereby, such communities resist the onset of neoliberal modernity, even as their indigenous knowledges become entwined in the neoliberal power relations. There is much in this paradoxical relationship to power that resembles mobilizations of indigenous knowledges during the colonial period.

Conclusions

This volume problematizes historical narratives of timeless, insular, and ecologically harmonious indigenous knowledges and practices that always challenged the imposition of environmentally deleterious colonial and scientific knowledges. The history of indigenous knowledge appears to contrast with that of scientific knowledges. If we accept, however, the multifaceted and global histories of indigenous knowledges in a fashion similar to the histories of scientific discourses, the oppositional relationship between indigenous knowledges and Western science no longer seems as clear. Nonetheless, the hybrid nature of knowledge, scientific and indigenous, remains disguised, inadvertently or deliberately, in either case with a resultant increase in its political salience. Modern indigenous and scientific knowledges were located in a contested landscape of environmental struggle and change during early modern colonialism and in its aftermath. Their identification as indigenous (or scientific) was essential to the engagement of knowledge with power in diverse encounters between peoples and environments.

The environmental historian remains with the many predicaments of indigenous knowledges. Because indigenous knowledges mean so much to so many, they escape definition. They represent unique challenges and opportunities for the scholar. Rather than ignoring indigenous knowledges, claiming that they do not exist, or replacing them with arguably less-contested labels, more neutral or historically "accurate," contributors to this volume explore the conceptual slipperiness and political manipulations of indigenous knowledges, illuminating the many similar struggles against marginalization undertaken by modernity's others.

Notes

1. Michael R. Dove, "The Life-Cycle of Indigenous Knowledge, and the Case of Natural Rubber Production," in *Indigenous Environmental Knowledge and Its Transformations: Critical Anthropological Perspectives*, ed. Roy Ellen, Peter Parkes, and Alan Bicker (Amsterdam: Harwood Academic Publishers, 2000), 241.

2. Arun Agrawal, "Dismantling the Divide Between Indigenous and Scientific Knowledge," *Development and Change* 26 (1995): 413–39. For a thoughtful case study of these issues, see Paul Nadasdy, *Hunters and Bureaucrats: Power, Knowledge, and Aboriginal-State Relations in the Southwest Yukon* (Vancouver: University of British Columbia Press, 2003).

3. Ellen, Parkes, and Bicker, *Indigenous Environmental Knowledge*; Michael R. Dove, "Indigenous People and Environmental Politics," *Annual Review of Anthropology* 35 (2006): 191–208; Paul Sillitoe, ed., *Local Science vs Global Science: Approaches to Indigenous Knowledge in International Development* (New York: Berghahn Books, 2007).

4. Earlier comparative efforts include William Beinart and Peter Coates, *Environment and History: The Taming of Nature in the USA and South Africa* (London: Routledge, 1995); Howard Lamar and Leonard Thompson, *The Frontier in History: North America and Southern Africa Compared* (New Haven, CT: Yale University Press, 1981).

5. See, for example, Glauco Sanga and Gherardo Ortalli, eds., *Nature Knowledge: Ethnoscience, Cognition, and Utility* (New York: Berghahn Books, 2004); Sillitoe, *Local Science vs Global Science*; Ellen, Parkes, and Bicker, *Indigenous Environmental Knowledge*. See also Dorothy L. Hodgson, "Introduction: Comparative Perspectives on the Indigenous Rights Movement in Africa and the Americas," *American Anthropologist* 104 (2002): 1037–49.

6. For a brief exception, see Andrys Onsman, *Defining Indigeneity in the Twenty-First Century: A Case Study of the Free Frisians* (Lewiston, NY: Mellen Press, 2004).

7. For an example of such controversies in biology, see the long-running debate over the "invasive" periwinkle, *Littorina littorea*, most recently in C. W. Cunningham, "How to Use Genetic Data to Distinguish Between Natural and Human-Mediated Introduction of *Littorina littorea* to North America," *Biological Invasions* 10, no. 1 (2008): 1–6.

8. See, for example, in central Africa, the development of notions of original inhabitants and newcomers in relationships between Bantu and Batwa in Kairn A. Klieman, *"The Pygmies Were Our Compass": Bantu and Batwa in the History of West Central Africa, Early Times to c. 1900 C.E.* (Portsmouth, NH: Heinemann, 2003).

9. *Oxford English Dictionary Online*, s.v. "indigeneity," "indigenous." Accessed October 4, 2011.

10. Roy Ellen and Holly Harris, introduction to *Indigenous Environmental Knowledge*, ed. Ellen, Parkes, and Bicker, 3.

11. Ibid.

12. Ibid.; see also Agrawal, "Dismantling the Divide"; and Dove, "Indigenous People and Environmental Politics."

13. Dorothy L. Hodgson, "Becoming Indigenous in Africa," *African Studies Review* 52, no. 3 (2009): 1–32. An instructive example is South African Coloured campaigns for indigenous status, manifest especially in the struggle to repatriate Sara Baartman's remains, in Clifton Crais and Pamela Scully, *Sara Baartman and the Hottentot Venus* (Princeton, NJ: Princeton University Press, 2009), 156–57.

14. Adam Kuper, "The Return of the Native," *Current Anthropology* 44 (2003): 389–402; Francesca Merlan, "Indigeneity: Global and Local," *Current Anthropology* 50 (2009): 303–33; Brian Donahoe et al., "Size and Place in the

Construction of Indigeneity in the Russian Federation," *Current Anthropology* 49 (2008): 993–1020.

15. Hodgson, "Becoming Indigenous," 8.

16. André Béteille, "The Idea of Indigenous People," *Current Anthropology* 39, no. 2 (1998): 187–91, esp. 190, 191.

17. In this volume, and in her book, Karen E. Flint, *Healing Traditions: African Medicine, Cultural Exchange, and Competition in South Africa, 1820–1948* (Athens: Ohio University Press, 2008).

18. John Knight, "'Indigenous Regionalism in Japan,'" in *Indigenous Environmental Knowledge*, ed. Ellen, Parkes, and Bicker, 167.

19. Béteille, "The Idea of Indigenous People," 191.

20. Eric J. Hobsbawm and Terence O. Ranger, eds., *The Invention of Tradition* (Cambridge: Cambridge University Press, 1983).

21. The seminal work is by Jan Vansina, published most recently as *Oral Tradition as History* (Madison: University of Wisconsin Press, 1985), an elaboration of his first book, *De la Tradition Oral: Essai de Methode Historique* (Tervuren: Annales du Musée Royal de l'Afrique Central, 1961). A starting point for the extensive comparative anthropology of orality was Jack R. Goody, *The Domestication of the Savage Mind* (Cambridge: Cambridge University Press, 1977).

22. For the best and most nuanced example, see the list of qualities of indigenous knowledge in Ellen and Harris, introduction to *Indigenous Environmental Knowledge*, ed. Ellen, Parkes, and Bicker, 4–5. For a discussion of these oppositions, see Agrawal, "Dismantling the Divide."

23. Arne Kalland, "Indigenous Knowledge: Prospects and Limitations," in *Indigenous Environmental Knowledge*, ed. Ellen, Parkes, and Bicker, 319–35.

24. Alix Cooper, *Inventing the Indigenous: Local Knowledge and Natural History in Early Modern Europe* (Cambridge: Cambridge University Press, 2007).

25. Judith A. Carney, *Black Rice: The African Origins of Rice Cultivation in the Americas* (Cambridge, MA: Harvard University Press, 2001). For debate over Carney's argument, but acknowledgment of the influence of African risiculture, see "AHR Exchange: The Question of 'Black Rice,'" *American Historical Review* 115, no. 1 (2010): 123–71.

26. James C. Scott, *Seeing Like a State: How Certain Schemes to Improve the Human Condition Have Failed* (New Haven, CT: Yale University Press, 1998).

27. Ibid., 323.

28. For the conventional academic wisdom on the colonial marginalization of indigenous knowledges, see Ellen and Harris, introduction to *Indigenous Environmental Knowledge*, ed. Ellen, Parkes, and Bicker, 11–12.

29. A seminal article in this regard is Madhav Gadgil, Fikret Berkes, and Carl Folke, "Indigenous Knowledge for Biodiversity Conservation," *Ambio* 22, nos.

2–3 (May 1993): 151–56. See also Kristiina A. Vogt et al., "Indigenous Knowledge Informing Management of Tropical Forests: The Link Between Rhythms in Plant Secondary Chemistry and Lunar Cycles," *Ambio* 31 (2002): 485–90.

30. Robert E. Johannes, ed., *Traditional Ecological Knowledge: A Collection of Essays* (Gland, Switzerland: International Union for Conservation of Nature, 1989).

31. An unexceptional but widely cited and influential example is Gadgil, Berkes, and Folke, "Indigenous Knowledge."

32. Scott, *Seeing Like a State*.

33. Paul Sillitoe, "The Development of Indigenous Knowledge: A New Applied Anthropology," *Current Anthropology* 39, no. 2 (1998): 223–52.

34. Arun Agrawal, "Indigenous Knowledge and Power" (keynote address at "Indigenous Environments" conference, Bowdoin College, Brunswick, Maine, April 3, 2008). Also see Nadasdy, *Hunters and Bureaucrats*.

35. John L. Comaroff and Jean Comaroff, *Ethnicity, Inc.* (Chicago: University of Chicago Press, 2009).

36. For a recent example, see Diana K. Davis, *Resurrecting the Granary of Rome: Environmental History and French Colonial Expansion in North Africa* (Athens: Ohio University Press, 2007).

37. There is an extensive literature that includes Roderick P. Neumann, *Imposing Wilderness: Struggles over Livelihood and Nature Preservation in Africa* (Berkeley: University of California press, 1998); William Beinart, "Soil Erosion, Conservationism and Ideas About Development: A Southern African Exploration, 1900–1960," *Journal of Southern African Studies* 11 (1984): 52–83.

38. William Cronon, *Changes in the Land: Indians, Colonists, and the Ecology of New England* (New York: Hill and Wang, 1983); Robert W. Harms, *Games Against Nature: An Eco-Cultural History of the Nunu of Equatorial Africa* (Cambridge: Cambridge University Press, 1987).

39. Tamara Giles-Vernick, *Cutting the Vines of the Past: Environmental Histories of the Central African Rain Forest* (Charlottesville: University of Virginia Press, 2002), 4.

40. Raymond Hames, "The Ecologically Noble Savage Debate," *Annual Review of Anthropology* 36 (2007): 178; Dove, "Indigenous People and Environmental Politics," 197; Shepard Krech III, *The Ecological Indian: Myth and History* (New York: Norton, 1999); Michael E. Harkin and David R. Lewis, eds., *Native Americans and the Environment: Perspectives on the Ecological Indian* (Lincoln: University of Nebraska Press, 2007); Shepard Krech III, "Beyond the Ecological Indian," in *Native Americans and the Environment*, ed. Harkin and Lewis, 3–31.

41. Giles-Vernick, *Cutting the Vines of the Past*, 7.

42. David M. Gordon, *Nachituti's Gift: Economy, Society, and Environment in Central Africa* (Madison: University of Wisconsin Press, 2006), 141–69.

43. Michael J. Sheridan, "Sacred Groves in Africa: The Opposite of Witchcraft" (paper presented at "Indigenous Environments" conference, Bowdoin College, New Brunswick, Maine, April 3–5, 2008). Also see Michael J. Sheridan, "The Environmental and Social History of African Sacred Groves: A Tanzanian Case Study," *African Studies Review* 52, no. 1 (2009): 73–98; and Michael J. Sheridan and Celia Nyamweru, *African Sacred Groves: Ecological Dynamics and Social Change* (Oxford: James Currey, 2008).

44. Mary Louise Pratt, *Imperial Eyes: Travel Writing and Transculturation* (London: Routledge, 1992); Richard White, *The Middle Ground: Indians, Empires, and Republics in the Great Lakes Region, 1650–1815* (Cambridge: Cambridge University Press, 1991). For Africanist literature on colonial origins of scientific disciplines, see, among others, Richard H. Grove, *Green Imperialism: Colonial Expansion, Tropical Island Edens and the Origins of Environmentalism, 1600–1860* (Cambridge: Cambridge University Press, 1995); Patrick Harries, *Butterflies and Barbarians: Swiss Missionaries and Systems of Knowledge in South-East Africa* (Athens: Ohio University Press, 2007); Saul Dubow, *A Commonwealth of Knowledge: Science, Sensibility, and White South Africa, 1820–2000* (New York: Oxford University Press, 2006); and many studies by Elizabeth Green Musselman, most recently, "Indigenous Knowledge and Contact Zones: The Case of the Cold Bokkeveld Meteorite, Cape Colony, 1838," *Itinerario* 33 (2009): 31–44.

45. William H. McNeill, *Plagues and Peoples* (New York: Anchor Books, 1976); Alfred W. Crosby, *The Columbian Exchange: Biological and Cultural Consequences of 1492* (Westport, CT: Greenwood, 1972); James L. A. Webb, Jr., *Humanity's Burden: A Global History of Malaria* (New York: Cambridge University Press, 2008).

46. Concerning the example of corn in Africa, see James C. McCann, *Maize and Grace: Africa's Encounter with a New World Crop, 1500–2000* (Cambridge, MA: Harvard University Press, 2007).

47. Cooper, *Inventing the Indigenous*.

48. For the codification of custom into colonial law in Africa, see Martin Chanock, *Law, Custom and Social Order: The Colonial Experience in Malawi and Zambia* (Cambridge: Cambridge University Press, 1985). Much has been written on the rise of colonial chieftaincy, including Mahmood Mamdani, *Citizen and Subject: Contemporary Africa and the Legacy of Late Colonialism* (Princeton, NJ: Princeton University Press, 1996).

49. Marsha Weisiger's contribution to this volume is based on her book *Dreaming of Sheep in Navajo Country* (Seattle: University of Washington Press, 2009).

50. See, for example, Edward Said's criticism of Bernard Lewis in *Orientalism* (New York: Vintage Books, 1979), repeated in many other reviews and publications. More recently, see Ussama Makdisi's contributions in "AHR Conversation: Religious Identities and Violence," *American Historical Review*, 112 (2007): 1432–481.

51. See, for example, Susan Sleeper-Smith, ed., *Contesting Knowledge: Museums and Indigenous Perspectives* (Lincoln: University of Nebraska Press, 2009).

52. As illustrated by Talal Asad, *Formations of the Secular: Christianity, Islam, Modernity* (Stanford, CA: Stanford University Press, 2003).

53. For the romantic and often spiritual opposition to Western thought, see Ian Buruma and Avishai Margalit, *Occidentalism: A Short History of Anti-Westernism* (New York: Penguin, 2004).

54. See, for example, Fikret Berkes, *Sacred Ecology*, 2nd ed. (New York: Routledge, 2008), xvi–xvii. The background to this is also explored in Krech, *The Ecological Indian*.

55. As pointed out in another context in Agrawal, "Dismantling the Divide."

56. Or elsewhere on Chumash tradition: Brian D. Haley and Larry R. Wilcoxon, "Anthropology and the Making of Chumash Tradition," *Current Anthropology* 38 (1997): 761–94; and Jon M. Erlandson, "The Making of Chumash Tradition: Replies to Haley and Wilcoxon," *Current Anthropology* 39 (1998): 477–510.

Part I

Middle Ground

CHAPTER 1

Looking Like a White Man

Geopolitical Strategies of the Iowa Indians during American Incorporation

David Bernstein

IN THE winter of 2007, ninety-one thousand people visited an innovative exhibit at the Field Museum in Chicago that explored the history of maps and mapping around the world. Midway through the exhibition, these visitors would have come across one of the most uncommon maps ever created (see fig. 1.1). Named after the Iowa Indian leader who presented it to Secretary of War Joel Poinsett in 1837, Notchininga's Map is unique for a number of reasons. First, it is one of a handful of artifacts that remain from a time and place in which Native spatial knowledge was primarily transmitted orally. Graphic aids—sketches drawn in the sand or ceremonial performances—generally lasted only a few hours or until the next steady rain. Second, unlike most other examples of North American Indian cartography that were created explicitly as navigational aids, Notchininga's Map represents a more generalized spatial construction, allowing us a slightly larger window into the worldview of its creator(s).[1]

The map depicts the river systems of a large section of what is now considered the upper Midwest of the United States, and with it, the historical

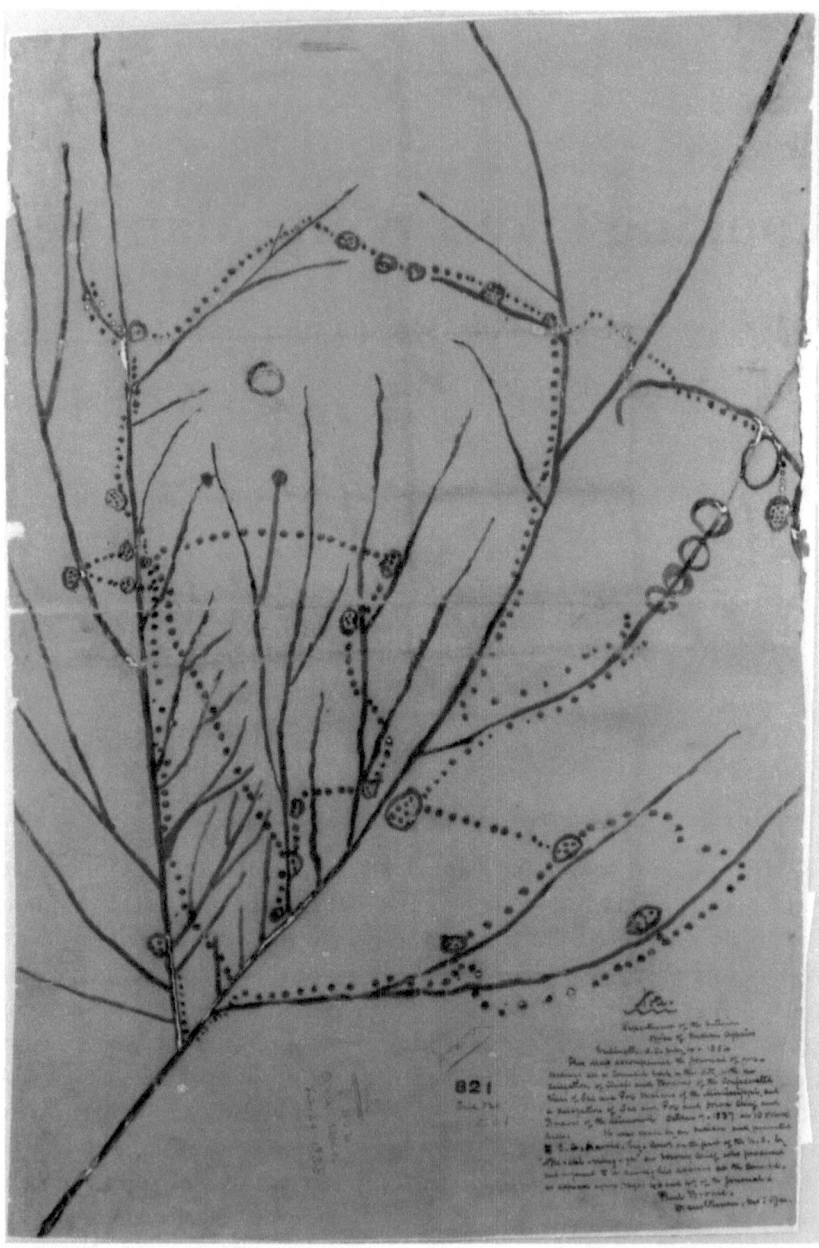

Fig. 1.1. Nothcininga's Map, 1837, Size of the Original 41x 27 inches. Courtesy of the National Archives and Records Administration, Cartographic and Architectural Branch, Washington, D.C. RG 75, Map 821, Tube 520.

migration of the Iowa people and the villages they had occupied since the fifteenth century. A dotted line begins near present-day Green Bay, Wisconsin, and continues south to the Iowas' village on the Wolf River where they lived in 1837 when they presented the map to the Americans. "This is the route of my forefathers," Notchininga stated at the meeting. "It is the land we have always claimed from old times—we have always owned this land—it is ours—it bears our name." Unfortunately, according to the accompanying label, the map "failed to allay the pressure from either other Native Americans or white settlers, and the Ioway were further displaced to Kansas and Oklahoma." At first glance, then, the map seems to be a graphic distillation of what we have come to expect from nineteenth-century Indian-white relations; Native assertion of ancestral territorial claims violently subsumed in an incompatible "clash of cultures," resulting in Indian displacement and dispossession.[2]

Yet first glances are deceiving. What appears to epitomize a traditional narrative of antagonistic "Indian" and "white" worldviews in fact confounds such simple categorizations. Notchininga's Map was part of larger set of social and political tactics the Iowas employed that cannot be placed into such binary categories. Faced with declining wildlife resources and the continued encroachment of more-powerful Indian neighbors, the Iowas in the 1820s began reshaping the economies toward what they hoped would be a more stable agricultural future. At the same time, they adopted new geopolitical strategies aimed at gaining support from American representatives, most notably conscientious appropriation of Euro-American territoriality and cartography. By creating a document in the discourse understood by the colonizing culture, a Ptolemaic map drawn on paper, the Iowas distanced themselves from other native groups. Rather than a dichotomous vision of Indian-white relations, Iowa leaders understood that their communities had potentially much to gain from aspects of white expansion. They met with Secretary of War Poinsett and other American officials to mitigate their recurring and immediate tensions with powerful Indian adversaries. The primary purpose of this article, therefore, is to look beyond circumscribed definitions of Indian-white relations by highlighting this new strategy and to explore how the Iowas used diplomatic—most significantly cartographic—tactics to help shape their rapidly changing world. In so doing, I suggest a new evidentiary source for a growing number of scholars who have gone beyond traditional narratives in which Indians are forced to choose between the extremes of "acculturating to" or "resisting" American westward expansion.[3]

In addition to illuminating specific geopolitical maneuvers made by the Iowas, by highlighting the Indians' appropriation of certain aspects of

Euro-American territorial constructs, I address a larger issue within the study of Native American cartography. Though there has been no lack of interest in the map—in addition to the exhibit, it has been reproduced in at least six scholarly and popular works, including volume 2 of the seminal work of David Woodward and G. Malcolm Lewis, *The History of Cartography*—it has received limited historical analysis. While non-Native maps have come under close post-structuralist scrutiny as documents that contain political and social agendas particular for a historical moment, indigenous maps have been viewed as "authentic" cultural snapshots; pure representations of how a group of Indians understood their spatial existence. Thus, while virtually all of the pieces have noted the similarities between the map and modern, scientific depictions of the region's hydrography—a "western" projection is unique among Native maps—scholars have simply accepted this irregularity as a characteristic of Iowa spatial constructions. This paper argues that extant examples of Indian cartography, including Notchininga's Map, contain the same hidden agendas as their Euro-American counterparts and must be considered in the same deconstructionist light if we hope to fully grasp their historical significance. In other words, in order to understand the importance of Native maps, we must do what we do with any document; consider it in the context in which it was created.[4]

Native Mapping in Historiographic Context

Since the 1970s, historians of cartography have utilized the ideas of Michel Foucault, Jacques Derrida, Edward Said, and Anthony Giddens to resituate the map as a form of discourse that contains power, rhetoric, and value, rather than as an objective representation of reality. Two articles by J. Brian Harley exemplified this epistemological shift. In "Deconstructing the Map," Harley called for the examination and acknowledgment of "the omnipresence of power in all knowledge, even though that power is invisible or implied, including the particular knowledge, encoded in maps and atlases." A "deconstruction" must occur whereby the map is examined within broader movements and structures. In this way, the rhetoric of maps will become much more apparent. Stating simply that "cartographers manufacture power," Harley concluded that the map's most important rhetorical function lies in its subjectivity.[5]

A second article by Harley more explicitly explored the political power contained within maps. Building on the premise that maps need to be understood within the larger family of value-laden images, Harley explored how maps facilitated the geographical expansion of political systems. Tying map creation into other imperial processes such as military expansion and exacting taxation, Harley determined that cartography was (and remains) a "teleological discourse, reifying power, reinforcing the *status quo*, and freezing social interactions within charted lines." And unlike music, art, or other expressions employed by those without alternative forms of resistance, maps have almost exclusively been used as a form of oppression by those in power. Thus, Harley argued, mapping's "ideological arrows," flew only in one direction.[6]

Though some criticized Harley's approach for its designation of maps as texts (which disregards the process of map creation), scholars began to follow Harley's lead by exploring maps' hegemonic functions—the way in which colonizing powers gain and maintain control—in specific historical circumstances.[7] In 1992, for instance, Gregory Nobles published an article in the *Journal of American History* that focused on mapping as a form of spatial control in colonial America. Examining the political order of the "Anglo-American Frontier," Nobles proposed that Euro-Americans established political and social boundaries well before actual settlement patterns. By creating what appeared to be a priori plans of what the North American interior looked like, Anglo-American mapmakers established a vision of future dominance. Nobles states, "By drawing lines across the continent and imposing themselves in print, they literally mapped out a New World order." Nobles's article was accompanied by explorations into the hegemonic function of maps in a variety of colonial settings.[8]

At the same time that scholars were examining maps as tools for colonial and imperial powers, there was a resurgence in the study of maps made by Native North Americans. Led by G. Malcolm Lewis and followed by such scholars as Richard Ruggles, Barbara Belyea, and Gregory Waselkov, this group used post-structuralist models to investigate indigenous maps on their own terms. Rather than immature versions of the measured, mathematical spatial representations of European scientific cartography, these scholars viewed Native maps as sophisticated cultural documents that revealed an entirely different understanding of the world around them than those created by contemporary Euro-Americans. This new understanding of Indian maps has led to reexaminations of Lewis and Clark's expedition, land transfers in colonial New England, and Spanish explorations of the American Southeast, to name just a few examples.[9]

As scholars revisit documents long dismissed as having little evidentiary value, three related lines of inquiry have emerged: (1) evaluating and comparing Native American spatial constructions; (2) exploring these constructions' influence on maps made by Euro-Americans and their incorporation into imperial territorial appropriation; and (3) Native American maintenance of indigenous spatial constructs in the face of colonial oppression.[10] A fundamental premise running through all three explorations is the belief that we can identify and isolate epistemologically unique forms of indigenous spatial knowledge.

G. Malcolm Lewis has argued, for example, that all Native maps created after 1925 can at best be considered as "pidgins," as they have been "too acculturated" to afford evidence of "traditional forms." Scholars such as Keith Basso and Hugh Brody—whose work documents the continued use of Native place-names—would no doubt refute Lewis's assertion that contemporary Indian spatial and territorial constructions are "pidgins," but they would certainly agree with his underlying premise of the existence of a uniquely Indian way of interacting with and representing geographical knowledge. Barbara Belyea goes so far as to say that not only are Indian and Euro-American constructions of space and place different, but "there is no 'common ground.' . . . Instead of continuing to translate the native cartographic convention into our own, we must acknowledge a gap between these conventions is essentially unbridgeable." Thus, while there has been considerable—and sometimes heated—debate about the definition and characterization of Indian mapping, this divisive rhetoric has masked a common assumption: Native constructions of space, and their representations, are inherently different from Euro-American constructs.[11]

While the existence (or lack) of an epistemologically indigenous worldview is beyond the scope of this paper, I will demonstrate how an unconditional acceptance of such a view limits our understanding of Native cartography.[12] By essentializing Indian spatial understanding to either a knowable or unknowable "other," we are continuing the practice of idealizing Indian knowledge as something that lies outside of history. While historians and anthropologists have generally gone beyond the segregation of ethnology and history, most cartographic scholars have maintained strict intellectual boundaries around Indian maps, considering them ahistorical cultural documents.[13] For example, the 131-page entry on "Native North American Maps" in *The History of Cartography* considers nothing beyond the cultural characteristics of Indian maps. The volume on Renaissance mapping, on the other hand, has separate sections for the political economic, military, and religious contexts of maps made in Italy, Portugal, Spain, German lands, Low Countries, France, the British Isles, Scandinavia, East-Central Europe, and Russia.[14]

I argue that without taking the historical context into consideration—the specific political, economic, and social circumstances in which a particular map was created—we relegate the creators of Indian cartography to a timeless distant past rather than taking them seriously as historical actors.

There have been a number of works that have astutely examined the political context of Indian mapping. Yet these pieces have invariably reified a dichotomous vision of Native and white concepts of space by exploring how Indians, either consciously or not, used their constructs to maintain "Indianness" in the face of colonial hegemony.[15] In so doing, these studies limit our historical analyses to the well-worn path of cultural continuity. By placing Notchininga's Maps in a particular historical moment, within a specific geopolitical landscape, we can continue to move beyond the Native/non-Native binary to explore the various ways the Iowas shaped their rapidly changing world. It is to this geopolitical landscape we now turn.

The Challenges of Imperial Incorporation and a New Political Alliance, 1700–1815

Throughout the eighteenth century, the Iowa Indians lived in semipermanent villages in present-day Iowa and Kansas, controlling much of the region.[16] They subsisted by hunting; farming maize, beans, and pumpkins; and, to a lesser degree, trading deer, beaver, otter, and raccoon skins with English and French traders. From fall to early spring, bands established seasonal camps in what is now southern Wisconsin and northern Iowa to hunt and make maple sugar. They returned to their villages in the early summers to tend small garden patches, then moved to the plains west of the Missouri for the summer buffalo hunt. Finally, the Iowas returned once again to their villages in late summer and early fall for harvesting.[17]

Recalling the Iowas' strength in the eighteenth century, future commissioner of Indian Affairs Thomas Mckenney declared, "Of all the tribes that hunt between the Mississippi and Missouri Rivers ... next to the Sioux ... the Ioway were once the most numerous and powerful."[18] In the first years of the eighteenth century, French explorer Pierre Charles Le Sueur also reported that the Mississippi was under control of the Scioux (Sioux), the Ayavois (Iowas), and the Otoctatas (Otoes). Le Sueur claimed that for the Indians, "it was not their custom to hunt on ground belonging to other, unless invited to do so by the owners." To travel the river without following this protocol, the Frenchman continued, put one "in danger of being killed."[19] Along with the Teton and Yanktonai Sioux, the Iowas controlled the land between the Mississippi and Missouri Rivers.

Le Sueur's comments not only illustrate the authority the Iowas wielded in the region, they also indicate a system of land use in which groups controlled fairly defined territories. While anthropological investigations into Indian land claims before the reservation era have highlighted the fluidity of property ownership throughout the upper Mississippi, these studies also affirm that conquest through warfare was a viable form of land acquisition.[20] For smaller groups to compete with larger bands for resources, therefore, they had little choice but to attach themselves to larger populations and create what anthropologist Patricia Albers calls a "merger."[21] According to Albers, such mergers fell into a four-step continuum. In the most developed stage of "complete ethnogenesis," once-distinct groups became socially and culturally indistinguishable. Albers terms the least developed merger a "polyethnic alliance formation," in which groups remained culturally separate but cooperated in the exploitation of resources in the region, performed various ceremonial activities together, and engaged in joint military action.[22] The Iowas employed such alliances throughout the 1700s.

This period of military strength, however, was cut short by the now well-known story of virgin-soil epidemics. As France, Spain, and England vied for colonial control of the Mississippi, the diseases their traders and explorers brought with them recalibrated an already elaborate system of alliances between various Indian groups and imperial powers.[23] By the middle of the 1760s, the first of two smallpox epidemics struck the Iowas, halving their population.[24] Recounting this period decades later, Iowa leaders explained, "Although once the most powerful and warlike Indians on the Mississippi and Missouri Rivers, [we were] reduced to nothing, a mere handful of that Nation that was once masters of the land."[25] When a second wave of smallpox struck in the first years of the nineteenth century, the Iowas numbers were once again halved, leaving just eight hundred people.

Unlike the Iowas who lived in two or three major villages where germs and bacteria spread quickly, Teton and Yanktonai Sioux lived in small nomadic groups and thus were less vulnerable to disease. These western Sioux quickly used their numeric advantages to become the dominant trappers and traders in the region, acquiring European guns and forcing smaller groups such as the Iowas, Omahas, Otoes, and Missouris to either merge with one another or look for protection under more populous groups of Indians. For the Iowas, that protection came in the form of the merged

Sac and Fox peoples, who themselves had only recently formed an alliance when the Sacs offered the Foxes refuge from massacring French armies at the end of the seventeenth century. Major Zebulon Pike reported the Iowas' new alliance in 1807 when he wrote that they "hunt on the west side of the Mississippi, the river De Moyen, and westward to the Missouri; their wars and alliances are the same as the Sauks and Reynards [Foxes]; under whose special protection they conceive themselves to be."[26]

Though the Iowas merger with the Sac and the Fox gave them satisfactory protection from the western Sioux for the first few years of the nineteenth century, their relationship had already begun to change in 1804 with the signing of a controversial Sac treaty. This treaty ultimately divided the Sac tribe and precipitated tensions between factions of Sacs and Iowas that continued for decades. These tensions became important factors in the Iowas' decision to begin a new relationship of protection with the United States in 1815 and ultimately the creation of Notchininga's Map.

In 1804, a group of Sacs living on the west side of the Mississippi traveled to St. Louis to meet with Governor William Henry Harrison to discuss the release of a Sac prisoner. While the details of the proceedings remain unclear, the resulting treaty left little doubt about the magnitude of the meeting. In the treaty, the Sacs ceded all claims to land on the east side of the Mississippi in exchange for annuities of one thousand dollars and gifts totaling just under thirty-five hundred dollars.[27]

There are many reasons why this small group of Missouri River Sacs may have signed the 1804 treaty. Living hundreds of miles west of the Mississippi, the representatives wanted to potentially get annuities and protection in exchange for lands east of the Mississippi that were of no consequence to them. Perhaps, as a letter from an American general attests, the Sacs were so disgusted by the news of an Osage party leaving St. Louis "loaded with presents," and "puffed up with ideas of their great superiority," they were driven to "make a treaty that wou'd shelter them from . . . the Osages, now consider'd by them as under the protection of the United States."[28] Or, perhaps the Sacs simply did not understand what they were signing, as they professed in a letter to the Secretary of War a year later. Regardless of the reasons, the treaty not only fractured the Sac-Fox alliance but, more important for the Iowas, caused such division within the Sac tribe that the Iowas were now under the protection of a band no larger than their own. The Iowas, therefore, were once again vulnerable to Yanktonai and Teton attacks.

Approximately 6,000 Sacs living on the Rock River on the east side of the Mississippi contested the treaty. The Iowas and the remainder of the

Sac and Fox populations living between the rivers totaled closer to 2,000, with only 600 warriors.[29] So with a population of perhaps a quarter of what it had been a century earlier, continual pressure for hunting grounds from the Sioux in the north, the Pawnee and Omaha in the west, and now the Mississippi Sac in the east, the Iowas did what vulnerable bands of Indians in the region had done for generations: attached themselves to a powerful neighbor.[30] In this case, that neighbor was the United States.

On December 16, 1815, just months after a particularly devastating Sioux attack, the Iowa Indians entered into their first treaty with the United States at a meeting also attended by Kickapoos, Big and Little Osages, and both groups of Sacs. In a series of letters to Secretary of War Henry Calhoun, Treaty Commissioner William Clark explained that his treaty proposals were met with "a considerable backwardness, if not positive reluctance," by several of the tribes, most notably the Mississippi Sacs. However, despite confining the parameters of the treaties to the "sole object of peace," as directed, Clark reported that unlike the other participants of the meeting, the Iowa Indians were "extremely solicitous that they embrace other subjects." According to Clark, the Iowas proposed a "spontaneous offer" to come more closely under the protection of the United States in exchange for annuities and the cession of a small portion of their lands.[31]

The Iowas' "spontaneous offer" to Treaty Commissioner Clark to cede some of their lands for promises of protection must be understood within the context of a dwindling population forced to find security in a region of growing violence. It was, therefore, neither a "spontaneous" nor an unqualified "offer." By signing the treaty of 1815 with the United States, the Iowas agreed to share some of their lands with the Americans in exchange for an alliance in warfare. The treaty between the Iowas and the Americans was, therefore, similar to the same "merger" process that the Iowas had been relying on since the first smallpox epidemic decimated their population sixty years earlier, and on September 16, 1815, a treaty of "peace and friendship" was signed by Clark and fifteen representatives of the Iowa people.[32]

It is easy, with the benefit of hindsight, to view the 1815 treaty as evidence of the Iowas' acceptance of, and even culpability in, the eventual American dominance in the region. Such a view, however, distorts the reality in which the Iowas lived. The Iowas' proposal to cede some of their lands in exchange for protection is best understood within the context of earlier Iowa responses to changes brought about by disease and warfare. Also, in the first quarter of the nineteenth century, the Americans were not the Iowas' primary concern. According to Richard White, Indians whose territory bordered the northern and central Great Plains felt that the crucial invasion of their lands came not from whites, but from the Sioux, who "remained their most feared enemy."[33] The Iowas' alliance with the Americans and other surrounding tribes illustrates their overwhelming concern for a Sioux intrusion onto their lands. It is this geopolitical reality we must understand in order to fully grasp the tactics of the Iowas for the next two decades, including the creation of Notchininga's Map.

Though the Iowas had made an alliance with the United States to gain territorial security, this agreement did little to stop the violence between rival Indian groups. The Iowas lived in what one traveler called a state of "perpetual warfare," as they engaged in conflicts with their neighbors on all sides.[34] The Kansa and Big and Little Osages threatened from the south, while the Yanktonai and Teton Sioux came from the north, the Pawnees from the west, and the Mississippi Sacs continued pressing their claims from the east.[35] Ceaseless bloodshed prompted Iowa chief Hard Heart to approach Indian Agent George Sibley in 1819 and reiterate the tribe's desire for protection and assistance. In a letter to now governor William Clark, Sibley forwarded an explanation of Hard Heart's request:

> They are surrounded [Hard Heart] says on every side by enemies, who are continually making war upon them; which compels them to be always on the watch, sleeping with one eye open, and one hand on their guns; so that they have but little time to hunt for the subsistence of their families.[36]

Hard Heart's words were more prescient than he knew, for early the next year he was killed by a band of Yankton Sioux.[37]

After five years of piecemeal attempts to end the growing violence, Governor Clark decided to call a council of all the Indian groups in the region, in which he hoped to establish "permanent" boundaries between the tribes. It would be during this treaty session, called to clarify boundaries, that a seemingly innocuous agreement between the Sacs, the Foxes, and the Iowas would result in massive land loss for the latter, and initiate more than a century of diplomatic and legal wrangling.[38]

Familiar with dozens of treaties in the region over the last twenty years, the Iowas, Sacs, and Foxes knew of the American tactic of recognizing territorial claims of larger groups over those of smaller ones. Overlooking previous disagreements, the leaders of the three tribes knew they must speak with one voice if they hoped to counter the Sioux's strength. The leaders saw this council as an opportunity to guarantee Sioux exclusion from the region. To do so, the Iowas would have to align their fortunes with the Sacs and the Foxes. When Clark arrived at Prairie du Chien on July 30, 1825, nearly one thousand Chippewa, Sioux, Winnebago, Menominee, Potawatomi, and Ottawa Indians had already established themselves on the grounds, but the Sac, Fox, and Iowa delegations had not arrived. Then, on August 4, a flotilla of seventy canoes came rushing down the Mississippi carrying the missing participants, who were armed with spears, clubs, guns, and knives, and singing war songs. According to one report, "No tribes attracted so intense a degree of interest as the Iowas and the Sacs and Foxes, tribes of radically diverse languages, yet united in league against the Sioux.... They beat drums. They uttered yells at definite points. They landed in compact ranks. They looked the very spirit of defiance."[39] For a moment, at least, the battle lines were drawn as the Sacs, Foxes, and Iowas joined in concert against the Sioux.

Fortunately for the Iowas, the strategy worked. The Sioux boundary line was established at the upper fork of the Des Moines River, north of the Iowas' primary hunting ground. To achieve this demarcation, however, the Iowas agreed that they would not define the boundary between themselves and the Sacs and Foxes at that time, and they would "peaceably occupy the same, until some satisfactory arrangement can be made between them for a division of their respective claims to country."[40] Therefore, while the 1825 Treaty of Prairie du Chien secured the southern portion of the land between the rivers from Sioux warriors, it did nothing to augment the Iowas' shrinking supply of game, which they now had to share with both the Missouri Sacs, who had remained in the region from the divisive 1804 Sac treaty, and the Rock River Sacs, who now agreed to move to the land between the rivers. The search for a "satisfactory arrangement" became a point of contention between the tribes and determined the Iowas' political tactics for the next fifteen years, culminating in the creation of Notchininga's Map.

It quickly became apparent that neither the Iowas nor the Sacs were willing to give up control of the shared region. Just five years after they agreed to "peaceably occupy the same," both groups petitioned Governor Clark to clarify boundaries between the groups, resulting in the second Treaty of Prairie du Chien in 1830. It was at this treaty session that the Iowas' new political strategy emerged: they would emulate some aspects of American society, and in so doing, hoped to place themselves above the Sac and the Sioux in the eyes of the American representatives. This tactic became apparent as soon as the treaty session began.

While other leaders claimed large portions of the territory as necessary hunting grounds, insisting that additional available lands were needed for hunting game, Iowa representatives highlighted their communities' agricultural activities. Iowa chief White Cloud contrasted his tribe's success at farming with the other Indian groups by declaring, "Look upon me and you look upon almost a white man. . . . I have learned to plough and I now eat my own bread and it makes me large and strong. These people (pointing to delegates of the Sacs and the Foxes) eat everything, and yet are lean. They can't get fat even by eating their own words." White Cloud hoped that by illustrating the Iowas' recent transition to an economy based in sedentary agriculture rather than hunting, the treaty commissioner would accept their land claims over others'. The Iowa chief understood that American recognition of a larger territorial base would give his tribe more bargaining power in any future treaty negotiations. Another chief, The Crane, extended the Iowas' claim by explaining, "Our Great Father has been trying, and we have been trying for several years to make us like the white people. We wish you to continue it a little longer, and you will perhaps see some of our young men profit by it."[41]

The words of White Cloud and The Crane reveal a complex set of motivations that defy a binary categorization.[42] By "learning to plow" and becoming metaphorically "like the white people," the chiefs expressed conscious decisions about their tribes' political policies as well as cultural changes they believed the Iowas should employ to meet changing social and environmental pressures. White Cloud's metaphorical assertion of being "almost a white man," did not signify his desire to assimilate into white culture. Instead, for the Iowas, being "like the white people" involved a set of activities, some of which could be "continued a little longer" or stopped at will. In fact, just moments after making his pledge to continue such activities, The Crane also declared to the assembly, "You know we are not like white people to lay up money."[43] So while the chiefs claimed to act "as white people" in some circumstances, they distanced themselves from such comparisons when necessary. For these representatives of the Iowas, being "like the white people" referred to a specific set of actions, such as farming with a plow, not cultural assimilation. Rather than a dichotomous vision of Indian-white relations, Iowa leaders understood that their communities had potentially much to gain from aspects of white expansion, particularly security from the rapidly expanding western Sioux.

As with the first meeting at Prairie du Chien, however, American representatives continued to delay the delineation of separate Iowa and Sac lands, proposing a common hunting ground encompassing the modern state of Iowa, with intertribal boundaries to be "marked as soon as the President of the United States may deem it expedient." In an inversion of stereotypical land-use portrayals, therefore, Iowa and Sac Indians were demanding a type of private corporate ownership while the U.S. government was, at least for the time being, interested in maintaining a communal hunting ground. Knowing the tenuous nature of such an agreement, in April 1834, the Iowas approached Agent Andrew Hughes and asked for a meeting to discuss this possibility of selling all of their land that was not part of the common hunting ground. According to Hughes, the Iowas wished to sell their land because "they were tired of the chase and wish to become like whitemen." In return, the tribe asked for domestic animals, an educational fund for their children, and farming equipment. They also wanted to maintain a small portion of their territory for agricultural purposes.[44]

For the second time in four years, then, the Iowas asserted their desire to make agriculture their primary mode of living. Hughes granted that request, and on September 17, 1836, the Iowas ceded all of their land lying between the Missouri River and the northern boundary of the state of Missouri and agreed to move to a strip of land on the west side of the Missouri River, abutting the Wolf River. They were to also receive seventy-five hundred dollars, rations for a year, a farmer, a blacksmith, a schoolmaster, an interpreter, a ferryboat, a mill, and five "comfortable houses." In addition, two hundred acres of ground were to be broken for farming and the tribe was to be supplied with one hundred cows and calves, five bulls, and one hundred stock hogs.[45] According to a letter from Agent Hughes, the Iowas quickly moved to their new land, where they seemed "highly pleased with their situation." On the land, they erected forty-one bark houses, each one with a small field or a patch of corn.[46]

At the same time the Iowas were treating with the United States, the Mississippi Sacs were also trying to solidify their land claims. Keokuk, who had gained control of the band after the failed "Blackhawk Wars," attempted to cede the land jointly controlled by the Sacs and the Iowas to the United States; a maneuver that greatly disturbed the Iowas. While they agreed that the treaty of 1825 allowed the Sacs to hunt on lands west of the Mississippi, the Iowas asserted that they had not intended to give up any ownership of the land. Further, the Iowas held that the Mississippi Sacs never took the land by conquest, the most important factor of land claims by Indians in the region.[47] As support for their claim, the Iowas asked William Clark—now the superintendent of the St. Louis Bureau of Indian Affairs—to write a letter on their behalf. In the letter, Clark explained that when he first arrived in the area, the Iowas possessed "an immense tract of land" between the Mississippi and the Missouri in which they still held an undivided interest. Clark's letter persuaded the commissioner of Indian Affairs to invite the Iowas and the Sacs to Washington.[48] The Iowas needed to convince the commissioner that they had historic control of the land between the rivers, thereby producing an exclusive Iowa claim, making further negotiations with the Americans more beneficial. For their part, the Sacs hoped to prove that they had taken the area by force, justifying their ability to bargain with Americans for the region. The success of the Iowas' claim was now contingent upon their political maneuvering as well as their ability to clarify their competing territorial claims with the Sacs. To do so, they turned to a tool they had seen the United States employ to great effect in two previous meetings: a Ptolemaic map.

Looking Like a White Man: Adoption of Euro-American Spatial Constructions

In a rented Presbyterian church on the morning of October 7, 1837, representatives of the Iowa and the Sac Indians met with U.S. Secretary of War Joel Poinsett and Commissioner of Indian Affairs Carey A. Harris to discuss the extent of each group's land claims. Notchininga, the second chief under White Cloud, and several other Ioway chiefs had come to Washington to dispute the terms of the 1825 Treaty of Prairie du Chien, and the subsequent treaty of 1830. The Iowas argued that the Sacs had ceded lands to the U.S. government that rightfully could not be traded away without the Iowas' consent. Notchininga presented a map to the Americans that he claimed showed the extent of Iowa lands. The map depicted an area extending from what is now northeastern Wisconsin on Lake Michigan, to western Nebraska on the Missouri River, and from southern Minnesota on the Mississippi River to an area just south of St. Louis, Missouri. The map represented the geographical and historical migration of the Iowa people and the villages they had occupied since the fifteenth century. "This is the route of my forefathers," Notchininga stated, pointing to a series of dotted lines. "It is the land we have always claimed from old times—we have always owned this land—it is ours—it bears our name." Finding settlements that could only have belonged to the Iowas, twentieth-century archaeologists have reinforced Notchininga's depiction of the Iowas' migration.[49]

Notchininga's Map, or No Heart's Map as it has come to be known, does not share many of the characteristics of other American Indian maps. While scholar Barbara Belyea acknowledges the extreme hazards of generalizing about the myriad of indigenous cultures in North America and the

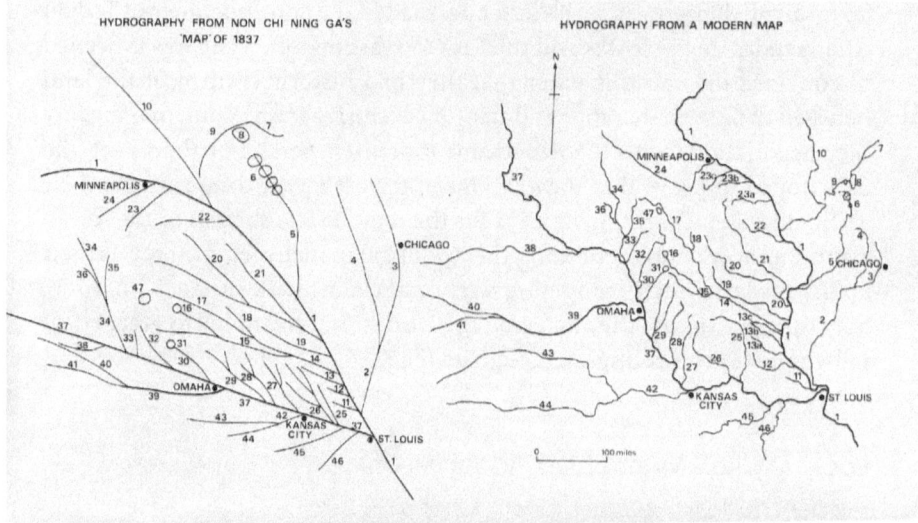

Fig. 1.2. Contemporary Interpretation of Notchininga's Map with Modern Hydrography Map. Reprinted Courtesy of David Turnbull and the University of Chicago Press. Reproduced from David Turnbull, *Maps Are Territories: Science Is an Atlas* (Chicago: University of Chicago Press, 1993); figure 4.8.

maps they created, she nonetheless argues for the existence of a fully developed Amerindian cartographic convention—including the lack of frame or other indicators of spatial existence outside of the map's projection and a constantly shifting scale derived from a principle of "linear coherence."[50] This principle can be illustrated by a map in which objects closer to a point of origin appear bigger than those farther away, but are still depicted in the order that they would be found if one were to travel in a straight line. Notchininga's Map contradicts both of these conventions of Amerindian cartography. While there is neither a formal frame nor lines of longitude or latitude that might represent the knowledge of the map as a section of a larger spatial construction, the lines depicting rivers bleed directly off the page—essentially using the edges of the paper to create a frame. This convention indicates an understanding of a world beyond the boundaries of the paper.

Perhaps most important, once the map is flipped on a vertical axis, we can see that the spatial representation does not follow the model of linear coherence, but instead, it follows more closely a European convention. In other words, rather than a representation in which the scale is dependent upon one's point of view, Notchininga's Map uses a constant scale with the familiar perspective from above.[51] In fact, Notchininga's Map is so spatially accurate, it differs from a modern hydrography map of the region only in details (see fig. 1.2).[52] The question one must ask, therefore, is why does this map lack the most important characteristic of other "Indian" maps? The answer lies not in abstract claims about indigenous cultures, but in the specific shifting geopolitical concerns of the Iowas.

It is impossible to know precisely why the Iowas created the map as they did. However, based on the Iowas' political maneuvers used at other meetings with the Americans, we can see how the creation of this map fits into a larger strategy. By adapting aspects of European spatial constructions, the Iowas were continuing the tactic they had used seven years earlier at the second Treaty of Prairie du Chien. At the earlier meeting, White Cloud and The Crane tried to separate themselves from the Sacs in the eyes of the Americans by claiming they were like "white men," while the Sacs were untrustworthy. With the creation of the map, the Iowas emulated another aspect of Euro-American culture in order to position themselves in a more favorable light to the Americans. By creating a document similar to ones Americans used to create territorial boundaries at previous meetings in 1825 and again in 1830, the Iowas demonstrated their understanding of Euro-American territoriality. Further evidence of this aim is Notchininga's demarcation of all the previous Iowa villages, dating back hundreds of years, but not the villages in the area ceded in 1830.[53] This indicates that, despite his claim against the Sacs, Notchininga respected the Iowas' cession to the Americans and their concept of land ownership.

Cartographic strategies aside, Notchininga was more direct in his verbal claim to the area. While he did not dispute the Sacs' current military dominance over the Iowas, Notchininga rested his argument on his tribe's historic control of the region, and on an arrangement the Iowas and the Sacs initially reached in 1825 when they agreed to use the territory as a shared hunting ground. Sac leader Keokuk, citing the importance of territorial conquest, rebutted that regardless of the Iowas' past claims or agreements, the Sacs had forcefully taken the Iowas' land, thereby rightfully gaining control of the region. Perhaps legitimizing their own process of conquest, the Americans decided that Keokuk's claim was strong enough to give the Sacs control of the remaining land between the rivers. Thus the meeting, called by both the Iowas and the Sacs in order to clarify each tribe's territory, ended with the Sacs gaining control of land that they had occupied with the Iowas for less than two decades, allowing the Sacs to dictate the terms of cessions to the Americans. Disgusted, the Iowas withdrew from the treaty council, turning down numerous cession proposals, and refused to participate in further meetings in Washington.[54]

While the Iowas now "owned" a fraction of the land that they had controlled just twenty-five years earlier, their attempts to adapt to the social pressures around them reveals a perseverance that counters the legacy of land loss. Despite their anger, the Iowas knew that American support was still necessary to aid their transition into an agrarian economy. Otherwise, as the Iowas confessed to one of the Indian agents, they knew that they would be forced to move back to the Des Moines River, where they would be unable to compete with the Sioux and the Sacs for resources.[55] So, rather than complete dispossession and diaspora, the Iowas secured a small portion of their former lands. A few months after the 1837 Sac treaty in Washington, the Iowas agreed to move south of the Missouri River, to the Great Nemaha, where they created a permanent village. In exchange, the Iowas were to receive $157,000 in investments, with at least 5 percent interest paid annually to the tribe in perpetuity. Also, the Americans were to provide funds for education, agriculture, blacksmith facilities, and "the construction of ten houses with good floors, one door and two windows."[56]

For many Iowas, life on the Great Nemaha was very different from the one they had envisioned just twenty-three years earlier when they entered into their first treaty with the Americans. In the first years of the century, they hunted across hundreds of thousands of acres; by 1840 they lived primarily as farmers on a few hundred acres. However, to frame the history of the Iowas in the first half of the nineteenth century entirely as a narrative of dispossession disregards their social adaptation and political maneuverings. Such a framework not only ignores the creativity of Iowa leadership, but also simplifies the social landscape to an Indian-white binary. The Iowas repeatedly allied themselves with the United States to gain political leverage. They made conscious decisions about which political and social strategies to employ in order to counter a dwindling supply of game and encroachment onto their lands.

Notchininga's Map, while not part of a successful attempt to retain territorial control, is still an important political document. It demonstrates creative geopolitical tactics that defy easy categorization in a historical period that is frequently depicted in black and white—or, in this case, red and white—terms. As with farming and metaphorically becoming "like white men," the creation of Notchininga's Map should be understood as a distinct political tactic that can't be described as either "resisting" or "acculturating to" American expansion.

I do not mean to suggest that on the morning of October 7, 1837, Iowa Indians relinquished indigenous forms of spatial knowledge. As with all people, the Iowas had multiple ways of understanding the world around them, and, epistemologically different or not, some of those forms were unique to the Iowas and their Siouan relations. Such constructions, however, were not bound by a single essentialized meaning. We must keep in mind that all historical texts have multiple and sometimes competing lines of discourse. Notchininga's Map is no different. There is no reason to accept Native maps as transparent snapshots of an Indian worldview. Similarly, there is no reason to think that a singular map can define how all Indians, or one band, or even one person, understood his or her spatial existence. European maps have come under close postmodern scrutiny as documents of power and control, either consciously or unconsciously full of political and social agendas. American Indian maps, on the other hand, are generally investigated as apolitical cultural artifacts, a somehow pure or transparent representation of Indian beliefs. It is important that we extend the same deconstructionist framework that we use to explore Euro-American cartography when we investigate indigenous maps. We must investigate them as we do any historical document. That is, they were made in and made for a very specific historical moment with the same political and social agendas that we come to expect from any other document. If we ignore the maps' political agenda, we are left with little more than another version of timeless Indians struggling to hold on to a timeless past.

Notes

1. "Ioway Communities in the Upper Mississippi Valley," part of the *Maps: Finding Our Place in the World* exhibit, Field Museum, Chicago, Illinois, 2007–2008. Map on loan from National Archives, Cartographic Branch, College Park, Maryland (Record Group 75, map 821, tube 520). Number of visitors gathered from museum's press department.

2. "Documents Relating to Ratified and Unratified Treaties," part of the *Maps: Finding Our Place in the World* exhibit. T494 Roll 3, Journal of Proceedings at Council, October 7, 1837 (National Archives [NA], Bureau of Indian Affairs [BIA], record group [RG] 75).

3. While many of the practitioners of the so-called "new Indian history" have moved beyond these extremes, their studies have generally focused on

periods either before 1815 or after 1880. For the earlier period, see, for example, Claudio Saunt, *A New Order of Things: Property, Power, and the Transformation of the Creek Indians, 1733–1816* (New York: Cambridge University Press, 1999); Richard White, *The Middle Ground: Indians, Empires, and Republics in the Great Lakes Region, 1650–1815* (New York: Cambridge University Press, 1991); and Daniel K. Richter, *The Ordeal of the Longhouse: The Peoples of the Iroquois League in the Era of European Colonization* (Chapel Hill: University of North Carolina Press, 1992). For later periods, see, for example, Melissa L. Meyer, *The White Earth Tragedy: Ethnicity and Dispossession at a Minnesota Anishinaabe Reservation, 1889–1920* (Lincoln: University of Nebraska Press, 1994); Brian C. Hosmer, *American Indians in the Marketplace: Persistence and Innovation Among the Menominees and Metlakatlans, 1870–1920* (Lawrence: University of Kansas Press, 1999); David R. Lewis, "Reservation Leadership and the Progressive-Traditional Dichotomy," *Ethnohistory* 38 (Winter 1991): 124–48; and Alexandra Harmon, "American Indians and Land Monopolies in the Gilded Age," *Journal of American History* 90, no. 1 (2003): 106–33. For a work that breaks down the Indian-white binary in the middle of the nineteenth century, see John P. Bowes, *Exiles and Pioneers: Eastern Indians in the Trans-Mississippi West* (New York: Cambridge University Press, 2007).

4. Notchininga's Map has been reproduced in: David Woodward and G. Malcolm Lewis, *The History of Cartography*, vol. 2, bk. 3 (Chicago: University of Chicago Press, 1998); G. Malcolm Lewis, ed., *Cartographic Encounters: Perspectives on Native American Mapmaking and Map Use* (Chicago: University of Chicago Press, 1989); G. Malcolm Lewis, "Indian Maps: Their Place in the History of Plains Cartography," in *Mapping the North American Plains: Essays in the History of Cartography*, ed. Frederick C. Luebke et al. (Norman: University of Oklahoma Press, 1983); William Green, untitled article on Iowa Map of 1837, in *An Atlas of Early Maps of the American Midwest: Part 2*, Illinois State Museum Scientific Papers 29, compiled by W. Raymond Wood (Springfield: Illinois State Museum, 2001); David Turnbull, *Maps Are Territories: Science Is an Atlas* (Chicago: University of Chicago Press, 1989); and Mark Warhus, *Another America: Native American Maps and the History of Our Land* (New York: St. Martin's Press, 1997).

5. J. Brian Harley, "Deconstructing the Map," *Cartographica* 26, no. 2 (1989): 1–20. The most cited postmodern works include Michel Foucault, *Discipline and Punish: The Birth of the Prison*, trans. Alan Sheridan (New York: Vintage Books, 1977); Anthony Giddens, *A Contemporary Critique of Historical Materialism: Power, Property and the State* (London: Macmillan, 1981); and Edward Said, *Orientalism* (New York: Vintage Books, 1979). Harley was not the only scholar to apply postmodern theory to the study of cartography. Like Harley, historian Thongchai Winichakul used Robert D. Sack's idea of territoriality—a

strategy used to control geographical space and, by extension, people and resources within that that space— as a conceptual framework in his examination of the role of mapping in the creation of the "geo-body" of Siam. Thongchai Winichakul, *Siam Mapped: A History of the Geo-Body of a Nation* (Honolulu: University of Hawaii Press, 1994).

6. J. Brian Harley, "Maps, Knowledge, and Power," in *The Iconography of Landscape: Essays on the Symbolic Representation, Design and Use of Past Environments*, ed. Denis Cosgrove and Stephen Daniels (New York: Cambridge University Press, 1988), 301–3. A posthumously published collection of Harley's work contains versions of both articles mentioned and other foundational works: J. Brian Harley, *The New Nature of Maps: Essays in the History of Cartography*, ed. Paul Laxton (Baltimore: Johns Hopkins University Press, 2001).

7. For a description of the map as process rather than text, see Robert A. Rundstrom, "Mapping, Postmodernism, Indigenous People and the Changing Direction of North American Cartography," *Cartographica* 28, no. 2 (Summer 1991): 1–12; and Matthew H. Edney, "Cartography without 'Progress': Reinterpreting the Nature and Historical Development of Mapmaking," *Cartographica* 30, nos. 2–3 (1993): 54–68. A summary of critiques of Harley can be found in Mathew H. Edney, "The Origins and Development of J. B. Harley's Cartographic Theories," *Cartographica* 40, nos. 1–2 (2005); with further discussion in Denis Cosgrove, "Epistemology, Geography, and Cartography: Matthew H. Edney on Brian Harley's Cartographic Theories," *Annals of the Association of American Geographers* 97, no. 1 (2007): 202–9.

8. Gregory H. Nobles, "Straight Lines and Stability: Mapping the Political Order of the Anglo-American Frontier," *Journal of American History* 80, no. 1 (June 1993): 9–35; William Boelhower, "Inventing America: A Model of Cartographic Semiosis," *Word and Image* 4, no. 2 (1988): 475–97; Matthew G. Hannah, "Space and Social Control in the Administration of the Oglala Lakota (Sioux), 1871–1879," *Journal of Historical Geography* 19, no. 4 (1993): 412–32. For studies outside of the United States, see Matthew H. Edney, *Mapping an Empire: The Geographical Construction of British India, 1765–1843* (Chicago: University of Chicago Press, 1990); Matthew Sparke, "A Map That Roared and an Original Atlas: Canada, Cartography, and the Narration of Nation, *Annals of the Association of American Geographers* 88 (1998): 463–95; D. Graham Burnett, *Masters of All They Surveyed: Explorations, Geography, and a British El Dorado* (Chicago: University of Chicago Press, 2000); and Raymond B. Craib, *Cartographic Mexico: A History of State Fixations and Fugitive Landscapes* (Durham, NC: Duke University Press, 2004).

9. In addition to works cited elsewhere in the notes, see James P. Ronda, "'A Chart in His Way': Indian Cartography and the Lewis and Clark Expedition,"

in *Mapping the North American Plains*, ed. Frederick C. Luebke, Frances W. Kaye, and Gary E. Moulton (Norman: University of Oklahoma Press, 1987); Emerson W. Baker et al., eds., *American Beginnings: Exploration, Culture, and Cartography in the Land of Norumbega* (Lincoln: University of Nebraska Press,1994); and William P. Cumming, *The Southeast in Early Maps* (Chapel Hill: University of North Carolina Press, 1998).

10. For an excellent analysis of the state of the field, see Raymond B. Craib, "Relocating Cartography," *Postcolonial Studies* 12, no. 4 (2009): 481–90.

11. Lewis, *Cartographic Encounters*, 9–32. For other examples of reintroduction of indigenous toponyms, see Keith H. Basso, *Wisdom Sits in Places: Landscape and Language Among the Western Apache* (Albuquerque: University of New Mexico Press, 1996); and Hugh Brody, *Maps and Dreams: Indians and the British Columbia Frontier* (Prospect Heights, IL: Waveland Press, 1981); Barbara Belyea, *Dark Storm Moving West* (Calgary: University of Calgary Press, 2007), 73; and Belyea, "Amerindian Maps: The Explorer as Translator," *Journal of Historical Geography* 18, no. 3 (1992): 267–77. Belyea in particular has been a vocal critic of those she perceives as categorizing Indian maps as immature versions of Western geographic knowledge, including G. Malcolm Lewis and Denis Wood. See Barbara Belyea, "Review Article of Denis Wood's *The Power of Maps*, and the Author's Reply," *Cartographica* 29, nos. 3–4 (1992): 94–99. For a further discussion of this debate, see Edney, "Cartography Without 'Progress.'"

12. In many ways, this conclusion was at the heart of the conference from which this collection was drawn, "Indigenous Environments: African and North American Environmental Knowledge and Practices Compared," held at Bowdoin College, New Brunswick, Maine, April 3–5, 2008. Also see the work of Arun Agrawal, "Dismantling the Divide Between Indigenous and Scientific Knowledge," *Development and Change* 26 (1995): 413–39.

13. A noteworthy exception to the practice of placing Indians within larger multicultural histories has been Calvin Martin. Martin argues that by disregarding the uniqueness of Indian "thought-worlds," historians are simply continuing the practice of colonization. The only way to write authentic histories of Indians, Martin argues, is to "get out of history, as we know it." Calvin Martin, ed., *The American Indian and the Problem of History* (New York: Oxford University Press, 1987), 6, 27. For a discussion of the boundaries between history and anthropology, see Melissa L. Meyer and Kerwin L. Klein, "Native American Studies and the End of Ethnohistory," in *Studying Native America: Problems and Prospects*, ed. Russell Thornton (Madison: University of Wisconsin Press, 1998), 182–216.

14. Woodward and Lewis, *The History of Cartography*, 51–181.

15. In addition to others mentioned in the notes, see Benjamin S. Orlove, "Mapping Reeds and Reading Maps: The Politics of Representation in Lake

Titicaca," *American Ethnologist* 18, no. 1 (1991): 3–38; Orlove, "The Ethnography of Maps: The Cultural and Social Contexts of Cartographic Representation in Peru," *Cartographica* 30, no. 1 (1993): 29–46; and Karl H. Offen, "Creating Mosquitia: Mapping Amerindian Spatial Practices in Eastern Central America, 1629–1779," *Journal of Historical Geography* 33, no. 2 (2007): 254–82.

16. While there are more than seventy spellings of "Iowa" used to designate the tribe, these variations were phoenetic pronunciations of the name used by the Indians themselves, such as "*aj u wej*." See Mildred Mott Wedel, "A Synonym of Names for the Iowa Indians," *Journal of the Iowa Archaeological Society* (1978): 48–72. I will use the name Iowa, unless referred to differently in the original documents.

17. Alanson Skinner, "Ethnology of the Ioway Indians," *Bulletin of the Public Museum of the City of Milwaukee* 5, no. 4 (1926): 183–85. For further anthropological information, including creation stories, see James Owen Dorsey Papers, group 4800, Anthropology Archives, Smithsonian Institution, Suitland, Maryland, esp. subgroups 294 and 296. For an ethnohistory of the Iowas, see Martha Royce Blaine, *The Ioway Indians* (Norman: University of Oklahoma Press, 1979); Mildred Mott Wedel, "The Iowa Indians," in *Handbook of North American Indians*, vol. 13, bk. 1 (Washington, DC: Smithsonian Institution, 2001): 432–46; and Duane C. Anderson, "Ioway Ethnohistory: A Review," pts. 1 and 2, *Annals of Iowa* 41, no. 8 (Spring 1973): 1228–41; *Annals of Iowa* 42, no. 1 (Summer 1973): 41–59.

18. Thomas L. McKenney and James Hall, *Biographical Sketches and Anecdotes of Ninety-Five of 120 Principal Chiefs from the Indian Tribes of North America* (Philadelphia: Frederick W. Greenough, 1838), 146.

19. "McCarter & English Indian Claims Cases," Princeton Collections of Western Americana (hereafter cited as PCWA), docket 135, exhibit 18.

20. These investigations have interrogated the primacy of tribal allegiance in regional social structures. A particularly concise account of the inquiry can be found in Patricia Albers and Jeanne Kay, "Sharing the Land: A Study in American Indian Territoriality," in *A Cultural Geography of North American Indians*, ed. Thomas E. Ross and Tyrel G. Moore (Boulder, CO: Westview Press, 1987), 53:

> In order to understand American Indian territoriality it is necessary to look at land-use from a regional rather than tribally-based perspective, and to distinguish between ideological claims to and the actual use of a specific territory.... In areas which have a history of multiple tribal use, the conditions of "sharing" must be analyzed to determine what kinds of land-claims members of different tribes hold and on what basis these rights are being asserted.

What are the sociopolitical bodies which hold land in common and are these groups always organized along single tribal lines? Can relationships, then, such as those based on kinship, manage land-rights independent of tribal allegiances?

See also Patricia C. Albers, "Changing Patterns of Ethnicity in the Northeastern Plains, 1780–1870," in *History Power and Identity: Ethnogenesis in the Americas, 1492–1992*, ed. Jonathan D. Hill (Iowa City: University of Iowa Press, 1996); and Theodore Binnema, *Common and Contested Ground; A Human and Environmental History of the Northwestern Plains* (Norman: University of Oklahoma Press, 2001).

21. Albers and Kay, "Sharing the Land."

22. Ibid.

23. See White, *The Middle Ground*. For an interesting case study tracing the ravages of smallpox, see Elizabeth A. Fenn, *Pox Americana: The Great Smallpox Epidemic of 1775–82* (New York: Hill and Wang, 2001).

24. Anthony F. C. Wallace, "The Iowa and Sac-and-Fox Indians in Iowa and Missouri." Unpublished findings as expert witness before U.S. Claims Commission, October 1954, 17–21 (PCWA, box 39, folder 11).

25. "Letters Sent by the Great Nemaha Agency," M234 R362, December 14, 1836 (NA, BIA, RG 75).

26. Zebulon M. Pike, *An Account of Expeditions to the Source of the Mississippi, and Through the Western Parts of Louisiana, to the Sources of the Arkansas, Kans, La Platte, and Pierre Juan Rivers: Performed by Order of the Government of the United States During the Years 1805, 1806, and 1807* (Philadelphia: C. & A. Conrad, 1810), 57.

27. Charles J. Kappler, *Indian Affairs: Laws and Treaties*, vols. 1 and 2 (Washington, DC: Government Printing Office), 1904; vol. 3, 1913; vol. 4, 1919; digital version, http://digital.library.okstate.edu/kappler/index.htm.

28. Edwin C. Carter, ed., *The Territorial Papers of the United States*, vol. 8 (Washington, DC: Government Printing Office, 1951), 76–80.

29. We must recognize that "divisions" within tribes in the early years of the eighteenth century is a bit of a misnomer, as the U.S. government–created delineation of "tribe" had not gained importance within the Indian social structure of decentralized bands. Scholars now recognize that intertribal kinship ties and individual relationships of reciprocity played a significant, if not primary, factor in the political, social, and economic interactions of both Indians and whites at this time. Therefore, reports such as those by Indian agent Nicolas Boilivin, claiming that the "Ioway and Sacs were hostile towards each other," must not be taken as indications of full-fledged tribal warfare, but were probably false generalizations about the Iowas' interactions

with various parties of Rock River Sac, who were not bound by the same ties of kinship as the Missouri Sac. See Meriwether Lewis, *Original Journals of Lewis and Clark Expedition*, ed. Reuben Gold Thwaites, vol. 7 (Scituate, MA: Digital Scanning, Inc., 2001), 374; and Blaine, *The Ioway Indians*, 99.

30. For a description of the continued violence in the region, see Blaine, *The Ioway Indians*, 113–26.

31. "William Clark to Secretary of War," St. Louis, October 18, 1815. Original location unknown (PCWA, docket 135, exhibit 46).

32. In addition to the protection sought from the Americans, the Iowas may have understood the 1815 treaty as an alliance of reciprocity. In an effort to maintain control of the valuable Mississippi and Missouri watersheds during the War of 1812, Americans provided various tribes in the region with twenty thousand dollars' worth of goods. A select few chiefs, including Hard Heart of the Iowas, received peace medals that professed their status as leaders and their ability to negotiate with others of the same rank. Perhaps not coincidentally, Hard Heart's is one of the fifteen signatures on the 1815 treaty. It is not hard to imagine that Hard Heart's personal bonds of reciprocity with the Americans, established during the War of 1812, played a role in his decision to seek protection from the Americans in 1815.

33. Richard White, "The Winning of the West: The Expansion of the Western Sioux in the Eighteenth and Nineteenth Centuries," *Journal of American History* 65 (1978): 320.

34. Paul Wilhelm (Duke of Wurttemberg), *Travels in North America, 1822–1824*, ed. Savoie Lottinville, trans. W. Robert Nitske (Norman: University of Oklahoma Press, 1973), 302.

35. Wallace, "The Iowa and Sac-and-Fox Indians," 14–39.

36. Edwin C. Carter, ed., *The Territorial Papers of the United States*, vol. 15 (Washington, DC: Government Printing Office, 1951), 562–64.

37. Wilhelm, *Travels in North America*, 316.

38. In 1955, the United States Indian Claims Commission finally decided on the annuities due each tribe. Most of the proceedings centered around the question of historic territorial control, with the 1825 treaty playing an important role.

39. Henry R. Schoolcraft, *Thirty Years with the Indian Tribes*, 215–16, as cited in Emma H. Blair, *The Indian Tribes of the Upper Mississippi Valley and the Region of the Great Lakes*, vol. 2 (Cleveland, OH: Arthur H. Clark, 1912), 356–57.

40. Kappler, *Indian Affairs*, Treaty with the Iowa, 1824, articles 2 and 3, http://digital.library.okstate.edu/kappler/Vol2/treaties/iow0208.htm.

41. "Documents Relating to Ratified and Unratified Treaties," T494 Roll 2, Minutes of Council held at Prairie du Chien, July 7–16, 1830 (NA, BIA, RG 75).

42. For studies that complicate such a view, see, for example, Lucy Eldersveld Murphy, *A Gathering of Rivers: Indians, Métis, and Mining in the Western Great*

Lakes, 1737–1832 (Lincoln: University of Nebraska Press, 2000), in which she describes the Fox Indians' successful mining operations; and Frederick E. Hoxie, *Parading Through History; The Making of the Crow Nation in America, 1805–1935* (New York: Cambridge University Press, 1995). Also see Gary C. Anderson, *Kinsmen of Another Kind: Dakota-White Relations in the Upper Mississippi Valley, 1650–1862* (Lincoln: University of Nebraska Press, 1984); and Tanis C. Thorne, *The Many Hands of My Relations: French and Indians on the Lower Missouri* (Columbia: University of Missouri Press, 1996). For a discussion of American expansionism in the early republics, see Reginald Horsman, *Expansion and American Indian Policy, 1783–1812* (Norman: University of Oklahoma Press, 1992).

43. "Documents Relating to Ratified and Unratified Treaties."

44. "Letters Sent by Office of the BIA," M21 R12, Hughes to Secretary of War Cass, April 12, 1834 (NA, BIA, RG 75).

45. Kappler, *Indian Affairs*, Treaty with the Iowa, etc., 1836, http://digital.library.okstate.edu/kappler/Vol2/treaties/iow0208.htm.

46. "Letters Received, Great Nemaha," Hughes to Clark, August 26, 1837 (PCWA, docket 153, exhibit 162; original NA, BIA, RG 75).

47. "Letters Received, Great Nemaha," H-62 Document A, 1837 (PCWA, docket 138, exhibit 153; original, NA, BIA, RG 75).

48. "Letters Received, Great Nemaha," H-62 Document B, 1837 (PCWA, docket 138, exhibit 155; original NA, BIA, RG 75).

49. "Documents Relating to Ratified and Unratified Treaties," T494, Roll 3; see Mildred Mott Wedel, "The Relation of Historic Indian Tribes to Archaeological Manifestations in Iowa," *Iowa Journal of History and Politics* 36, no.1 (1962): 227–314; Mildred Mott Wedel, "Indian Villages on the Upper Iowa River" *Palimpsest* 47, no. 12 (1961): 561–92.

50. Barbara Belyea, "Inland Journeys, Native Maps," in *Cartographic Encounters: Perspectives on Native American Mapmaking and Map Use*, ed. G. Malcolm Lewis (Chicago: University of Chicago Press, 1989), 141.

51. An example of a map in which the scale is dependent upon the viewer's point of view is the famous 1976 Saul Steinburg illustration "View of the World," published as the cover of the March 29, 1976, issue of the *New Yorker*.

52. Turnbull, *Maps are Territories*, 23.

53. Green, Untitled Article on Iowa Map of 1837.

54. Blaine, *The Ioway Indians*, 169.

55. "Letters Received, Great Nemaha 1837," Dougherty to Clark, May 30, 1838 (PCWA, docket 153, exhibit 175; original NA, BIA, RG 75).

56. Kappler, *Indian Affairs*, Treaty with the Iowa, 1838, http://digital.library.okstate.edu/kappler/Vol2/treaties/iow0208.htm.

CHAPTER 2

On Biomedicine, Transfers of Knowledge, and Malaria Treatments in Eastern North America and Tropical Africa

James L. A. Webb, Jr.

DURING THE early years of the "Columbian Exchange," malaria parasites crossed the Atlantic Ocean in the bloodstreams of European colonists and African captives. In the Americas, anopheline mosquitoes took blood meals from these immigrants and proved biologically capable of hosting the parasites. The infected mosquitoes then took blood meals from noninfected individuals and spread malaria to them.

This introduction of malaria in the Americas was far less spectacular in its initial demographic impact than the first waves of smallpox and measles that killed large numbers of Native Americans. Over time, however, malaria became an endemic disease in the New World and at least by the nineteenth century had become the principal disease burden of eastern North America. This relatively rapid integration of European and tropical African malarial zones in the Americas stands in sharp contrast to the lack of disease integration between the European and the tropical African malarial zones in the Old World. There, the European and North African mosquito vectors were less efficient in transmitting malaria, and they were unable to host the genotypes of the falciparum malaria parasites of tropical Africa below the Sahara. The result was that malaria in tropical Africa remained particularly deadly to nonimmune Europeans, and this epidemiological barrier prevented the colonization of tropical Africa before the late nineteenth century.[1]

Treatment of malaria was a major concern for the African and European societies that suffered the infections. During the first era of European exploration, conquest, and colonial rule (1450–1800), as Europeans encountered new disease environments, they sought to expand their knowledge of the flora of the wider world. One of the principal motivations was the quest for medically useful plants.[2] In the late sixteenth century, the Spaniards learned that the bark of the cinchona tree that grew wild on the eastern slopes of the Andes was effective in treating malaria, and cinchona bark slowly entered the Western medical practice as the first disease-specific drug in the materia medica. This remedy, however, remained relatively scarce and expensive before the last quarter of the nineteenth century, and thus beyond the means of most sufferers.[3]

This essay develops a framework for considering the transfers of knowledge about malaria treatments that took place between European Americans and Native Americans in eastern North America and between Europeans and Africans in tropical Africa. It considers the nature of premodern therapeutic systems, the different malarial environments of eastern North America and tropical Africa, and the broad contexts in which the transfers of knowledge about malaria treatments may be understood.

Premodern Therapeutic Systems

Premodern therapeutic systems appear to have shared two meta-elements. The first was a broad distinction between two fundamental categories of illnesses: one that was caused by interventions from the spirit world, and one that was "natural."[4] The idea of a category of disease linked to the spirit world appears to be anciently rooted in our deep human past, a part of our common inheritance of a worldview shaped by animism.[5] This worldview likely traveled with the earliest migrants out of Africa into Eurasia and the Americas, and the need to intervene in the spirit world became a foundational element of healing cultures around the world. This category of spirit-induced illness persists today in "modern" cultures, in several modalities of belief about the spiritual dimensions of disease.[6] By contrast, the second category of diseases included those that were unexceptional and relatively mild. They were generally accepted as mundane conditions of life.

The second meta-element was a broad distinction between two categories of therapies. The first category was based upon the use of behavior modifications, dietary restrictions, and/or biomedicines that were prepared from plants or animal products. This biomedical knowledge was a blend of empirical observations, imputations, and beliefs about the biophysical effects of behavior change and remedies based on plant and animal products. The relief that some sufferers of common ailments and conditions gained from palliative treatment or practical cure validated the therapeutics. The second therapeutic category was of ritual, spiritual interventions to effect cures. Shamanist specialists who possessed occult knowledge typically carried out these interventions.

The boundaries between categories of disease and categories of therapy were mutable. Some "simple" or "natural" illnesses might progress in severity and be considered anew as spirit-caused. Similarly, some "natural" illness that normally required a biomedicine or dietary prescription might progress in severity and be seen to require a ritual intervention (sometimes in combination with biomedicines). In practice, many therapeutic approaches blended ritual and biomedicine, and in this sense all premodern systems might properly be considered as medically pluralistic.

Biomedical knowledge about plants that could be used for routine medical treatment and in combination with spiritual therapy everywhere must have evolved over time. Healers selected plants from local floral domains for regular use, and exotics, too, must have entered into the very earliest exchanges that took place over medium and long distances. In this respect, the systems of indigenous knowledge in various world regions might best be thought of as the legacies of regional experimentation and exchange rather than the proprietary knowledge of tribes or ethnic groups. The eastern North American and tropical African therapeutic systems, too, must have changed over time (as did the Afro-Eurasian systems); yet, because social scientists have generally considered these systems of indigenous knowledge to be beyond the reach of historical study in the eras before European invasion, we know few specifics about their historical evolution.

Malaria Zones

The introduction of malaria to North America in the early seventeenth century lagged by about one hundred years the introduction of malaria into the Caribbean and South and Central American tropics. In North America, two zones of malarial infection developed—one of predominantly *Plasmodium vivax* infections (with some *P. malariae* infections) from northern Europe, and another of mixed infections of *P. vivax*, *P.*

malariae, and *P. falciparum* from southern Europe and new genotypes of *P. falciparum* infections from tropical Africa—that were lateral, blended extensions of the Afro-Eurasian zones. In North America, the biological division between these two zones, determined by the different minimum temperature requirements for the sexual reproduction of the vivax and falciparum parasites in the mosquito, ran approximately through what would become the state of Maryland.

The two malarial zones of North America grew to be distinctively different from their Eurasian progenitors, because the malarial mosaics were also determined in part by the biological makeup of the human beings who became infected and served as secondary hosts and reservoirs of infection. In sharp contrast to the African and the African American communities that formed in North America, the European and the Native American communities had no genetic defenses against any of the malaria parasites. The only successful accommodation was hard-won immunities that could be achieved after repeated infections. To the north of Maryland, where vivax infections (known colloquially as the "ague"—from the French *aïgu*, for an acute fever) were predominant, the vast majority of infections for Europeans and Native Americans resulted in anemia-induced lassitude, after passing through the nightmarishly acute phases of fevers and chills.

In the colony of Maryland and farther south, falciparum entered the mix of malarial infections. Falciparum infections were deadly, and could produce mortality of up to 50 percent in nonimmunes, which included all Europeans and Native Americans who had not already had their first encounter. In these southern colonies, a stream of African immigrants came to North America armed with an array of genetic defenses against malaria. Virtually all carried a genetic mutation known as Duffy antigen negativity, which provided complete protection against vivax infections. Thus, where African populations predominated, falciparum infections were more common. In addition, because of the high rates of endemic falciparum infection in western Africa, virtually all immigrants from Africa possessed acquired immunities to falciparum, and many African immigrants carried genetic defenses against falciparum infections, including sickle-cell hemoglobin.[7]

Therapeutic Zones and Knowledge Transfers

Tree barks were an important source of medicines throughout the Americas, and some barks were in common use over large regions. In eastern North America, for example, before 1492 the ill had drunk tinctures from the bark of the dogwood tree (*Cornus florida*) as a painkiller and sleep aid.

The zone of dogwood bark use fundamentally matched the habitat range for the dogwood tree and did not coincide with any single cultural zone, language family, or ethnic group. In this regard, the use of dogwood bark likely indicates a broader therapeutic zone with some threads of common culture that stretched from the Amazon through the Caribbean to what is today Canada. With the arrival of malaria parasites in eastern North America, dogwood bark began to be used to treat the symptoms of fever and chills.

The zone of therapeutic use of dogwood bark in the Americas was a rough analogue to a similar therapeutic zone in Eurasia, in which opium was a common palliative for malaria over a vast region that stretched from China to India. During the course of the European maritime expansion into the Indian Ocean world, the opium therapeutic zone expanded farther. Biomedical knowledge about opium to treat malaria reached Europe and was incorporated into European folk therapeutics. When Europeans encountered malaria in eastern North America, they brought their biomedical knowledge of opium treatment from Asia to bear on the problem. In eastern North America, European American therapies treated malaria parasites from western Eurasia and tropical Africa with biomedical knowledge from Asia.

Other elements of what was originally Asian biomedical knowledge became globalized through maritime trade and were incorporated into the "indigenous knowledge" of Native Americans. The example of American ginseng (*Panax quinquefolius* L.) is instructive. The Cherokees used a decoction of the root to treat headaches, cramps, and menstrual problems and blew chewed root on the spot to treat pains in the side. The Cherokees, who produced and sold ginseng to traders, knew the plant by its abbreviation "sang." As James Mooney recorded in his 1891 publication on the sacred formulas of the Cherokees: "The Cherokees sell large quantities of sang to the traders for 50 cents per pound, nearly equivalent there to two days' wages, a fact which has doubtless increased their idea of its importance.... The Chinese name, ginseng, is said to refer to the fancied resemblance of the root to a human figure, while in the Cherokee formulas it is addressed as the 'great man' or 'little man,' and this resemblance no doubt has much to do with the estimation in which it is held by both peoples."[8]

Malaria Treatment in Eastern North America

Native Americans, without prior experience of malaria, drew upon their biomedical knowledge about how to treat other diseases in an effort to counteract the exotic. They used the barks of the dogwood tree (*Cornus florida*), the yellow poplar or tulip tree (*Liriodendron tulipifera*), the wild cherry tree (*Prunus virginiana*), and the oak tree (*Querus*)—which were held to be efficacious in the treatment of fevers and to relieve headache—to counteract malarial fevers and chills.[9] Among northern Native Americans, boneset was widely used as a fever remedy, and indeed, an early nineteenth-century writer noted that the Indian name for boneset translated as "ague-weed."[10] All apparently were effective in reducing malarial symptoms; none, however, were medically active against the parasites themselves.[11]

Dogwood bark as a malaria therapy entered into common use among European immigrants and Native Americans in eastern North America. Some European Americans, such as the Pennsylvania Germans, used dogwood bark more broadly as a general fever remedy.[12] In southeastern North America, dogwood bark was blended with cinchona bark from the rain forests of the eastern Andes and alcohol to treat malarial fever. This was the potion that was recommended by the U.S. forces in Florida during the Second Seminole War (1835–1842).

European Americans initially conceived of their borrowings from the Native American pharmacopoeia as "Indian medicine." European American popular confidence in Native American medicine was high in the early nineteenth century. A succession of books record this enthusiasm: in 1813 in Cincinnati, *The Indian Doctor's Dispensary* was published; in 1836, *The Indian Guide to Health*; in 1838, *The North American Indian Doctor, or Nature's Method of Curing and Preventing Disease According to the Indians*.[13]

At least by the mid-nineteenth century, European Americans had adopted a variety of Native American biomedicals for use as antimalarials. As Daniel Drake noted:

> Many of our native bitters have been more or less extensively used to arrest the paroxysms of intermittent fever. The favorites are, or have been, the bark of the *Cornus Florida*, or dogwood; *Liriodendron Tulipifera*, or yellow poplar; *Prunus Virginiana*, or wild cherry tree, and the herbs *Eupatorium perefoliatum*, or thoroughwart, and *Sabbatia angularis* (formerly *Chironia ang.*) or American centaury. As it was an old professional opinion that the superior efficacy of the cinchona bark, over other bitters, arose from the union of an astringent principle, it has been customary to combine, with the bark of the trees just

mentioned, a quantity of oak or some other astringent bark, and to render the whole stimulating with wine or whisky; frequently, indeed, to administer them in the form of tincture.[14]

During the second quarter of the nineteenth century, as the laboratory techniques for isolating the pure alkaloids (quinine and cinchonine) from cinchona bark became known, the cinchona alkaloids began to replace tree bark in the treatment of malaria, although the cinchona alkaloids remained relatively expensive and beyond the means of some European American sufferers. During the U.S. Civil War (1861–1865), the Northern forces choked off the flow of cinchona alkaloids to the South and thereby forced a return to tree bark use. Malaria was one of—and perhaps the most important of—the killing and debilitating wartime diseases. Dogwood bark was the principal drug used by the Confederate army.[15]

Native American knowledge of the analgesic action of tree barks such as dogwood was part of a body of practical knowledge about the medically active properties of plants, and part of a larger transfer of Native American biomedical knowledge to European Americans that was incorporated into the official pharmacopoeia of the United States.[16] In North America, the barks of the sarsaparilla and poplar trees, as well as of willows, were employed to fight fever; they contained active chemical compounds similar to those in aspirin.[17] These barks entered into therapeutic cultures of the European Americans and had broad applications, although later studies have concluded that, like dogwood bark, they were ineffective against the malaria parasites.[18]

Initially credited to Native Americans, over time the "Indian medicine" came to be thought of as *knowledge of the land* that would be gained naturally by virtue of lengthy residence, and by the early twentieth century the knowledge of native plants was passing into a corpus of scientific knowledge. Even as late as the 1920s, however, some medical authorities expressed their appreciation of the importance of some Native American medical practices. For example, Fielding H. Garrison, the author of *An Introduction to the History of Medicine*, wrote appreciatively: "The Indian knew, for example, the importance of keeping the skin, bowels, and kidneys open, and, to this end, the geyser, the warm spring, and the sweat oven were his natural substitutes for a Turkish bath. Emesis, or catharsis, followed by a vapor bath and a cold plunge, set off by a dose of willow-bark decoction (salicin), was the North American Indian's successful therapeutic scheme in the case of intermittent and remittent fevers; a vapor bath and cimicifuga were his mainstays against rheumatism."[19]

Elements of European indigenous folk knowledge about malaria likewise seem to have passed to the Native Americans. Europeans, including the English from the southeastern reaches of Great Britain, had had a long and miserable experience with malaria, and they had developed palliative treatments based upon the use of alcohol, herbs, and, at least by the early nineteenth century, opium. Yet the most significant element of "knowledge" about malaria that had been gained in western Europe and confirmed in North America was an epidemiological notion that the disease came about as a result of exposure to marshland and other wetlands. This was expressed as "miasmatic theory." The core idea was that miasmas, which were often foul-smelling as a result of decomposing vegetative matter, gave rise to disease, particularly to malaria. This general notion diffused easily across cultural lines. Native Americans associated marshlands with mosquitoes, and some Native American groups, such as the Cherokees, also associated disease with insects. There was thus a rich nexus of common associations that predated the discovery in 1897 that the female anopheline mosquito was the insect vector for malaria.

Other important cultural borrowings of biomedical knowledge took place in eastern North America. African and African American slaves, far from their native flora, borrowed the biomedical knowledge of Native Americans and adopted some European medical practices such as purging and bleeding. They developed a cosmology of "African magic" that was an amalgam of elements from different tropical African belief systems based upon the two categories of "natural" and "spirit-caused" illnesses. In this respect, the African American ethnomedical system, too, was an expression of "globalization."[20] There was little borrowing, however, by European Americans from the African American synthesis, perhaps because of white fear of African "magic" and poisoning.[21]

In sum, during the nineteenth century in eastern North America, knowledge about the treatment of malaria was an amalgam of ideas that blended Asian, Native South American, and Native North American therapies with European ideas about epidemiology. This early stage in the globalization of malaria therapeutic practice was short-lived and never fully realized. With the rise of scientific medical practice in the early twentieth century, plant medicines other than the cinchona alkaloids began to drop out of the pharmacopoeia. Native American biomedical practice eventually was downgraded to an indigenous body of knowledge principally of ethnographic interest, rather than practical use. The earlier era of cross-cultural influences on biomedical practices faded from memory.

Malaria Treatment in Tropical Africa

How do the eastern North American experiences of therapeutic zones and knowledge transfers compare with those in tropical Africa? The inhabitants of tropical Africa suffered more from the ravages of malaria than any other peoples in the world. They deployed a variety of cultural practices that mitigated the impact of the disease. These ranged from the avoidance by highland peoples of malarial lowlands to the use of biomedicals. Throughout tropical Africa, a wide array of plants were used to treat the symptoms of malaria. Recent scientific investigations indicate that some of these plants do have antimalarial properties, although the plant medicines are not as efficacious as cinchona alkaloids and bark. They were, however, effective in reducing the severity of acute attacks in individuals. The disease burden, nonetheless, remained heavy. In the era of the Atlantic slave trade (1450–1880), malaria claimed the lives of hundreds of thousands of Africans annually and produced millions of cases of acute sickness.

Although modern science recognized that malaria was (and is) an acute problem in tropical Africa, most Africans did not consider it to be so. This is in large measure because the symptoms of malaria are highly varied, and as is true of many today, most Africans in the past did not think of malaria as a killing disease. The experience of malaria as an adult is so common that it is difficult to appreciate its role as a childhood killer.

Tropical Africans did not develop versions of miasmatic theory. The principal mosquito vectors for malaria in Africa were *Anopheles gambiae* and *Anopheles funestus*, which typically bred in small depressions in the soil (even as small as a human heelprint) and in fresh water. Some vectors bred in coastal swamps, but this was hardly the rule. African epidemiological thinking about malaria tended to focus on the experience of fever and link it to other sources of heat, rather than focus on malarial topography. A common belief was that malaria was caused by exposure to the sun.

During the early era of the Atlantic slave trade (1450–1750), some European traders, particularly those who intermarried and formed Afro-European communities along the western African coast, probably came to appreciate some of the practical elements of African biomedical knowledge.[22] Europeans who were not longtime residents and were directly engaged in the export trades in slaves and tropical goods showed scant interest in African plants except those of obvious economic importance, at least before the mid-eighteenth century. Europeans collected and sent back to Europe a total of eleven plants from tropical Africa before the publication of Linnaeus's *Species Plantarum* in 1753.[23] From the mid-eighteenth to the early nineteenth century, a handful of Europeans who were temporarily resident undertook notable botanical investigations along the western African coast. In Senegal, the naturalist Michel Adanson (1749–1754) explored the local flora, and near Christiansborg Castle, in contemporary Ghana, the Danish botanists Paul E. Isert (1783–1787) and Peter Thonning (1799–1803) collected African plants, at least in part with a goal of finding medicinal herbs.[24]

Although African biomedical knowledge included knowledge of plants that could reduce the suffering from acute malaria attacks (and may have been able to reduce the parasite load), no African antimalarial medicine entered into general European practice, nor did any other kind of African biomedical treatment.[25] Consequently, Europeans appear to have made no efforts to transplant medically active tropical African plants in the European colonies.[26] For Europeans resident along the western African coast, the reliable standby treatment for malaria throughout the eighteenth and nineteenth centuries remained cinchona bark and, from the mid-nineteenth century, the cinchona alkaloids.[27]

In tropical Africa, as in eastern North America, the realm of ritual spiritual interventions was culturally closed to Europeans. In western Africa, practitioners of the occult arts were organized into secret societies, and a major element of their practice was concerned with healing. Similarly, in central and southern Africa, the *ngoma* "cults of affliction" provided healing rituals to their adherents, but the social and cultural contexts were too vastly different to admit European participation.[28]

As in eastern North America, by the late nineteenth century, the rise of pseudoscientific racism and scientific medicine led to a loss of interest in practical indigenous biomedical knowledge. The military conquest of tropical Africa and the establishment of European rule over African subjects likewise militated against European borrowing from African biomedical knowledge. In the early twentieth century, new understandings about the transmission of malaria led Europeans to efforts at mosquito control and prophylaxis. Measurements of the high parasite loads of infected African children led Europeans to identify them as the principal threat to European health, and Europeans sought to live at safe distances from African communities. The discovery of adult African immunities to malaria reinforced the focus of tropical medicine on the protection of Europeans.

The broad historical outlines of the interaction of medical traditions in tropical Africa are substantially different from those in eastern North America. Malaria was the principal threat to Europeans along the West African coast. The malarial environment was far more dangerous in West

Africa than in eastern North America. Most Europeans had not previously experienced falciparum infections and had no acquired immunity. Their first encounters were often fatal. Their best strategy was to limit their exposure to disease along the African coast by shortening their lengths of visit to the greatest extent possible.

The deadly malarial environment also meant that African palliative or suppressive therapies were of marginal utility for nonimmune Europeans. It is likely that for this reason, among others, they were largely ignored. By the late nineteenth century, when the European colonization of tropical Africa began in earnest, the colonizers had quinine (as well as rudimentary public health measures), which greatly reduced their risks of sickness and death, although their risks were still elevated compared to their age cohorts in Europe.[29] In an era before the discovery of genetic and immunological defenses against malarial infections, the greater resiliency of tropical Africans was cast in racial terms, a judgment that seemed to be borne out by the experience of Africans in the Americas. Whatever the nature of African medicines, they were assumed to have little relevance for European colonizers. European colonial settlement in the highlands of tropical East and southeast Africa began only in the 1920s, when European knowledge of the vectors, parasites, and treatment regimens was growing rapidly. They saw little to learn about malaria therapeutics from the communities around them. These judgments were reinforced when the intensity of endemic infections among older children and adults and the high rate of child mortality came into clearer focus.

In contrast to the situation in eastern North America, where malaria became a progressively less serious health problem in the first half of the twentieth century, malaria remained a deadly concern in tropical Africa. In the immediate aftermath of the Second World War, the new techniques of indoor residual spraying with insecticides to kill adult anopheline mosquitoes and thereby reduce or eliminate the transmission of malaria spread quickly within sub-Saharan Africa. They were first practiced in the white settler colonies of South Africa and Rhodesia, at the southern edge of tropical Africa, in urban areas, and in regions where expatriate firms had investments in mining or agriculture. The malaria control projects were run by malariologists and had a technologically narrow purchase. The experts did not survey the state of African biomedical knowledge about malaria treatment. They drew a handful of Western-educated Africans into scientific training, in which they learned Western medical conceptions about malaria. In the heyday of scientific modernism, the common juxtaposition was of Western "science" and African "superstition."

In the aftermath of the Second World War, the synthetic antimalarial drug chloroquine became widely available. It was both inexpensive and highly effective in preventing and curing falciparum malaria. It became the frontline drug in the struggle against malaria during the global eradication campaign (1955–1969). And when other interventions, such as indoor residual spraying with DDT, proved unable to eradicate the disease and the recurrent costs were deemed too high to bear, chloroquine continued to serve its purpose. After the independence of the former British and French African colonies, merchants continued to import chloroquine, which was available in rural and urban tropical Africa so inexpensively that most sufferers had access to it. Many Africans, however, continued to use the biomedicines of the fields and forests as well.

In the late 1980s, the malaria parasites developed resistance to chloroquine, and this resistance soon spread widely in tropical Africa. By the mid-1990s, chloroquine was unreliable as a malaria therapy, and death rates in tropical Africa began to climb steeply, reaching levels that were comparable to the 1930s, before the era of Western medical intervention. This, then, was the general context for the emergence of international interest in African biomedical knowledge.

Conclusions

This brief essay explores different patterns of cross-cultural borrowing of malaria therapeutic practices in eastern North America and tropical Africa. Over the course of the eighteenth and nineteenth centuries, European Americans and Native Americans suffered malarial infections, and European Americans borrowed freely from Native American biomedical knowledge. Indigenous Native American medicines became an integral part of malaria treatment for European Americans. Native plants and their medically active properties were described in the United States Pharmacopoeia into the early decades of the twentieth century. By the mid-twentieth century, these borrowings had largely slipped away from historical memory.

By contrast, Europeans did not borrow tropical African biomedical knowledge. In part, this was owing to the hostile epidemiological environment that foreclosed the possibility of significant European settlement. From the eighteenth century, Europeans had knowledge of cinchona bark and, from the mid-nineteenth century, quinine, and thus tropical African malaria therapies appeared to be of little significance for them. Only in the late twentieth century, coincident with the emergence of malarial parasite resistance to the frontline antimalarial drug, chloroquine, was interest stimulated in indigenous African medical knowledge.

Notes

1. James L. A. Webb, Jr., *Humanity's Burden: A Global History of Malaria* (New York: Cambridge University Press, 2009), 42–65.

2. Early in the era of direct maritime trade with southern Asia, various European trading companies and imperial ventures set up botanical gardens in Asia—and the Dutch East India Company set out a garden at the Cape of Good Hope—with an eye to exploiting the medicinal properties of local plants. See Richard H. Grove, *Green Imperialism: Colonial Expansion, Tropical Island Edens and the Origins of Environmentalism, 1600–1860* (Cambridge: Cambridge University Press, 1995); G. Scott and M. L. Hewett, "Pioneers in Ethnopharmacology: The Dutch East India Company (VOC) at the Cape from 1650 to 1800," *Journal of Ethnopharmacology* 115, no. 3 (2008): 339–60.

Europeans also carried out extensive "bioprospecting" in the New World. See Londa L. Schiebinger, *Plants and Empire: Colonial Bioprospecting in the Atlantic World* (Cambridge, MA: Harvard University Press, 2004).

3. Webb, *Humanity's Burden*, 66–91.

4. The category of spirit-caused disease is, of course, extremely broad, and some groups drew finer distinctions. The Cherokees, for example, according to James Mooney and Frans M. Olbrechts, recognized "natural," "supernatural," and "preternatural" causes of disease (James Mooney, *The Swimmer Manuscript: Cherokee Sacred Formulas and Medicinal Prescriptions*, revised, completed, and edited by Frans M. Olbrechts [Washington, DC: United States Government Printing Office, 1932], 14–39).

5. John R. McNeill and William H. McNeill, *The Human Web: A Bird's-Eye View of World History* (New York: Norton, 2003), 17–18.

6. Anne Harrington, *The Cure Within: A History of Mind-Body Medicine* (Cambridge, MA: Harvard University Press, 2008).

7. By contrast with North America, the malarial environment in tropical Africa was rich in parasites. Falciparum infections predominated and were so heavy that virtually all Africans were parasitized. A mother's acquired immunities protected the young child up to approximately eighteen months of age, after which the child had to pass through the trials of repeated infections. Most childhood deaths occurred between the ages of eighteen months and five years. Thereafter, acquired immunities afforded a considerable degree of protection; Africans over the age of five were regularly parasitized but only infrequently symptomatic.

8. James Mooney, "Sacred Formulas of the Cherokees," *Seventh Annual Report of the Bureau of Ethnology to the Secretary of the Smithsonian Institution 1885–'86* (Washington, DC: Government Printing Office, 1891), 326–27.

9. Daniel Drake, *A Systematic Treatise, Historical, Etiological, and Practical, on the Principal Diseases of the Interior Valley of North America* (Cincinnati, 1850), 750, cited by Virgil J. Vogel, *American Indian Medicine* (Norman: University of Oklahoma Press, 1970), 98.

10. Benjamin S. Barton, *Collections for an Essay Towards a Materia Medica of the United States* (Philadelphia, 1810), 3rd ed., part 1, 28; and part 2, 22–26, 55, cited by Vogel, *American Indian Medicine*, 284.

11. Our understanding of these Native American therapies comes to us principally via European American accounts. A major exception is the Cherokee materia medica, a part of which was transcribed via the Cherokee syllabary, perhaps in the 1850s or earlier. Even as late as the 1880s the Cherokees were using the regional barks to treat malaria. James Mooney described the Cherokee treatment for "Unawa'stï, 'that which chills one,' . . . a generic name for intermittent fever, otherwise known as fever and ague":

> The doctor beats up some bark from the trunk of the wild cherry and puts it into water together with seven coals of fire, the latter intended to warm the decoction. The leaves of Tsâl-agayû'nli (Indian tobacco—*Nicotiana rustica*) are sometimes used in place of the wild cherry bark. The patient is placed facing the sunrise, and the doctor, taking the medicine in his mouth, blows it over the body of the sick man. . . . Only as much as will be needed is made at a time, and the patient always drinks what remains after the blowing. Connected with the preparation and care of the medicine are a number of ceremonies which need not be detailed here. The wild cherry bark must always be procured fresh; but the Tsâl-agayû'nli ("Old Tobacco") leaves may be dry. (Mooney, "Sacred Formulas," 362–63)

12. Vogel, *American Indian Medicine*, 300.

13. A. Irving Hallowell, "The Backwash of the Frontier: The Impact of the Indian on American Culture," in *The Frontier in Perspective*, ed. Walker D. Wyman and Clifton B. Kroeber (Madison: University of Wisconsin Press, 1957), 240.

14. Drake, *A Systematic Treatise*, 749–50.

15. Michael A. Flannery, *Civil War Pharmacy: A History of Drugs, Drug Supply and Provision, and Therapeutics for the Union and the Confederacy* (New York: Pharmaceuticals Products Press, 2004), 226–27. It remained part of the herbal materia medica into the twentieth century. See Finley Ellingwood and

John U. Lloyd, *The American Materia Medica, Therapeutics, and Pharmacognosy* (Chicago, IL: Ellingwood's Therapeutist, 1919), 272–73.

16. Vogel, *American Indian Medicine*, 267, 336–37, 354–56, and 384–85, cited by Clara Sue Kidwell, "Native American Systems of Knowledge," in *A Companion to American Indian History*, ed. Philip J. Deloria and Neal Salisbury (Malden, MA: Blackwell, 2002), 97.

17. Aspirin, first produced in 1897, is acetylsalisylic acid. It is a synthetic analogue of the naturally occurring salisylic acid that is found in the poplar, willow, and myrtle trees; salisylic acid, like aspirin, has anti-inflammatory and antibacterial properties.

18. Another Cherokee medicine for more-generic fever and pain, a decoction of Virginia or black snakeroot (*Aristolochia serpentaria*), entered into Euro-American antimalarial treatment as a supplement to cinchona alkaloids and bark. As the U.S. Dispensatory described it: "A stimulant tonic, acting also as a diaphoretic or diuretic, according to the mode of application; ... also been highly recommended in intermittent fevers, and though itself generally inadequate to the cure often proves serviceable as an adjunct to Peruvian bark or sulphate of quinia" (Mooney, "Sacred Formulas," 324).

19. Fielding H. Garrison, *An Introduction to the History of Medicine*, 4th ed. (Philadelphia, PA: W. B. Saunders, 1929), 26. The *Cimicifuga* are a small genus of herbs of the family Ranunculaceae. They were used for treating severe back and neck pain.

20. Holly F. Mathews, "Rootwork: Description of an Ethnomedical System in the American South," *Southern Medical Journal* 80, no. 7 (1987): 885–91. On herbal medicine in the Georgia Sea Islands, see Faith Mitchell, *Hoodoo Medicine: Gullah Herbal Remedies* (Columbia, SC: Summerhouse Press, 1999).

Tropical Africa made numerous contributions of economically valuable plants to the Americas, notably "red rice" (*Oryza glaberrima*). See Judith A. Carney, "African Rice in the Columbian Exchange," *Journal of African History* 42, no. 3 (2001): 377–96; for a list of African exported domesticates other than rice, see 391–94. Some of the other African food crops that made their way to the Americas had medicinal uses, although these medicinal uses remained largely unknown to the Europeans who held Africans in bondage in the Americas.

21. Robert A. Voeks has explored how, in Brazil, "slave medicine" did not flow from the enslaved to the masters, probably because of fear of African "magic" and poisoning. In Bahía, for example, the Portuguese were willing to learn and borrow from the indigenous populations, but not from the evolving system of candomblé that blended Africa, Native American, and European elements. See Voeks, *Sacred Leaves of Candomblé: African Magic,*

Medicine, and Religion in Brazil (Austin: University of Texas Press, 1997), 36–41, 45–49.

22. George E. Brooks, *Eurafricans in Western Africa: Commerce, Social Status, Gender, and Religious Observance from the Sixteenth to the Eighteenth Century* (Athens: Ohio University Press, 2003), 16–17.

23. F. N. Hepper, "Africa," in *Systematic Botany, Plant Utilization and Biosphere Conservation*, ed. Inga Hedborgh (Stockholm: Almqvist and Wiksell, 1979), 41–42. For a survey of botanical collectors in West Africa before 1860, see R. W. J. Keay, "Botanical Collectors in West Africa Prior to 1860," *Comptes Rendus de la IVème Réunion Plénière de L'Association pour l'Etude Taxonomique de la Flore d'Afrique Tropicale* (Lisbon, 1962), 55–68.

24. F. N. Hepper, "The Niger and the Nile: Botanical Exploration Around Two African Rivers," *Annals of the Missouri Botanical Garden* 78 (1): 81.

25. See, for example, Thonning's annotations for *Cassia occidentalis*: "Is used by the natives in different ways. . . . The bark of the root has a bitterly stringent taste, it is said to be recommended as a good substitute for chinabark [Chinchona]. The leaves have a stupefying odour , which much resembles opium"; and *Ocimum gratissimum*: "The most important use of this plant is in a malignant bilious fever connected with jaundice, which is very prevalent near R. Volta after inundation of the river." F. N. Hepper, *The West African Herbaria of Isert and Thonning* (Kew: Robert MacLehose, 1976), 34, 65.

26. The Dutch seaborne empire was among the largest imperial networks in the seventeenth and eighteenth centuries, and yet a recent comprehensive survey of the commerce, medicine, and science in the Dutch Golden Age makes no mention of any medically active plant from tropical Africa that entered the Dutch networks of global trade. See Harold J. Cook, *Matters of Exchange: Commerce, Medicine, and Science in the Dutch Golden Age* (New Haven, CT: Yale University Press, 2007).

27. See, for example, Paul E. Isert, *Journey to Guinea and the Caribbean Islands in Columbia (1788)*, translated from the German and edited by Selena A. Winsnes (Oxford: Oxford University Press, 1992), 153–54.

28. John M. Janzen, *Ngoma: Discourses of Healing in Central and Southern Africa* (Berkeley: University of California Press, 1992).

29. Philip D. Curtin, *Death by Migration: Europe's Encounter with the Tropical World in the Nineteenth Century* (New York: Cambridge University Press, 1989).

CHAPTER 3

Indigenous Ethnoornithology in the American South

Shepard Krech III

GIVEN THE global encounter, past and continuing, between indigenous and nonindigenous people, as well as the importance of comprehending human-environmental relations, it is critical to understand the extent to which the ideas held by nonindigenous newcomers toward the natural world affected autochthonous cultures. The question of impact is increasingly posed, and seems to loom largest, when the newcomers possess environmental assumptions based in science rather than local knowledge—but is no less important when they do not.

I explore this question in the American South, where through time indigenous people and newcomers of European and African descent encountered one another. This region was settled initially by American Indians and later by colonists from Europe and slaves from Africa. Investigating the impact of non-Native on Native thought concerning "the natural world" or "the environment" is too daunting for a brief essay, for which reason I focus on one area or domain: the gloss represented in English as "birds" (embraced by the class Aves in Western biological classification) and its equivalents in different cultural systems of knowledge. In order to elucidate knowledge and meaning relating to birds my approach is ethnoscientific, that is, it draws on evidence from naming, taxonomy, and cultural meaning in order to reveal not just indigenous ornithologies but the influence on them (if any) of non-Native ornithologies.[1]

The South is a complex region. In the first place it is vast—some five hundred thousand square miles; it is environmentally diverse, from the coastal plains to the Appalachian heights; and it is inhabited throughout by birds—more than three hundred unevenly distributed species representing most North American families (e.g., woodpeckers, falcons). The region is also complex in its human inhabitants. Indians have lived there for over eleven thousand years, first as mobile hunters and collectors and then as increasingly sedentary cultivators of maize, squash, beans, and other domesticated plants, and builders of platform-mound towns that were specialized economically, stratified, and warlike. Societies emerged, evolved, and fell apart—all before newcomers arrived in the sixteenth century.

The new immigrants came from throughout Europe, especially England, Scotland, Ireland, and France. In turn they imported slaves from Africa—principally West Africa—initiating processes that caught up Native Southerners in the Atlantic play for commodities, power, and empire from the sixteenth through eighteenth centuries. With these new people came ideas about the possession and control of land and resources that, while not entirely unfamiliar, were intense in application. With them also arrived novel diseases, which proved devastating. Formerly sovereign Native societies disappeared, some to coalesce with others in new entities whose names are familiar today—the Catawbas, Cherokees, Chickasaws, Choctaws, and Creeks in particular. In the nineteenth century, the American government forcibly moved most remaining Native people west to Indian Territory in today's Oklahoma, in order to open up their lands to privileged new non-Native immigrants. While this essay is concerned mainly with the era that came to an end with these relocations, it draws on evidence from the postrelocation era that sheds light on indigenous ornithologies.

Ethnoscience and Ethnoornithology

Ethnoscience refers both to a set of methods designed to reveal knowledge systems, or what is often called the native point of view, and to that point of view—how a given people conceive of and perceive their culture. The methods are intended to reveal how people distinguish, name, and classify cultural domains (categories of classification systems). In the abstract the domains are limitless. Classic examples investigated are kinship terminology, color terms, firewood, disease diagnosis, and cuisine—as well as plants (ethnobotany), animals in general (ethnozoology), birds (ethnoornithology), and other domains pertaining to nature or the environment. The "ethno-" in these terms signifies the focus on knowledge in *ethnoi,* or nations regarded predominantly as people who are native, indigenous, aboriginal, tribal, or in the minority; above all as autochthonous to a particular place. Notwithstanding, ethnoscience also embraces the cultures of those who live in the West, even if they regard neither themselves as ethnic nor their knowledge as anything but scientific.[2]

On the knowledge side, ethnoornithology focuses on birds—"things that fly," perhaps, although for some people those things include bats, insects, winds, and other things classified with birds. No ethnoornithological snapshot of the American South could possibly reveal its complexity. Southern Indians as well as immigrant nonindigenous people of European and African descent varied linguistically and culturally—and formed families in time mixed not just in genes but in language and culture, including (potentially) ethnoornithological understanding. Thus, among the possible historical outcomes is a mélange of ideas about birds: a blurring of indigenous conceptions and perceptions as a result of the diffusion of ethnoornithological understandings possessed by newcomers from Europe and Africa; ethnoornithologies with origins in both the Old and the New Worlds. Among the newcomers I have most to say about the ornithologies of those from the British Isles (Britain and Ireland) and their descendants, but I also draw on fragmented data to speak to people of African descent.

The distinction between conception and perception is deliberate (if thorny and debated).[3] To conceive of a particular bird is to form, or hold, a general idea of its attributes. Generally, it is to label (or name) it and to relate it to other birds in a taxonomy or classification. To perceive a bird is to apprehend it on the basis of one's senses, in the formation of which experience and cultural understanding interlace. The distinction can be boiled down to the difference between, on the one hand, naming a bird and assigning it to a category or to categories on different levels of specificity because of having internalized (learned) some conceptual schemata; and, on the other, having a relationship (association) with a bird because of accumulated experience, history, and knowledge, all of which (like the categories) are densely cultural and highly situational.

Conceiving or assigning to categories can lead one to taxonomies with levels ranging in inclusiveness (or exclusiveness). To take a purely hypothetical example, in one society a partial taxonomy of "things that fly" ("bird"), from most to least inclusive categories, might be bird, land bird, raptor, falcon, peregrine falcon, eastern form of the peregrine falcon, and adult male eastern peregrine falcon. In a second society that partial taxonomy might simply be bird (most inclusive) and peregrine falcon (least inclusive). Perceiving a particular bird, on the other hand, leads to specific cultural understandings about and relationships with that bird. Thus in one society the peregrine falcon might be perceived as linked to status, power, aggression, hostility, warfare, and other matters of vital interest—as arguably was the case in the native American South prior to the arrival of people of European extraction—and in the second society the peregrine falcon might be regarded principally as a top-line predator of hundreds of vulnerable avian species.

Naming: Native People

We begin with conceptions revealed in names for, and classifications of, birds. The earliest written evidence of indigenous bird names in the South dates from the sixteenth and seventeenth centuries, was recorded by Europeans who possessed unusual curiosity or training in natural history, and is spare and fragmentary. For example, John White, governor of the English Roanoke colony in 1587 and an artist, left a number of drawings and paintings of birds, for some twenty of which he recorded Algonquian names. They included the common loon, surf scoter, osprey, sandhill crane, pileated woodpecker, eastern towhee, red-winged blackbird, northern cardinal, and blue jay. White's birds range from water to land birds, from large to small birds, and from raptors to passerines; but he does not specify if the native names are specific to particular birds or embrace others.

A few years later, in 1610–1611, William Strachey, an Englishman curious about nature and resident in Jamestown, also recorded Algonquian names of birds—but many more than White. In translation they include more than one dozen waterbirds, such as "duck" (mallard?), "wigeon" (American wigeon), "brant," "goose," "swan," and "gull"; raptors like "eagle," "sparrow hawk," and "owl"; game birds like "turkey cock"; wading birds such as "crane"; land birds including "pigeon" (mourning dove?), "wood pigeon" (passenger pigeon?), "parrot" (Carolina parakeet), and "robin red breast" (American robin); and an exotic bird, the "chicken." Diverse, often obscure, Strachey's Indian names tilt toward waterfowl, raptors, and other birds deemed useful or noticeable—a typical European bias.

In the nineteenth and twentieth centuries the evidence improves greatly with ethnographic and linguistic research with key native consultants. For example, one mid-twentieth-century list, which reflects unusual avian knowledge on the part of a Catawba consultant named Sam Blue and the ethnographer, provides names for more than sixty kinds of birds ranging from ducks, herons, and raptors to shorebirds and a small land birds. Some names, such as those for killdeer and screech owl, are onomatopoeic; others, like "big chicken" (in translation) for turkey or "bird black with red wings" for red-winged blackbird, are descriptive; yet others signal some behavioral characteristic, like "tree bird" for wood duck or "fish-catching bird" for belted kingfisher. The turkey vulture is "wild ancient sure enough eats all carrion," which references both its foraging behavior and a mythological role. Blue's names do not always correspond to species in Western ornithological science. He often extended the name for one bird to others thought of as related (e.g., great horned owl and barred owl; whip-poor-will and chuck-will's-widow; turkey vulture and black vulture). Furthermore, many birds remained unnamed.[4]

Data on the Cherokees are richer because of collaborative work by people knowledgeable about birds. In the past, the Cherokees collectively distinguished at least 110 kinds of *jisgwa* (bird)—one of five major kinds of animals—including mythological birds and spirit-birds. They named both highly visible species like various hawks (sharp-shinned, Cooper's, red-tailed, red-shouldered, broad-winged, and marsh hawks are all distinguished), falcons, eagles, and the osprey, as well as less-flashy or conspicuous birds like the winter wren, golden-crowned kinglet, least flycatcher, bank swallow, and pine siskin. Their names tend to be either onomatopoeic or descriptive of appearance or perceived behavior: *duweyela*, "climbing up and down on a round thing" (white-breasted nuthatch); *wadahyeli*, "imitator" (brown thrasher); *unegoda*, "white dirt" or "white soil" (northern flicker; from the conspicuous white rump of this ground feeder); *uwelaaski*, "love sick" (red-tailed hawk; from its whistle, perceived as a sign of loneliness); and *atsila ustili*, "fire on head" (golden-crowned kinglet). The northern mockingbird is *tsusko digis'ski*, "head eating," from the belief that to eat the head of this bird is to make one intelligent.[5]

Given the richness of the data from the Cherokees, it is somewhat surprising that late twentieth-century dictionaries list no more than sixty different kinds of birds and add relatively little to ethnoornithology. For example, a Chickasaw dictionary uses the same label, *foshi*, for "finch," "nuthatch," "sparrow," "thrasher," and "thrush," as for "bird"—a remarkable lack of specificity. Other names translate directly from a bird's habitat (*oka foshi*, literally "waterbird," is "gull") or appearance (*chulha losa* [losa is "black"] is "blackbird," "grackle," and "brown-headed cowbird"; *foshi lakna*, "yellow bird," is perhaps the American goldfinch).

Another Chickasaw dictionary that names many familiar birds (e.g., bluebird, cardinal, chickadee, crow, raven, scissor-tailed flycatcher [*hilowi-foshi'*, "thunder bird"; or *foshi' ishkalasha' hasimbish*, "scissors tail bird"], great horned owl, hummingbird, whip-poor-will, mockingbird [including *foshi' taloowa'*, "bird-singer"; and *fosh-ato'chi'*, "mortgage bird," to which I return) but reserves greatest lexical elaboration for raptors and woodpeckers. There are four different kinds of owls: great horned, screech, short-eared, and a fourth. Four eagles (*osi'*) are distinguished: bald (literally, white-headed), red-headed, striped with one stripe around the body, and big. Three hawks (*akankabi'*, "chicken-kill") are differentiated: "chicken" ("chicken-kill"—an example of a label used at two taxonomic levels), red-tailed ("chicken-kill tail red"), and "smaller chicken-kill." The woodpeckers (*bakbak* or *aboowa bo'li'* "house pound") include: *bakbak ishkobo'homma*, "woodpecker head red"; *bakbak ishto'*, "woodpecker big"; *chapchap* (a small woodpecker); *itti' cha'li'*, "tree pound"; and the flicker, which has two names.[6]

There are also names for new birds, for exotics, like the canary (lumped with warblers), the *aachompa' foshi'*, "town/store/trading post bird," presumably the monochromatic, nondescript, small European house sparrow introduced in America in the 1850s–1860s and continental by 1900;[7] and the chicken, endemic to Southeast Asia, which acquired a place in most American Indian ethnoornithologies—not everywhere, however, immediately. For the Chickasaws, lexical elaboration among birds was greatest for the domesticated chicken (*akanka'*)—an onomatopoeic name?—and they distinguished striped, bearded, spotted, yellow, red, black, white rock, tailless, curly-headed, and other types.[8]

Lexical interests reveal cultural interests: for raptors and woodpeckers, the interest is of long standing; for Western birds (e.g., scissor-tailed flycatcher) or an exotic that lives in one's midst (house sparrow), it is for new birds in new circumstances in Indian Territory; for the chicken, it is for an important introduced (and then indigenized) domesticated species. That contemporary dictionaries do not reveal more is surely due to the scant ornithological knowledge of the linguists and others who compiled them, the removal itself, an erosion of knowledge of birds in lands left behind, and, perhaps the linguistic and cultural impact of other native people with whom southern Indians came into contact following removal.

Naming: The British

In turning to the impact of newcomers on indigenous bird names in the South (other than that in time, English everywhere has taken the place of native languages), we begin with names used by English speakers for American birds. As in Britain, bird names in America have ranged from conventional to idiosyncratically vernacular. The first has been more typical of natural history and science and the second of local knowledge, but at any moment in time the two coexisted in different sectors of the population (urban/rural, literate/nonliterate, etc.). Bird names have been applied to categories known in Western science as the species, genus, or family, as well as used more rarely for birds of different age and sex, as the following three examples from the early eighteenth through the mid-twentieth centuries illustrate.

First is the early eighteenth-century naturalist-explorer John Lawson's list of 120 different kinds of Carolina birds, which ranged from waterfowl, shorebirds, pigeons, and raptors to thrushes, woodpeckers, swallows, and the martin, catbird, mockingbird, and oriole. Lawson even noted "Hedge-Sparrows"—New World sparrows resembling the European dunnock (a small widespread bird streaked brown and gray commonly known as the hedge sparrow)—at a time when few others bothered with them or flycatchers, warblers, sparrows, wrens, vireos, and other families of small land birds.[9]

Lawson's list is similar to earlier ones that owe a great deal to European birds. His familiar British names made sense because many American birds were morphologically similar to ones that he knew from the Old Country: the gannet, mallard, teal, wigeon, woodcock, swift, turkey (an exotic in Britain), will willet (willet), gray plover, and raven are examples. Even when the differences were greater Lawson fell back on common English names, for example, pigeon (passenger pigeon), tomtit (Carolina chickadee), turtle dove (mourning dove), and kingfisher (belted kingfisher)—or generic (family) categories like goose, gull, crow, curlue (curlew), snipe, crane, stork, and hern (heron/egret). New birds known in America but not in Britain received new names, including the Baltimore-bird (Baltimore oriole), parrakeeto (Carolina parakeet), summer duck (wood duck), bald-eagle, cat-bird, mocking-bird, blue-bird, whippoo-will, and turkey-buzzard.[10]

The second example is provided by the late eighteenth-century naturalist William Bartram, who differs from Lawson in creatively combining European with emergent American names for birds, for example, whooting owl (barred owl), carrion crow (black vulture), forked tail hawk (swallow-tailed kite), sharp winged hawk (Mississippi kite), little jay (Florida scrub jay), purple jackdaw (boat-tailed grackle), little grey butcher bird (loggerhead shrike), summer redbird (summer tanager), nonpareil (Fr., "without equal") or painted finch (painted bunting), yellow hooded titmouse (?), great savanna crane (sandhill crane), marsh bittern or Indian hen (American bittern), crying bird (limpkin), white brant goose (snow goose), and great black cormorant (double-crested cormorant). In this list, carrion crow, jackdaw, jay, titmouse, butcher bird, brant goose, whooting, cormorant, forked tail, and bittern all reference British birds but summer redbird, sharp winged, crying, and other descriptive terms owe more to an evolving American vernacular than to names for Old Country species.[11]

The third list was elicited in the 1940s from a "pioneer" family on a Piedmont farm in the southern Appalachians. Like Bartram's, it reveals both continuity and change, the first in bird names originating in Great Britain, for example, crane (heron); blue crane (great blue heron); white crane (egrets and the immature little blue heron); didapper (pied-billed grebe [little grebe in Great Britain]); wild duck (mallard); carrion crow (black vulture); fish hawk (osprey); raincrow (yellow-billed cuckoo [green woodpecker is the rain bird in Great Britain]); blue darter (sharp-shinned and Cooper's hawks [sparrow hawk and other raptors are "blue hawk" in Great Britain]); killdee (killdeer); hooting owl (great horned owl [tawny owl in Britain]); turtle dove (mourning dove); wren (Carolina wren); tomtit (Carolina or black-capped chickadee); field lark (meadowlark). The names derive from the similarity of New and Old World species.

Other pioneer bird names are American in origin and were used for birds lacking exact counterparts in Britain, including hell-diver (pied-billed grebe), shike-poke (green heron), hen hawk (red-tailed hawk), laughing owl (barred owl), bullbat (common nighthawk), chimney sweep (chimney swift), yellow-hammer (northern flicker), Indian hen (pileated woodpecker), shirt-tail (red-headed woodpecker), bee-martin (eastern kingbird), gourd martin (purple martin), redbird (northern cardinal), hang-nest (Baltimore and orchard orioles), town sparrow (house sparrow), rice bird (bobolink), swamp blackbird (red-winged blackbird), joree (towhee), cherry bird (cedar waxwing), and yellow mocking-bird (yellow-breasted chat).

For this pioneer family, many birds remained unnamed. Apparently they lacked salience or escaped notice. Even if noted some birds were not named, as with blue-headed and yellow-throated vireos (regarded as male and female forms of the same unnamed bird).[12] Lack of notice or salience was common: on the whole, small birds went underreported, unreported, or overgeneralized, in particular sparrows and others known as skulkers or unremarkable in plumage or behavior; the classic "dicky birds" or "little brown jobs."[13]

Naming: English and African Influences on Indian Names

At this stage we can draw several conclusions on bird names. First, with respect to names in English, the influence of the "Old Country"—Great Britain—has remained strong through time, even in folk or vernacular bird names originating in Great Britain.[14] Second, again pertaining to the names in English, some betray an apparent New World origin, such as Indian pullet and Indian hen for green herons and yellow-crowned and black-crowned night herons—names said moreover to be "facetious" rather than to reflect domestication.[15]

The third and—given the objectives of this essay—most important assessment concerns the influence of newcomer bird names on American Indian bird names (or vice versa). Eliding, first, the eventual replacement of Native names by English names, which has been universal in this region of North America as Native languages have declined, or, second, the impact of relocation on the inventory of birds and therefore their names, the inescapable conclusion is that on the surface the overlap or convergence between Indian and English names is negligible.

But there are exceptions, which are well worth mention. The first three concern onomatopoeia. For example, *dzatana'* or *djataga'*, an unanalyzable but probably onomatopoeic Cherokee name for the introduced chicken, is arguably parallel to and debatably derivative of one of a string of ancient onomatopoeic names in English for this clucking bird.[16] Second, an alternative form for eastern towhee in Cherokee is very similar to a vernacular form for this bird in English: *Jori'* (Cherokee) and *joree* (English). An English origin for *jori'* (rather than the reverse) is suggested by the presence of an unrelated name for eastern towhee in Cherokee.[17] Third is the name chickadee, which stands in opposition to the hypothesized influence of *joree* on *jori'*. In English, chickadee, a generic label applied to two closely related species, the Carolina and the black-capped chickadee, surely originated in an Indian language in the American East, such as Cherokee (*tc'igalili, jigilili, tsikilili*), Delaware (*-tcililisis*), Penobscot (*ktcigigi-*), or Oneida (*tskleleli*).[18] Onomatopes, it seems, move with greater flexibility between unrelated languages than names that are descriptive, of obscure origin, or unanalyzable.

A fourth exception shifts the focus from newcomers who spoke English to those whose speech was based in African and African American tongues. As mentioned, as a result of the slave trade, Africans were forcibly transported to the South where, in time, they lived among people of American Indian and European descent as slaves, runaways, free people, neighbors, and consanguineal or affinal kin. The question here is whether or not they influenced indigenous conceptions or understandings of birds. They had at least one influence on names of birds in English: one common vernacular name in English for the great blue heron is poor Joe or po' Joe, whose proximate origin was probably *pojo* (heron) in the language called Gullah that developed in the Georgia and South Carolina low country, and ultimate origin *podzo* in West African Vai. (The opposite movement—from English to Gullah—is suggested in *bidibidi*, which in Gullah means a small bird or chicken and in Kikongo means a bird, and *biddy*, which in English has meant chicken or fowl since the sixteenth century.)[19]

But did names for birds diffuse from Gullah or an African tongue to American Indian languages? The answer is: Perhaps. In Gullah (with a Kikongo origin), woodpecker is *bababa*, and in Chickasaw and Choctaw the red-headed woodpecker is *bakbak*. In Gullah (with an origin in Vai), owl is *huhu*, and in Cherokee screech owl is *wahuhu, wahahu,* or *wahuhi*; and in Catawba barred owl is *hoho* and screech owl is *hohu*. Orthography and phonetics aside, the superficial similarities between these forms are striking.[20]

One final example exploring the possibility of African or African American influence on American Indian naming concerns the northern mockingbird, whose imitative ("mocking") abilities are caught in its names in southern Indian languages. The Creeks called it *fus-svhayv*, "mocking bird, imitating bird"; the Cherokee *tsusko' digiski'*, "head eating," from the belief that to eat its head is to make one clever and intelligent; the Choctaw *hushi balbaha* "bird that talks in a foreign language"; and the Chickasaw *foshi' taloowa'*, "singer bird"; or *fosh-ato'chi'*, "mortgage bird."[21]

One can readily understand linking this around-the-clock vocalist with singing, imitating, speaking in a foreign language, or intelligence. On the other hand, mortgage bird at first glance is puzzling—yet the idea of the mockingbird as the mortgage bird might have entered Chickasaw from African-American culture. In stories told by Reconstruction-era African-Americans living near preremoval Chickasaw territory in Alabama, the northern mockingbird, personified as "Mister Mockin' Bird," figured prominently in African-American thought. His deeds and misdeeds were ancient: he stole corn planted by Dove; he sang far better than Catbird, who, because of his color and size, could not occupy the top limb; he could imitate a chicken, bluebird, sparrow, lark, chuck-will's-widow, whip-poor-will, and bobwhite; and, if eaten, the mockingbird's eggs would force the consumer to tell all he knew.

Mr. Mockingbird was perceived as the "Master Bird" because he was present in the "first times," because he sang, fought, and was a year-round resident—and because he figured significantly in financial affairs and financial ruin. One story framed in the context of debt-caused ruin, and free blacks scandalously taking on debts that others could not settle, related that Mr. Mockingbird did the same thing in the days when there was said to be a pot of gold buried under every stump. He signed all the promissory notes he could, in a "reckless" fashion took on debt, worked hard to keep up interest payments, and was worth so much that the state insured him and levied a fine of five dollars on anyone who killed him. But Mr. Mockingbird, the most "impudentes'" bird, denied that he was insured or that he cared, and he skipped and sang away. He had put his name on "all de birds' notes"—on all their mortgages.

This story offers a strong clue to the meaning and origin of a puzzling Chickasaw name for the northern mockingbird.[22] Just as African and American Indian genes blended in the South, so did culture, including, it seems, bird names and meanings. This resulted in part from the enslavement of thousands of African Americans by the elite of the so-called Five Civilized Tribes, including the Chickasaw, and in part from kinship and familial ties at first forged mainly by African men and Indian women, which enabled complex cultural interweavings seen in, among other domains, indigenous ornithology.

Classifying: Native People and Newcomers

The second aspect of ethnoornithological conception explored here is taxonomy. Assessments are difficult for the simple reason that classificatory data on birds are rare for the native South at any period. As with names, the exception is for the Cherokees, whose "birds," rather than being coterminous with "birds" (the class Aves) in Western scientific taxonomy, embraced spirit-birds and beings with birdlike attributes—that is, they had feathers or flew—prominent among which was a mythical raptor, and at first excluded chickens and other exotic domesticated fowls. These extensions to other-than-avian (Aves) beings and exclusions of exotic or invasive forms mark the first departures from Western science.

That said, most birds named by the Cherokees correspond to Western science's species or (the next more inclusive category) to the genus represented by a single species, such as the wild turkey, American goldfinch, and pileated woodpecker. At times, the Cherokees departed from this to lump two or more species in a single category: for example, they gave one name ("tanager") to the scarlet tanager and the summer tanager; one to the downy woodpecker and the hairy woodpecker; one ("blackbird") for the red-winged blackbird, rusty blackbird, brown-headed cowbird, and common grackle; one, apparently generalized from the moorhen, to it, the coot, and several species of rails; one (sandpiper, "they put their legs in water") to nine kinds (species) of shorebirds; and apparently one to more than one dozen species of sparrows and allied birds. Sparrows present an interesting case: collectively they were "the real or principal bird" or "really the bird," perhaps because of vast wintertime numbers. The song sparrow, which bore the same name as all sparrows, might have been the type species and source for the category "sparrow." The Cherokees apparently distinguished the song, fox, and white-throated sparrows by name but not others in this numerous but inconspicuous category of small brown birds.[23]

Individual Cherokees varied in their ability to identify birds and did not always agree on naming. Some, for example, considered the red-winged blackbird and the common grackle as the same kind of bird, others assigned the same name to the red-winged blackbird and brown-headed cowbird, and at least one person distinguished these birds according to where they lived (e.g. in the swamp) or by their color tint (e.g., bluish). Some called the red-headed woodpecker, yellow-bellied sapsucker, and red-breasted nuthatch by the same name, "deaf," because they seemed fearless in the presence of humans, but other birds did not.

No matter how robust these data seem, all bird lists are based on the limited knowledge of a few—and, with regard to the distribution of knowledge and naming of things like birds, no single person is omniscient in any society. This, together with the erosion of cultural knowledge and the supplantation of traditional names by oft-vague (in a taxonomic sense) English bird names (e.g., "gull," "finch," "sparrow," "warbler"), leaves firm conclusions on traditional classification difficult. Moreover, collaboration between Native people and ethnographers knowledgeable about birds aside, no Cherokee names have been recorded for approximately one-half of the species that lived in or passed through their territory. We do not know for certain why there is no record of their names. The Cherokees distinguished by name birds that were not obviously visible or important in subsistence, the economy, material culture, size, coloration, or behavior, but ones marked by features not obviously "salient." Like indigenous people elsewhere, they surely possessed profound knowledge of their homeland, including knowledge of birds corresponding often to the species or genera of Western science, assembled in what seems to have been a shallow classification, that is, with few levels between "bird" and each individual terminal (specific) kind.[24]

As for the impact of taxonomies of people of European descent on Indian classification, much is unknown. A great deal has been written about how in the early-modern era (ca. AD 1500–1800), the foundations of European ideas about the natural world were shifting from folk knowledge to natural history. The span was great, the changes gradual and uneven. At one extreme was the development of an increasingly scientific ornithology that resulted in substantial syntheses of bird names, taxonomy, and knowledge of habits and behavior. In the British Isles more than one dozen heavily illustrated natural histories of British birds appeared, containing bird names, lists, classifications, illustrations, and observations.[25]

But the impact of this work on the American South must be inferred. However direct it might have been at the end of the continuum defined by natural history and science, it surely was negligible at the other end where folk knowledge reigned among rural people unaware of the evolving ornithological sensibility in natural history and science. Even among the cognoscenti, alternative classifications of birds presented themselves. Eighteenth-century choices included dividing birds into waterbirds and land birds, then into birds with crooked bills and talons versus birds with straight beaks and claws; separating birds into groups by those that had two, three, or four toes, webbed, simple, lobed, or connected; distinguishing birds by legs feathered or naked; or (Linnaeus) distinguishing six orders of birds: (1) raptors and parrots; (2) woodpeckers, corvids, and other birds; (3) birds that swim; (4) shorebirds and wading birds; (5) gallinaceous birds; and (6) a catch-all category of "passerines," petrels, and others. These various schemes did not exhaust the possibilities.

Regardless of the preferred taxonomy, the use of a label such as "ducks" for kinds not further named, or "waterbirds" or "land birds" for those frequenting such habitats, betrays categories intermediate to ones above and below. For example, here are at least four levels of classification: bird, waterbird, duck, and teal. Not only is this deeper—that is, more layered—than much indigenous ethnoornithological taxonomy, but there is no obvious overlap with it in the American South, except in the primacy of the species or of the genus—worldwide, the basic folk generic category.[26]

Perceptions: Native People

In the American South, Indians perceived or apprehended birds in many ways. They defined many as edible and with gustatory interest killed and consumed many, from turkeys, passenger pigeons, and waterfowl to a range of small birds, using a refined technology of blowguns, traps, and other weapons and tools. They attracted some to nest in gourds over their gardens and defend territory as well as, increasingly, domesticated chickens against avian intruders. Some—cranes or storks perhaps—they might have domesticated, but the evidence is thin at best. Southern Indians also manufactured artifacts from the feathers, bones, and other body parts of cranes, herons, egrets, swans, raptors, and other birds, fabricating clothing, robes, headdresses, crowns, arrow points, fletching, fans, tubes, and a variety of decorations. Many selected the same birds—swans, egrets, turkeys, and eagles and other raptors were favored—in part for natural characteristics like the size and color of plumage (if not just the right color, it could be pigmented), and in part for cultural associations between particular birds and peace, hostility, aggression, flight, and other human states.

An even greater number and variety of species were significant in contexts ranging from social and political to religious and curative. Some birds again stood out. For example, eagles were positively charged, with the golden eagle, where it could be found and prior to its extirpation, the eagle of choice. Raptors—probably eagles—marked public squares and houses where authority, sacred or secular (or both), was concentrated. Eagle feathers signaled accomplishment, authority (sacred and secular), and power. People used eagle-feather fans in ceremony and wore eagle claws on breechclouts. Eagles or their feathers were presented to others in order to validate the words that accompanied them.

In contrast, indigenous Southerners cast other birds in negative terms, relating vultures (commonly known as buzzards) to death and construing owls and others as malevolent night birds. As widespread in the region as these beliefs might have been, they were not universal or without nuance. Indeed, some assigned to the vulture a productive role in the long-ago formation of mountains and valleys, and granted it a beneficial part in curing the ailing. Moreover, not all kinds of owls were automatically or equally evil. They appeared often in the material culture of the region, sculpted in and on small figurines, ceramic jars, pipes, and massive wooden images, and figured in contexts ranging from malevolent to benevolent, diviner to witch, or inauspicious augur to protector. However construed, owls were often, if not always, the occasion of heightened attention.

Birds appeared throughout in contexts meaningful to individuals from before birth to after death. That the number and kinds of species were great is evident from Cherokee magical formulas designed to achieve ends positive for the agent but perhaps negative for the person toward whom a formula or incantation was directed. Birds figuring in the formulas ranged across the category *jisgwa*, or "birds": the osprey, kestrel, screech owl, long-eared owl, great horned owl, barred owl, common raven, kingfisher, pileated woodpecker, hairy woodpecker, red-headed woodpecker, Carolina wren, indigo bunting, eastern bluebird, loggerhead shrike, mourning dove, ruby-throated hummingbird, eastern wood pewee, great crested flycatcher, purple martin, chimney swift, yellow-breasted chat, northern cardinal, eastern meadowlark, several bird spirits or spirit-birds, eagles, gulls, and others.

The interest in birds is ancient, if we can judge by the archaeological material record that survived the millennia. Despite the difficulty in arriving at ironclad conclusions on the identity of many specific prominent species, during a period of some two and one-half millennia, native people in the South showed strong interest in certain families or orders. First were hawks, eagles, owls, falcons, vultures, and other raptors (and raptorial spirit-birds), which were sculpted, stamped, incised, woven, and tattooed in or on wood, stone, shell, ceramic, and other media. In some cases, a copper or stone talon, or a wing, was sufficient to signal the "raptor" referenced. Second were big woodpeckers with prominent crests (the pileated or the ivory-billed, probably the latter). Third was the wild turkey. Fourth were the wood duck and other waterfowl. Other less prominent though still recognizable birds included mergansers, pelicans, and the roseate spoonbill. The identity of all these birds is reasonable at the level of the order or family; in some instances the genus and even the species are quite clear.

As argued elsewhere, people were interested in some of these birds because in pre-European times (especially during the era known as the Mississippian), war was endemic and there was a connection between the elite in society and birds with notable strengths and aggressive tendencies. Moreover, everywhere birds numbered among the animals associated with descent. Other birds stood out on aesthetic grounds or because of anomalous characteristics; the wood duck, which is not only spectacularly plumaged but nests, unlike most ducks, in trees, is one example. Finally, people interacted with, and assigned meaning to, an even greater variety of birds because of the constant need to influence beings that, as animate other-than-human persons, could make one miserable in the absence of attention or propitiation, or that could help one achieve certain positive or negative ends.[27]

Perceptions: The Newcomers

As with naming and taxonomy, we turn to the question: Did people of European or African descent influence indigenous ethnoornithological perceptions of birds? The question is complex, and the answers are tentative and based on the newcomers from the British Isles, many of whom, mercantilists especially, worked among, lived with, and married Native people, and left mixed-blood descendants. These newcomers possessed tastes similar to those of Native people for birds deemed "useful," that is, edible or desirable in domestic consumption. They shared gustatory interest in waterfowl and game land birds even while they differed in which birds, feathers, and other parts they commodified. More important for the questions posed here is that neither they nor Southern Indians embraced all possible birds in their respective ornithologies, nor were their ornithologies identical in any sense to today's Western ornithology based in biology, ethology, and other sciences—not indigenous ornithologies with their separate logics, not the classifications and perceptions of nonliterate rural newcomers, not the schemes of those aware of early-modern natural-historical taxonomies.

Prior to the time when Western science overwhelmed folk knowledge, to what extent might the perceptions of birds in British culture—Irish, Welsh, Scottish, or English perceptions—have had an impact on perceptions in Cherokee, Creek, or another indigenous cultures? The nineteenth-century painter-ornithologist Alexander Wilson saw little difference between American Indians and some people in Europe when it came to their thoughts about some birds. Indians, he remarked, wanted as "little to do as possible" with nocturnal birds such as whip-poor-wills and owls, which they regarded with "suspicious awe." The night plagues the mind, Wilson thought, leaving these birds similar to ghosts and other other-than-human beings. Yes, some Indians thought these ideas "silly," but most, Wilson implied, did not—nor, he deduced, would "an illiterate German, a Scots Highlander, or the less informed of any other nation," for whom what "is strange and not comprehended, is usually attributed to supernatural agency; and an unexpected sight, or uncommon incident, is often ominous of good, but more generally of bad fortune."[28]

There is ample evidence in support of Wilson's hypothesis for parallel perceptions in the British Isles and the Native American South. Prior to the nineteenth century, the British widely anthropomorphized birds, assigned them moral characteristics, and considered some auspicious and others unlucky. British folk beliefs about birds were remarkably varied: swans lived for three hundred years; swallow ashes were a remedy for failing sight; and a medicine prepared from one hundred swallows, castor oil, and white wine cured epilepsy; one who ate the heart of a nightingale would sleep only two hours a night; loons hatched their young through holes beneath their wings; jack snipe and snipe were male and female of the same species; if killed, a robin (an ill omen for many) or swallow would bring bad luck; gannets grew by their bills on certain cliffs; the comings and goings of red-throated loons forecast weather changes; goose embryos formed in the fruit of willow trees; if swallows or martins build under the eaves of a house its inhabitants will prosper; a sparrow kept alive will bring the death of the parents of the sparrow-catcher; the bittern shone a light from its breast to see its prey, or made its booming call by inserting its bill into a reed or the mud (to some this bird was the "night raven" and was feared as an omen of death).[29] Because of resemblances between many Old and New World birds, it is reasonable to suppose that many of these beliefs had few impediments crossing the Atlantic. Ernest Ingersoll, speaking of the cuckoo as a harbinger of rain, suggested as much: "The old maxims carried into the New World: when British or Italian immigrants became colonists in America, and found cuckoos here, they continued the sayings, regardless of differences in climate and other circumstances."[30]

Perceptions: Convergence

It is common to argue that the various meanings assigned to things like birds by indigenous people like Southern Indians were analogous to ones held elsewhere by indigenous people. Thus, despite oft-demonstrated encyclopedic knowledge of the environment, including birds, such people have been shown to assert as fact (as in eastern Indonesia and Papua New Guinea) that certain birds are celibate or switch sexes, that males in nature are really females and vice versa, that a falcon decapitates its prey with its wing, or that a bird produces low-pitched vocalizations with its anus.[31]

It is far less common to suggest that in their beliefs, indigenous people like Southern Indians were similar to Westerners who arrived in their midst as expansion-minded settlers and colonists. But British folk beliefs discussed above put the lie to sharp separation of the two—one native or indigenous, the other non-Native and expansionist. The sheer range and variety of British folk beliefs about birds was impressive. Whereas such perceptions might not have been compatible with beliefs circulating in natural historical or scientific circles, they were tenacious and widespread among rural folk lacking exposure to the more cosmopolitan ideas. Moreover—perhaps the most crucial point—certain aspects of British folk belief that concern augury, power, transmutation, and the deluge also figured strongly in Southern Indian ethnoornithologies.

To begin, the belief that birds were augural was ancient in Europe and strong in Britain. The cuckoo foretold the arrival of spring and a good harvest; a green woodpecker calling, a blackbird or chaffinch singing loudly, or a grey heron or swallow flying low foretold rain; gulls, storm petrels, and the osprey all forecast changes in weather by their flight, behavior, or postures. If pale, a duck's cooked breastbone meant a mild winter and if dark, a severe winter. A kingfisher hung by its bill would swivel to indicate with its breast the future direction of the wind. Other augural birds included the pied wagtail: to the person keeping count, one that wagged its tail other than nine times after it landed was unlucky. That ideas like these probably carried across the Atlantic could be seen among settlers in the southern Alleghenies, for whom the augural whip-poor-will indicated with its calls the number of years before marriage.[32]

Second, the British regarded the eagle—for them the golden eagle—as the king of birds. A keen-sighted, proverbial bird ("eagle-eyed") that could gaze at the sun's rays, set its feathers afire, and plunge into the sea to renew itself, the eagle was undeniably courageous and strong. Even though its prominence in the British Isles was tempered by more influential corvids (the raven, rook, and chough), or rendered ambivalent by the wren, who bested it in the contest to fly to the heavens by hiding in the eagle's feathers, only to emerge at the last instant as victor, belief in the eagle's power persisted and when this bird appeared in heraldry, either single- or double-headed, it was as a compelling symbol of authority and power. In broader and deeper historical context, the eagle or a related large bird of prey like a lammergeier or griffon vulture served as messenger for Zeus; as the means, through its wings, of the flight from Egypt recounted in Exodus; as able to ascend to God, according to Saint Jerome; and as first among birds in a twelfth-century Latin bestiary that presented its offspring to the rays of the sun and descended from on high like a thunderbolt.[33]

Also powerful, but negatively, were birds considered to be gravely ominous—in particular owls and goatsuckers, but also corvids. Despite contradiction and ambivalence, the carrion crow and rook were quite ill omens. So was the raven, widely linked with evil, death, and witchcraft—yet still considered (perhaps because of natural strengths) as a powerful and useful bird in divination. The magpie was not simply an ill omen but was believed to morph into human form. Owls, however, long since messengers of ill fortune and death, and connected to witchcraft, comprised an especially dangerous category, especially the most nocturnal of them (even the diurnal little owl sacred to Athena did not escape deep ambivalence). In Wales, tawny and barn owls were called "corpse birds." In early nineteenth-century Pennsylvania, a tract in German noted that a sleeping person on whom the heart and right foot of a barn owl had been placed would answer any question put to him. Finally, the nightjar, the lone representative of goatsuckers, was "corpse-hound" or "corpse fowl" to some, and was believed to cause distemper in calves, suck goats dry of their milk at night, or house the wandering souls of unbaptized infants.[34]

Third, beliefs in transmutation and metempsychosis were widespread in British ethnoornithology: barnacle geese grew from and dropped off barnacles and metamorphosed into feathered birds; robins morphed into redstarts; garden warblers changed into blackcaps; and in winter corncrakes became water rails until spring, when they changed back into corncrakes (the Scots, in their fashion, thought that the corncrake, a lucky bird, semi-hibernated in a torpid state in winter). So was the belief in metempsychosis common: swans embodied the spirits of the dead; storm petrels, albatrosses, gannets, gulls, and other birds were souls of dead mariners; and deceased children's souls became kittiwakes.[35]

The final belief discussed here that is similar in the British Isles and the indigenous American South is the discovery by a dove of reemergent land after a primordial flood. In Britain the story is biblical: at the end of the Noachian deluge the dove, not the raven (the first bird sent by Noah), finds and returns with the evidence of land—an olive leaf. The tale is familiar in the New World, where it is old yet has clear parallels with the account of Noah in Genesis. The Choctaws say that a dove discovered grass after a large black bird denied a call for assistance or flew off never to return; the Chitimacha that a dove brought corn to earth and its people. African Americans also assign to "Sis' Dove" an important role related to corn: she is clairvoyant and can divine not just when a person will die—she moans for souls—but crop yields, which she communicates by cooing on the right of a man plowing if the yield will be good, on the left if poor. Sister Dove is able to do this because she is said to have been the first to plant a grain of corn. Here the interwoven and complex causal connections between Native American, African American, and European-American folk systems seem inextricable.[36]

Conclusions

The questions raised by similar and parallel naming practices and cultural perceptions—not, however, by taxonomy—among people of Indian, European, and African descent are in most instances difficult to answer satisfactorily. Indians in the American South and people of European or African descent—the indigenous people and the newcomers, respectively—shared some bird names and some cultural apprehensions of birds. The data bearing on both are intriguing. The names led rarely to English and more often to Gullah and African languages. As for cultural perceptions, stories in both Britain and the American South connected birds in the same biological family (Columbidae) with ancient floods. In both Britain and the American South, birds were augural, but specific kinds varied greatly, and why some were chosen but others not is often mysterious. In both could be found powerful birds, positive and negative, yet unlike augury the specific kinds were remarkable in their similarity: owls, goatsuckers, and some corvids as negative; the eagle as positive—and the influence of African beliefs about these particular birds needs exploration. Moreover, in both Britain and the indigenous American South could be found beliefs in metamorphosis, transmutation, and metempsychosis.

Yet despite the plausible influence of newcomers on naming and perceptions, the evidence is far from ironclad. What was the relationship between the late eighteenth-century Choctaw belief that the dried corpse of a kingfisher was a useful deterrent against moths in clothes and the identical mid-nineteenth-century (or earlier) European belief? How was the belief of a twentieth-century Pamunkey from Virginia that soras (rails) turned into frogs, and frogs into soras, when each appeared or disappeared related to the strikingly similar beliefs in transmutation held by people who came to Virginia from Britain?[37]

Wilson, I think, was on the right track in suggesting a parallel sensibility about birds in Indian and European folk belief, even as his language reflected the growing tension between folk-biological and natural-historical—in time, scientific—explanation. Naturalists of European descent eventually considered early-modern European beliefs quaint and then bizarre, but for centuries this avian folklore led observers to fear certain birds, admire and privilege others, and deem many barely worthy of notice. And certain beliefs proved remarkably difficult to dislodge, like the one about swallows entering torpor and submersing in water or muck during winter rather than migrating to some warmer, insect-filled clime—an explanation encouraged in America, as the historian Andrew Lewis suggests, by a climate of intellectual permissiveness in natural history.[38]

While native names and taxonomy can prove resilient, much depends on language, memory, and cultural knowledge and interest—in this case, about, of, and in birds. Unfortunately, much knowledge of the past that is of greatest interest in this essay has probably disappeared. Native people themselves lament the loss of native language and knowledge of the "things" that people once knew.[39] Time and enforced relocation west to a new biome with novel avian species in Oklahoma both represent enemies to the retention of traditional knowledge about things like birds from a former locale. The paucity of names for birds and knowledge of different species in contemporary dictionaries is in part a reflection of these processes. Yet perhaps by bringing the cultural knowledge concerning birds of people of European and African descent into the frame of the knowledge possessed by Native people, the indigenous ethnoornithology that emerges becomes a richer and more faithful reflection of the complex historical processes at work.

Notes

1. This essay builds on the following recent research on the American South (and see, unless stated otherwise, for additional references): Shepard Krech III, *Spirits of the Air: Birds and American Indians in the South* (Athens: University of Georgia Press, 2009).

2. *Oxford English Dictionary Online*, s.v. "ethnic" and "ethno-"; William C. Sturtevant, "Studies in Ethnoscience," *American Anthropologist* 66, no. 3, part 2 (1964): 99–131; Shepard Krech III, "The State of Ethnohistory," *Annual Review of Anthropology* 20 (1991): 345–75.

3. Tim Ingold, "Introduction to Culture," in *Companion Encyclopedia of Anthropology*, ed. Tim Ingold (New York: Routledge, 1994), 329–49.

4. Much remains speculative in Chief Blue's list. For example, his word for the turkey is "big chicken," which might reference an exotic species (chicken), the greater prairie chicken or heath hen, or the exotic domesticated version of the subspecies of the wild turkey transported by people of European descent to the American South. When another exotic bird, the distinctive-looking Muscovy duck (originally from the Caribbean and Central and South America), reached the American South from Europe, the Creeks placed this hissing duck in a taxon that included ducks and the limpkin and called it *fuco sule*, "duck-vulture," a lexical sign of its turkey vulture–like red facial skin. See Jack B. Martin and Margaret McKane Maudlin, *A Dictionary of Creek/Muskogee* (Lincoln: University of Nebraska Press, 2000); and Krech, *Spirits of the Air*.

5. James Mooney, *Myths of the Cherokee* (New York: Dover, 1995); John Witthoft, "Bird Lore of the Eastern Cherokee," *Journal of the Washington Academy of Sciences* 36 (1946): 372–84; Arlene Fradkin, *Cherokee Folk Zoology: The Animal World of a Native American People, 1700–1838* (New York: Garland, 1990). See Krech, *Spirits of the Air*, 30–32, and passim.

6. Jesse Humes and Vinnie May (James) Humes, *A Chickasaw Dictionary* (Norman, OK: Chickasaw Nation, 1973). The Creeks also lumped the exotic canary in with the endemic "warbler" (Martin and Maudlin, *A Dictionary of Creek/Muskogean*). See Krech, *Spirits of the Air*, 27, 29.

7. Peter Coates, "Eastenders Go West: English Sparrows, Immigrants, and the Nature of Fear," *Journal of American Studies* 39 (2005): 431–62.

8. Pamela Munroe and Catherine Willmond, *Chickasaw: An Analytical Dictionary* (Norman: University of Oklahoma Press, 1994); and Krech, *Spirits of the Air*, 29.

9. John Lawson, *A New Voyage to Carolina*, ed. Hugh Talmadge Lefler (Chapel Hill: University of North Carolina Press, 1967), 140–55. On dunnock/hedge sparrow, see Mark Cocker and Richard Mabey, *Birds Britannica* (London: Chatto and Windus, 2005), 333–34; H. Kirke Swann, *A Dictionary of English and Folk-Names of British Birds* (Detroit: Gale Research, 1968), 79, 120.

10. W. L. McAtee, "The Birds in Lawson's 'New Voyage to Carolina,' 1709," *Chat* (December 1955): 74–77; W. L. McAtee, "The Birds in Lawson's 'New Voyage to Carolina,' 1709—Last Installment," *Chat* (June 1956): 23–27.

11. Francis Harper, "William Bartram's Names of Birds," *Proceedings of the Rochester Academy of Science* 8 (1943): 208–21.

12. A. L. Pickens, "A Comparison of Cherokee and Pioneer Bird-Nomenclature," *Southern Folklore Quarterly* 7 (1943): 213–21; Swann, *A Dictionary*; Charles Swainson, *The Folk Lore and Provincial Names of British Birds* (Whitefish, MT: Kessinger, 2004).

13. Kevin R. McNamara, "The Feathered Scribe: The Discourses of American Ornithology Before 1800," *William and Mary Quarterly* 47 (1990): 210–34. The term "dicky (dickey) bird" has been in use since the eighteenth century for generic small birds like sparrows, pipits, warblers, and others (*Oxford English Dictionary Online*, s.v. "dicky-bird, dickey-bird").

14. Vernacular bird names of British origin other than ones mentioned in the text include diver (loon), didapper, dipper, and dabchick (various grebes), gray duck (gadwall), English duck (mallard), broadbill (northern shoveler), black duck (greater and lesser scaup), duck hawk (peregrine falcon), ring plover (semi-palmated plover), peet weet (spotted sandpiper) ox-eye (semipalmated sandpiper), sea swallow (common, Forster's, and least terns), goatsucker (nighthawk), and robin redbreast (American robin). W. L. McAtee, "Folk Names of Florida Birds," *Florida Naturalist*, no. 2 (April 1955): 35–37, 64; McAtee, "Folk Names of Florida Birds, Part 2," *Florida Naturalist*, no. 3 (July 1955): 83–87, 91; McAtee, "Folk Names of Florida Birds, Part 3," *Florida Naturalist*, no. 4 (October 1955): 103, 121–23; McAtee, "Folk Names of Florida Birds, Conclusion," *Florida Naturalist*, no. 1 (January 1956): 25–28; Swainson, *The Folk Lore and Provincial*

Names of British Birds. Thanks to T. Grand, Julie Wraithmell, and Charles Lee for locating the January 1956 number of the *Florida Naturalist*.

15. McAtee, "Folk Names of Florida Birds" (April 1955): 37, 64.

16. Witthoft, "Bird Lore," 384.

17. Witthoft, "Bird Lore," 383–84; Pickens, "A Comparison," 221; McAtee, "Folk Names of Florida Birds, Conclusion," 28. Compare the gray jay, whose common vernacular name in English is "whiskey jack." Indians north of the St. Lawrence River called this bird both *wiskedjak* (the probable source of whiskey jack) and a term that translates "offal bird."

18. Mooney, *Myths of the Cherokee*, 295–96; Witthoft, "Bird Lore," 381; Frank G. Speck, "Bird Nomenclature and Song Interpretation of the Canadian Delaware: An Essay in Ethno-ornithology," *Journal of the Washington Academy of Sciences* 36 (1946): 256.

19. Lorenzo D. Turner, *Africanisms in the Gullah Dialect* (Ann Arbor: University of Michigan Press, 1974), 63, 191, 199, 237; *Oxford English Dictionary Online*, s.v. "biddy."

20. W. L. McAtee, "Folk Names" (1955): 36–37; Turner, *Africanisms*, 65, 194; Munroe and Willmond, *Chickasaw*; Frank G. Speck, *Catawba Texts* (New York: Columbia University Press, 1934); Cyrus Byington, *Dictionary of Choctaw*, ed. John R. Swanton and Henry S. Halbert, Smithsonian Institution, Bureau of American Ethnology, bulletin no. 46. (Washington, DC: Government Printing Office, 1915); Mooney, *Myths of the Cherokee*, passim; Witthoft, "Bird Lore"; Andrew Lee Pickens, "Contributions to Catawba Ethnozoology," in "Indian and Nature Lore from Old Catawba Country, or Out-of-Doors in the Southern Piedmont: Indians, Animals, Plants," *Neighborhood Research* 18, nos. 1–5 (1957): 6 pages; Fradkin, *Cherokee Folk Zoology*.

21. Martin and Maudlin, *A Dictionary*; Witthoft, "Bird Lore," 382; Byington, *Dictionary of Choctaw*; Munro and Willard, *Chickasaw*.

22. Martha Young, *Plantation Bird Legends* (New York: R. H. Russell, 1902), 11, 40, 43, 55, 76–78, 193–96.

23. If sparrows were "real" or "principal" birds because their type bird, the song sparrow, and the others named are the "most widely found" (Pickens), then they present less of a "puzzle" than I suggested initially (cf. Krech, *Spirits of the Air*, 31).

24. On the shallowness of taxonomy, see Shepard Krech III, "Traditional Environmental Knowledge," in *Encyclopedia of World Environmental History*, vol. 3, ed. Shepard Krech III, John McNeill, and Carolyn Merchant (New York: Routledge, 2004), 1213–16.

25. Michael Walters, *A Concise History of Ornithology* (New Haven, CT: Yale University Press, 2003), 11–51; Peter Bircham, *A History of Ornithology*

(London: Collins, 2007), 24–138. See also Keith Thomas, *Man and the Natural World: A History of the Modern Sensibility* (New York: Pantheon Books, 1983), 51–148.

26. Harriet Ritvo, *The Platypus and the Mermaid and Other Figments of the Classifying Imagination* (Cambridge, MA: Harvard University Press, 1997). Walters, *Concise History*, 37–68; Krech, "Traditional Environmental Knowledge."

27. The preceding section draws on Krech, *Spirits of the Air*, passim.

28. Alexander Wilson, *American Ornithology, or, The Natural History of Birds in the United States*, vol. 5 (Philadelphia: Bradford and Inskeep, 1808–1814), 74–75.

29. Swann, *A Dictionary*, 18, 131, 164, 166, 198–99, 231–33; Swainson, *Folk Lore*, 22, 53, 61, 144, 146, 193, 214; Ernest Ingersoll, *Birds in Legend, Fable, and Folklore* (New York: Longman, 1923), 63–66, 80, 181, 184; Edward A. Armstrong, *The Folklore of Birds: An Enquiry into the Origin and Distribution of Some Magico-Religious Traditions*, 2nd ed. (New York: Dover, 1970), 62.

30. Ingersoll, *Birds in Legend*, 225.

31. Paul Sillitoe, "From Head-Dresses to Head-Messages: The Art of Self-decoration in the Highlands of New Guinea," *Man* 23 (1988): 298–318; Steven Feld, "Cockatoo, Hornbill, Kingfisher," in *Man and a Half*, ed. Andrew Pauley (Aukland: Polynesian Society, 1991), 207–13; Gregory Forth, *Nage Birds: Classification and Symbolism Among an Eastern Indonesian People* (New York: Routledge, 2004), 115–37; Krech, *Spirits of the Air*, 32–33.

32. Swann, *A Dictionary*, 55, 180, 186; Swainson, *Folk Lore*, 7, 63, 105–6, 111, 145, 157, 205, 211; Ingersoll, *Birds in Legend*, 6, 214–25; Armstrong, *Folklore*, 208.

33. These eagle beliefs are widespread in Europe and western Asia. Swann, *A Dictionary*, 97–98; Swainson, *Folk Lore*, 35–43, 134–35; Ingersoll, *Birds in Legend*, 28–36; Armstrong, *Folklore*, 125–40;

34. Swann, *A Dictionary*, 2, 13, 42, 91–92, 96, 149, 151–52, 167, 187–88, 201; Swainson, *Folk Lore*, 77, 84, 88–92, 97–98, 123–31; Ingersoll, *Birds in Legend*, 74, 154, 163–67, 180–88; Armstrong, *Folklore*, 71–93.

35. Swann, *A Dictionary*, 138, 198–99; Swainson, *Folk Lore*, 149–50, 177; Ingersoll, *Birds in Legend*, 65–66, 93; Armstrong, *Folklore*, 211–14.

36. Ingersoll, *Birds in Legend*, 5, 99–101; Alice Parmalee, *All the Birds of the Bible: Their Stories, Identifications, and Meaning* (New Canaan, CT: Keats, 1959), 53–58; Krech, *Spirits of the Air*, 167–70; Young, *Plantation Bird Legends*, 13–15.

37. Ingersoll, *Birds in Legend*, 23; Krech, *Spirits of the Air*, 76; Frank G. Speck and John Witthoft, "Some Notable Life-Histories in Zoological Folklore," *Journal of American Folklore* 60, no. 238 (1947): 345–49.

38. Andrew J. Lewis, "A Democracy of Facts, an Empire of Reason: Swallow Submersion and Natural History in the Early American Republic," *William and Mary Quarterly* 62 (2005): 663–96. See also Swainson, *Folk Lore*, 51.

39. Krech, *Spirits of the Air*, 164–65.

CHAPTER 4

Nation-Building Knowledge

Dutch Indigenous Knowledge and the Invention of White South Africanism, 1890–1909

Lance van Sittert

RECENT SCHOLARSHIP has strongly argued that "science," by providing "objective" knowledge to inform state policy, played a significant role in the invention of a settler nation-state in South Africa both before and after 1910. This argument has been made exclusively on readings of elite discourse and in the face of substantial counterevidence of the popular rejection of imperial Anglo science by the Dutch-cum-Afrikaner settler population. The role of science in settler nation-building was considerably more complicated than its localization through the creation of research institutions and training of practitioners. Indigenization also involved the validation of previously denigrated bodies of Dutch indigenous knowledge as science. The practice of water divining in the Cape Colony was one such case of Dutch folk knowledge, denounced as an impediment to development in the 1890s, which was rehabilitated as an aid to development after the South African War in official discourse. Rehabilitation, by compelling practitioners to translate water divining into the dominant scientific idiom of the official discourse on agriculture, had the primary instrumental effect of legitimating both the imperial Anglo scientific idiom and the settler nation-building project energetically embarked on in the 1900s among a hostile Dutch population in the Cape countryside. The historical example is instructive for the current postapartheid nation-building moment and its equally enthusiastic embrace of previous despised African indigenous knowledge, as demonstrated by Karen Flint's essay on African indigenous medicine in this volume.

Science and Folk Knowledge in the Late Colonial Cape Colony

Much of the recent scholarship on the late colonial Cape has been devoted to an inventory of the official application of scientific knowledge to agriculture, variously styled "progressivism" (by its adherents) and "conservationism" (by its scholars).[1] In a dominant mode of inquiry reminiscent of the old liberal historiography in its join-the-dots empiricism and privileging of the professional biography of white practitioners over social context, this scholarship has doggedly cataloged the efforts of state botanists, foresters, hydraulic engineers, and veterinary surgeons to improve colonial agriculture during the roughly two decades following the establishment of a Department of Agriculture in the colony in 1889 and beyond. In this telling, the individual scientists (both amateur and professional) occupy center stage in narratives driven by the process of scientific theorizing, testing, and translation into policy, a process portrayed as essentially socially and environmentally benign.

This neoliberal revision of late colonial Cape history has been subject to criticism on a number of fronts. One line of attack has indicted it for ignoring the broader social context of colonial conquest and racism shaping scientific inquiry as well as the limited political and financial capacity of the colonial state to either sustain such inquiry or give effect to its findings.[2] Another has disputed its portrayal of scientific agricultural policies as socially and environmentally benign by counting the social cost of progressivism brutally imposed on the predominantly black rural underclass, which it stripped of subsistence rights to a now enclosed commons.[3] A third has stressed the Creole nature of colonial science born not fully formed from the burning glass minds of its white male practitioners, but begat rather through their promiscuous intellectual miscegenation with indigenous folk knowledge.[4] Yet a fourth has pointed out the prominent place of the irrational in progressivism's supposedly rational scientific approach to agriculture.[5]

It is the latter two lines of critical inquiry that I want to pursue here: the hybrid nature of colonial scientific knowledge and the context and process in which previously derided bodies of indigenous folk knowledge come to be revalued if not as scientific then at least as having equivalent social status as a way of further elaborating the critique of neoliberalism. The conventional answer is a utilitarian one: if folk knowledge was shown to have practical utility, it would be incorporated into the scientific canon. The context most familiar to African historians in which this process of the identification and incorporation of useful folk knowledge might occur was the social emergency of the livestock or human disease pandemic. Such events dramatically overrode entrenched racism to prompt and/or permit colonial scientists to prospect folk knowledge for useful ideas about disease etiology and prophylaxis and elevated their gleanings to the status of scientific knowledge.[6] Such emergency forays into and borrowings from folk knowledge, however, tended to be marked by stark asymmetries of power between white scientific and African folk practitioners and the complete erasure of the latter's authorship and ownership of any looted fragments translated into scientific discourse. In their frequent failure to yield any useful information, such emergency-induced interactions also tended to more often confirm and reinforce than call into question scientific prejudices against folk knowledge.

The transformation of water divining in the Cape Colony during the heyday of agricultural progressivism from Dutch quackery to the lodestar of imperial hydraulic engineering in the desert suggests an altogether different political answer to the question of the context and process in which folk knowledge becomes hybridized and translated into scientific knowledge.[7] That is to say that water divining's utility in the lead up to Union in 1910 was both practical and political; it was, on the one hand, a good guide to tapping subterranean water in the colony's semidesert interior and as, or perhaps even more, important, on the other, it was a means of drawing a disaffected rural settler population into the process of imperial nation-building in the immediate aftermath of a protracted and bitter guerrilla war in the Cape countryside.[8]

Rather than being simply different kinds of utility, the practical benefits of water divining were mutually exclusive from the political in the sense that the former had long been, were, and would continue to be available to individual settlers seeking to sink boreholes on their land without the latter, the implicit endorsement of the practice by the premier mouthpiece of agricultural progressivism in the colony—the *Agricultural Journal of the Cape of Good Hope* (hereafter *AJCGH*)—and the colonial state's public works department. The setting of the imperial imprimatur on the practice, however, was crucially determined by its practical utility and affected a double cross-hybridization simultaneously indigenizing progressivism through its incorporation of folk practice and rationalizing water divining through its translation into the dominant discourse of science.

Water divining is an instructive example of folk/indigenous knowledge for other reasons, too. Unusually for Africa, it represents a body of imported European folk knowledge and so disrupts the powerful implicit assumption about indigenous knowledge and the irrational in this context being a peculiarity of the black other.[9] Because the majority of European settlers at the Cape enjoyed the rights of citizens denied the indigenous black majority, they also spoke for themselves in the protracted *AJCGH* debate about water divining, their robust sense of self and agency in stark contrast to the effacement of black authorship and ownership of folk knowledge elsewhere in colonial Africa.[10] Water divining thus offers a unique insider's view of a folk practice, albeit one still forcibly fitted to the procrustean beds of the English language and scientific discourse. As a discussion stretching over many years with multiple participants and even more readers, the *AJCGH* debate offers a popular agrarian venue of late imperial national imagining as corrective to the surfeit of elite urban imaginings, which have garnered the lion's share of the scholarly attention to date.

The Practical Appeal of Water Divining

The practice had taken up of water divining likely arrived at the Cape with the first European settlers in the mid-seventeenth century. It has a long, documented history in Europe, and indigenous folk hydrology in southern Africa is primarily concerned with rainmaking, not subterranean water prospecting.[11] The status of water divining as official and popular practice and its miscegenations with indigenous folk hydrological practices at the Cape during the long eighteenth century under the Dutch East India Company are unknown, but with the arrival of the British as imperial overlords at the end of the eighteenth century, it was summarily dismissed as a fraud practiced by charlatans on an ignorant and gullible Dutch settler population. Hence, Barrow reported that a man he claimed to be an Irish deserter

> had taken up the profession of a *water-wyzer* or discoverer of water, and had shown sagacity enough to establish a sort of reputation in the country. By speaking little, looking wise, and frequent application to the eye of a double convex lens, which happened to have an air-bubble within it, he had practised with great [success] on the credulity and ignorance of the Dutch farmers, and had obtained from them, by this and other means, a pair of horses and several hundred rix-dollars

of paper money. Lighting their pipes at the sun by means of his glass, and the persuasion that the air-bubble within it was a drop of water that possessed the sympathetic quality of always turning towards its kindred element, had such an irresistible effect on the rude minds of the African boors, that the Irishman, like a true quack, appreciated this consequence so highly, that he never deigned to pay a visit to any farmer, in order to examine the state of his water, without a previous fee.[12]

Far from disappearing, however, water divining persisted, and a century later, when Barrow's successors in the colonial civil service returned to the countryside in a bid to boldly reengineer its subterranean water sources in order to drought-proof settler agriculture, they again encountered the figure of the *water-wyzer*, his powers undiminished by a century of scientific imperialism and, initially at least, responded in like fashion to Barrow. They rudely denounced the practice as "quackery pure and simple," and complained that it hampered their own scientific efforts by fostering a "very crude idea of the conditions relating to the existence of underground supplies of water [that] exists among farmers ... in many instances a rooted conviction of huge underground rivers pervades their minds ... bolstered by the extraordinary statements of certain persons who style themselves 'Water Wysers.'"[13]

The strength of the denunciations reflected the weakness of the intellectual and material resources deployed by the Cape colonial state to progressivism's hydraulic front. Denied a geological survey by a settler Parliament skeptical of the value of geologists from past experience, the colonial state relied instead on the lone hydraulic engineer in its employ and the part-time labors of a professor at the South African College in Cape Town for all its scientific geology. The results were consequently sparse and unsophisticated, being distilled into the official orthodoxy of the so-called "dolerite intrusion theory," which generated basic rules of thumb for operating drills in the field designed to maximize returns while minimizing costs. The drills themselves were put in the hands of foremen recruited from the ranks of expatriate mechanics at the Salt River railway works in Cape Town and hastily tutored in geology by the hydraulic engineer "with elementary books on geology ... the reports of the Geological Commission ... as well as boxes of rock specimens so that they can recognize the rocks they meet with in boring" and then dispatched to the countryside.[14]

The number of drills deployed by the colonial state was also always far short of what was needed to service farmer demand, forcing their rapid rotation through the countryside and hence severely limiting the time that foremen could spend on any one farm. That official complaints against water diviners clustered in the years immediately after the Jameson Raid and before the South African War is also significant. Rhodes's failed coup attempt against the South African Republic led to both the collapse of his alliance with the Afrikaner Bond in the Cape and a sharp rise in anti-English sentiment in the countryside, making the job of the English-speaking missionaries of hydraulic modernization to the Dutch gentry all the more difficult and a preference for the advice of water diviners over drill foremen as much a political as a practical choice on the part of the antiprogressive heathen.

Following the end of the South African War in 1902, the colonial state reluctantly acceded to the long-standing demand of settler farmers and entrepreneurs and the harsh reality of its own straitened postwar financial circumstances and agreed to instead of only subsidizing the wells that it drilled for farmers, to also subsidize those bored by private contractors. Thus removed from the front line of the underground water rush and itself increasingly involved in prospecting water in the dry west, where there were no dolerite intrusions to guide drilling, the colonial state was then able and willing to make a more measured appraisal of water divining and belatedly recognized its popular support among farmers and practical utility to its own drilling operations. As a result of this changed context, the *AJCGH* opened its correspondence pages to proponents and skeptics alike in late 1906 and published no fewer than fifty-five letters over the next five years on the subject of water divining, two-thirds from practitioners and converts. Nor did this exhaust farmer interest. The editor of the new Union agricultural department's journal perfunctorily ending the "desultory skirmishing" on the "hardy annual" in 1911, but the rival commercial agricultural press continued to carry copious correspondence on the topic well into the 1920s.[15]

This opening up also coincided with the lead up to Union in 1910: the British confection of an independent settler nation-state out of its two colonies (Cape and Natal) and the two conquered Boer republics (Orange Free State and South African Republic), and can also be read as explicitly political in intent, one of a multitude of official efforts to heal the rift between the Anglo and the Dutch sectors of the settler population caused by the South African War. In the charged postwar atmosphere of the Cape countryside, the act of official recognition, by an Anglo urban elite championing science and the market, of a body of Dutch rural folk knowledge grounded in Christian faith and exchanged within a moral economy of mutual assistance, modeled the promise and practice of the coexistence of difference for common purpose that the architects of Union envisioned as the founding idea of the new settler state. Also, unlike hydraulic science, with its rejection of belief, dead earth, and dictatorship of experts, water divining, in its ideas of faith, the circulation of vital fluid, and the intercession of anointed lay intermediaries, furnished the colonial state with handy metaphors for imagining the new nation in the idiom of the rural moral economy.

The Political Appeal of Water Divining

The *AJCGH* was published as the official mouthpiece of the Cape Colony's department of agriculture from its establishment in 1889 until its absorption into a new national department in 1910 and has recently been the subject of heated debate among scholars of the late colonial Cape.[16] While it has served as a key source on progressivism for neoliberals, their critics have disputed its material impact on farming practices in the colony, pointing to its small print-run (five thousand; two thousand in Dutch) relative to the total settler farm population, and accused neoliberals of mistaking its promotion of progressivism for the reality of progressivism in the countryside. The issue of circulation is less relevant to the present discussion, however, both because it is concerned with ideas of the nation, not the reality of agricultural modernization, and because the water-divining debate furnishes abundant evidence of the *AJCGH*'s wide rural audience, not least in the frequent and spirited participation by the organic intellectuals of hydraulic modernization in the countryside, the diviners themselves.

A production question that is relevant to the present discussion and cannot be answered on the available evidence is the extent to which the agricultural department exercised its editorial authority to shape the water-divining debate as it appeared in print in the journal. In other words, was the published correspondence merely a selection of mailings or did the department publish every letter it received on the subject from readers? While a definitive answer to this question is impossible in the absence of a surviving journal archive, there is strong internal evidence in the published correspondence itself, not least in the often brief, confused, and/or contradictory nature of the communications, to suggest the department published everything it received. Further circumstantial evidence for this surmise comes from what we know of the department's small staff and the journal's breadth of coverage, as well as the complete absence of any clear, coherent, or consistent line on water divining running through the debate. The duration of the correspondence also suggests an absence of editorial censorship of any kind; backveld correspondents knew that if they wrote in to the *AJCGH* they would be published in full without official censorship or comment. Anything less and the correspondence would quickly have dried up, the large number of correspondents who preferred noms de plume to their names' being published in the journal, suggesting that there was a high perceived risk of public ridicule or ostracism involved in participating in the debate, even with an uncritical editorial policy.

The attraction of the water-divining debate to the agricultural department would appear to have been both practical and political. With the shift to subsidizing private drilling contractors in 1904, the department was removed from direct superintendence of boring activities and urgently needed to find another way to protect both farmers and the public purse against the fraudulent practices of "land sharks" attracted to the postwar underground water rush.[17] As one public works official reported in 1905, "At present time I do not think there is a Division in the Cape that has not its water diviner. One might almost say that each ward has its expert."[18] Under these circumstances simply ignoring or occasionally denouncing water diviners no longer sufficed, hence the need to educate settler farmers about the practice in order to avoid a shark feeding frenzy at their expense.

That the correspondence, in both volume and duration, far exceeded what might reasonably be construed as necessary to address this practical concern, points second to the political utility of the subject to the colonial state. Having tentatively broached the subject in its journal for practical reasons, the agricultural department, quite by accident, discovered in water divining a subject immensely popular with its rural readership and one that elicited a continuous stream of correspondence, from the Dutch countryside to Anglo urban Cape Town, at a time when such unsolicited and fraternal communication was rare and hence all the more valuable. That such correspondence was also incidentally rich in metaphorical resonances with the incipient process of settler nation-building only further recommended it to officials in the capital. They thus continued to provide it with a public forum in the years leading up to Union—the "valuable space" of the journal so frequently commented on by correspondents—and conspicuously avoided forcing the debate to either closure or consensus, to the great chagrin of some of the progressive readership who wanted both in the form of a return to the journal's prewar practices of excluding water divining and promoting science.

Thus "Another Sceptic" wrote in 1907 to "protest" the "continuous stream of letters" intended to "bolster up this absurd superstition" and to express himself as disgusted at finding letters on this subject appearing month after month in an official publication of the Cape Government; and although it is not overlooked that you, Mr. Editor, are in no way responsible for the opinions expressed in the "Correspondence" column, and that you invite letters from all on questions of interest, I think it would meet with the approval of the majority of your readers, could you see your way to exclude the subject from your Journal, until at least there is something more to go on than "the unsupported word of the operators."[19]

In response, the *AJCGH* editor chided "Another Sceptic" as being too "severe," and declared, "No advantage can be gained by arbitrarily suppressing such a discussion, and some good may yet result if the subject is fully debated."[20] This brief and enigmatic editorial comment constitutes the only official pronouncement on the logic of publishing the protracted debate on water divining in the journal, but, given the volume, duration, and ultimate inconclusiveness of the "discussion," it is unlikely that the envisaged official "good" was confined merely to matters of water supply and public accounting. For water divining also operated with ideas of faith, the circulation of vital fluid, and the intercession of anointed lay intermediaries, all of which resonated with the broader settler nation-building project and, while some worried that "the argument is becoming acute. It is threatening to form another line of cleavage in the country," there is evidence to suggest that it had exactly the opposite effect.[21]

While some advocates of water divining espoused explicitly Christian interpretations of the phenomenon or associated the practice specifically with the church,[22] the majority of correspondents were uncomfortable with what one called "an undercurrent of supernaturalism in some of the letters which have appeared in the Journal upon this subject." Water divining's association with Christianity was instead important in furnishing a model of optimism in the unknown, or "faith," that was readily adopted by proponents of water divining as an alternative to the scientific skepticism of their detractors. Whereas the latter refused all belief in the absence of objective evidence, the profession of "faith" in water divining, like that in a Christian god, was one based on a personal experience of the phenomena and in defiance of objective evidence to rationally explain it. Divining rod advocates thus spoke of themselves as "believers," and their correspondence largely consisted of public professions of "faith" in which they narrated the tales of their conversion from "unbelievers" (as distinct from "skeptics," who were rational atheists about divining) into "believers."

Declared one believer, "I have faith in the divining rod, and shall never attempt to dig for water without first consulting my piece of fencing wire," while a sympathetic unbeliever noted that "like religion, if a man believes in it, it is alright."[23] The "farming public," as one skeptic lamented, "were mostly indifferent about the phenomenon of the 'Divining Rod,' although, at the same time cherishing a form of faith in the stick, for the want of a reasonable explanation regarding the causes of its apparent vitality."[24]

Divining rod skeptics, eager to dispel this faith and quash the debate through scientific research or a public trial, found all their efforts in this regard stymied by the colonial state. Not only did the agricultural department provide water divining a permanent public platform in the journal from which to proselytize, but the public works department, Cape Town and Port Elizabeth municipalities, and the Port Elizabeth Agricultural Society all refused to stage the definitive test desired by both skeptics and the more entrepreneurial of divining practitioners to settle the matter. In the face of this indifference and obstruction, skeptics were reduced to appeals to metropolitan scientific research or opinion, further alienating themselves from their fellows and the rising mood of settler nationalism. That the latter also required an act of faith was not coincidental. Readers of the *AJCGH* found in the long-running water-divining debate the opportunity and encouragement to publicly profess their faith in a new secular experiential community of "believers" fundamentally different from old orthodox progressive skepticism about both the colony and its inhabitants, and in so doing were able to model the choice they would be asked to make at Union in 1910 and find the strength and courage to profess their faith on the new national stage, too, just as they had first done on the smaller colonial one.

Water divining also rejected scientific geology's insistence on underground water as a scarce and unevenly spread agricultural resource, and the colony as consequently fractured into scattered pockets of hydrological prosperity amid vast zones of water poverty. In stark contrast to scientific geology's model of an ancient dead earth, indifferent and threatening to settler agrarian endeavor, water divining conjured a fundamentally different vision of the earth as alive with water flowing everywhere underground in "veins" (Dutch "*aars*") and so available to anyone who knew where and how to find it. This alternative hydrological vision of the colonial agrarian economy undergirded by a dense subterranean arterial web of flowing water both drew on the metaphor of the human vascular system and in turn offered a metaphor for the body politic of the embryonic nation-state. The region's subterranean water topography, in the telling of the water diviners, prefigured the coming nation-state by linking the many disparate parts of the new "South Africa" into a single unified hydro-system full and flowing with the vital fluid that was the guarantee of the settler rural economy's health and prosperity. More than wishful thinking, divining's hydro-vascular vision of the earth appeared to be miraculously affirmed by every successful water strike made in defiance and contradiction of the prevailing geological orthodoxy.

The figure of the water diviner that emerged from the *AJCGH* debate also invited readers' attention and contemplation. While a minority of correspondents held that divining was merely a trade that could be practiced by anyone (even blacks and women) and sought to codify, patent, and sell the knowledge, the overwhelming majority regarded it as a gift possessed by only a select few. That those thus anointed employed their gift in the service of their fellow farmers without any expectation or demand for monetary reward was widely believed to be the reliable rule of thumb for distinguishing diviners from frauds in the Cape countryside, even by critics of the practice. The water diviner, by refusing to accept money for the life-giving service she or he provided, taught the most elementary lesson in the nationalist catechism: that individual security came not from personal but collective prosperity. Said one, who described himself as "an amateur water finder" of six to seven years' experience, "I write having 'no axe to grind,' except that of benefiting the South African farmer."[25] Or, as the motto on the new Union coat of arms proclaimed, "Unity is strength." In their simple solidarity with and selfless service of the settler collective, the water diviner thus furnished the journal's readership with a model of the ideal citizen of the coming nation-state, against which they could measure themselves and to which they could aspire.

There is an irony to all this, of course, in that the colonial state's practical and political appropriation of faith, mysticism, and moral economy of water divining for nation-building in the lead up to Union merely accelerated the transformation of folk practice already begun by the postwar underground water rush. The most obvious of these transformations involved the translation from oral into written form and concomitant commodification. The *AJCGH* debate did both, publishing copious written accounts of water divining intended to guide and assist novices and allowing entrepreneurial practitioners to effectively advertise and tout their services for business.[26] More insidiously, but no less significantly, the journal put a burden of empirical proof on practitioners, which, even if they ultimately rejected it, they were nonetheless forced to bear. In entering the debate in the journal's pages, correspondents thus did not enter a neutral space, but one already constituted and configured by the discourse of science and hence innately hostile to proponents of divining who could not at least offer plausible speculations about the likely rational causality of the phenomenon. Even those advocates who cited Scripture in defiance of science were nonetheless bending to this evidentiary demand. Although the debate fell far short of the skeptics' insistence that it "must leave no room for mysterious and unknown forces to beat a retreat to that nebulous realm so long their harbour of refuge whenever the arrows of scientific criticism have been shot at them," in all these ways it did demystify water divining and so "break this mysterious force to utilitarian harness."[27]

Conclusions

The appropriation through legitimation of folk knowledge is never a politically neutral act and always involves folk knowledge's translation into the dominant language and discourse of power. In the case of water divining, this was an ancient if largely ignored practice in the colonial Cape countryside, which acquired a sudden practical and political utility to imperial power in the final decade of British colonial rule at the Cape, as the political economy of water boring and the state system were reconfigured following the end of the South African War. Legitimated as a useful guide to both farmers and the state in tapping the subterranean water horizon, water divining also furnished the Anglo urban colonial state with an unexpected Dutch rural audience and handy folk models of faith, unity, and citizenship that prefigured and hence assisted correspondents and readers in imagining Union. Appropriation by the colonial state also initiated or accelerated processes of translation, commodification, and rationalization, transforming the practice and rapidly stripping it of the very faith, mysticism, and moral economy that gave it postwar popular purchase on the backveld and hence the colonial state, too.

Set against the broader scholarship on progressivism and settler nationalism in this period, both of which emphasize the central place of science in these ideologies, the discussion of water divining by the flagship journal of agricultural progressivism in the Cape colony appears as a strange and inexplicable anomaly. It should not. The neoliberal feting of progressivism's scientific experts has massively overinflated their significance as in the case here of water, where the role of the lone hydraulic engineer and part-time geologist was completely eclipsed by the para-geologist drill foremen and water diviners, or, in the more celebrated case of veterinary science, where the more numerous veterinary surgeons on the public payroll were nonetheless vastly outnumbered by the more than two hundred para-veterinary sheep inspectors in state employ. Similarly, scholars of settler nationalism have confined themselves to readings of elite Anglo urban–cum-metropolitan science without a rural readership or metaphorical resonance, lending their bold claims an inherent implausibility. Had they deigned to read popular rural science texts like the *AJCGH*, they would have recognized the limited appeal and utility of scientific skepticism for nation-building in the countryside and the need to selectively appropriate folk knowledge and practice in order to effect both agrarian modernization and national imagining.

Notes

1. The urtexts of this scholarship are William Beinart, *The Rise of Conservation in South Africa: Settlers, Livestock and the Environment* (Oxford: Oxford University Press, 2003); and Saul Dubow, *A Commonwealth of Knowledge: Science, Sensibility and White South Africa, 1820–2000* (Oxford: Oxford University Press, 2006); and the many earlier versions of their chapters, which appeared in journals and edited collections over the decade prior to publication.

2. See Lance van Sittert, "The Nature of Power: Cape Environmental History, the History of Ideas and Neoliberal Historiography," *Journal of African History* 45, no. 4 (2004): 305–14; William Beinart, "Academic Amnesia and the Poverty of Polemics," *Journal of African History* 46, no. 1 (2005): 127–35; Lance van Sittert, "Reply," *Journal of African History* 46, no. 1 (2005): 135–38; and Martin Legassick, "Science and 'South Africanism': White 'Self-Identity' or White Class and Race Domination?," *Kronos* 33 (2007): 245–58.

3. See, for example, Nancy Jacobs, *Environment, Power and Injustice: A South African History* (Cambridge: Cambridge University Press, 2003); and Jacob Tropp, *Natures of Colonial Change: Environmental Relations in the Making of the Transkei* (Athens: Ohio University Press, 2006).

4. Elizabeth Green Musselman, "Plant Knowledge at the Cape: A Study in African and European Collaboration," *International Journal of African Historical Studies* 36, no. 1 (2003): 367–92.

5. Lance van Sittert, "Class and Canicide in Little Bess: The 1893 Port Elizabeth Rabies Epidemic," *South African Historical Journal* 48, no. 2 (2003):

207–34; and Lance van Sittert, "The Supernatural State: Water Divining and the Cape Underground Water Rush, 1891–1910," *Journal of Social History* 37, no. 4 (2004): 915–37.

6. See John Mackenzie, "Experts and Amateurs: Tsetse, Ngana and Sleeping Sickness in East and Central Africa," in *Imperialism and the Natural World*, ed. John MacKenzie (Manchester: Manchester University Press, 1990), 187–212; and Dan Gilfoyle, "Veterinary Research and the African Rinderpest Epizootic: The Cape Colony, 1896–1898," *Journal of Southern African Studies* 29, no. 1 (2003): 133–54, for classic cases.

7. See Van Sittert, "The Supernatural State," for a utilitarian interpretation of the official endorsement of water divining in the progressive-era Cape Colony.

8. See Bill Nasson, *Abraham Esau's War: A Black South African's War in the Cape, 1899–1902* (Cambridge: Cambridge University Press, 1991); and Rodney J. Constantine, "The Guerrilla War in the Cape Colony During the South African War of 1899–1902: A Case Study of the Republican and Rebel Commando Movement" (MA thesis, University of Cape Town, 1996), for the war; and Saul Dubow, "Imaging the New South Africa in the Era of Reconstruction," in *The Impact of the South African War*, ed. Daniel Omissi and Andrew S. Thompson (Basingstoke: Palgrave, 2002), 76–95, for postwar white nation-building.

9. See Udo Krautwurst, "Water-Witching, Modernist Epistemologies and Dowsing Rationality: Exporting Models of Non-Rationality Through Colonial and Development Discourses" (paper presented to the Canadian Anthropology Society, University of Toronto, May 7, 1998). All page references here are to this source, although an abridged version was subsequently published in *Political and Legal Anthropology Review* 21, no. 2 (1998): 71–82. Thanks to Nancy Jacobs for first alerting me to Udo's work and to Udo for so generously sharing it with a complete stranger.

10. See Musselman, "Plant Knowledge at the Cape"; and Nancy Jacobs, "The Initimate Politics of Ornithology in Africa," *Comparative Studies in Society and History* 48, no. 4 (2006): 564–603, for efforts to recover black folk knowledge authorship from the scientific record.

11. See, for example, Jean-Pierre Goubert, *The Conquest of Water: The Advent of Health in the Industrial Age* (Princeton, NJ: Princeton University Press, 1989), 31–34; M. R. Lynn, "Divining the Enlightenment: Public Opinion and Popular Science in Old Regime France," *Isis* 92, no. 1 (2001): 34–54; and Warren A. Dym, "Scholars and Miners: Dowsing and the Freiburg Mining Academy," *Technology and Culture* 49, no. 4 (2008): 833–59, for the European origins of the practice; and Paul S. Landau, "When Rain Falls: Rainmaking and Community in a Southern Tswana Village, c.1870 to Recent Times,"

International Journal of African Historical Studies 26, no. 1 (1993): 1–30; and Patrick Jolly, "Some Photographers of Late Nineteenth Century San Rainmakers," *South African Archaeological Bulletin* 47, no. 156 (1992): 89–93, for the African practice.

12. John Barrow, *An Account of Travels in the Interior of Southern Africa in the Years 1797 and 1798*, vol. 1 (London: Cadell and Davies, 1801), 376–77. See Nigel Penn, "Mapping the Cape: John Barrow and the First British occupation of the Colony, 1795–1803," *Pretexts* 4, no. 1 (1993): 20–43, for Barrow's biography and context.

13. Cape of Good Hope, *Report of the Inspector of Water Drills, 1895* [G22-96], 4.

14. Cape of Good Hope, *Report of the Select Committee on the System of Deep Well Boring and the use of Diamond Drills, 1903* [C1-03], 21.

15. See letter to the editor, "The Divining Rod Problem," *South African Agricultural Journal* 2, no. 4 (April 1911): 512, for the quote.

16. Van Sittert, "The Nature of Power"; Beinart, "Academic Amnesia"; Van Sittert, "Reply"; and D. Nel, "You Cannot Make the People Scientific by Act of Parliament: Farmers, the State and Livestock Enumeration in the North-Western Cape, 1850–1900" (MA thesis, University of Cape Town, 1998).

17. C. A. Scanlen, "Pumping Tests on Boreholes," *Agricultural Journal of the Cape of Good Hope* [hereafter cited as *AJCGH*] 36, no. 5 (May 1910): 608, for the quote.

18. C. Warner, "The Origin of Igneous Dykes and Their Relation to the Underground Water Supply of the Cape Colony," *AJCGH* 26, no. 2 (February 1905): 264.

19. Another Sceptic, "The Divining Rod—Is It a Fraud?," *AJCGH* 31, no. 5 (November 1907): 596.

20. Ibid.

21. Henry Francis, "The Divining Rod," *AJCGH* 31, no. 3 (September 1907): 346.

22. See Edgar H. R. Evans, "The Divining Rod on Trial," *AJCGH* 32, no. 1 (January 1908): 120, for the quote.

23. Letter to the editor, "The Divining Rod Problem," 684; and Cape of Good Hope, *Report of the Select Committee on Water-boring and Diamond Drills, 1904* [C7-1904], 11.

24. C. E. Liebenberg, "The Divining Rod," *AJCGH* 29, no. 6 (December 1906): 822.

25. Frank Biggs, "The Divining Rod Again," *AJCGH* 31, no. 2 (August 1907): 206–7.

26. See Sinclair, "Water Finding by the Divining Rod," *AJCGH* 29, no. 4 (October 1906): 538; B. M. Bowker, "The Divining Rod Not a Fraud," *AJCGH* 30, no. 6 (June 1907): 824–25; John M. Bowker, "The Divining Rod—a Challenge," *AJCGH* 31, no. 6 (December 1907): 720; Frank Biggs, "Suggested Comprehensive Test for the Divining Rod," *AJCGH* 31, no. 6 (December 1907): 723–25; B. M. Bowker, "The Divining Rod and Underground Water Supply," *AJCGH* 32, no. 4 (April 1908): 514; Quod Sciam, "Water Finding with the Rod," *AJCGH* 32, no. 6 (June 1908): 775; J. G. Webster, "The Divining Rod Proves a Success," *AJCGH* 33, no. 22 (August 1908): 242; W. St Leger Seaton, "The Divining Rod," *AJCGH* 34, no. 1 (January 1909): 215, for advertising and touting.

27. See Edgar H. R. Evans, "The Divining Rod—Is It a Fraud?," *AJCGH* 31, no. 5 (November 1907): 594–95; and Henry Francis, "The Divining Rod," *AJCGH* 31, no. 3 (September 1907): 346, for the quotes.

Part II

Conflict

CHAPTER 5

Locust Invasions and Tensions over Environmental and Bodily Health in the Colonial Transkei

Jacob Tropp

THE 1890s witnessed an unusually destructive invasion of locusts in many parts of South Africa. In the Eastern Cape a series of locust swarms wreaked havoc on agricultural production by both European and African farmers alike. In the recently colonized Xhosa-speaking polities of the Transkei, by this time taking shape as a growing labor "reserve" for the larger white settler economy, Cape colonial officials responded to these invasions by attempting to enforce locust eradication in African communities. Such actions were necessary, officials argued, to reduce the threats locust depredations posed not just to Africans' crops but also, and even more so, to neighboring European farms in the Transkei and eastern districts of the Cape Colony.

Yet such campaigns generated deep strains in colonial relations in particular communities in the Transkei, where the presence of locusts, the problems they posed, and the appropriate means and processes by which to respond were all understood in quite different terms. When officials demanded that Africans destroy locusts in their fields, the government interfered with preexisting local ways of ritually contending with environmental distress and therapeutic practices that linked ecological and bodily healing. In parts of Thembuland and Pondoland, ritual specialists, prominent chiefs, and many communities expressed their resistance to colonial locust campaigns through the assertion of alternative agricultural rituals and prophecies that centered on the power of young women's fertility. In some areas of Fingoland, local residents opposed the colonial state by drawing explicit connections between locust plagues and the increased incidence of childhood disease, using the syncretic language of Christian and indigenous prophetic traditions. Taken together, these cases suggest that popular responses and resistance to colonial locust policies grew out of a much wider range of existing ritual and spiritual practices than officials ever anticipated or understood. In the face of intense biophysical stresses and expanding colonial domination, local people asserted and defended their own cultural means of controlling the health of their natural environs and themselves.

The Power of Agricultural Rituals

Locusts were by no means new to African farmers in the newly colonized Transkei. Yet the early 1890s brought a rather unique pest to the region—swarms of the red locust, a particularly voracious and destructive species that had not been seen in the Eastern Cape for a few decades. These new invaders not only presented unique swarming tendencies that often baffled both colonial authorities and African communities alike, but they also severely attacked all vegetation in sight, from crops and pasturage to the trees and bushes upon which they settled at night.[1] As officials strove to contain this damage and block the swarms' spread to neighboring white settler farming districts, they faced an additional obstacle that would recur throughout these formative colonial years—with limited colonial personnel on the ground to implement official policies, they would have to rely upon Africans' participation. By the end of the decade authorities would increasingly employ new entomological research and techniques for destroying locusts in many locales of the Transkei, such as laying out lethal fungus and spraying arsenite of soda.[2] From the initial assault of red locusts in the early 1890s, however, and even as such substances were used in subsequent years, officials consistently found the most practical and effective approach for eradicating locusts was to directly enlist Africans' labor and skills, under the supervision of locally stationed colonial personnel and willing African headmen. In fact, when swarms first began ravaging Africans' fields, authorities took special note of local people's particular ways of destroying the pests—such as driving their small livestock and dragging sledges over them, beating them with bushes, digging them into trenches, and driving them into the dry grass and setting fire to them by night—and promoted the adoption of such methods in colonial eradication campaigns across the region.[3] From the outset, colonial success in locust destruction was thus predicated on colonial appropriation of local environmental knowledge.[4]

African compliance and colonial appreciation of Africans' knowledge both had their limits, however. While Africans in many parts of the Transkei followed government directives to rid locusts from their lands or independently engaged in such activities, noncompliance became a recurring problem for officials in some locales, and colonial authorities regularly blamed local "witch doctors" for fanning the flames of such popular resistance. Some of the sharpest and most vocal critics of colonial locust policies were indeed those ritual specialists—*amagqirha* ("diviner-healers") and *amaxhwele* ("herbalists")—who assumed various responsibilities for ensuring that local landscapes and populations were protected from any debilitating forces, including such pests as locusts. As the government expanded its locust directives, some of these specialists felt direct threats to their spheres of influence in local communities and even attempted to mobilize anticolonial popular responses. Unwittingly, colonial locust policies had intruded into the sensitive politicized terrain of local ritual and environmental knowledge.

In multiple areas of Thembuland and Pondoland, for instance, officials repeatedly complained about the prominent role played by one so-called "locust doctor," Kama, in turning local populations against locust destruction. Though based in the Mqanduli district in Lower Thembuland, Kama was reported to influence events in various districts, directing Africans far and wide to refrain from complying with government locust measures and instructing them in alternative ritual responses to the invading pests. At some point in the early 1890s, in fact, Kama was even imprisoned for such activities.[5] As one magistrate commented in early 1896, Kama's popularity represented a growing threat to official locust eradication and colonial authority more broadly: "His influence and reputation are so great that people from all parts flock to his Kraal and consult him to obtain charms to remove the locusts. . . . Kama is so thoroughly believed in that unless something is done to check his evil influence matters will assume a grave aspect."[6]

As his services grew in demand, Kama also seized the opportunity to publicly assert his ritual authority and the direct thwarting of colonial power it signified. In February 1896, as confidentially reported to the magistrate by an African observer, Kama claimed before a group of followers:

> That he has a white bird which tells him secrets at night time, and that he was informed that beyond the swarm of locusts he saw a very large Impi [army] of Natives who were going to attack the Europeans in this country and in the Colony generally and that a big war was coming on, and that they were now to take this message to their parents and to tell them what he has mentioned to them. That he Kama [was] a man of great influence amongst the Natives, and that he would endeavour to influence all Chiefs in the Country, as he was well known by them, to rise and go to war. . . . I am going to stir up the people (Natives) to turn out and fight the Europeans and turn them out of the Country, that all of the Natives who will assist the Europeans will die. I will therefore advice [sic] all the Natives men and women to buy assegais [spears], and there were a large Number of men at this meeting armed with guns and assegais who were called by him for this purpose. . . . Kama further told the people to induce all the Natives to stand up and fight on one day that he would burn some herbs on a fire which will cause every Native to fight against the Europeans.[7]

Kama here directly confronted government efforts to curb his ways of dealing with locusts and environmental distress, asserting the power and primacy of his ritual knowledge—signified by the white bird, a symbol often associated with *amagqirha*[8]—and even claiming it would be the springboard to a broader victory over colonialism. More than any other individual at this time, Kama starkly articulated the tremendous stakes involved when the government interceded in Africans' own means of managing and healing their landscapes.[9]

Beyond the high politics of Kama's inflammatory rhetoric, local communities' complex ways of ritually contending with the locust threat in Thembuland and Pondoland reveal how colonial locust campaigns intervened into much deeper cultural worlds of environmental healing than officials ever expected. While Kama's outspoken and continuous opposition to government agendas disturbed officials and missionaries, they were also especially distraught at the behavior of the young females who followed his ritual instructions. Magistrates and missionaries regularly decried what appears to have been a common ritual practice in many areas of Thembuland

and western Pondoland: young unmarried females, wearing only a beaded girdle, would proceed through their communities' croplands, performing particular songs and dances for the purpose, while they waved specially chosen plants or mealie stalks, carried and scattered red clay, or otherwise "doctored" the fields with particular roots or "medicines."[10] Most significant here is the fact that young females played the central roles in these rites—referred to in some locales as the *ixoshombo* ceremony but more widely recorded as *inqoloqho*.

Ethnographic evidence from various Xhosa- and Zulu-speaking groups from this period onward suggests that young unmarried females, about to be initiated into womanhood and embodying fertility in their communities, were often seen in the late nineteenth and early twentieth centuries as ritually pivotal in protecting fields from many types of destructive natural predators, from maize grubs to locusts.[11] The practice of *ixoshombo* and *inqoloqho* in the Transkei purposefully emphasized this fertility and incorporated symbols that were recognizable in other ceremonies marking the beginning of womanhood, such as the beaded girdle and the use of red clay.[12] Colonial locust policies thus tread into the domain of long-running, preexisting ritual practices that extended well beyond the immediate, material impact of locusts and deep into local Africans' linked ideas about fertility, gender roles, and environmental health.

One of the more difficult dimensions to interpret in these rituals is the significance of particular gender inversions that have often played central roles. Subsequent ethnographers of Thembu, Bomvana, Tshezi, Mpondo, and neighboring Zulu communities have recorded how *ixoshombo*, *inqoloqho*, and related ceremonies highlighted young women's ritual power by providing a space for them to transgress accepted social norms and gender boundaries. In certain Bomvana locales, for instance, young women essentially took over control of the fields through which they wandered and sang, with all others prohibited from entering the fields while they were present. According to the ethnographer Peter A. W. Cook: "If any stray cattle were found there these were captured by the girls and driven back to their kraal. The owner of the cattle had to pay a goat as a fine to release them. This goat was killed and the girls ate a portion of it, the rest going to the people of the kraal."[13] Thus *ixoshombo* and *inqoloqho*, at least for a controlled time and space, seemingly elevated young females' position in society and inverted reigning norms regarding married men's control over land and livestock.[14]

Through his research on Zulu women's agricultural rituals in the 1930s and 1940s, Max Gluckman was one of the earliest and most influential theorists regarding the meaning of such ritualized gender dynamics in southern

Africa and beyond. For Gluckman, the Zulu *Nomkubulwana* ceremony, in which women and girls took on stereotypical "male" behaviors as they ceremonially honored a spiritual "princess" protector of the community's young field crops, represented a cathartic "ritual of rebellion"—"an instituted protest demanded of sacred tradition," which on the surface contested but fundamentally only reinforced the gender status quo.[15] Recently Todd Sanders, examining women's rain rituals among the Ihanzu of Tanzania, has criticized the enduring currency of Gluckman's interpretation, pointing to its flawed assumptions that women necessarily utilize rituals to contest the patriarchal structures they face in their everyday lives and that there is a singular, monolithic gender "system," which women strive to invert. Rather than viewing "male" and "female" playing oppositional roles in ritual practice, Sanders and others have stressed that in some cultures gender complementarity, mixing, and confusion are often collectively understood and expected as the basis of a ritual's transformative power and potential.[16]

Such reinterpretations help point us toward the broader communal purposes behind *ixoshombo* and *inqoloqho* practices of a century ago and how they related to the intruding locust initiatives of the colonial state. While it is difficult, given the limits of the source material, to assess in detail the perspectives and intentions of the young women at the center of these rites, there are significant clues suggesting the wider community's stake in such ceremonies and their transformative ritual power at this particular moment of mounting environmental distress and colonial pressure. In most instances *ixoshombo* and *inqoloqho* were highly organized through various social networks and hierarchies of senior men and women, with young women playing the starring ritual roles in an ensemble cast.

First, there was the prominent role assumed by Kama in many locales, evidenced not just by the volume of colonial irritation at his influence but even more so by the widespread and long-lasting invocation of his name in ritual practice. For example, in her 1978 master's thesis on Xhosa drama, Dorcas Jafta gave an account of the *inqoloqho* ritual based on oral testimonies from elderly African men and women from various districts in the former Ciskei and Transkei who had participated in the ceremony when it was still practiced in earlier decades. According to her sources, this was the song women would sing while "doctoring" the fields:

Sizinqoloqho mama	(We are the inqoloqho mama
Siziintombi zakwaNkama	We are the girls of Nkama
Sivela kwaMbombo	We come from Mbombo
Sisebenzel' umbona.	We work for mielies [corn].)[17]

Employing Kama and supporting his legitimacy in many areas, particularly in western Pondoland, were often high-ranking chiefs. In the Ngqeleni district of western Pondoland in the summer of 1895–1896, as local communities contended with severe crop losses from locust swarms, relations between the resident magistrate and Mpondo leaders grew increasingly testy as the latter refused to comply with official locust eradication and disavow their association with the by now infamous Kama.[18] At a more local level, evidence suggests that prominent men of a location or sublocation and the wider community were also often instrumental in *inqoloqho* ceremonies. As Joan Broster recorded among Thembu communities several decades later, headmen and other male leaders would convene to choose an appropriate *ixhwele* (herbalist) to "doctor" the fields; a small committee of men would then be appointed to follow the *ixhwele*'s instructions, including rounding up the young women in the community to perform the central rites; and then a special seclusion hut would be chosen and a responsible older man and woman would be placed in authority over these young women, providing them protection and cooking them food provided by the wider community.[19] It was also regularly recorded in the late nineteenth and early twentieth centuries that homesteads and parents whose daughters were involved in *inqoloqho* rites for their community would each take on some of the burden of paying for the ritual specialist's services, in exchange for having their fields ritually protected from locusts and other misfortune.[20]

My point here is to stress the broader community effort behind the organization and practice of such ceremonies to rid locusts from people's lands. Young women's fertility served as the symbolic vehicle for *ixoshombo* and *inqoloqho*, and any accepted mixing of gender norms and boundaries within this context, while allowing junior females some space to temporarily invert everyday power dynamics, also seems to have been aimed at enhancing the ritual potency brought to this communal purpose. As the colonial government attempted to enforce its particular ways of understanding and contending with locust depredations, many communities instead chose to invest in these preexisting ritual ways of healing the landscape, collectively asserting and identifying with their own strategies of communal well-being.[21] And, as Kama and prominent chiefs' involvement suggests, these rituals could also be more strategically invoked in purposeful opposition to colonial state power.

Protecting Children's Health in Fingoland

A rather different series of responses to government-sponsored locust destruction emerged in certain Fingoland communities in the mid-1890s and again in 1899–1900. During these years, African residents faced massive locust swarms amid a combination of multiple rural stresses, including drought and the increased incidence of specific diseases.[22] While many people cooperated with government efforts to eradicate invading locusts, colonial authorities also noted that in certain locales many residents adamantly refused to comply, claiming that locust destruction directly caused the spread of illness. One noteworthy episode in the Butterworth district in 1900 involved a recurring theme of locusts "retaliating" in response to the government's interventions. According to the Butterworth magistrate, W. T. Brownlee:

> It was with great difficulty in many instances that the natives could be got to undertake locust destruction, as they have been taken possession of by all sorts of superstitious and idle fancies, one of these being that the destruction of the locusts brought disease and death among the people. In this connection rather a curious incident occurred. Soon after the business of destruction began a swarm of hoppers marched across the Market-square in Butterworth and swarmed into the verandah of the Court-house. "Ha," said the natives, "they have come to lodge a complaint"; a gang of prisoners was employed and in a short while destroyed the whole swarm. A day or two thereafter the Magistrate was seized with an acute attack of illness, and then said the natives "Ha! what is it? Here it is: this is that thing that we said would happen."[23]

It is telling here that Magistrate Brownlee himself was represented as a primary victim of the locusts' "revenge," following his push to eradicate them in the district. What more immediate proof did one need that the enforcement of locust destruction caused widespread illness and misery, even infecting the bodies of colonial officials themselves?

To understand this repeatedly expressed connection between locusts, their destruction, and poor health, it is useful to look more closely at the much better documented ferment surrounding colonial locust campaigns in Fingoland in the mid-1890s. Such resistance in these years in part echoed broader antigovernment discontent percolating throughout Mfengu districts and other parts of the Transkei, as people critically responded to the proposed implementation of the Glen Grey Act, amid a particularly acute moment of rural distress, through protest and rumor.[24] Yet the specific ways in which many people complained about and associated locusts and disease also bore particular significance. For instance, according to the Tsomo district magistrate in late 1894:

> Last year an attempt was made to induce the natives to destroy the young locusts, and in some locations they did something in that direction; but this year they decline to interfere with them in any way, being firmly impressed with the idea that the locusts destroyed last year have revenged themselves upon them by causing the great mortality which has occurred this year amongst their children. (The children died in most instances of measles.)[25]

A year and a half later, in the neighboring Nqamakwe district, the magistrate similarly complained that Africans in the district had "completely ceased" from destroying the young locusts hatching in various locales:

> I have reason to believe that this is owing to some superstitious idea to the effect that some misfortune will fall upon them if they interfere with the swarms.... The fact that a year or two ago a very fatal epidemic of measles, with pulmonary complications supervening, followed the destruction of local swarms, and carried off a large number of children, may have something to do with this unhappy development.[26]

Throughout these years, popular complaints about the government destroying locusts continually emphasized such associations with the increased incidence of childhood disease and mortality.[27] The virulence of certain illnesses, especially measles and smallpox, had indeed spiked in these and neighboring districts over the previous few years, and young children were repeatedly cited as the disproportionate victims. For instance, the Nqamakwe magistrate tragically noted in April 1894 "the very serious and alarming rate at which the Native children have been dying in the District. Within the last few months upwards of four hundred deaths of children alone, have been reported at this office, not counting adults. The mortality is chiefly confined to young children from the age of ten years down to babyhood and the disease if not epidemic appears to be certainly very contagious."[28] Official attempts to vaccinate or quarantine local populations, though successful in some areas, were also regularly avoided in many locales, with residents viewing such schemes as ineffective in combating the spread of disease or, more cynically, as efforts by the government to more completely exert its control over local populations, their mobility, and their service to the colonial economy.[29]

Intense drought conditions and locust swarms in the mid-1890s compounded the increase in children's illness and mortality, destroying the primary sources of good health and nutrition and enabling diseases to have a more devastating impact. In some locations in the Nqamakwe and Tsomo districts in early 1896, officials described how the unusually intense locust swarms "have completely destroyed all the grain, beans, pumpkins, potatoes and have almost entirely eaten up the pasturage. Reports come on from all sides that everything is ruined."[30] For many African parents witnessing this sudden and widespread debilitation of their "young crop" in both their fields and their homes, the problem of locusts and childhood disease could thus be seen as directly related phenomena, both physically disabling the vitality of their families' lives and severely straining their capacity to control and ensure their future existence.[31] In an era when the colonial government increasingly exerted its influence over rural people's lives and landscapes, many African residents were strongly disinclined to support further efforts by officials to determine how people should respond to such distress. Resistance to colonial locust campaigns was therefore embedded in people's wider critical perspectives concerning Africans' diminishing control over their environments and their bodies amid this era of deepening colonial domination.

One particular story circulating in the Tsomo district in the mid-1890s underscored the fact that many people sought alternative ways of explaining and asserting control over such combined threats to their lives and livelihoods. A rumor spreading to many areas, and eventually reaching the desk of local officials, related the story of an African woman giving birth to a three-headed son, one of which was in the form of a locust's head. The mother was at first afraid, but the child then spoke and assuaged her fears, instructing his mother to assemble all of the men of the village to hear his prophecy: "I am a messenger from God: God has sent me to deliver this message to you, do not kill the locusts, they will not destroy your crops."[32] This rumor and prophecy, centered on a newborn child, speaks to the above-mentioned associations often made between locust invasions and childhood illness.

As in other prophecies in the Eastern Cape in the nineteenth and early twentieth centuries, the story is infused with Christian themes (the three heads may suggest the Trinity, for instance) and promises some form of "salvation" from ecological and economic crisis through an adherence to particular norms when responding to such pressures, although these are not clearly described in the archival record. In this story, the newborn child is strong, vital, even comforting, and steers the course for the future welfare of the community, in stark contrast to the conditions many families faced in the wake of locust depredations and often fatal smallpox outbreaks among their young. While anecdotal, this particular episode does suggest how many people in Fingoland and elsewhere strove to assert some control over their fate when facing these rural pressures, far beyond the colonial government's efforts to diagnose and manage such problems.

Conclusions

Looking at these varied episodes from the colonial Transkei reveals that popular responses to locusts were deeply situated within complex practices associated with the healing and welfare of both people's landscapes and their own bodies—in many cases, in fact, these aspirations were intimately connected.[33] In their agricultural campaign to have locusts destroyed in African districts, colonial officials thus entered into unanticipated arenas of often intense cultural politics, as different groups drew from diverse ritual, therapeutic, and prophetic repertoires to question the propriety of the government's intervention and assert their own ways of understanding and coping with intensifying threats to their well-being.

Understanding such levels of meaning in local environmental knowledge and resistance can offer insights into the tensions of not only these early colonial years but also subsequent episodes of state-peasant conflict in the Eastern Cape. For example, in the late 1910s and early 1920s, following the turbulent convergence of a ravaging influenza epidemic and violent state repression of rural Africans in the region, the colonial state again attempted to force local residents to destroy invading locust swarms. And once again, though with much greater organization, many Africans expressed their opposition to this intrusion through their allegiance to an alternative set of environmental and bodily healing practices, in this instance one rooted in an independent religious movement led by a female Xhosa Christian prophet.[34] Such historical recurrences deserve further reflection: they suggest that popular responses to state environmental intervention need to be located within local people's wider experiences and perceptions of distress as well as their deeper understandings of, and desires for, legitimate routes to spiritual and physical wellness.

Notes

1. Jacobus C. Faure, *The Life History of the Red Locust [Nomadacris septemfasciata (Serville)]* (Pretoria: Union of South Africa, Department of Agriculture, 1935), 9, 14, 21. As one Transkeian magistrate noted in 1896, the locusts' "appearance and characteristics would almost lead one to suppose that a new species had been produced by some process of evolution. They differ in many points from the locusts which are so well known in the Colony. . . . I should think there is hardly anything of their size under the sun that can surpass them in voracity. They devour leaves, grass or crops without discrimination." Cape of Good Hope, Native Affairs Department, *Blue Book on Native Affairs (BBNA) 1896*, report of the Resident Magistrate (RM) of Kokstad, 139–40.

2. Cape of Good Hope, Forest Department, *Report of the Chief Conservator of Forests for 1896*, 156; Cape Town Archives Repository (hereafter cited as CTAR), Records of the Conservator of Forests, Transkei (FCT) 2/1/1/2, Conservator C. C. Henkel to the Under-Secretary of Agriculture (USA), February 25, 1897; *BBNA 1900*, RM Port St. John's, February 2, 1900, 40; *BBNA 1901*, RM Butterworth, January 5, 1901, 37–38; CTAR, Records of the Resident Magistrate of the Kentani District 5/1/1/18, RM Kentani to the Secretary of Native Affairs, November 13, 1907; *BBNA 1908*, "Reports of Resident Magistrates," 36. On the rising importance of entomological science to Cape colonial efforts to support settler agriculture, see Karen Brown, "Political Entomology: The Insectile Challenge to Agricultural Development in the Cape Colony, 1895–1910," *Journal of Southern African Studies* 29, no. 2 (2003): 529–49.

3. CTAR, Records of the Secretary of Agriculture 110, 420, RM Idutywa to Under-Secretary for Lands, Mines, and Agriculture, November 7, 1892, and RM Butterworth to Chief Magistrate of the Transkei (CMT), November 6, 1893; *BBNA 1894*, RM Idutywa, 51 and RM Nqamakwe, 55; CTAR, Records of the Resident Magistrate of Butterworth District 5/1/15, September 28, 1900, CMT circular to all RMs; *BBNA 1901*, W. T. Brownlee, RM Butterworth, January 5, 1901, 37–38.

4. For a similar theme in the contemporaneous field of Cape colonial medicine, see Premesh Lalu, "Medical Anthropology, Subaltern Traces, and the Making and Meaning of Western Medicine in South Africa: 1895–1899," *History in Africa* 25 (1998): 133–59.

5. CTAR, Records of the Chief Magistrate of the Transkeian Territories (CMT) 3/141, RM Ngqeleni to CMT, letters of February 18, 21, and April 20, 1896; CTAR, CMT 3/196A, Letters Received, Confidential, 1892–1905, RM Mqanduli to CMT, February 27, 1895, attaching "Statement made by [no name given] before C. F. Blakeway Esq. R. M. Mqanduli," February 15, 1895; CTAR,

FCT 2/1/1/2, FCT to USA, February 21, 1896; CTAR, Records of the Resident Magistrate of Umtata District (1/UTA) 4/1/8/1/4, Charles Chambers to RM Sweeney, December 26, 1893. Kama's influence was also subsequently noted in Joan A. Broster, *The Tembu: Their Beadwork, Songs and Dances* (Cape Town: Purnell, 1976), 36–38; Monica Hunter, *Reaction to Conquest: Effects of Contact with Europeans on the Pondo of South Africa* (London: Oxford University Press, 1936), 77–78; Peter A. W. Cook, *Social Organisation and Ceremonial Institutions of the Bomvana* (Cape Town: Juta, 1931), 140–41.

6. CTAR, CMT 3/141, RM Ngqeleni to CMT, February 21, 1896.

7. CTAR, CMT 3/196A, Letters Received, Confidential, 1892–1905, RM Mqanduli to CMT, February 27, 1895, attaching "Statement made by [no name given] before C. F. Blakeway Esq. R. M. Mqanduli," February 15, 1895.

8. Mongameli Mabona, *Diviners and Prophets among the Xhosa (1593–1856): A Study in Xhosa Cultural History* (Piscataway: Transaction Publishers, 2004), 351.

9. There is also an intriguingly contemporaneous role played by ritual specialists in combating locust infestations during the Chimurenga rebellion across the Limpopo River in what is today Zimbabwe. David Beach has discussed how during the summer of 1895–1896, amid intense locust attacks on crops, the pursuit and distribution of anti-locust "medicine" served as important means of contact between Ndebele and Shona political and spiritual leaders. David N. Beach, "'Chimurenga': The Shona Rising of 1896–97," *Journal of African History* 20, no. 3 (1979): 395–420, particularly 406–9. See also Steven Feierman, *Peasant Intellectuals: Anthropology and History in Tanzania* (Madison: University of Wisconsin Press, 1990), 100, on healers historically dispensing locust medicines in the Pare mountains.

10. CTAR, 1/UTA 4/1/8/1/4, Samuel Baudert, Baziya, to RM Umtata, December 26, 1893; CTAR, CMT 3/141, RM Ngqeleni to CMT, letters of February 18, 21, and April 20, 1896; CTAR, FCT 2/1/1/2, FCT to USA, February 21, 1896.

11. Basil Holt, *The Tshezi of the Transkei: An Ethnographic Study* (Johannesburg, 1969); Broster, *The Tembu*, 36–38; Cook, *Social Organisation*, 77–78; Max Gluckman, "Zulu Women in Hoe Culture Ritual," *Bantu Studies* 9 (1935): 255–71; A. T. Bryant, *The Zulu People, As They Were Before the White Man Came* (Pietermaritzburg: Shuter and Shooter, 1949), 662–66. Eileen Krige described in the 1960s how for Zulu communities interpreting many agricultural misfortunes as the result of moral transgressions, particularly sexual defilement, the "chief actors in getting rid of them are quite appropriately, therefore, virgin girls who draw attention to their moral uprightness by going naked." Eileen J. Krige, "Girls' Puberty Songs and Their Relation to Fertility, Health, Morality and Religion Among the Zulu," *Africa: Journal of the International African*

Institute 38, no. 2 (1968): 173–98, quote on 180. On similar rituals related to chief's first-fruit ceremonies in various Nguni societies, see Hunter, *Reaction to Conquest*, 404–5; W. D. Hammond-Tooke, *Bhaca Society: A People of the Transkeian Uplands* (Cape Town: Oxford University Press, 1962), 175, 178; Brian Marwick, *The Swazi: An Ethnographic Account of the Natives of the Swaziland Protectorate* (London: Cass, 1966), chap. 5; Hilda Kuper, *An African Aristocracy: Rank Among the Swazi* (London: Oxford University Press, 1947), chap. 13.

12. Broster, *The Tembu*.

13. Cook, *Social Organisation*, 140–41.

14. Though, as Eileen Krige has suggested, broader cultural taboos in the region regarding females and livestock have not historically applied to all females in the same way. Young Zulu girls, for instance, had long herded livestock when family circumstances required it. Krige, "Girls' Puberty Songs," 184.

15. Max Gluckman, "Rituals of Rebellion in South-East Africa," chap. 3 in his *Order and Rebellion in Tribal Africa* (New York: Free Press of Glencoe, 1963), quote from page 114; Gluckman, "Zulu Women."

16. Todd Sanders, "Rains Gone Bad, Women Gone Mad: Rethinking Gender Rituals of Rebellion and Patriarchy," *Journal of the Royal Anthropological Institute* 6, no. 3 (September 2000): 469–86; Todd Sanders, "'Doing Gender' in Africa: Embodying Categories and the Categorically Disembodied," in *Those Who Play with Fire: Gender, Fertility and Transformation in East and Southern Africa*, London School of Economics Monographs on Social Anthropology, vol. 69, ed. Henrietta L. Moore, Todd Sanders, and Bwire Kaare (New Brunswick, NJ: Athlone Press, 1999), 41–82. For similar insights into the ritual potency of gender complementarity, see Camilla Power and Ian Watts, "First Gender, Wrong Sex," and Bwire Kaare, "*Saisee Tororeita*: An Analysis of Complementarity in Akie Gender Ideology," in *Those Who Play with Fire*, ed. Moore et al., 101–32 and 133–52 respectively.

17. Dorcas Nompumelelo Jafta, "A Survey of Xhosa Drama" (MA thesis, University of Zululand, 1978), 1–2, and "appendix," 169–70. For other references to songs stressing Kama's importance, see Broster, *The Tembu*, 37; Hunter, *Reaction to Conquest*, 77–78; Cook, *Social Organisation*, 140–41; Mabona, *Diviners and Prophets*, 197.

18. CTAR, CMT 3/141, RM Ngqeleni to CMT, February 21, 1896, meeting of RM Ngqeleni and Mpondo chiefs.

19. Broster, *The Tembu*, 36; Jafta, "A Survey of Xhosa Drama," 76.

20. CTAR, 1/UTA 4/1/8/1/4, Charles Chambers to RM Sweeney, December 26, 1893; CTAR, CMT 3/196A, Letters Received, Confidential, 1892–1905, RM Mqanduli to CMT, February 27, 1895, attaching "Statement made by [no name given] before C. F. Blakeway Esq. R.M. Mqanduli," February 15, 1895; CTAR,

CMT 3/141, RM Ngqeleni to CMT, February 21, 1896; CTAR, FCT 2/1/1/2, Conservator C. C. Henkel to USA, February 21, 1896; Cook, *Social Organisation*, 140–41.

21. I owe this line of thinking regarding collective identity to Derick Fay, who observed a revived *inqoloqho* ceremony in 1999 and interprets its meaning in "'The Trust Is Over! We Want to Plough': Land, Livelihoods and Reverse Resettlement in South Africa's Transkei" (PhD diss., Boston University, 2003), 240–44. Fay explores how people used *inqoloqho* not just to deal with environmental distress, but also as a way of marking who legitimately belonged in a community and who did not. Perhaps similar interests were at play in such ceremonies of a century ago, though the historical sources are too thin to probe this too far.

22. *BBNA 1901*, 35, "Report of the CM for 1900," February 15, 1900; Ibid., 37–38, W. T. Brownlee, RM Butterworth, January 5, 1901.

23. *BBNA 1901*, 37–38, W. T. Brownlee, RM Butterworth, January 5,1901.

24. See William Beinart and Colin Bundy, *Hidden Struggles in Rural South Africa: Politics and Popular Movements in the Transkei and Eastern Cape, 1890–1930* (London: James Currey, 1987), 138–65; and my discussion of some of these pressures and popular responses in "Dogs, Poison and the Meaning of Colonial Intervention in the Transkei, South Africa," *Journal of African History* 43, no. 3 (2002): 451–72.

25. *BBNA 1895*, 64, RM Tsomo, November 22, 1894.

26. CTAR, CMT 3/147, RM Nqamakwe to CMT, April 24, 1896.

27. For another prominent example, see CTAR, CMT 3/164, RM Tsomo to CMT, April 20, 1896.

28. CTAR, CMT 3/146, RM Nqamakwe to CMT, April 9, 1894, original emphasis.

29. *BBNA 1889*, 32, RM Tsomo, January 1, 1889; *BBNA 1890*, 28, RM Tsomo, January 3, 1890; *BBNA 1891*, 32, RM Tsomo, January 2, 1891; *BBNA 1893*, 54, RM Nqamakwe; CTAR, CMT 3/58, RM Butterworth to CMT, Blue Book report for 1894, December 12, 1894; CTAR, CMT 3/58, RM Butterworth to CMT, Blue book report for 1895, December 31, 1895; *BBNA 1895*, 64, RM Tsomo, November 22, 1894; CTAR, CMT 3/105, RM Kentani to CMT, December 18, 1894; CTAR, CMT 3/147, Nqamakwe district, correspondence throughout 1894 and 1895 describe recurrent smallpox concerns in the district; CTAR, Records of the Magistrate of the Engcobo District, 5/1/3/2, RM Engcobo to CMT, July 30, 1895; *Umtata Herald*, "The Next Delusion," March 23, 1895; CTAR, Records of the Magistrate of the Nqamakwe District (1/NKE) 5/1/2/3, RM Nqamakwe to CMT, October 19, 1895; Records of the Magistrate of the Tsomo District 6/1/1/7, RM Tsomo to CMT, February 7, 1895.

30. CTAR, CMT 3/164, RM Tsomo to CMT, January 10, 1896. On the unusual virulence of locust swarms at this time, see also CTAR, 1/NKE 5/1/2/3, "Increase Locust Pest," petition from fifteen Europeans in the Nqamakwe District to RM Nqamakwe; CTAR, 1/NKE 5/1/2/3, William Ndzimela, Nqamakwe Gaol, to RM Nqamakwe, March 17, 1896, on the concern that local people "will die from starvation caused by this drought and locusts."

31. A parallel can be seen in Gabriel Rugalema's recent description of popular understandings of AIDS in particular communities in East Africa:

> Since the late 1980s the preferred name for the disease has been *ekiuka* (a pest). The evolution of the term *ekiuka* is an analogy drawn between HIV infection of the human population on one hand and the infestation of the banana crop by weevils and nematodes on the other. The destructive combination of the weevil and nematodes leads to the falling over of immature banana plants. . . . As AIDS kills young adults, similarly banana weevil and nematodes kill young banana plants prematurely. As my informants explained, Buhaya is faced by two kinds of *ekiuka*: one is destroying the *kibanja* (banana/coffee farm) while the other is destroying human beings.
>
> "Understanding the African HIV Pandemic: An Appraisal of the Contexts and Lay Explanation of the HIV/AIDS Pandemic with Examples from Tanzania and Kenya," in *HIV and AIDS in Africa: Beyond Epidemiology*, ed. Ezekiel Kalipeni et al. (Malden: Blackwell, 2004), 191–203, quote from 196. Thanks to David Eaton for this reference.

32. CTAR, CMT 3/66, RM Cofimvaba to CMT, April 27, 1896, attaching statement made before RM Cofimvaba, Ncora Hotel by "Mahliki," April 25, 1896, concerning the events in the neighboring Tsomo district.

33. Julie Livingston, for instance, has explored how people "experience history in their bodies and how they, in turn, make historical sense out of their changing bodily experiences" as they contend with shifting "ecologies of misfortune," in *Debility and the Moral Imagination in Botswana* (Bloomington: Indiana University Press, 2005), quotes from pages 1, 145.

34. Robert R. Edgar and Hilary Sapire, *African Apocalypse: The Story of Nontetha Nkwenkwe, a Twentieth-Century South African Prophet* (Athens: Ohio University Press, 2000), esp. chaps. 1 and 2.

CHAPTER 6

Navajos, New Dealers, and the Metaphysics of Nature

Marsha Weisiger

"THE TALK about grazing conditions was not true," asserted Frank Goldtooth in the early 1970s. "There was plenty of vegetation and water. The ranges and valleys were covered with tall grass and beautiful flowers." The elderly Diné (Navajo) man recalled the traumatic New Deal era of the 1930s, when officials with the U.S. Bureau of Indian Affairs (BIA) and the Soil Conservation Service (SCS) pressured Navajos to slash herds in an effort to conserve severely overgrazed rangelands on the Navajo Reservation. Located on the Colorado Plateau, the reservation encloses some twenty-five thousand square miles at the intersection of Arizona, New Mexico, and Utah. Goldtooth had helped implement the program to reduce livestock and restrict stockowners to circumscribed areas, but looking back, he concluded that the government program had been misguided. Federal conservationists had misread the land and the relationship of the Diné to it.

The Diné themselves, he told his visitor, long conserved the range by moving in an annual cycle, yet government policy-makers, disdainful of traditional ways, disrupted those patterns, and in so doing they degraded the land. In the old days, he explained, "the people moved with their sheep whenever and wherever they wished with the seasons." It seemed clear to him, in fact, that the Diné knew how to live in harmony with the land. "A homesite," he explained, "is not good when a family lives in the same place too long. The vegetation is tramped on too much, and it never gets a chance to grow again. Long ago, moving with the stock from one place to another was much better than what we do now. It gave the vegetation time to grow again."[1]

But in the 1930s, federal conservationists portrayed a landscape much different from the one Goldtooth remembered. Rather than reporting lush vegetation, John Provinse, an official with the Navajo Service, exclaimed in a radio broadcast that anyone "could look around and see that great barren areas existed on the Reservation, that the grass was short and becoming shorter, that the wind was whipping sand out of dry washes and from barren spots and piling it up into sand dunes, that there were gullies everywhere." Provinse described a weary waste of sheet erosion, exotic and unpalatable vegetation, and large areas of grassland, once in excellent condition, but "now so denuded of grass that they will scarcely support a saddle horse."[2]

Each of these narrators told a radically different story about the land, and each presumed an utterly different solution, much as Jacob Tropp found in the Transkei (chap. 5 this volume). For Provinse and the conservationists, the earth was eroding before their eyes. Only a drastic cut in the numbers of livestock and a written permit tying each stockowner to a particular piece of land would restore the grasslands and avert disaster. Many Diné disagreed. Like Goldtooth, they maintained that the land remained healthy, that the problem was temporary drought. It was as though Goldtooth and Provinse saw completely different landscapes.

Two sets of "experts," one scientific and one native, offered diametrical descriptions of the land. Each reflected different values and understandings about the way nature works and the relationships of humans to nature. Conservationists employed scientific theories of equilibrium, succession, carrying capacity, and arroyo development to depict the Navajo range as seriously overgrazed. Diné, by contrast, drew on their understandings of cosmology, the mosaic of landscapes, and the interrelationships between livestock and land learned through generations of experience grazing the southern Colorado Plateau, and they concluded that they were witnessing nature's cycle: rain would follow drought, and all would be well again. Neither the Diné nor the New Dealers fully grasped the complexities of nature. Each, no doubt, held pieces of the puzzle, but neither could see the value of the other's.

Today, the Navajo Nation is, if anything, in worse shape than it was in the 1930s. Conservationists managed to bring livestock numbers down to the so-called carrying capacity, and yet they failed to stem the process of desertification. Grazing and periodic drought brought a spiraling decline in the ability of the soils to produce their historical forage, so that by the late 1950s, a decade of severe drought, range conditions crossed an ecological threshold, the point at which an ecosystem becomes irreversibly changed.[3] The result has been a chronically degraded range.

One key to understanding what went wrong with the program to save the soil on the Navajo Reservation lies in the disjuncture between these two stories of land, native and scientific. Each narrator related a conception of the world that the other found incomprehensible. That was not necessarily an unbridgeable divide, for they shared common ground—the desire to maintain some sort of "balance of nature"—although the means to that end certainly differed. Federal authorities alone, however, had the plenary power to prescribe their view of nature. They largely ignored or even dismissed the Navajos' understandings of the natural world and their local knowledge of the land.[4] By "local knowledge," I do not mean the modern, strategic deployment of "indigenous knowledge," as such. Indeed, that phrase would have puzzled Navajos in the 1930s. I mean, instead, the experiential and often practical knowledge that the political theorist James C. Scott calls "mētis."[5] Ignoring local knowledge, along with Diné epistemology and cultural issues, had important consequences. The Diné resisted and rejected the range conservation program, and so the conservationists proved unsuccessful in actually restoring the range.

In developing their program for the Navajo Reservation, New Deal conservationists told themselves tales of a precipitous decline from a formerly luxuriant grassland to a wretched wasteland. These scientific storytellers were not unique, of course. We may like to think of science as an objective, nonideological pursuit, and yet all science (including the scientific data I myself use in this essay) is socially constructed among communities of scholars, who consciously or unconsciously bring to their work values, experiences, and assumptions that shape their conclusions, even though they may tell themselves otherwise.[6] That does not mean that soil scientists fabricated fables, in the sense of purposeful falsehoods. On the contrary, they narrated stories about the land that seemed to them most plausible, in light of the evidence that they found most persuasive. Nonetheless, the credibility of that evidence depended on their point of view.

The conservationists believed that Navajo rangelands had been overstocked for more than fifty years. By 1930, William Zeh, a BIA forester, concluded that erosion was spreading like a cancer across the reservation. He argued that the Navajos' 1.3 million sheep and goats exceeded the range's carrying capacity by a factor of two or three. And that shocking figure excluded the large numbers of Navajo horses, as well as cattle, mules, and other stock. In light of such disparities, he wrote, erosion was "inevitable." Zeh worried that the reservation would become uninhabitable, forcing the government, as legal guardian, to either relocate Navajos onto new lands or support them on the dole.[7]

In early June 1933, Commissioner of Indian Affairs John Collier asked Hugh Hammond Bennett, head of the newly created Soil Erosion Service (later renamed the Soil Conservation Service), to spearhead a study of erosion on the Navajo Reservation. Bennett's study consisted of a whirlwind tour lasting less than a week, but everywhere he looked, he saw destruction. All in all, he estimated that some 70 percent of the land suffered from serious erosion. Even beyond the denuded areas around hogans and watering holes, ground that once supported blue grama and galleta grasses now yielded mostly snakeweed and other toxic or unpalatable plants. Sadly, he predicted, a large part of the range would never fully recover.[8]

Before long, the SCS, working in cooperation with the BIA and the Biological Survey, sent a legion of experts to the reservation to describe, measure, classify, and analyze the land. Range technicians, soil specialists, engineers, agronomists, and biologists—many of them among the best in the region—swarmed across Navajo Country. They studied the soil, the range, and the forests. They recorded the topography, drainage patterns, and vegetation. They documented Navajo land use and identified potential dam sites and arable soils. Perhaps most important, these troops of trained professionals *measured* the land, reducing the mesas and canyons, the forests and badlands, the meadows and arroyos, the grasses, forbs, and shrubs to a series of numbers in an effort to arrive at a precise, scientific calculation of the range's carrying capacity.[9] These numbers then became the cornerstone of the stock reduction program.

Reduction, however, was already well under way when the first comprehensive studies of the reservation began to roll off the typewriters. Two qualities of these reports are most striking: their focus on riparian areas and their narrative structure. Collectively, these studies told a story that went something like this: In the beginning, the alluvial valleys had been covered by heavy stands of grass. During torrential rains, these grasses slowed the runoff, allowing the water to spread across the valley floors and trickle slowly into the loamy soils. But the Navajos allowed their sheep to overpopulate the land. Overgrazing removed the vegetation or reduced its vitality, which led to an invasion of unpalatable and poisonous weeds, exposed the soil to the wind, and encouraged flows of water to cut great gullies, washing the red soil through the watershed of the Colorado River.[10]

This story of a decline from an Edenic pastoral landscape contained a large measure of truth. Grazing does invariably alter the environment, and overgrazing can and did accelerate erosion and bring desertification. When livestock continuously defoliate favored forbs, grasses, and shrubs, they eventually kill the native vegetation they prefer and encourage the invasion and spread of less-palatable plants, both native and exotic. As vegetation density decreases, larger areas of soil are exposed to the baking sun, making them more arid. And as the patches of bare ground become wider, the wind begins to carry away the topsoil. Trampling hooves also compact soils, thereby reducing aeration and water infiltration and encouraging runoff and sheet erosion. Overgrazing, then, can destroy the land, just as the soil conservationists narrated it.[11]

And yet, all stories—whether they trace progression toward a better life or tell of decline toward something worse—take their starting point from a set of assumptions and values that consciously foreshadow the conclusion. A story of catastrophically eroding lands necessarily begins with a healthy environment, or one that is at least stable. As any dramatist knows, such a happy beginning is a necessary prelude to a compelling plotline of tragic declension. The conservationists, however, had little actual knowledge of the condition of the land before the Diné began grazing their livestock on it. Instead, as they constructed their stories about Navajo Country, the scientists relied on assumptions about the land's historical condition that they barely acknowledged and never scrutinized.[12]

Following the influential theories of the pioneering ecologist Frederic Clements, the scientists assumed that the stands of shrubs extending across the reservation had invaded once lush grasslands, and they defined those plant communities not dominated by grasses as degraded. Clements, whose "climax theory" shaped ecological studies for more than a generation, argued that mature vegetation communities remain stable, or in a state of equilibrium, unless disturbed by something like fire or overgrazing. Following a disturbance, a given vegetation community would redevelop through a series of stages until it again reached its mature or climax state. According to Clements, the sagebrush-dominated lands of the Colorado Plateau—which he called "sagebrush savanna"—were the product of overgrazing. In its pristine, mature state, he contended, the region was predominantly grassland.[13]

Mid-nineteenth-century descriptions of the land also swayed the conservationists. Comparisons with early travel accounts persuaded them that the carrying capacity had dropped by one-third to one-half since the reservation was established in 1868.[14] However, a close reading of early explorers' accounts suggests that travelers generally focused attention on riparian areas and springs—a small fragment of the overall landscape—where they found good forage and water for their horses and mules. The scientists' story of an overgrazed range, then, relied in part on the misguided notion that a more ideal pastoral landscape once characterized all of Navajo Country.

Consider the account written in 1857 by Lt. Edward Beale, whose descriptions of a well-watered pasture of plenty had a marked effect on conservationists' perceptions of the historical landscape. In a publicity pamphlet, the BIA juxtaposed passages from Beale's journal, written along a proposed wagon route paralleling the Little Colorado River, with images by government photographer Milton Snow. These pictures, according to the BIA, told "a story of wasted rangeland, crumbling walls of mud, and nature thrown out of balance by man's wanton misuse of his resources." Beale's rhapsodic descriptions of verdant meadows, "undulating prairie land, covered with grass," and easily passable rivers contrasted sharply with photographs depicting "giant fingers of erosion," unpalatable snakeweed, and arroyos "cutting the country like a knife." The differences offered "graphic proof," in case the reader missed the point, "that no cycle of drouth, but man's stupid misuse of nature's resources, made the Beale Trail what it is today."[15]

And yet government officials were quite selective in choosing the lieutenant's words to construct a dramatic story of environmental destruction, aimed at mollifying congressional critics of the stock reduction program. They omitted those elements of the historic landscape that might have muddied their picture of decline from Eden. Beale found abundant greasewood, as well as grama, indicating shrub-grasslands, not pure pastures. And while he described most of the terrain as flat or gently rolling, he also encountered deep gullies.[16] It's worth noting, too, that Beale's route generally followed stream courses; thus, most of the good grazing he described was in riparian areas or around springs. Snow's photographs leave no doubt that the grassy meadows along these rivers had vanished by the 1930s, but they also imply that vast areas of the reservation extending away from these streams were part of the same story.

But we know little even now about the historical conditions of that larger mosaic of shrub-grasslands, woodlands, and badlands. Only a few travelers ventured off the riparian trails. Lt. Joseph Ives, for example, had surveyed the area earlier that same year, prior to the summer monsoons, but unlike Beale, he struck off toward the Hopi villages. Along that path, he wrote, "the scene was one of utter desolation.... There was not a spear of grass, and from the porousness of the soil . . . it was impossible that there should be a drop of water."[17] It would be hard to deny that Snow's powerful photographs documented the desertification of the southern edge of Navajo Country, but his selective viewpoint revealed and reinforced a somewhat distorted understanding of the changes that had taken place since Beale's journey.[18]

Historical observations shaped soil conservationists' perceptions in one more important way: washes and streams that travelers described as shallow in the 1840s and 1850s had become deeply entrenched by the early 1900s, following a boom in the Navajo livestock population. This pattern could be seen across the West, which witnessed an explosion in the numbers of cattle in the late nineteenth century. Government scientists thus assumed that arroyos, from ten to one hundred feet in depth, constituted unambiguous evidence of overgrazing on the Navajo Reservation.[19]

Although the only evidence that livestock had *caused* southwestern arroyos was the coincidence in timing, these scientists dismissed a competing theory that climate change had initiated gullying. Two noted geologists, Herbert Gregory and Kirk Bryan, attributed the arroyos to climate, noting that they appeared to be universal across the Colorado Plateau, even in areas left ungrazed because of the absence of stock water, and that similar episodes of arroyo cutting had occurred around 1100, long before the introduction of livestock.[20] Similarly, the geomorphologist John Tilton Hack, who studied the ancient sand dunes near the Painted Desert, suggested that the role of grazing was minor, compared with long-term geological processes that had been structuring this region for thousands of years. Scientists with the SCS, led by the renowned climatologist C. Warren Thornthwaite, rejected these arguments, finding no evidence of a new trend toward drought that would cause severe erosion in the absence of overgrazing.[21]

Scholars have since concluded that climate change—a long period of intense drought followed by a new pattern of high-energy, convective summer storms—likely initiated the network of arroyos that even now scar the land. According to the tree-ring data, severe drought in the 1870s, 1880s, and especially 1899–1904, weakened plants. Not since the 1660s—and before then, the 1250s—had the region suffered such painful drought. Then came an abnormally and prolonged wet period, from 1905 to 1920—the likes of which had been unseen for nearly a century—when intense summer downpours brought flash flooding. As roiling waters surged through once shallow washes, weakened plants no longer held the soil in place, allowing water to carve away at the upstream heads, undercut the banks, scour channels, and thereby lengthen, widen, and deepen trenches. And as gullies cut deeper into the earth, they lowered the water table below the shallow roots of native bunchgrasses and encouraged the spread of more xeric plants with long taproots.[22] None of this information on precipitation was available in the 1930s, but the evidence offered by the esteemed geologists Bryan and Gregory provided clues.

Thornthwaite, however, was absolutely right in one important particular. Navajo Country did not experience deep drought during the 1930s, according to the tree-ring record. True, there were droughty years, especially 1934 (the century's warmest) and 1936. But generally speaking, the region received average rainfall over the course of the decade. What made it *seem* so dry was the marked contrast with the extreme wetness of previous decades; a generation of Diné had grown up during an aberrant period when rainfall and snow were well above average. But beginning in 1925, a shift in atmospheric wind patterns brought a steep decline in the availability of moisture, unprecedented since the last millennium.[23] Climate change thereby transformed the landscape, chiseling arroyos deep into the earth and robbing desert grasses of life-sustaining water, but that change began much earlier than the 1930s. No doubt, heavy grazing exacerbated this process by weakening and thinning vegetation. But in rejecting the role of climate change, conservationists simplified a more complicated story.

Federal conservationists, then, made a number of problematic and contested assumptions as they constructed their stories about the Navajo range. Nonetheless, their studies reveal that overgrazing at least *accelerated* the course of natural erosion by removing and killing vegetation that might otherwise hold the soil in place. The conservationists exaggerated the Navajos' role in causing erosion, and yet their studies leave little doubt that overgrazing contributed significantly to the sorry state of the land.

Why, then, did the Navajos not see it?

Federal conservationists seemed baffled by that question, but what is striking in their reports is how little they tried to understand the one variable that mattered more than anything: the Navajos themselves. BIA Commissioner John Collier, to be sure, was fairly knowledgeable about Navajo culture and society, and he realized that the conservation program's success depended, in part, on even more knowledge. Unfortunately, Collier proved unable to secure the appropriations necessary to hire anthropologists until 1935, well after stock reduction began to transform the Diné economy.[24] Still, even if Collier had managed to initiate cultural research far earlier, it seems doubtful whether it would have made much difference. His own insistence on "practical" information impeded any effort to understand Navajos on their own terms.

Overseeing the anthropological effort was Eshref Shevky, who held a doctorate in experimental medicine but had no background in Navajo ethnography, no formal anthropological training, no interest in traditional academic questions about customs, beliefs, myths, or kinship. That kind of information, in his opinion, was useless for developing a workable range management program. Instead, he insisted on "hard facts."[25] The questionnaires he designed for his study, known as the "human dependency survey," asked for quantifiable information about population, economic resources, income distribution, and little else.[26] It read more like a census schedule than an instrument for discovering meaningful information about Navajos or their relationships to the land.

To his credit, though, Shevky hired a pair of dedicated anthropologists, Solon Kimball and John Provinse, who endeavored to understand Navajo culture on its own terms by using a more ethnographic approach to their research in one part of the reservation, as a pilot project. They spent time with Navajo families, talking with the men and observing how their families functioned. That effort helped them to recognize what they called the "land-use community," clustered groups of families related through women who shared the same range, worked cooperatively at such tasks as shearing and dipping sheep, and joined together for ceremonies. But before Kimball and Provinse could expand their research into other areas of the reservation, their superiors within the SCS suspended their work, allegedly over petty turf issues.[27]

Even Kimball and Provinse remained ignorant of many of the most important aspects of Navajo culture, despite their efforts to understand indigenous land use. Kimball would later defend his limited knowledge, arguing that information on Navajo thought and cultural dynamics was either unavailable or "*irrelevant to the problems of an action program.*"[28] The claim that this information was unavailable ignored the presence of Father Berard Haile and Gladys Reichard, two of the century's authorities on Navajo culture, both of whom had for some time been delving into Navajo religion, kinship, and social organization. Nor was information on Navajo thought and culture irrelevant. Haile's and Reichard's insights could have helped Kimball develop a richer understanding of Navajo life and thought. By ignoring the importance of cultural information on seemingly esoteric matters such as spiritual beliefs, the New Dealers created an incomplete picture of Navajos and their relationships with livestock and land.

Importantly, they failed to adequately consider that Navajos might have their own tales to tell about their relationships with nature. Those stories expressed a view of the natural world gained through keen observations of a stingy land that nonetheless nurtured them as hunters, gatherers, farmers, and, later, shepherds for at least four centuries. And yet, Diné, too, misread the landscape, often ascribing the desolate condition of the range solely to drought or spiritual disorder. Like the scientists, they had an incomplete understanding of the rapidly changing ecological conditions of the first half of the twentieth century. Few were even willing to acknowledge that a more xeric landscape required a different strategy for managing the range. Still, they possessed a local knowledge of the land, an experiential understanding that the soil conservationists largely ignored.[29]

Diné were intimately familiar with their environment, and they expressed it by descriptively naming every clump of trees, every spring and seep, indeed every locale, no matter how minute. These word pictures mapped the landscape in ways that no line drawing could ever capture. Not surprisingly in this arid land, Diné emphasized places where water may be found. Tó Dínéeshzhee', or Kayenta, describes "waters spread out in rivulets, fan-like." Tó Haach'i', or "water is scratched out," describes a sandy creekbed where water can be dug out by hand. And Dibé Bichaan Bii' Tó, meaning "sheep manure spring," locates an apparently popular watering hole. Diné also observed the plants on which they depended, and their names for plants both discriminated between species and generalized among allied species in ways that Western science echoes. Those names told stories about the plants as well, describing not only their physical characteristics but also, for example, their value for healing and for feeding livestock.[30] In naming nature, Diné delineated the richness that they saw in a landscape that outsiders often viewed as impoverished waste.

Diné knew nature not only through their connections with the physical environment but also through their ties to the metaphysical world. Blessingway, perhaps the most important of the Diné ceremonies, framed their understanding of the relationships between livestock and land in much the same way science framed the way that federal conservationists comprehended their environment. Blessingway recounts the epic story of creation and chronicles the life of Changing Woman, the most revered of the Holy People and, significantly, the being most identified with the earth. According to that saga, Changing Woman first gave life to sheep and goats, and in the process created the plants that cover the ground. As the sheep and goats were born, their amniotic fluid soaked into the soil, and from the moistened earth, vegetation grew.³¹ In that way, plants and animals multiplied together.

Like the conservationists, Diné recognized that plant life had become increasingly desiccated and sparse by the early 1930s, but they had a fundamentally different understanding of the underlying problem and the appropriate solutions. Most believed the problem was drought. Drought had come and gone periodically since the 1870s—and even long before that—and this era, while prolonged, did not seem different. Where soil conservationists saw dead grass and shrubs, Diné saw dormant vegetation that would revive with rain. And Diné responded as they always had. When drought caused corn crops to dwindle, Diné traditionally slaughtered more sheep and goats for food, and they bartered animals, wool, and pelts for grain at trading posts. In consuming livestock, Diné decreased their herds and extended webs of reciprocity as stockowners shared their bounty with poorer kin. Diné also typically responded to drought by moving long distances to find better forage. In the early 1820s, for instance, drought spurred the Diné leader Narbona to move his family and his flock of some 2,250 sheep and goats more than two hundred miles from the eastern slopes of the Chuskas to the western edge of the Hopi mesas.³² Drought brought hardship, but the shepherds always coped somehow.

Many Diné believed that underlying the apparent drought of the 1930s was a more fundamental disorder, *hóchxọ*, or spiritual chaos. Such disorder sprang from imbalances in the social relationships among people, between humans and the Holy People, or between humans and the nonhuman world, disequilibriums that only ceremonies could set aright. If hóchxọ was drying up the rain and causing the plants to wither and die, the most important action that Diné could take was to perform Blessingway and other ceremonies to restore order, or *hózhọ*. Hózhọ is the central concept of Diné philosophy. Although often glossed as "beauty," essentially, it refers to the balance or harmony or perfection that surrounds all life, animates the universe, and brings long life and happiness. Diné do not imagine hózhọ as a static condition; it requires continual maintenance through ritual action. When things become disordered, people restore order, or hózhọ, by singing Blessingway, which reenacts creation, not figuratively, but literally. This process of re-creation through Blessingway is an important concept that those of us who are not Diné sometimes find difficult to grasp. For Diné who follow the traditional ways, mind and matter are inseparable. Thought, speech, and song *actually create physical reality.*³³

Traditionally Diné exercised control over their world through thought and speech. In Blessingway, for example, things occur when people think or talk about them, particularly when they repeat a request four times. The spiritual healers known as *hataałii*, moreover, cure their patients by reenacting creation through song. And even ordinary people in their everyday lives could make things happen, good or bad, through the simple act of thinking or talking about them. Praying for rain would make it rain, and people could ensure the health of their horses and sheep or even expand their herds by singing the proper Blessingway songs that reenacted the creation of livestock. This faith in the power of ritual songs persisted through the 1930s and much longer.[34] To the Diné way of thinking, Blessingway songs were—and are—crucial to the well-being of their animals and the land.

Consequently, as drought seemed to grip the reservation and stock began to starve, Diné responded with a flood of ceremonies. This outpouring of ritual struck scientists as mere superstition; songs could do nothing to increase forage. William McGinnies, director of the reservation's land management program, barely contained his disdain when he observed that "forage production . . . can in no way be increased by prayers or religious fervor."[35] But Diné had a different understanding of the environmental problems they were experiencing. A Diné woman from around Farmington, New Mexico, revealed that one of the Holy People, Banded Rock Boy, visited her and explained the reason that the rains no longer came: "We do not live the right way anymore," she reported. "People have forgotten the right way to live and everyone *thinks the wrong thoughts*." And Banded Rock Boy prescribed the solution, as well: "The people should hold ceremonies," he told her. "They must pray for things to be good again."[36] If livestock were a gift of the Holy People, then surely the wanton destruction of that gift would bring misery. Importantly, many like the woman from Farmington believed that the people had forgotten the right way to live, had forgotten how to sing the right songs, and so the earth tilted off balance.

Just as New Dealers viewed these ideas as wholly irrational, Diné thought stock reduction itself seemed anything but logical. It flew in the face of everything they understood about their world. Many saw the root of the problem in stock reduction itself. Listen to the story that Gambler Woman narrated:

> Before the reduction period there was a lot of grass, and I think it was the stock reduction that caused our pasture vegetation to be reduced. . . . The Anglos are not telling the truth when they say that the reason for the stock reduction was too much

livestock and not enough vegetation to provide for it. There was an abundance of greasewood and other vegetation. During the mid-summers[,] vegetation, like the sunflowers, colored the place. . . . There is very little now for a sheep to take a bite of. All this is due to the lack of precipitation from above. Maybe they reduced that, too.³⁷

This story expressed a common conception among Diné. Many had a completely different sense of the timing of environmental change than the conservationists had. Soil scientists viewed the degraded range as the result of an ecological decline that reached back to the 1880s, but Diné, recalling a recently luxuriant land, believed that desertification began only in the 1930s. Many viewed the land in a light refracted through the prism of memory. Some likely looked back to the particularly wet period between 1905 and 1920, years when Fred Deeschii'nii had seen grasses "so tall in some areas that all you could see was a horse's back."³⁸ They remembered patches of land in especially well-watered places at higher elevations and in relatively pristine areas without stock water, for the effects of grazing were unevenly distributed across the landscape. Many saw a correlation between stock reduction and the advent of an extended drought, but they saw them in that order, as cause and effect, transposing the actual course of events. Viewing the landscape through the lens of their spiritual beliefs, they reasoned that, in mercilessly slashing livestock, the New Dealers created hóchxǫ, or chaos, and thereby dried up the rain.³⁹

Diné blamed drought, disharmony, and the arrival of the conservationists themselves for the decline, while they defended their own stewardship with descriptions of lush vegetation. In doing so, they overlooked environmental changes that had been taking place since the early twentieth century, in part because the incremental scale of those changes eluded day-to-day observations. Many failed especially to acknowledge that growing numbers of people and flocks placed intense pressure on the forage, thereby reshaping the relationships between plants, soils, and water. At the same time, in telling themselves that the problem was temporary drought, they did not recognize that long-term climatic conditions were changing, any more than the conservationists did. Diné needed to adjust their herds to relatively droughty conditions over the long term. New conditions called for new ways of imagining their world.

Diné had long imagined that world as a mosaic of grasses, forbs, and brush through which they maneuvered with age-old movements that conserved and even created forage, but those seasonal shifts became increasingly difficult by the 1930s. Transhumance probably *had* conserved the range, at least through much of the second half of the nineteenth century, and expansion into new lands had delayed the day of reckoning. After all, if nutritious forage had declined rapidly as they built their herds, the incredible boom in the numbers of livestock could not have occurred, because the land could not have sustained high rates of reproduction. Between 1868 and 1930, the Diné population itself multiplied fivefold, from about 8,000 to perhaps 39,000 people; and their herds increased perhaps fifteenfold, from about 50,000 to nearly 750,000 sheep and goats. But the efficacy of transhumance began to change in the 1880s and 1890s. Over time, Diné population growth and the encroachment of Anglo and Hispanic ranchers on the periphery began to limit the amount of range available to each family, and seasonal movements became constricted.[40] As a consequence, even by the early 1880s, Diné shepherds found it harder and harder to find new forage. Eventually some began to complain openly that the reservation was overgrazed and demanded an extension of the reservation boundary to give Diné exclusive rights to much of the public domain on the periphery.[41] But this proposed expansion could not really solve this population problem, since Diné families and Anglo and Hispanic ranchers already occupied those lands.

Competition for forage was bound to place intense pressure on ecological systems. Many Diné observed the changes, even if they did not fully recognize the cause. Ernest Nelson inadvertently documented the effects of overgrazing when he described the reservation's lush range conditions before government meddlers destroyed everything: "You could see the golden blossoms of sunflowers growing for miles and miles around," he reminisced. There was lots of grass, he recalled, but also "pigweed grass grew thickly everywhere you looked."[42] Without realizing it, Nelson confirmed what the conservationists saw. Overgrazing had encouraged the spread of both native and exotic weeds, like pigweed, which thrives on disturbed, denuded soils. It brought locoweed, which colored the land with beautiful flowers, but poisoned the livestock that ate them.

Diné, of course, were well aware of which plants sickened their stock and avoided those areas where large stands of toxins thrived, but there were also weeds that they welcomed. Many of the plants that thrived on overgrazed ground—native plants such as sunflowers, greasewood, snakeweed, and rabbitbrush—had cultural meanings as medicines, food, or dyes. Diné women, for example, prized rabbitbrush for dying blanket wool, as well as for curing headaches and treating colds, and they used snakeweed to treat snake and insect bites, headaches, and cuts.[43] One culture's field of noxious plants was another's pharmacopoeia.

The Diné and the conservationists looked at the world through cultural lenses that shaped their understandings of the land. Neither group fully understood nature's contingencies and complexities, though they acted as though they were certain they did. Each told themselves a profoundly different story about the earth and the proper way to care for it. Many of us, educated in the catechism of science, are inclined to accept the conservationists' tale. And yet both narratives, native and scientific, can be used to explain today's poor range conditions. For conservationists, the denuded range itself was proof of the damage wrought by overgrazing. But it is interesting that those Diné who believed that stock reduction itself unleashed chaos across the land also pointed to the range as proof.

Federal authorities possessed the power to impose their story on the Navajos, and yet they never quite grasped the symbolic meanings embodied by livestock, meanings that would linger long after sheep no longer meant much economically. Livestock offered long life and happiness; they were the substance of Diné thoughts and prayers. The conservationists and even the BIA anthropologists never saw the point of understanding those prayers. They never saw the point of understanding the ceremonies and traditional stories. As far as they were concerned, those stories were merely esoteric "myths" and "legends," with no meaning for conservation. Had they listened to those stories, they would have discovered a great deal about the Navajos and their ways of knowing nature.

Indeed, in retrospect Solon Kimball mused that the conservationists might have framed a program around the fundamental Diné belief in hózhǫ, a concept not all that unlike the scientific notion of equilibrium.[44] Finding common ground, of course, would have required the conservationists to set aside the notion that Western science offers all the answers, indeed the only answers, to ecological problems. That would have been, perhaps, too much to expect, but all systems of knowledge seek to explain the same physical reality of the nonhuman world, and it is hubris to believe that only Western science comprehends the workings of nature. As the biologist and cultural theorist Donna Haraway has remarked, nature does not speak through scientists, like a ventriloquist, unmediated by culture. Western science, like Diné metaphysics, is a product of culture.[45]

The conservationists possessed important knowledge about the workings of the natural world, but so, too, did Diné ways of knowing nature offer wisdom. Diné, for example, perceived the "discordant harmony of nature," to borrow the ecologist Daniel Botkin's phrase, something that scientists are just now beginning to grasp. They knew that hózhǫ and hóchxǫ, order and chaos, were both inherent to the natural world.[46] No doubt, their spiritual metaphors did not fully comprehend the complexities of nature any more than the New Dealers' mechanistic metaphors did. Both imagined an idealized nature, and both sought to control it, one through technology, the other through ceremony. Both believed in a kind of homeostasis. But unlike the conservationists, who thought that nature remained static in the absence of human disturbance, the Diné fathomed the flukiness of the natural world.

When New Deal conservationists dismissed Navajo understandings of nature, they made a grievous mistake. For when the next administration turned the range management program over to the Navajos, they relinquished the reins to people for whom conservation had come to seem anathema. Even today, traumatic memories of stock reduction complicate efforts to conserve the range. As one Diné employee of the Navajo Department of Forestry observed, most people now will not "touch grazing issues on the reservation with a ten foot pole."[47] The program that might have been a means to restore hózhǫ came to be viewed as the origin of a seemingly perpetual state of hóchxǫ.

Notes

1. Frank Goldtooth, interview in *Navajo Livestock Reduction: A National Disgrace*, ed. Ruth Roessel and Broderick Johnson (Chinle, AZ: Navajo Community College Press, 1974), 98–107. The bureau has been called the Indian Service, the Office of Indian Affairs, and now the Bureau of Indian Affairs. For simplicity, I use the present name throughout this essay.

2. John H. Provinse, "Physical Condition of the Reservation," Window Rock, October 18, 1938, pp. 1 and 4, folder 20, box 1, Thomas Dodge Collection (MS 33), Department of Archives and Manuscripts, Hayden Library, Arizona State University, Tempe.

3. Tamzen K. Stringham, William C. Krueger, and Patrick L. Shaver, "State and Transition Modeling: An Ecological Process Approach," *Journal of Range Management* 56 (2003): 106–13; and Brandon T. Bestelmeyer et al., "Development and Use of State-and-Transition Models for Rangelands," ibid.: 114–26.

4. The federal government held plenary power over the Navajos and most native groups. Chief Justice John Marshall famously defined Indian tribes as "domestic dependent nations" whose relationship to the federal government was "that of a ward to his guardian." *Cherokee Nation v. Georgia*, 30 *U.S. Reports* 1 (March 18, 1831).

5. James C. Scott, *Seeing Like a State: How Certain Schemes to Improve the Human Condition Have Failed* (New Haven, CT: Yale University Press, 1998), 4–7.

6. On the social construction of grasslands ecology, see Ronald C. Tobey, *Saving the Prairies: The Life Cycle of the Founding School of American Plant Ecology, 1895–1955* (Berkeley: University of California Press, 1981).

7. William H. Zeh to J. P. Kinney, May 19, 1932, Central Classified Files (CCF) 301.14 Range Management, Navajo, Prior to June 1, 1941, box 166, Forestry and Grazing Division, Record Group (RG) 75, National Archives, Pacific Region (NARA-PR), Laguna Niguel, California; Zeh, "General Report Covering the Grazing Situation on the Navajo Indian Reservation," in U.S. Congress, Senate, Committee on Indian Affairs, *Survey of Conditions of the Indians of the United States*, pt. 18, *Navajos in Arizona and New Mexico*, pp. 9123–27, 9131.

8. [H. H. Bennett], "Report to the Navajo Council by Conservation Advisory Committee for the Navajo Reservation," 1933, pp. 2–4, folder 3, box 18, U.S. Soil Conservation Service Records (MSS 289), Center for Southwest Research, Zimmerman Library, University of New Mexico, Albuquerque. From 1933 until 1935, the agency was called the Soil Erosion Service; for simplicity, I use its subsequent name, "Soil Conservation Service," throughout this essay. My information on plant characteristics is based on: William A. Dick-Peddie, *New Mexico Vegetation: Past, Present, and Future* (Albuquerque: University of New Mexico Press, 1993); William W. Dunmire and Gail D. Tierney, *Wild Plants and Native Peoples of the Four Corners* (Santa Fe: Museum of New Mexico Press, 1997); Frances H. Elmore, *Shrubs and Trees of the Southwest Uplands* (Tucson: Southwest Parks and Monuments Association, 1976); Robert R. Humphrey, *Arizona Range Grasses: Their Description, Forage Value, and Management* (Tucson: University of Arizona Press, 1970); "Living from Livestock" (Natural Resources Conservation Service, n.d.); James Stubbendieck, Stephan L. Hatch, and Charles H. Butterfield, *North American Range Plants* (Lincoln: University of Nebraska Press, 1981); and Tom D. Whitson et al., eds., *Weeds of the West* (Newark, CA: Western Society of Weed Science, 1996).

9. McGinnies, "The Problem of Soil Erosion on the Navajo Indian Reservation and Methods Being Used for Its Solution," 1936, p. 5, folder 11, box 8; Hugh G. Calkins and F. D. Matthews, "Report on Proposed Erosion Control Methods, Navajo Reservation," January 18, 1935, pp. 5–8, folder 37, box 7, both in SCS Records, UNM.

10. See, for example, McGinnies, "Problem of Soil Erosion," pp. 1–2; and Charles W. Collier, "Soil Conservation in the Navajo Country," *Soil Conservation* (SCS) 1 (October 1935): 1–2.

11. For a thorough discussion of the effects of overgrazing, see Marsha Weisiger, *Dreaming of Sheep in Navajo Country* (Seattle: University of Washington Press, 2009), chap. 6.

12. William Cronon, "A Place for Stories: Nature, History, and Narrative," *Journal of American History* 78 (1992): 1347–76; also see Diana K. Davis, "Potential Forests: Degradation Narratives, Science, and Environmental Policy in Protectorate Morocco, 1912–1956," *Environmental History* 10 (2005): 211–38.

13. Frederic E. Clements, "Nature and Structure of the Climax," in *Foundations of Ecology: Classic Papers with Commentaries*, ed. Leslie A. Real and James H. Brown (Chicago: University of Chicago Press, 1991), 59–97; Clements, "Plant Indicators," "Climaxes, Succession and Conservation," and "The Relict Method in Dynamic Ecology," all in *Dynamics of Vegetation: Selections from the Writings of Frederic E. Clements*, ed. B. W. Allred and Edith S. Clements (New York City: H. W. Wilson, 1949), 91, 96, 189, 204, 206. For background on Clements and his influence on soil conservationists, consult Donald Worster, *Nature's Economy: A History of Ecological Ideas* (Cambridge: Cambridge University Press, 1994), chap. 11; Tony L. Burgess, "Desert Grassland, Mixed Shrub Savanna, Shrub Steppe, or Semidesert Scrub? The Dilemma of Coexisting Growth Forms," in *The Desert Grassland*, ed. Mitchel P. McClaran and Thomas R. Van Devender (Tucson: University of Arizona Press, 1995), 51–56; and Jason G. Hamilton, "Changing Perceptions of Pre-European Grasslands in California," *Madroño* 44 (1997): 311–33. For the Soil Conservation Service's expression of equilibrium theory in Navajo Country, see "Land Management in the Navajo Area," [draft of pamphlet, c. 1937], CCF 300, box 117, Navajo Area Office, RG75, NARA-PR.

14. Provinse, "Physical Condition," pp. 4–5.

15. H. C. Lockett and Milton Snow, *Along the Beale Trail: A Photographic Account of Wasted Range Land* (Lawrence, KS: U.S. Office of Indian Affairs, 1939), 2–3, 12–19, 48–49.

16. U.S. Congress, *Wagon Road from Fort Defiance*, Executive Document 124, Serial Set 959, 35th Congress, 1st Session (1858); the quote is from p. 40.

17. U.S. Congress, Senate, *Report upon the Colorado River of the West*, by Joseph C. Ives, Executive Document, 36th Congress, 1st Session (1861), 117, 128.

18. Passing references to the long-standing history of overgrazing since the late nineteenth century can be found in Calkins and Matthews, "Report on Proposed Erosion Control Methods," p. 3, UNM, and "Justification of Present Plan of District Range Control," Reference File of Commissioner John Collier, 49–54, box 11, RG75, National Archives (NA), Washington, DC.

19. Herbert E. Gregory, *Geology of the Navajo Country: A Reconnaissance of Parts of Arizona New Mexico, and Utah*, U.S. Geological Survey, Professional

Paper 93 (1917), 130–31; U.S. Department of Agriculture (USDA), *Western Range: A Great but Neglected Natural Resource*, Senate Document 199, 74th Congress, 2nd Session (1936), 119, 308–12; Calkins and Matthews, "Report on Proposed Erosion Control Methods," pp. 4–5, UNM. Also see, for example, H. F. Johnson and Lucian A. Hill, "Work Report, Soil and Erosion Survey, Land Management Unit No. 4," 1936, pp. 17–18, folder 32, box 8, SCS Records, UNM. C. Warren Thornthwaite, C. F. Stewart Sharpe, and Earl F. Dosch offer an excellent discussion of channel-cutting in *Climate and Accelerated Erosion in the Arid and Semi-Arid Southwest with Special Reference to the Polacca Wash Drainage Basin, Arizona*, Technical Bulletin No. 808 (USDA, 1942), 95–99.

20. See, for example, Gregory, *Geology of Navajo Country*, 131–32; Kirk Bryan, "Recent Deposits of Chaco Canyon, New Mexico, in Relation to the Life of the Pre-Historic Peoples of Pueblo Bonito," *Journal of the Washington Academy of Sciences* 16 (February 4, 1926): 75–76; Bryan, "Date of Channel Trenching (Arroyo Cutting) in the Arid Southwest," *Science* 62 (1925): 338–44. Also see Stephen A. Hall, "Late Quaternary Sedimentation and Paleoecologic History of Chaco Canyon, New Mexico," *Geological Society of America Bulletin* 88 (1977): 1593–618; and Yi-Fu Tuan, "New Mexican Gullies: A Critical Review and Some Recent Observations," *Annals* (Association of American Geographers) 56 (1966): 591.

21. John T. Hack, "Dunes of the Western Navajo Country," *Geographical Review* 31 (1941): 240–63; D. G. Anderson, "Range Management Branch Report, Land Management Unit No. 3," January 1938, p. 11, vol. 7, box 1; and Anderson, "Range Management Report, Land Management Unit No. 1," May 1937, pp. 6–7, vol. 3, both in Soil Conservation Service Collection (AZ 124), Special Collections, University of Arizona Library, Tucson; C. W. Thornthwaite, C. F. S. Sharpe, and Earl F. Dosch, "Climate of the Southwest in Relation to Accelerated Erosion," *Soil Conservation* (SCS) 6 (1941): 300–301; Thornthwaite, Sharpe, and Dosch, *Climate and Accelerated Erosion*, 123–24.

22. William L. Graf offers an excellent history of the study of arroyo development in "The Arroyo Problem: Palaeohydrology and Palaeohydraulics in the Short Term," in *Background to Palaeohydrology: A Perspective*, ed. K. J. Gregory (Chichester: John Wiley, 1983), 279–302. The literature on southwestern arroyos is vast. Particularly useful is Denevan, "Livestock Numbers in Nineteenth-Century New Mexico, and the Problem of Gullying in the Southwest," *Annals* (Association of American Geographers) 57 (December 1967): 691–763; Richard Hereford and Robert H. Webb, "Historic Variation of Warm-Season Rainfall, Southern Colorado Plateau, Southwestern U.S.A.," *Climatic Change* 22 (1992): 239–56; and Luna B. Leopold, "Rainfall Frequency: An Aspect of Climatic Variation," *Transactions* (American Geophysical Union) 32

(1951): 347, 350–51. For a countervailing argument regarding environmental changes in southeastern Arizona, however, see Conrad Joseph Bahre, *A Legacy of Change: Historic Human Impact on Vegetation of the Arizona Borderlands* (Tucson: University of Arizona Press, 1991), esp. chap. 5.

23. Western Regional Climate Center (http:www.wrcc.dri.edu/summary/Climsmaz.html), precipitation tables for Chaco Canyon, Crownpoint, Farmington 3NE, and Shiprock; Paul R. Sheppard et al., "The Climate of the US Southwest," *Climate Research* 21 (2002): 229–30. Fort Defiance and Kayenta also recorded especially dry growing seasons in the 1930s.

24. Collier to H. H. Bennett, December 20, 1935, CCF 31777-1935-344, Cooperative Plan for Soil Conservation with the Dept. of Agriculture, RG75, NA; Lawrence C. Kelly, "Anthropology in the Soil Conservation Service," *Agricultural History* 59 (1985): 140.

25. Kelly, "Anthropology in the Soil Conservation Service"; also Kelly, "Anthropology and Anthropologists in the Indian New Deal," *Journal of the History of the Behavioral Sciences* 16 (1980): 14; "Sociological Survey of the Navajo Reservation: A Statement of Procedure," Regional Conservation Bulletin No. 32, Conservation Economics Series No. 5, May 1936, pp. 8, 15, folder 18, box 8, and BIA, Division of Socio-Economic Surveys, *Statistical Summary: Human Dependency Survey, Navajo Reservation and Grazing District 7*, 1940, box 10, both in SCS Records, UNM; Emma Reh, "Navajo Consumption Habits (for District 1)," draft report, October 24, 1939, Navajo Consumption Habits folder, box 32, U.S. Soil Conservation Service Records (MS 190), Rio Grande Collections, Branson Library, New Mexico State University (NMSU), Las Cruces; Kimball, "Land Use Management: The Navajo Reservation," in *The Uses of Anthropology*, ed. Walter Goldschmidt (Washington, DC: American Anthropological Association, 1979), 65–66, 69–70.

26. Kimball, "Land Use Management," 65–66, 69–70; "Sociological Survey Procedure," p. 15, UNM; BIA, *Statistical Summary: Human Dependency Survey*, UNM; Emma Reh, "Navajo Consumption Habits (District 1)," NMSU.

27. Kimball, "Land Use Management," 72–75.

28. Kelly, "Anthropology in the Soil Conservation Service," 141; Kelly, "Anthropology and Anthropologists in the Indian New Deal," 16; Kimball, "Land Use Management," 64–67, 73–75, emphasis in original. Also see Solon T. Kimball and John H. Provinse, "Navajo Social Organization in Land Use Planning," *Applied Anthropology* 1 (1942): 18–25.

29. James C. Scott perceptively explores the contours of indigenous, practical knowledge—mētis—which, he holds, can be acquired only through practice and "represents a wide array of practical skills and acquired intelligence

in responding to a constantly changing natural and human environment." See Scott, *Seeing Like a State*, 311–41.

30. Alan Wilson and Gene Dennison, *Navajo Place Names: An Observer's Guide* (Guilford, CT: Jeffrey Norton, 1995). For a similar, yet more thorough, analysis of Western Apache epistemology, consult Keith H. Basso, *Wisdom Sits in Places: Landscape and Language Among the Western Apache* (Albuquerque: University of New Mexico Press, 1996). For Navajo "ethnoscience," see Washington Matthews, "Navajo Names for Plants," *American Naturalist* 20 (1886): 767–77; and Matthews, "Natural Naturalists" (unpub. ms. read before the Philosophical Society of Washington, October 25, 1884), in *Washington Matthews: Studies of Navajo Culture, 1880–1894*, ed. Katherine Spencer Halpern and Susan Brown McGreevy (Albuquerque: University of New Mexico Press, 1997), 193–201.

31. Slim Curley, Version I, in *Blessingway*, ed. Lelan C. Wyman (Tucson: University of Arizona Press, 1970), 245–46.

32. See, for example, Kay Bennett, *Kaibah: Recollection of a Navajo Girlhood* (Los Angeles: Westernlore Press, 1964), 240–41; Walter Dyk, *Son of Old Man Hat: A Navaho Autobiography* (1938; reprint, Lincoln: University of Nebraska Press, 1966), 104–13, 129–31, 153–58, 173–78; Franc Johnson Newcomb, *Hosteen Klah: Navaho Medicine Man and Sand Painter* (Norman: University of Oklahoma Press, 1964), 11–12.

33. My rather cursory discussion here draws heavily on Gary Witherspoon, *Language and Art in the Navajo Universe* (Ann Arbor: University of Michigan Press, 1977), p. 9 and chap. 1. My discussion of hózhǫ and hóchxǫ is also informed by Milford B. Muskett, "Identity, *Hózhǫ́*, Change, and Land: Navajo Environmental Perspectives" (PhD diss., University of Wisconsin, Madison, 2003), 136–37, 159–60. The role that thought, speech, and—by extension—breath play in creating reality can be seen throughout Blessingway, but consult especially Frank Mitchell, Version II, in *Blessingway*, ed. Wyman, 354–55. I am also indebted to James C. Faris in "Taking Navajo Truths Seriously: The Consequences of the Accretions of Disbelief," in *Papers from the Third, Fourth, and Sixth Navajo Studies Conferences*, ed. June-el Piper (Window Rock, AZ: Navajo Nation Historic Preservation Department, 1993), 181–86.

34. See, for example, Slim Curley, Version I, in *Blessingway*, ed. Wyman, 248–64; Henry Zah, in *Navajo Livestock Reduction*, ed. Roessel and Johnson, 122.

35. W. G. McGinnies, "The Agricultural and Range Resources of the Navajo Reservation in Relation to the Subsistence Needs of the Navajo Indians," May 12, 1936, pp. 2-3, folder 11, box 8, SCS Records, UNM.

36. Don Watson, "Navahos Pray for the Good of the World," *Mesa Verde Notes* 7, no. 1 (1937): 16–18. Emphasis mine.

37. Ason Attakai, in *Navajo Livestock Reduction*, ed. Roessel and Johnson, 129.

38. Fred Descheene, in *Navajo Livestock Reduction*, ed. Roessel and Johnson, 194.

39. See, for example, John Arthur and wife, interview, July 5, 1953, folder 135, box 5, Collier and Ross field notes, Dorothea C. and Alexander H. Leighton Collection (MS 216), Special Collections, Cline Library, Northern Arizona University, Flagstaff. This viewpoint is a constant refrain in the interviews published by Roessel and Johnson in *Navajo Livestock Reduction*; see especially pp. 131, 146, 150, and 172.

40. Nancy Shoemaker, *American Indian Population Recovery in the Twentieth Century* (Albuquerque: University of New Mexico Press, 1999), 33. My figure on the magnitude of the increase in Navajo stock is necessarily hypothetical. It assumes that there were approximately fifty thousand sheep and goats by the early 1870s, including the number belonging to those who never went to the Bosque Redondo; that number is no more than a guess (see Weisiger, *Dreaming of Sheep*, chap. 6). The figure for 1930 includes lambs and kids.

41. Dyk, *Son of Old Man Hat*, 129–43; Petition to President from Chin Lee Valley, [ca. 1924?], box 30, folder 6, Franciscan Papers (AZ 500), Special Collections, University of Arizona Library, Tucson.

42. Ernest Nelson, in *Navajo Livestock Reduction*, ed. Roessel and Johnson, 159.

43. Clyde Kluckhohn and Dorothea Leighton, *The Navajo* (Cambridge, MA: Harvard University Press, 1946), 30–31.

44. Kimball, "Land Use Management," 65.

45. Donna J. Haraway, "Universal Donors in a Vampire Culture: It's All in the Family: Biological Kinship Categories in the Twentieth-Century United States," in *Uncommon Ground: Toward Reinventing Nature*, ed. William Cronon (New York: Norton, 1995), 323.

46. Daniel B. Botkin, *Discordant Harmonies: A New Ecology for the Twenty-first Century* (New York: Oxford University Press, 1990), 127.

47. Patrick Gordon Pynes, "Erosion, Extraction, and Reciprocation: An Ethno/Environmental History of the Navajo Nation's Ponderosa Pine Forests" (PhD diss., University of New Mexico, 2000), 172.

CHAPTER 7

Cherokee Medicine and the 1824 Smallpox Epidemic

Paul Kelton

IN JUNE 1824, an alarming message came to Cherokees and Christian missionaries residing at Springplace, a Moravian boarding school in northern Georgia. Smallpox had struck communities in western North Carolina. Both Cherokees and missionaries worried about this ominous news. They feared that the lethal disease was on its way into Georgia, and both took actions to halt the spread of the epidemic. Missionaries obtained vaccine and vaccinated some 130 Euro, Afro, and Native Americans.[1] Meanwhile, an estimated 300 to 400 Cherokees would have nothing to do with the missionaries' medicine and instead flocked to one of their own religious leaders, who held the *Itohvnv*, or "smallpox dance." This ceremony involved seven nights of praying, fasting, and taking indigenous medicines. The missionaries of course dismissed practices such as the smallpox dance as ancient superstitions and concluded that their speedy action had halted the spread of the disease, which, fortunately for all those around Springplace, had remained away. Many Cherokees, however, gave credit to their own medicine for stopping an impending tragedy.[2]

Although coming to an anticlimactic finish, the 1824 smallpox epidemic presents a window to discuss three of the major themes presented in this volume. First, the Cherokees' smallpox dance demonstrates the dynamic nature rather than the static timelessness of indigenous knowledge. This ritual had been crafted sometime in the not too distant past since smallpox was introduced during the era of European colonization.[3] Second, the Cherokees' response to smallpox represents how indigenous peoples employed their knowledge to challenge an outside group's imposition of power. By adhering to their medical beliefs and practices, the Cherokees expressed their displeasure with the growing influence of Christian missionaries who loudly condemned "heathen" practices.[4] Third, the 1824 epidemic presented a lost opportunity for hybridization. The missionaries, with their intolerance of native ways, provided no middle ground for indigenous peoples to incorporate something new and certainly beneficial into their own beliefs and actions.[5]

Invention of the Smallpox Dance

Exactly when the Cherokees invented their smallpox dance cannot be determined with certainty, but the eighteenth-century documentary record suggests that the ceremony's origins lay in a murky period between a devastating smallpox epidemic that they experienced in 1738 and a threatened return of the germ in late 1758 and early 1759.[6] In the former episode, no record of the smallpox dance exists, although the English trader James Adair vividly described the event in his classic work of early American ethnography, *The History of the American Indians*.[7] Prior to the latter episode, the Cherokees indeed responded with something similar if not nearly identical to the smallpox dance that nineteenth-century missionaries described.

James Adair's description of the 1738 epidemic presents a stark contrast to what we know of the Cherokees' response in 1824. The English trader reported that "almost one half" of their nation perished within a year from what was to them "a foreign" and "strange disease."[8] Adair reported that "holy men" made several efforts to arrest the spread of the disease and cure those who became infected, but they proved "deficient in proper skill" and mortality escalated. Cherokee healers, according to the English trader, essentially sentenced their patients to death with their final prescription of having them plunge themselves into frigid water. Adair remarked that their "rivers being very cold in summer, by reason of the numberless springs, which pour from the hills and mountains—and the pores of their bodies being open to receive the cold, it rushing through the whole frame, they immediately expired."

After this failure, medicine men "broke their old consecrated physic-pots, and threw away all the other pretended holy things they had for physical use, imagining they had lost their divine power by being polluted." The English trader added that a "great many [Cherokees] killed themselves ... seeing themselves disfigured, without hope of regaining their former beauty, some shot themselves, others cut their throats, some stabbed themselves ... many threw themselves with sullen madness into the fire, and there slowly expired, as if they had been utterly divested of the native power of feeling pain."[9]

Adair's account should be read with care. His effort to convince his readers that native North Americans descended from the lost tribe of Israel gives readers a skewed view of indigenous cosmology. Adair's description of the Cherokees' response to the 1738 epidemic reads like a passage from the Old Testament. The English trader claimed that native holy men blamed the disease on the "adulterous intercourses of their young married people" in their neighbors' bean-plots at night. Adair added that medicine men viewed the disease as "divine anger" for "flagitious crimes." The Cherokees certainly viewed the epidemic as stemming from supernatural causes, but they were not likely to have believed it to be punishment for adultery.

Indigenous peoples had a different attitude to their English contemporaries when it came to sex and marriage. Married Cherokees could divorce their partners and choose another with little social stigma. Instead of such sinful conduct, native religious leaders were more concerned with appeasing the spirits believed to bring fertility. Sexual intercourse in the bean-plots was considered taboo because human fluids—blood and semen—were polluting and would violate the long-established fertility rites that ensured a good harvest.[10] The spirit world did not necessarily become angry, but instead irreverent conduct caused an imbalance in the cosmic forces that influenced their lives. Southeastern natives in general believed that their world existed in a precarious balance between competing spiritual powers. The spirits of the upper world existed in tension with those of the lower, while each of the winds that blew from the cardinal directions sought advantage over the others. When any of these spiritual powers grew stronger at the expense of others, misfortune occurred. Violation of fertility rites, those associated with tapping into the spiritual powers of the universe to bring bountiful harvests, thus represented egregious error among the Cherokees and brought their misfortune.[11]

The English trader omitted other crucial ethnographic information that would have given more of a context for native actions. When smallpox-stricken individuals plunged themselves under water, they performed a version of the Going-to-Water ceremony. Cherokees employed this ceremony on a regular basis—not just in the event of active sickness. It was in one sense a purification ritual. Natives cleansed themselves of the impurities that would endanger ceremonial activities, including those involved in healing. Going-to-Water also was a communal rite to restore the cosmic balance and avoid misfortune. A medicine person led his followers to a river, where every individual entered the water, plunged himself or herself under four times, emerged each time to face one of the cardinal directions, and prayed to the winds that blew from there.[12]

When Going-to-Water did not restore cosmic balance and check the epidemic, holy men likely did destroy their "consecrated physic-pots" and "pretended holy things" just as Adair claimed. But what the English trader does not tell his readers is that medicine people commonly discarded the materials and paraphernalia they used when they lost patients. Such healers did not practice medicine until a new moon, at which time they underwent ritual purification.[13] Having undergone the proper customs and regained their powers of healing from the spirit world, native doctors that failed their smallpox patients in 1738 likely returned to the practice of medicine. Going-to-Water, moreover, did not disappear from the Cherokees' ceremonial inventory. One English observer noted that in the 1750s they discontinued using this ritual when faced with smallpox, but it remained a central ritual among them in their efforts to ward off other diseases and other misfortunes.[14]

Despite the problems with Adair's account, it still remains a powerful description of how demoralizing early smallpox epidemics must have been for indigenous peoples. Other scholars have in fact utilized the account to illustrate the catastrophic nature of virgin soil epidemics. These epidemics occurred within communities who lacked prior exposure and thus acquired immunity to an introduced disease.[15] With widespread sickness and death, natives felt powerless and resorted to fatalistic behaviors. The Cherokees certainly may have had a prior exposure to smallpox, but the massive casualties they experienced in 1738 indicate that if a preceding episode had occurred, it was at least a generation before.[16] That the Cherokees thought of the disease as "foreign" and "strange" additionally suggests that smallpox had neither appeared to them very often nor with any regular frequency. The Cherokees had come up with a name for the frightful disease at some point, calling it "*Oonatàquára*," a derivation of their word for thunder, *Eentaquàróske*, thus suggesting that they thought of the disease as coming down upon them from the spirits of the upper world.[17] Nevertheless, the English trader Adair, who lived among the southeastern Indians for several generations and wrote voluminously on their customs, makes no reference to the smallpox dance.

In January 1759, a visiting Presbyterian minister made a passing comment suggesting that the Cherokees had made innovations since their devastating experience in 1738. The Reverend William Richardson remarked that "they are much given to conjuring & the conjurers have great Power over [them]." He added that they "have . . . been preparing a Physick [which] they say will drive away all their Disorders & the man to whose care it was committed has been every Night and Morning going round the Town House hollowing & crying & frequently in the Day to the great Man above for a blessing on the Physick, as they say." The ritual began a "few days" before Richardson made note of it on January 14 and ended on January 17, making it similar in length to the seven-day ritual that Cherokees practiced in response to smallpox in 1824.[18]

Epidemiological circumstances related to the Seven Years' War in North America (1754–1763) further suggest that the ritual Richardson observed was the smallpox dance. As British, French, and native men mobilized and traveled across the country fighting one another, the virus spread through England's mid-Atlantic and northeastern colonies and plodded west among a myriad of native villages from the upper Ohio to the Mississippi.[19] Hundreds of Cherokee stumbled into this ongoing epidemic during the spring and summer of 1758, when the English encouraged them with promises of copious presents to join them in Pennsylvania in an expedition to dislodge the French and their native allies from Fort Duquesne. When nearly one thousand Cherokees arrived, they found such promises unfulfilled and the dreaded smallpox circulating among British troops and colonial militia. A few Cherokees in fact became infected; most did not stay long and returned home. Remarkably, they did not bring the virus home with them, as no epidemic was reported throughout the remainder of 1758. What they almost certainly did bring home was news of the ongoing epidemic.[20] The Cherokees also likely heard about smallpox approaching them from the south. The dreaded disease broke out among settlers around Augusta, Georgia, leading South Carolina's officials to enact quarantine.[21]

When continual requests were made that they supply warriors, the Cherokees informed the English that "they never undertook anything of consequence, but they consulted their conjurers to know the pleasure of the Great Man above and they never departed from his opinion." And what the "conjurors" predicted was that "a pestilential distemper would get among their young men, that they would lose a great many and the rest would be so harassed with fatigue and sickness that they would get in very late if at all."[22] About sixty warriors to be sure did go north following the warning of their religious leaders, but not too long after they left, the Cherokees turned to a more formal ritual to deal with the specter of smallpox.[23]

The disease avoidance ritual that the Reverend William Richardson observed appears to us without much ethnographic information. Richardson provided few details, forcing one to turn to nineteenth-century sources to describe what the smallpox dance might have looked like. These accounts identify the particular spirit that spread smallpox as *Kosvkvskini*, which, according to some Cherokees, physically appeared in the forms of both a man and a woman. The female was of "a ripe chestnut burr colour, and similarly covered all over with fine prickels, whereupon she flitted the prickle, on touching any one, [and] raised the fine red pimple characteristic of the disease." The male was of "a ripe choke berry hue; and his touch, wherever that of the [female spirit] had preceded, gave the blackness which the pustules afterwards assumed."

Kosvkvskini originally dwelt in the upper world but descended into the world of the Cherokees when they violated taboos and desecrated their own ceremonies. Since the evil spirits "prowled in [a] wide and open public way," it was not safe for the Cherokees to travel. Instead, they stayed in their villages and performed the Itohvnv to purify themselves from past transgressions and regain sacred power. Members of a village gathered at their council house, consumed medicines, performed dances, and sang prayerful songs under the direction of specially consecrated medicine people. For seven days, women, men, and children dutifully performed various rituals to cleanse their community of impurities. Since Kosvkvskini rested only at midnight, Cherokees could leave their dwellings only then and only travel along "by-paths" in the woods to avoid a tragic encounter with evil spirits.[24]

From the nineteenth-century description of the smallpox dance, it becomes quite clear that the Cherokees viewed the disease as contagious. The Itohvnv was in some regards a ritualized form of quarantine. It functioned to quell contact between uninfected and infected villages. Indigenous peoples at the time did not understand contagion as we do today. Contact with a dreadfully sick or deceased person, especially one whose bodily fluids oozed out of them unabatedly, would pollute an individual. Such pollution, as previously mentioned, undermined ceremonies that tapped into spiritual power to ensure among other things good harvests, success in warfare, and good health for community members.[25] For this reason, menstruating women, wounded warriors, and others were secluded from villages and not allowed reentry until undergoing purification.[26] Cherokees recognized smallpox victims in the same way. During the 1738 epidemic, for example, medicine people grew "afraid, that the diseased would otherwise pollute the [council] house, and by that means, procure all their deaths."[27] They were thus ordered to remain outside of the village.

While Cherokees believed evil spirits to be the cause of smallpox, it cannot be ruled out that they understood the disease to be some kind of poison or particle that actually entered the body. Some diseases and ailments were believed to be the result of these foreign objects. These objects, however, got into the body through the agency of witches or evil spirits, making disease avoidance a complicated spiritual matter.[28] Cherokees, for example, may have sought to avoid traveling into English settlements not simply because they knew diseases including smallpox lurked there but also because of rumors deliberately spread by the French "that the Carolina People had Conjourors amongst them, that could send up different Bundles of Sickness to their Nation which they scattered amongst their Towns from which proceeds the Decrease of their People."[29] The smallpox dance thus was an attempt to tap into spiritual power, keep their own ceremonies pure, and protect themselves from the witches and evil spirits that would ruin the power of their medicine.

Missionaries and Medicine

When the Cherokees created their smallpox dance, they did so with no discernible influence from Euro-Americans. Europeans with whom they interacted in the eighteenth century generally made very little effort and had very little desire to change native customs. That all changed during the first three decades of the nineteenth century. Then, Protestant missionaries, with the support of the U.S. government, worked to transform indigenous peoples into "civilized" yeoman, Christian farmers.[30] Missionaries did not intend medicine to be a central component of their efforts, but it did become an important topic in the dialogue between natives and Euro-Americans. Many Cherokees showed some interest in the medicine that they thought missionaries possessed, but the advocates of "civilization" shut off any meaningful exchange. Their denunciation of "heathen" customs and denigration of native doctors prevented an opportunity for hybridization, while the Cherokees used their own medical knowledge and practices to express their opposition to the cultural imperialism of the missionaries.

Given the interrelationship between medicine and religion in indigenous societies, Cherokees looked upon missionaries as healers. Shortly after their arrival, for example, the Moravians were asked numerous times by natives for help.³¹ At first, the Moravians proved reluctant to do so. They feared that suspicion would fall upon them if they failed. "It is now a very difficult thing to advise the Indians in cases of illness," the missionaries claimed in 1806, "because one is suspected of having poisoned them if one is not successful."³² Despite their reluctance, Moravians had to administer medicine because students under their charge became sick and because requests for treatment and remedies continued from their indigenous neighbors, whom they did not want to alienate.

In some instances, Moravians and Cherokees displayed a mutual tolerance for each other's medicine and even shared their knowledge. In September 1809, for example, two schoolboys came down with severe fevers while attending Springplace. The children's fevers worsened, and the grandfather of one of the sick boys came and treated them with an emetic made from roots that he gathered nearby. The grandfather was satisfied that the medicine would work and that the missionaries would adequately care for them. Upon his departure, he asked the Moravians to share some of the medicinal herbs that they grew themselves and used in their own home remedies. The missionaries gladly obliged. Meanwhile, the Moravians were happy that the grandfather's remedy for the two boys had the desired effect. Within a month the two boys were fever-free and healthy. In another case, the missionaries recorded with little commentary a case in which the Tyger took his son Dawzizi home when he had a "strong influenza." A month later Dawzizi returned healthy, claiming that he had been treated by an "old Indian doctor" who scratched him with gar's teeth, rubbed the scars with a "juice of certain herbs," and extracted "a little horn of blood" from his body.³³

The Moravians' overall intolerance nonetheless cut off opportunities for hybridization. By using requests for medicine as opportunities to promote Christianity, they stifled significant exchanges of medical beliefs and practices. The missionaries rejoiced that one of the boys treated by his grandfather in 1809 did not go home when his brother was sent to fetch him. They believed the trip home would be too much of an ordeal and, worse, would deliver him into "heathen hands." It was best, they concluded, that Jesus would "treat them according to his love." Christianity was also the prescription for a man named Gunrod, whose son Young Wolf displayed a keen interest in the Moravians and brought his ill father to them for some elecampane roots. The missionaries informed Gunrod that his life and health were in God's hands and that they wished him a return to good health, but wished even more that he would "throw himself as a child into the arms of the Creator and Redeemer and ask Him that He Himself would bring him into His will." The Otterlifter also asked the Moravians for advice on treating his "very sick and weak little child" and also received a dose of Christianity. "We helped as well as we could," the Moravians proclaimed. "Our Dear Savior blessed the remedies."

One Cherokee who continually sought medical help from the Moravians became their first convert. Margaret Vann Crutchfield, or "Peggy," suffered terribly from tuberculosis, and the missionaries gave her not only locally produced herbal remedies but also drugs imported from the larger Euro-American pharmacopoeia, including the opium-based laudanum. "Since our Sister Crutchfield recovered with the help of this medicine through God's blessing," the Moravians recorded in their diary in 1818, "it has been reported far and wide." In 1820 Zaujuka followed Peggy Crutchfield's lead. Zaujuka became "seriously ill and could hardly speak any more" and asked the Moravians for help. The missionaries prepared "various kinds of medicine for her and wrote her a comforting letter and instructed her in how to pray to the Savior whether the illness leads to life or death." The woman survived her illness and later became baptized.[34]

Cherokee Christians became zealous opponents of indigenous medicine. Peggy Crutchfield often translated for the Moravians and chastised others who wanted to take their sick children home and have them treated by native doctors. Such chastisement did not stop Dawnee from taking her sick son, George, home to be "treated according to the heathen way." A little over a month later George returned with what the Moravians described as a "wild look." "We learned soon afterward that his mother had had a spell cast over him, and after that he seemed near death for ten days," the Moravians reported. While "the advice and help of a white man" supposedly restored his health, indigenous medicine had done its damage. The Moravians dismissed George because he "completely changed in a troubled way" and "continued in sin and shame."

Another Moravian student, however, remained much more steadfast to Christianity and challenged her own family's traditional practices. In 1820 Tuhsiwalliti came to Springplace to take his daughter Nancy home because, according to the Moravians, "the grandmother had ordered a conjurer to protect her granddaughter against illnesses." Nancy did not want to go home and the Moravians were faced with the difficult position of neither wanting to anger the father nor exposing the girl to "heathenism." "We had to persuade her just to go with her father," the Moravians decided, "that she would not be forced to submit herself to the trickery." Nancy indeed resisted. She volunteered to care for her ill grandmother instead of joining her family in the Going-to-Water ceremony. When her brother came back to relieve her of caring for the elderly woman, Nancy ran back to Springplace. Nancy later was baptized, received the new name of Anna Johanna, and helped persuade her father to become a Christian as well.[35]

The Moravians' most important convert, Charles Hicks, also denounced Cherokee medicine and criticized the practices of his people. Although the son of a Scottish trader, Hicks (1767–1827) spoke the language of his native mother fluently and acquired a considerable depth of knowledge about tribal customs and history. He served as an interpreter for his nation and elevated his stature in 1808 when he not only refused the bribes that American agents had given his countrymen to sell a large quantity of their hunting grounds, but he also publicly denounced those who had been bought off. In 1813 he became treasurer of his nation, and in 1817 he became second principal chief. The Cherokees accorded Hicks a great deal of respect for his staunch dedication to preserving their lands and their political sovereignty, but his enthusiasm for Christianity certainly put him outside the mainstream of his people. Having joined the Moravian Church in 1813, Hicks despaired about the indigenous medical practices of his own family. He informed the missionaries that he could not prevent "several old women" from giving "heathen treatment" to his sick grandson, whose care according to matrilineal customs was entrusted to his mother's side of the family.[36]

Hicks also took his fight against native medicine beyond his family members. In 1813, for example, he tried to convince the non-English-speaking Big Halfbreed of the futility of "the so called magic arts of the Indians." The Moravian convert claimed that native medicine people were "not in a position either to keep themselves healthy or to prolong their lives ... that they are no more in a position to help others." He concluded that "humans were not made just for this short life," but instead could be saved by Jesus and go to heaven. Three years later he resumed his discussion with Big Halfbreed and encouraged the man to seek salvation through Jesus. "Our Brother [Hicks] also pointed out to [Big Halfbreed] the futility of all conjuring, which the Indians hold in *very* high esteem," the Moravians reported. "He asked him whether he could believe that a conjuror's immersing a man into water could protect him from sickness or could save a man from death when he saw how many people got sick often and also died regardless of these tricks."

Big Halfbreed, whose daughter, Zuajuka, and wife, Qualiyuga, later converted, remarked that he still did not understand what Hicks was talking about and remained committed "for the time being to remain with the *ancient beliefs*." While Hicks by all accounts engaged the Big Halfbreed and other traditionalists politely, his advocacy of Christianity and public skepticism about indigenous healing methods nonetheless fueled the growing cultural war over medicine.[37]

This conflict grew even more intense with the arrival of a new group of missionaries. In 1817 the American Board of Commissioners for Foreign Missions (ABCFM)—an organization consisting of Presbyterians and Congregationalists largely from New England—sent several ministers and teachers into the Cherokee Nation. As they did with the Moravians, Cherokees approached these new missionaries with their health needs, and to an even greater extent than their predecessors the New Englanders denounced indigenous medicine and used such requests to further Christianity. "In this country far from civilized society and consequently Physicians," the Reverend J. C. Ellsworth reported, "a teacher must be called many times to visit the sick & Dying." The minister claimed to have made twenty visits within one year. "I think it a favorable circumstance, if we can gain the confidence of the people sufficiently to trust themselves in our hands in such [occasions] of danger, rather than apply to those called conjurors."[38]

ABCFM minister Elizur Butler was in fact a trained physician, and he applied both his crafts—saving bodies and souls—among the Cherokees. The doctor did not shy away from giving medical care; he was convinced that his skills were far superior to those of native doctors. Butler, for example, bled a Cherokee woman who suffered from severe stomach pains. This supposedly revived her, but when she did not return to full health, she resorted to Going-to-Water. The woman later died, and of course Butler blamed indigenous practices. The husband remained a supporter of Christianity and offered Reverend Ard Hoyt the opportunity to preach at his deceased wife's funeral. Seventy to eighty Cherokees gathered to hear the Christian message of salvation in the afterlife.[39]

ABCFM minister Moody Hall also provided medicine to those in his flock and those he hoped to add. In 1823 he continually stopped at Alexander Sanders's home to see his sick children and hopefully to give them medicine. A devout Cherokee Christian, Sanders welcomed such treatment, but his wife preferred that the children be treated with "the old practice."[40] The following year, Alexander's brother George came down with a serious illness, and while not yet a Christian, he sought the help of Hall. The minister gave the typical Euro-American prescription of bleeding and vomiting. Hall believed he had restored the Cherokee man's health, claiming, "He is now recovered & apparently feels that I was the instrument under God of saving his life."[41]

George Sanders, however, proved to be among a small minority. Wherever ABCFM missionaries went, they found that despite their loud and public denunciations of "heathenism," a majority of Cherokees still adhered to their own medical beliefs and practices. Hall, for example, found most of his young students absent from school in 1822 when a local "conjuror" called them away to attend a ceremony to ward off measles that was then epidemic throughout the area. Hall went to visit the families of those who had been attending his services and lamented, "I was lead [sic] to hope that the spirit of God was really striving with them. But a short time since [they] were among the first to attend all the frolics & foolish traditions of the country."

To be sure, some of the sick Cherokees did seek Hall's help, including one native man who took part in the "incantations" performed to "drive away the measles." Hall did give medicine—usually emetics believed to restore the body's humors to fight off even measles—and looked to such opportunities to promote Christianity, but his message must have given little relief. For in his words, his primary duty was "to impress on their minds the necessity of being prepared for death." Such a message undoubtedly fueled the belief among Cherokee medicine people that missionaries and their native listeners had weakened their community's medicine to the point where measles could not be stopped.[42]

When smallpox arrived in 1824, the cultural war between Cherokee medicine people and Christian missionaries became even more intense. "The Indians say an unbelievably big snake brought this horrible pest in the Nation," the Moravians reported. "It has a white head and is as thick as a human. Even its stench is supposed to be so unbearable that it kills people on the spot."[43] The "big snake" was likely the *Uktena*—a giant serpent with horns that had been sent to live with the sun but that left other creatures behind him on earth to inflict harm on people.[44] Although certainly differently from the being Kosvkvskini that caused smallpox in other Cherokee accounts, the Uktena represented the idea that the disease came from the upper world. In any event, the proper procedure to deal with these malevolent creatures was to tap into other spiritual powers to restore order and harmony, and that is just what the Cherokee children attending the Moravians' boarding school attempted to do. Not satisfied with Christian prayers alone, the children prayed to "a large eagle" and asked him "to keep illness away from them."[45]

In other areas of their nation the Cherokees held the more elaborate smallpox dance. The Moravians learned that "an old sorcerer" in the town of Talony arranged a dance "to drive away the Small pox." The missionaries believed that the dance involved "all sorts of amazing trickery," by which the medicine man seduced his followers into giving him deerskins and strings of beads. "On such occasion the sorcerer prays to the black dog in the north, the white one in the east, the gray one in the south, and the red one in the west," the Moravians reported.[46] Such prayers of course were not "trickery" to the Cherokees. The winds from the four cardinal points represented spiritual forces that needed to be venerated in order to restore a cosmic balance, one that missionaries and their converts had disrupted with their disdain for the practices that indigenous peoples believed brought order and harmony.[47]

The missionaries continued to denigrate native medicine and instead offered alternatives that combined vaccination with Christianity. Although both the Moravians and the ABCFM ministers claimed credit for initially coming up with the idea for retrieving cowpox from Tennessee, the two missionary organizations collaborated in an effort to vaccinate everyone they could in the Cherokee Nation.[48] Daniel Butrick, who apparently had never been vaccinated before, rode to Knoxville, where he was vaccinated with cowpox and then returned to Springplace, where he passed on the medicine to the boarding school children. Other Cherokee traveled to Springplace to be vaccinated, and by July 10, the Moravians had treated 130 people with the cowpox. On Sunday, July 11, the Moravians vaccinated another batch of people—whites, blacks, and natives—before and after church services. Some Cherokee parents retrieved their students from Springplace and took them home so that they could be the source of cowpox for the rest of their family and neighborhoods.[49] Vaccination spread through other Christian networks that had developed. ABCFM missionaries vaccinated children and families around at least three other mission stations.[50]

Christian ministers' aims of course involved more than saving bodies. It was about fighting a culture war against native adversaries, and no one engaged in this quest more fiercely than Moody Hall. Hall believed that the Cherokees' "ignorance" and "inattention" to the growing epidemic would result in the death of a thousand people. "I shall use all my influence to have all the Cherokees [vaccinated]," he vowed while waiting on Butrick to bring him cowpox. He certainly felt under pressure, because the "old Conjurer" of Talony had appointed another "great physic dance (as in the case of the measles) promising that all who join him shall not be afflicted with the disease." In the meantime, Hall took solace that his converts remained steadfast to their new beliefs, stating that "the Christians all say that they think more of a short sincere prayer than of their seven days of fasting & drinking physic."[51]

Having received vaccine from Butrick, Hall vaccinated all who would consent. If the opportunity had been presented in a way more tolerant of Cherokee beliefs and practices, more Cherokees might have consented than actually did. Back in 1806, for example, a number of leading Cherokees, including the principal chief, Pathkiller, who had remained unconverted throughout his life, appealed to the federal government for vaccine to deal with an earlier threat of smallpox.[52] Nevertheless, Hall, with his deep ethnocentrism, failed to change the minds of "great numbers" who gathered three miles from his mission to "conjure away the Small-pox." Hall dismissed the medicine man as a "liar, thief, and busybody" who employed his "foolish labor" two years before against measles and who now deluded "the multitude" into rejecting vaccine. The medicine man, though, countered Hall, arguing (falsely) that the missionary was a drunk to be disregarded. The medicine man's son added another accusation, accurately charging Hall and his family for failure to act hospitably to hungry natives who had previously visited the mission station. He added that the Cherokees had agreed to let Hall stay among them for only five years and that his "time was pretty near up."[53] Most Cherokees indeed were satisfied with their own medicine. They were not simply rejecting the vaccine but also the message and the antisocial behavior associated with those offering it.

Conclusions

The culture war over medicine continued after the 1824 epidemic. At times Christian evangelists even expressed dismay that they were losing to the "conjurors." In 1827, the Reverend Isaac Proctor lamented that even those who had become church members still practiced native medicine. "Their conjuring is as purely heathen as almost any thing to be met with on the River Ganges," he informed his mission board. "When conjuring they pray to almost every creature such as white dogs, butterflies, turtles, etc. etc."[54] Daniel Butrick, though, did not let such backsliding pass. In 1828 the minister suspended two church members who had engaged in "conjuring" and reported that "my preaching respecting idleness, Sabbath breaking, but especially conjuring and my determined & public opposition to them has excited some feeling against me." He admitted that church attendance dropped off but glossed over Cherokee opposition by claiming that "perfect order and regularity" existed "in our meetings because none attend but such as wish to receive instruction."[55]

Similarly, Charles Hicks's converted brother, William, informed a Moravian "that he had been endeavoring to relieve certain Heathen conjurors from their superstitious ways, but that as yet his exertions had been vain."[56] By the end of the 1820s, the Moravians and the ABCFM missionaries were joined by the Baptists and Methodists, but altogether they counted only 1,399 members among the nearly 15,000 Cherokees.[57] Such diminutive numbers indicate that a large majority of Cherokees remained wedded to what the missionaries considered ancient beliefs and customs.

Scholars should not accept the missionaries' claims of these medical beliefs and rituals as ancient. As the smallpox dance illustrates, the Cherokees adapted their indigenous knowledge to deal with the threats that colonialism and its germs presented. In 1824 Cherokees had further opportunity for creativity in the way they dealt with smallpox. Vaccine was available to them, and it was not out of the realm of possibility that offered to them under different circumstances, they would have accepted it. Because of the cultural war that the missionaries provoked, no middle ground existed in which natives could incorporate Euro-American medicine into their medicine. Indigenous knowledge and practices about smallpox remained one tool in the arsenal of Cherokee religious leaders in their counterattack against the growing influence of Christianity.

Notes

1. By 1824 vaccination had become a common practice in the United States. Perfected and popularized by Edward Jenner in England in 1796, vaccination entailed the insertion of cowpox matter into an incision on the body. This produced a mild infection that generated the production of antibodies that gave immunity to smallpox. Vaccination should not be confused with the earlier practice of inoculation. In this method, an individual was deliberately infected with smallpox matter much as one would be with cowpox. However, in the case of inoculation, one came down with a case of smallpox, although usually having milder and more survivable symptoms. Because an inoculated person was still contagious and could pass the disease on to a nonimmune person who would have a severe case of the disease, this practice was controversial. On the struggle against smallpox in the eighteenth- and nineteenth-century Anglo-American world, see Arthur Allen, *Vaccine: The Controversial Story of Medicine's Greatest Lifesaver* (New York: Norton, 2007), 11–69.

2. Springplace Diary, June 11, June 24, and July 10, 1824; and Johan Schmidt to Theodor Schulz, July 13, 1824, Moravian Archives, Winston-Salem, North Carolina (hereafter cited as MAS); Springplace Diary, June 30, 1824, Moravian Archives, Bethlehem, Pennsylvania (hereafter cited as MAB), box 193, fo. 15, microfilm. (I wish to thank William Keel of the University of Kansas

for translating this portion of the diary from its original German.) See also Edmund Schwarze, *Moravian Missions Among Southern Indian Tribes of the United States* (Bethlehem, PA: Time Publishing Company Printers, 1923), 174–75. On not spreading beyond North Carolina, see Charles Hicks to Joseph McMinn, September 26, 1824, M234 #71, fr. 0348; Johann Schmidt to Benade, August 23, 1824, MAS.

3. I have developed this idea elsewhere in regard to the eighteenth century and seek in this paper to move my analysis into the nineteenth century. See Paul Kelton, "Avoiding the Smallpox Spirits: Colonial Epidemics and Southeastern Indian Survival," *Ethnohistory* 51 (Winter 2004): 45–71. Some scholars have in fact dismissed native medicine people when it came to smallpox, characterizing their attitude as one of resignation in the face of a "white man's disease." The charge that native healers employed ineffective or counterproductive techniques against introduced disease appears frequently in the literature. Alfred Crosby, for example, posits native responses as exacerbating the impact of epidemics. See Alfred W. Crosby, "Virgin Soil Epidemics as a Factor in the Aboriginal Depopulation in America," *William and Mary Quarterly*, 3rd ser., 33 (April 1976): 289–99. In regard to the Cherokees, William McLoughlin wrongfully concludes that "the services of their medicine men were not considered effective against whitemen's diseases like measles and smallpox." See William McLoughlin, *Champions of the Cherokees: Evan and John B. Jones* (Princeton, NJ: Princeton University Press, 1990), 55.

4. On the role of missionaries in early nineteenth-century history, see Robert F. Berkhofer, *Salvation and the Savage: An Analysis of Protestant Missions and American Indian Response, 1787–1862* (New York: Atheneum, 1972); Bernard W. Sheehan, *Seeds of Extinction: Jeffersonian Philanthropy and the American Indian* (Chapel Hill: University of North Carolina Press, 1973); and William McLoughlin, *Cherokees and Missionaries* (New Haven, CT: Yale University Press, 1984).

5. Here I am using middle ground in a generic sense of peoples with differing worldviews arriving at mutual accommodation by adopting ideas and practices of each other for mutual benefit. Richard White develops how a specific middle ground emerged between Algonquians and French and later British in the Great Lakes region during the colonial era. In this middle ground mutual misunderstandings did not preclude participation that blended elements from both sides of the cultural divide. See Richard White, *The Middle Ground: Indians, Empires, and Republics in the Great Lakes Region, 1650–1815* (New York: Cambridge University Press, 1991). White later makes the point that his findings should not be taken out of their proper time and space. The degree to which middle grounds emerged between indigenous peoples and

colonial powers certainly varied over time and space. On this issue see "Forum: the Middle Ground Revisited," *William and Mary Quarterly*, 3rd Ser. 63 (January 2006): 3–96.

6. It is likely that at least a portion of the Cherokees suffered from smallpox in the late 1740s, but the evidence is not entirely clear. On documented epidemics among the Cherokees and other groups in the eighteenth-century Southeast, see Peter Wood, "The Impact of Smallpox on the Native Population of the 18th-Century South," *New York State Journal of Medicine* 87 (1987): 30–36.

7. James Adair, *History of the American Indians* (London, 1776); reprint, ed. Kathryn E. Holland Braund (Tuscaloosa: University of Alabama Press, 2005), 253.

8. James Adair estimated that one-half of the Cherokee Nation perished, but he may have inflated the death toll. An examination of other sources throws into question his estimate and suggests that depopulation may have been between 17 and 50 percent. See Adair, *A History of the North-American Indian*, 252; "A State of the Province of Georgia Attested Upon Oath in the Court of Savannah, November 10, 1740," in *American Colonial Tracts Monthly* 1 (July 1897): 6; Governor James Glenn to Board of Trade, February 3, 1748, in *Records in the British Public Record Office Relating to South Carolina, 1663–1782*, vol. 23, ed. William L. McDowell, (Columbia: South Carolina Department of History and Archives), 74–75. For a more general discussion of Cherokee population dynamics during the eighteenth century, see Peter Wood, "Changing Population of the Colonial Southeast," in *Powhatan's Mantle: Indians in the Colonial Southeast*, ed. Peter H. Wood, Gregory A. Waselkov, and M. Thomas Hatley (Lincoln: University of Nebraska Press, 1989), 35–103.

9. Adair, *History of the North American Indians*, 252–53.

10. Theda Perdue, *Cherokee Women: Gender and Culture Change, 1700–1835* (Lincoln: University of Nebraska Press, 1998), 57–58.

11. Here I agree with Charles Hudson, who suggests that the Cherokees would blame epidemics "as a consequence of breaking certain moral or ritual rules, thereby offending spiritual beings higher up in the spiritual pantheon than mere animal spirits." See Hudson, "Why Southeastern Indians Slaughtered Deer?" in *Indians, Animals, and the Fur Trade*, ed. Shepard Krech III (Athens: University of Georgia Press, 1981), 160. Hudson argues against the application of Calvin Martin's thesis that northeastern natives held animal spirits responsible for colonial-era epidemics of introduced diseases and thus waged a holy war against them. See Calvin Martin, *Keepers of the Game: Indian-Animal Relationships and the Fur Trade* (Berkeley: University of California Press, 1978). On Cherokee conceptions of the cosmos, power, and medicine, see Charles

Hudson, *The Southeastern Indians* (Knoxville: University of Tennessee Press, 1976), 122–39, 336–51; Raymond D. Fogelson, "Cherokee Notions of Power," in *The Anthropology of Power*, ed. Raymond D. Fogelson and Richard N. Adams (New York: Academic Press, 1977), 185–94.

12. James Mooney, "The Cherokee River Cult," *Journal of American Folklore* 13 (January–March 1900): 1–10.

13. John Howard Payne Papers, vol. 4, no. 14, Newberry Library, Chicago (hereafter cited as Payne Papers).

14. John Gerar William De Brahm, *De Brahm's Report of the General Survey in the Southern District of North America*, ed. Louis De Vorsey Jr. (Columbia: University of South Carolina Press, 1971), 107.

15. It is important to emphasize that natives lacked acquired immunity and not genetic immunity. For a discussion of this issue, see David Jones, "Virgin Soils Revisited," *William and Mary Quarterly*, 3rd Ser., 60 (October 2003): 703–42.

16. I have argued elsewhere that the Cherokees likely first experienced smallpox either in the late 1690s or around 1711. See Paul Kelton, *Epidemics and Enslavement: Biological Catastrophe in the Native Southeast, 1492–1715* (Lincoln: University of Nebraska Press, 2007).

17. Adair, *History of the American Indians*, 116.

18. Reverend William Richardson Journal, January 14, 1759, Indian Miscellaneous Manuscripts Collection, Cherokee Folder, New York Public Library.

19. John Duffy, *Epidemics in Colonial America* (Baton Rouge: Louisiana State University Press, 1953), 86–90.

20. Bouquet to Forbes, Fort Loudon (Pa.), June 14, 1758, in *The Forbes Expedition*, vol. 2 of *The Papers of Henry Bouquet*, ed. S. K. Stevens, Donald H. Kent, and Autumn L. Leonard (Harrisburg: Pennsylvania Historical and Museum Commission, 1951), 87–89.

21. John Lloyd to [Edmund Atkin], June 25, 1758; and William Henry Lyttelton to John Stewart, July 11, 1758, William Henry Lyttelton Papers, William L. Clements Library, Ann Arbor, Michigan; South Carolina *Gazette*, July 7, 1758.

22. Turner to Lyttelton, July 2, 1758, *Documents Relating to Indian Affairs, 1754–1765*, vol. 2, ed. William L. McDowell (Columbia: South Carolina Archives Department, 1958–1970), 471. Turner related this episode in other letters. See Turner to [Byrd], Fort Loudon [Cherokee Nation], June 23, 1758; and George Turner to [General John Forbes], June 23, 1758, Headquarters Papers of Brigadier-General John Forbes Relating to the Expedition against Fort Duquesne in 1758, Tracy W. McGregor Library, University of Virginia, microfilm, reel 2, item 326.

23. On the Cherokees' participation in the Great War for Empire, see John Oliphant, *Peace and War on the Anglo-Cherokee Frontier, 1756–63* (Baton Rouge: Louisiana State University Press, 2001).

24. Payne Papers, vol. 1, 159–60.

25. See notes 18 and 19 this chapter.

26. Adair, *History of the American Indians*, 164–65.

27. Ibid., 252.

28. For an elaboration on this point, see Kelton, "Avoiding the Smallpox Spirits," 47–55.

29. Intelligence from Judge's Friend to Captain Raymond Demere, December 10, 1756, *Documents Relating to Indian Affairs, 1754–1765*, II, 265.

30. For an overview of Cherokee history in the early nineteenth century, see William G. McLoughlin, *Cherokee Renascence in the New Republic* (Princeton, NJ: Princeton University Press, 1986).

31. Springplace Diary, July 6, 1802; October 16, 1802; February 24, 1803; March 5, 1803; August 14, 1803; MAS. "Minutes of the Mission Conference Held in Springplace," trans. and ed. Kenneth G. Hamilton, *Atlanta Historical Bulletin* (Winter 1970): 24, 26; Rowena McClinton, ed., *The Moravian Springplace Mission to the Cherokees*, 2 vols. (Lincoln: University of Nebraska Press, 2007), I, 119 and 142 (hereafter cited as *Moravian Springplace Mission*).

32. McClinton, *Moravian Springplace Mission*, I, 119 (quote), and 142.

33. Ibid., I, 332–35; II, 31, 36.

34. McClinton, *Moravian Springplace Mission*, I, 351, 568–69, 205, 362, 370, and 379–81.

35. Ibid., 220, 221, 237, 385; II, 246–47.

36. Ibid., II, 59.

37. Ibid., I, 562; II, 110.

38. J. C. Ellsworth to Jeremiah Everts, n.d. (probably 1824), The Papers of the American Board of Commissioners for Foreign Missions, vol. 4, Houghton Library, Harvard University, Cambridge, MA, microfilm, reel 739 (hereafter cited as *ABCFM*).

39. Joyce B. Phillips and Paul Gary Phillips, eds., *The Brainerd Journal: A Mission to the Cherokees, 1817–1823* (Lincoln: University of Nebraska Press, 1998), 272, 273, 280, 281, 284, 286.

40. Quoted in Perdue, *Cherokee Women*, 183.

41. Moody Hall to Jeremiah Everts, September 13, 1824, *ABCFM*, vol. 5, reel 739.

42. Moody Hall Journal, May 17, 30; November 5, 1822, *ABCFM*, vol. 3, reel 738.

43. Springplace Diary, June 11, 1824, MAS.

44. James Mooney, *History, Myths and Sacred Formulas of the Cherokees* (Washington, DC: Smithsonian Institution, 1900; reprint, Asheville, NC: Bright Mountain Books, 1992), 297.

45. Springplace Diary, June 20, 1824, MAS. On the spiritual significance of birds to the Cherokees, see Shepard Krech III, *Spirits of the Air: Birds and American Indians in the South* (Athens: University of Georgia Press, 2009), 134.

46. Springplace Diary, June 21, 1824, MAS.

47. Mooney, "The Cherokee River Cult," 1–10.

48. Johan Schmidt wrote to his mission board and claimed he had to persuade the reluctant Butrick, a Presbyterian, to go to Knoxville for cowpox, but ABCFM missionaries made no reference to Schmidt's role. See Schmidt to Schulz, July 13, 1824, MAS; J. C. Ellsworth to Jeremiah Everts, July 7, 1824, *ABCFM*, vol. 3, reel 738.

49. Springplace Diary, July 10, 1824; July 11, 1824, MAS.

50. J. C. Ellsworth to Jeremiah Everts, July 7, 1824, *ABCFM*, vol. 3, reel 738.

51. Moody Hall to Jeremiah Everts, June 29, 1824, *ABCFM*, vol. 3, reel 738.

52. Pathkiller and John Lowery to Return J. Meigs, February 17, 1806, in Tennessee Documentary History, accessed March 19, 2008, http://diglib.lib.utk.edu/cgi/t/text/text-idx?c=tdh;cc=tdh;sid=993136c581b04a73f8f9512944d2840f;q1=pox; rgn=main;view=text;idno=pa0018. See also The Glass, Dick Justice, John Boggs, and Charles Hicks to R. J. Meigs, March 5, 1806, Bureau of Indian Affairs, RG 75, Records of the Cherokee Agency in Tennessee, 1801–1835, National Archives, Washington, DC, microfilm M208, reel 3. Daniel Ross to R. J. Meigs, March 24, 1806, Tennessee Documentary History, accessed March 19, 2008, http://diglib.lib.utk.edu/cgi/t/text/text-idx?c=tdh;cc=tdh;sid=993136c581b04a73f8f9512944d2840f; q1=Ross;rgn=main;view=text;idno=pa0019.

53. Moody Hall Journal, July 9, 1824, *ABCFM*, vol. 3, reel 738 emphasis in original.

54. Isaac Proctor to Jeremiah Everts, July 28, 1827, *ABCFM*, vol. 4, reel 739.

55. Daniel Butrick to Jeremiah Everts, November 28, 1828, *ABCFM*, vol. 4, reel 739.

56. Clauder Diary, MAB, box 194, fo. 6.

57. McLoughlin, *Cherokees and Missionaries*, 157, 167, and 175. The breakdown is as follows: Moravians 45, ABCFM 167, Baptist 99, and Methodist 1,028. It should be noted that Baptist and Methodist activities remained rather limited before 1824 and their records are scarce before then. The growth of the Methodist can be attributed in part to the fact that their itinerant preachers turned a blind eye toward native medical practices.

Part III

Environmental Religion

CHAPTER 8

Spirit of the Salmon

Native Religion, Rights, and Resource Use in the Columbia River Basin

Andrew H. Fisher

IN EARLY April, the residents of Celilo Village hold a salmon feast to welcome the returning runs of spring chinook and thank them for their imminent sacrifice. The annual event draws hundreds of visitors to the tiny Indian community in the Columbia River Gorge, nine miles upstream from The Dalles, Oregon, and the eponymous dam that flooded the Celilo Falls fishery in 1957. Although the river has been silenced and the salmon have dwindled, people still gather in the village longhouse to participate in ceremonies that honor the five sacred foods of the *Wáašat* religion: water (*chuush*), salmon (*waykanash*), deer (*winat*), roots (*xnit*), and berries (*tmanit*). The Sahaptin songs and prayers that precede the feast remind worshippers of their responsibility to respect and care for the gifts of the Creator (*Nami Piap*). The longhouse leader "speaks in the ancient language's manner," observes writer Elizabeth Woody, a member of the Warm Springs confederated tribes:

> He speaks to all in *Ichiskiin*. He says, "We are following our ancestors. We respect the same Creator and the same religion, each in turn of their generation, and conduct the same service and dance to honor our relatives, the roots, and the salmon.

> The Creator at the beginning of time gave us instruction and the wisdom to live the best life. The Creator made man and woman with independent minds. We must choose to live by the law, as all the others, salmon, trees, water, air, all live by it. We must use all the power of our minds and hearts to bring the salmon back. Our earth needs our commitment. That is our teachings. We are each powerful and necessary."[1]

Journalists and the general public are invited to witness these ritual enactments of environmental stewardship, but the feast's educational function remains secondary. First and foremost, the ceremony affirms the spiritual beliefs that still inform Mid-Columbia Indian efforts to protect and restore the natural resources that traditionally sustained their culture, even as the tribes have harnessed modern technologies and scientific expertise to that end.

Wáašat expresses what anthropologist Stephen Langdon calls "a logic of relational sustainability," whereby "correct attitude, action, and ritual practice" perpetuate beneficial relationships between humans and the nonhuman beings they depend on for survival. This concept is nothing new to scholars—much less to indigenous peoples—but it bears further examination in light of the recent controversy surrounding the trope of the Ecological Indian. Shepard Krech's critique of that cultural icon sparked furious academic and public debates over the relative merits of Native Americans as conservationists and ecologists. My purpose in this essay is to take faith seriously as both an epistemological foundation and a discursive strategy that Mid-Columbia Indians have employed in defense of their reserved rights to harvest particular resources, as well as in their efforts to manage those resources cooperatively with state and federal agencies. At the same time, I explore some of the tensions within tribal communities between those who readily enlisted Western science as an ally and those who regarded technocratic solutions and tribal regulations as threats to their culture and religion. Native people have variously defended, modified, and departed from the spiritual beliefs of their ancestors. To avoid romanticizing or essentializing them, it is important to historicize the spiritual, economic, and environmental practices of Mid-Columbia Indians.[2]

Wáašat has acquired many names during its long history. Most adherents prefer the Sahaptin label, meaning "dance," but it is also known as the Seven Drums Religion, the Sacred Dance Religion, the Longhouse Religion, or simply "the Indian religion." This final name reflects the contemporary view that *Wáašat* is the most "traditional" of the various faiths practiced in Mid-Columbia Indian communities, even though it exhibits Christian influences. Some practitioners avoid the term "religion" altogether because of its narrow, compartmentalized connotation. "To non-Indians, the longhouse represents religion," explained Lewis Malatare, the head of a Wáašat congregation on the Yakama reservation. "To Yakamas, we prefer not to use the word religion but more a way of life—a life that was dictated to us by the natural surroundings of our environment."[3]

Most important, Wáašat is about honoring the foods that supplied the subsistence needs and shaped the culture of Mid-Columbia Indians for some ten thousand years before the arrival of Europeans. "Our food is part of our religion and is medicine to our body," explained Elsie David (Yakama) during a 2007 interview. "Everything to my people [is] interrelated—our religion, Mother Earth, the animals, the trees, the rocks—they all work together." Foodways and religion are also deeply intertwined with notions of "Indianness" in contemporary Plateau communities. "That's what identifies us," says David. "I don't think I would know a great deal of my culture if I just lived on cow and non-traditional food. My grandma used to say, 'You're not going to know anything about our people if you don't eat our food.' If you're going to eat cows, you're going to be dumb like a cow."[4]

For the sake of brevity, this essay focuses on salmon—the most economically valuable, ecologically vulnerable, and politically contested of the five sacred foods. Salmon ranks second only to water in Wáašat's ritual hierarchy. Although the antiquity of specific practices is uncertain, anthropologists Deward Walker and Helen Schuster suggest that first-food feasts are probably the oldest ceremonials within the Longhouse religion. These calendric rites, conducted to welcome the arrival of different foods during the spring and summer, express the common animistic belief that all things in nature possess spirit and power. Ritual forms and content have changed over time, however, starting before the arrival of Europeans and continuing to the present day. According to Walker and Schuster, Plateau Indians originally held first-food feasts and other services in the extended family lodge of a village headman. By the mid-nineteenth century, ceremonies had shifted to an enlarged mat lodge or "dance house" erected specifically for that purpose. Today, the roughly fifteen permanent longhouses located across the Columbia Plateau also serve as meeting halls and community centers. The feasts held there have ancient roots but likewise reflect centuries of cultural adaptation. As Walker and Schuster explain, the contemporary Wáašat religion constitutes "a complex mixture of older elements including vision questing, tutelary spirit power, and, in some locations, shamanistic curing, along with various Christian elements, in a distinctive nativistic framework in which the tribal language, behavioral norms, morality, relations, beliefs, and customs are perpetuated." The behavioral norms, beliefs, and customs at issue here are those relating to Native interactions with the natural world.[5]

The first Euro-Americans to observe Plateau religious rituals noted the importance placed on respectful treatment of food sources, especially the anadromous fish runs that supplied most of the Indians' protein. Traveling up the Columbia River in April 1806, members of the Lewis and Clark expedition witnessed a first salmon feast in the village of Wishram, just above The Dalles:

> There was great joy with the natives last night in consequence of the arrival of the Salmon; one of those fish was caught; this was the harbinger of good news to them. They informed us that these fish would arrive in great quantities in the course of about 5 days. [T]his fish was dressed and being divided into small pieces was given to each child in the village. [T]his custom is founded in superstitious opinion that it will hasten the arrival of the salmon.[6]

No one in the village could catch or consume any of their own fish until this ceremony had been performed, and fur traders during this period found that Native people would not sell any salmon until these ceremonies had been held.

Still, scholars debate whether the first salmon ceremony encouraged or effected deliberate resource conservation among Plateau Indians before it became necessary in the twentieth century. Shepard Krech suggests that reduced harvests were merely an incidental result of Northwest Indian religious ceremonies. True conservation is "by design," he contends, and "practices are conservationist not because they have sustainable consequences but if they meet intentionally formulated ends." By contrast, ethnographer Eugene Hunn and historian Joseph Taylor argue that first-food feasts and associated beliefs served a pragmatic ecological purpose. By postponing the start of the regular spring harvest and prohibiting fishing under certain circumstances, ritual proscriptions allowed the upriver escapement of many salmon that might otherwise have fallen prey to Native nets. More broadly, oral traditions about the consequences of wasteful hunting and hoarding taught that animal spirits would punish disrespectful behavior with bad luck or illness. Despite highly efficient fishing techniques and large catches, writes Taylor, "Indian culture and economy produced a sustainable tension between society and nature." Insisting upon a scientific basis for conservation misses the point that Mid-Columbia Indians were doing what they believed was necessary to perpetuate the resource. Although salmon runs fluctuated according to natural conditions, Native people had little reason to doubt the efficacy of their methods until the crisis that followed Euro-American colonization.[7]

Mid-Columbia Indians enforced principles of dependence, respect, and moderation through special "salmon chiefs" who presided over village fisheries. The vintage of this title, too, remains open to question. Some anthropologists identify the salmon chief as a modern creation, called into being by increasing competition and declining salmon runs in the late nineteenth century, whereas Mid-Columbia Indians insist on earlier origins. According to Howard Jim, the late leader of Celilo Village, "The fishing was always regulated by the chief." Evidence from elsewhere on the Plateau suggests that the role was likely an aboriginal one whose importance became magnified at Celilo Falls as declining runs and increasing competition raised the stakes. Nez Perce villages, for example, traditionally recognized a *lewtekenewé·t* ("fish headman"), who was responsible for distributing the catch. In the early 1800s, fur traders visiting Kettle Falls noted the presence of a salmon chief responsible for allocating fish, regulating individual stints on scaffolds, and overseeing the first salmon ceremony. By the early 1900s, when Tommy Thompson assumed this role at Celilo Falls, it had evidently become a hereditary post with well-defined responsibilities. The salmon chief determined the length of the fishing seasons and dictated when fishing should cease for a variety of ritual reasons. These "taboos" included fishing at night, on Sundays, and after drowning deaths (a fairly regular occurrence in the turbulent rapids of The Dalles–Celilo reach). Thompson had difficulty enforcing traditional regulations after the fishery became commercialized, but they clearly served the purpose of conservation.[8]

Meanwhile, the social context and religious philosophy underlying Plateau subsistence practices changed in response to European contact. Starting in the 1830s, Catholic and Protestant efforts to convert Indians accelerated a process of religious borrowing and blending that continued into the late nineteenth century. The handbells obtained from fur traders and Jesuit priests quickly made their way into Longhouse services, where leaders used them to signal the beginning and end of various phases. Similarly, Indians adopted Sunday as a regular day of worship and attached sacral significance to the numbers three and seven, which also figure prominently in the Christian faith. While five still appeared frequently in Wáašat songs and dances, seven became the standard number of drummers and the number of people assigned to collect foods for feasts. By 1855, when the U.S. government compelled Mid-Columbia Indians to sign treaties ceding most of their aboriginal territory, Christian concepts of mortal sin and divine wrath had likewise mingled with indigenous beliefs regarding the sacredness of creation.[9] Witness the sentiments expressed by Owhi, a signatory chief for the Upper Yakamas, during the 1855 Walla Walla Council:

> God named this land to us[;] that is the reason I am afraid to say anything about this land. I am afraid of the laws of the Almighty, this is the reason I am afraid to speak of the land. . . . Shall I steal this land and sell it? [O]r what shall I do? This is the reason that my heart is sad.
>
> My friends, God made our bodies from the earth as if they were different from the whites. What shall I do? Shall I give the lands that are a part of my body and leave myself poor and destitute? Shall I say I will give you my lands? I cannot say. I am afraid of the Almighty.[10]

The Creator had given Indians land (*tiichám*) to supply their sacred foods, and to trade it away invited punishment in the afterlife as well as political turmoil and economic hardship in this world.

Many headmen consented to the treaties only because they promised the Indians continuing access to traditional food sources located on their ceded lands. As a Tygh chief named Simtustus proclaimed during the Wasco council, "The [Deschutes rapids] have sustained us in fish. The Falls where we catch the fish, we would like to reserve it."[11] In making this accommodation, however, the treaties sowed the seeds of future controversy. The treaties did not *give* the tribes any special privileges, as critics later claimed, but the language of the treaty documents restructured aboriginal rights in significant ways. Specifically, the so-called "fishing clause" (virtually identical in all of the Plateau treaties) stated:

> The exclusive right of taking fish in all the streams, where running through or bordering said reservation, is further *secured to said confederated tribes and bands of Indians*, as also the right of taking fish at all usual and accustomed places, *in common with the citizens of the Territory*, and of erecting temporary buildings for curing them; together with the *privileges* of hunting,

gathering roots and berries, and pasturing their horses and cattle upon open and unclaimed land.[12]

By vesting subsistence rights in the confederated tribes and bands, this article nominally transformed what were traditionally individual and familial entitlements into tribal ones. At the same time, it raised the prospect of competition from American citizens through the phrase "in common" and introduced a false distinction between "rights" and "privileges." Within sixty years, hostile state governments would seize upon such language in order to restrict Mid-Columbia Indian fishing at off-reservation sites.

The non-Indian assault on treaty fishing rights resulted from the introduction of salmon to the capitalist marketplace. Starting in the mid-1860s, the application of industrial processing and canning techniques transformed the legendary runs of the Columbia River into a lucrative commodity. Initially, white commercial interests focused their activities in the estuary, but the introduction of fish wheels in 1879 made it possible to catch salmon in the upstream rapids where traps, seines, and gill nets generally could not function. When the Northern Pacific Railroad reached The Dalles in 1883, packers rushed to establish operations at or near indigenous fisheries. By 1900, five canneries and dozens of wheels lined the river between the Cascade rapids and Celilo Falls. Conflict erupted as the newcomers shoved aside Indian fishers, sometimes even dynamiting their stands to make way for wheels. Although many Natives earned money selling salmon to the canneries, most still depended on fishing for subsistence and resented the theft of their ancient fishing grounds. They also objected to the imposition of state regulations that followed from the effects of overfishing, habitat destruction, industrial pollution, and dam construction. Many conservation laws favored commercial and recreational interests of non-Indians over those of Indians, who found their off-reservation fishing increasingly constrained by a web of regulations governing illegal gear, trespassing, licensing, closed seasons, prohibited areas, catch limits, and the sale of fish. When Indians caught salmon and steelhead trout in violation of these laws, state authorities arrested and prosecuted them for poaching. Treaties, they contended, gave Indians only the same privileges as white "citizens of the Territory."[13]

The legal history of the Northwest Indian fishing rights controversy is well-documented and too lengthy to recount here. More important to this discussion is the spiritual language in which many tribal members couched their defense of treaty-reserved rights and resources. As Owhi had done during the Walla Walla council, tribal leaders and defendants frequently invoked the idea of a separate creation to challenge state jurisdiction over traditional foods and activities that antedated both federal treaties and state governments. Chief George Meninick, a witness to the Walla Walla council proceedings and the son of a Yakama treaty signer, articulated this view in his testimony during the Towessnute case, one of the first Indian trials under Washington's stringent 1915 fisheries code:

> God created the Indian country and it was like He spread out a big blanket. He put the Indians on it. They were created here in this country, truly and honestly, and that was the time this river started to run. Then God created fish in this river and put deer in these mountains and made law through which has come the increase of fish and game. Then the Creator gave us Indians life; we awakened and as soon as we saw the game and fish we knew that they were made for us. . . . We had the fish before the missionaries came, before the white man came. We were put here by the Creator and these were our rights as far as my memory to my great-grandfather. This was the food on which we lived. . . . My strength is from the fish; my blood is from the fish, from the roots and the berries. The fish and the game are the essence of my life. I was not brought from a foreign country and did not come here. I was put here by the Creator. We had no cattle, no hogs, no grain, only berries and roots and game and fish. We never thought we would be troubled about these things, and I tell my people, and I believe it, it is not wrong for us to get this food.[14]

The trial court agreed that treaty fishing constituted a "preserve," a reserved right that could not be restrained by state regulation, but on appeal the Washington State Supreme Court reinstated the charges and overturned the lower court's decision. Dripping with disdain for Indian treaties and Indian culture alike, the four-to-one majority opinion held that the state could impose any restrictions it wished on Native "children" operating under a "dubious document."[15]

Towessnute was merely the opening salvo in a seventy-year-long battle to control tribal fishing rights. Unbowed by the reversal, Meninick and three other Mid-Columbia Indians returned to the scene of the "crime" in 1917 with the intention of launching a test case. State officers arrested them for fishing within a mile of Prosser Dam, the former site of an indigenous fishery called Tóp-tut, and in 1921 their appeal again reached the state supreme court. Jim Wallahee, Meninick's codefendant and the nephew of Owhi, took the opportunity to reiterate their shared belief that white men had no business interfering with rights and resources that came from the Creator.[16] On the contrary, non-Indians had violated the law and endangered the salmon with their reckless behavior:

> Is it right for the white man to build a dam at the falls and then say that his act destroys the bounty of the Creator?
> I am telling the truth. Indians do not bother white people. Anything they raise we do not bother. I do not go into a white man's field or destroy his things. I keep out, but the salmon does not belong to him. It is sent free from the ocean by God for my use.[17]

Although the court still reaffirmed Towessnute, the Indians' religiously inflected rhetoric helped sway opinion in Olympia, where Meninick and other tribal members appeared in ceremonial regalia to lobby the state government. Shortly before his case reached the bench, the state legislature passed a law temporarily allowing Yakama Indians to fish for subsistence at Prosser Falls "by any reasonable means, at any time." It constituted a Pyrrhic victory at best, yet it revealed a strain of white sympathy that tribal activists would later exploit to good advantage.[18]

The Towessnute case and countless trials like it forced Native understandings of nature into conversation with the dominant discourses of science and law in the United States. Prosecuted again and again for violating state conservation laws, Mid-Columbia Indians began to frame their defense of treaty rights in terms the courts could recognize and respect. The word *conservation* also started to appear in public and private pronouncements concerning tribal fishing and tribal religion, as Native people explicitly identified their traditional beliefs and practices with the avowed goals of state regulation. After a Wáašat service in the 1960s, for example, longhouse leader Robert Jim told his sons, "This is what we believe; this is what is important: Cooperation, Sharing, Hospitality, Reciprocity, and Conservation, never take more than you need." Yakama tribal councilman Johnson Meninick echoed this sentiment in 1974 when he assured state officials that indigenous customs could effectively guide tribal regulation of the fishery: "I believe we've practiced lifelong [conservation]. We're born to it, we're raised with it, we die with it. Our people who were our forefathers have practiced this tradition. They know what to do, and they hand it down to us, and we're going to hand it down to the younger [generation]."

By that time, Native people had clearly learned the *language* of conservation, but it does not necessarily follow that they had learned the *concept* from their colonizers.[19]

The values that Robert Jim placed at the core of Native belief did suffer strain as forces of cultural change and commercial opportunity opened rifts among Mid-Columbia Indians. Starting in the 1920s, hundreds of tribal fishers began flocking to Celilo Falls to escape deteriorating conditions and increasing restrictions on the Yakima and Umatilla Rivers, which had been extensively dammed for irrigation purposes. For Tommy Thompson, the headman and salmon chief at Celilo, the growing influx of outsiders created numerous headaches. In his youth, perhaps three to five dozen men had regularly fished the islands across from the village. By the early 1940s, there would be two hundred to three hundred people crowding the rocks each season. While some could claim family rights through blood or marriage, the majority possessed only the "tribal" right outlined in the treaties. They could fish at traditional sites with permission or use one of five "hobo holes" on Chief Island, where Thompson allowed anyone with a net to take a turn. Local canneries encouraged intensive commercial fishing, however, and the more aggressive newcomers simply horned in on established locations. In the worst cases, they chased away the rightful owners or erected new fishing scaffolds that interfered with existing stands. Many visiting Indians refused to share their sites with others and ignored rules against fishing at night and on Sundays, which risked offending the "salmon people" and encouraged state crackdowns. Christian converts and younger reservation Indians seemed especially prone to dismiss them as a pack of superstitions. Their continued defiance, aggravated by the growing presence of non-Indians and non-treaty Indians claiming a right to fish "in common," drove Chief Thompson to distraction until The Dalles Dam ultimately flooded the falls.[20]

The case of the Albert brothers illustrates the clash of competing values as the Celilo fishery became increasingly crowded and commercialized. In September 1939, a dispute erupted over the control of customary fishing sites on Little Ateem Island, also known as Albert Island after its nominal owners. At the center of the controversy stood Isaac and Thomas Albert, young Yakama enrollees who had started the Portland Fish Company along with several Native partners. Acting on the advice of a cannery employee, the Alberts installed aerial cableways to Little Ateem but denied access to nonmembers and even destroyed their competitors' scaffolds. Their selfish behavior triggered intervention by the Celilo Fish Committee (CFC), an intertribal body created to assist Tommy Thompson in regulating the fishery and settling disputes. The CFC revoked its approval of the Alberts' cables, but they defied the order and refused to attend any committee meetings. Bolstered by the support of cannery buyers, they also shrugged off a scolding letter from U.S. District Attorney Carl Donaugh. "Under the law," he told them, "any one of the members of any one of the tribes has as much right to fish on the particular rocks that you fish on as you have.... I think that you should be loyal to your Yakima tribe and to the agreements that have been made on behalf of the Yakima people." In 1940 the CFC endorsed this line of reasoning by voting to give all the claimants equal privileges on Little Ateem. Threatened with exclusion if they failed to comply, the Alberts grudgingly agreed to respect the rights of others and to heed Chief Thompson's regulations—for a while.[21]

The death of Celilo Falls in 1957 failed to end either tribal fishing culture or the fight over treaty fishing rights. Despite the flooding of traditional stations and the displacement of ancient communities, some Mid-Columbia Indians steadfastly refused to leave the river. A few families migrated downstream to five "in-lieu" fishing sites the Army Corps had belatedly built to replace locations lost to the Bonneville Dam (completed in 1938). In 1945, the federal government had promised to purchase and improve roughly four hundred acres at six locations for tribal fishing and camping; by 1960, the Army Corps of Engineers had developed only four, amounting to less than forty acres. That year, six families moved into the drying sheds at Lone Pine, while more than a dozen others settled farther downstream at Underwood, Cooks (later called Cook's Landing), and Wind River. They endured awful living conditions because the sites had not been designed for year-round occupation. In fact, the Corps and the Bureau of Indian Affairs refused to make improvements because they opposed the creation of permanent communities there. Johnny Jackson, whose family lived at Underwood, later explained why people stayed: "When they built The Dalles Dam and they finished the dam, they felt all the people would probably move away and go back to the reservation. They failed to realize that a lot of us were from that [area], we lived here, we were always here. We lived here all our lives from generation to generation. And fishing was our life, a way of fishing and taking care of the land."[22]

Their determination to keep their homes on the river and their nets in the water turned these families into both champions and challengers of tribal treaty rights. As the long confrontation between state regulation and tribal sovereignty reached its climax in the 1960s and 1970s, the strident activism of the resident fishing families collided with the rising nationalism of the reservation tribes. Tribal governments, determined to exercise their sovereign powers, selectively supported treaty fishermen in their legal battles against state harassment. At the same time, however, the councils issued regulations that threatened the autonomy and spirituality of the "River People." In their opinion, fishing rights remained an individual prerogative controlled only by the rhythms of the river and the laws of the Creator. State-determined seasons and tribal permits represented an infringement of their religious liberty as well as a threat to their livelihood. "No man should be required to obtain a permit from another man to practice his religion," declared David Sohappy Sr., who soon emerged as the symbolic leader of the river-dwelling dissidents. They still believed in the "old ways," and they bristled at the allegation that their supposedly "unrestricted" fishing endangered the resource.[23]

The trials and tribulations of David Sohappy dramatically exposed the tension between traditionalist and statist perceptions of the salmon crisis, which peaked in the midst of the fishing rights controversy and stoked the anger of everyone concerned. As the grand-nephew of Smohalla, an important prophet of the Wáašat religion during the late nineteenth century, Sohappy followed the spiritual teachings and seasonal round of his ancestors. He began fishing at age five and spent much of his youth on the river at White Bluffs, where his grandparents maintained a drying shed. "That is where I learned about Indian language and religion," he later recalled. "I remember going to the longhouse from way back then, as my parents were firm believers in the Seven Drums or Wáašat religion. I used to attend every week.... We would have our ceremonies for the first food, preparing it all day Saturday for the Sunday event." Following a brief stint in the Army Air Corps, he farmed his family's allotment and worked various jobs for twenty years before deciding to become a full-time fisherman. In 1965, at age forty, he moved his wife, Myra, and their seven children to the in-lieu fishing site at Cook's Landing. There, his life took a dramatic turn as his family became embroiled in the running three-way battle between the states, the tribes, and the families along the river.[24]

Initially, the treaty tribes and the River People appeared to have identical interests. Both opposed state regulation of Indian fishing, and in 1968 Sohappy began his activist career like many Indians before him—serving time in a county jail for illegal fishing. Upon release, however, he and his nephew immediately filed a federal lawsuit with twelve other Cook's residents against a slate of Oregon fish and game officials headed by Fish Commissioner McKee A. Smith. *Sohappy v. Smith* reached federal district court along with *U.S. v. Oregon*, a supporting suit brought by the Justice Department on behalf of the four Columbia Basin treaty tribes.

Judge Robert C. Belloni merged the cases and handed the Indians an impressive victory, ruling that the states could regulate tribal fishing only when necessary for conservation and that they must guarantee the Indians a "fair and equitable share" of the salmon runs as well as the opportunity to participate in resource management. The decision set an important precedent for the tribes, who owed it largely to the initiative of river families, but their alliance was already showing signs of strain. River People resented that the tribes had barged in after refusing to support the *Sohappy* plaintiffs, forcing them to cover the court costs on their own. As Wilbur Slockish said recently, "They weren't interested in helping us until we started winning." Tribal officials, in turn, complained of the dissident group's seemingly reckless disregard for sound legal strategy and tribal sovereignty. Relations would get much worse before they got better.[25]

Over the next twenty years, many tribal officials came to regard the River People as loose cannons on their fledgling ships of state. Despite a set of common enemies and an overarching unity of purpose, the original plaintiffs remained at odds with the tribes over fishing regulations. For several years before the *Sohappy* case, the residents of Cook's Landing had ignored tribal ordinances, challenged them in court, and tried to pass their own measures through a rival regulatory body called the Columbia River General Council Fish Commission. Although their legal salvos missed the mark, many Columbia River Indians continued to defy the tribal councils into the 1970s, citing as justification their spiritual beliefs and their role as guardians of tradition. "Not all people have the same religion, and this is true of the Yakima Indians. Not all Indians have the same respect for Indian culture and Indian religion," Sohappy explained in 1976, the year his case was severed from *U.S. v. Oregon* at the behest of the intervening tribes. In his view, the fishing families knew better than the tribal councils how to conserve the salmon. Because they still lived on the river and followed traditional ways, River People could be trusted to regulate themselves. After all, they were not to blame for the depletion of the salmon runs. Conversely, since some tribal leaders had lost touch with fishing culture, they had no more right to control it than the states did. William Klein, the lead attorney for the Sohappy plaintiffs, expressed this view in 1978 when he insisted that the courts "must listen to those Indians who fish as well as those Indians who 'rule.'"[26]

Neither the states nor the tribal councils accepted the dissidents' arguments, and the people at Cook's Landing soon acquired a reputation as poachers. Fisheries enforcement officers periodically seized their boats and nets—costing the Sohappys alone some $138,000 over twenty years—but it proved fruitless to prosecute them for illegal fishing when that carried only a misdemeanor charge in county court. The government's big break came in 1982, after Sohappy and his son David sold fish caught with ceremonial permits to undercover agents engaged in a federal-state sting operation (later dubbed "Salmonscam"). Acting on the erroneous assumption that Indian fishers were responsible for the disappearance of forty thousand fish between the Bonneville and McNary Dam pools, federal authorities raided Cook's Landing and arrested seventy-five Indians. Nineteen ultimately faced charges under the Lacey Act, which Senator Slade Gorton of Washington had amended to make illegal fishing a felony offense.

Although biologists eventually found the "missing" salmon in tributary streams, where they had been diverted by fluoride spills from an aluminum smelter, the two Sohappys each received the maximum sentence of five years in prison for selling a total of 345 fish. "They labeled us as [an] Indian mafia family controlling fish prices, controlling access and all of that," remembered Wilbur Slockish, who served twenty-eight months of a three-year sentence. "They really tried to paint us as bad people." The conviction of five tribal members placed the Yakama Nation in an awkward position. Anxious to assert its jurisdiction, the tribal government insisted on holding its own trial before handing the defendants over to federal marshals in 1987. The jury found all five men innocent, and the tribal council immediately requested presidential pardons, but it was too late. The spectacle of traditionalists being tried by their own government filled River People with bitterness.[27]

Some also lashed out at the Columbia River Inter-Tribal Fish Commission (CRITFC), a cooperative resource management organization composed of representatives from the Yakama Nation, the Confederated Tribes of the Umatilla Indian Reservation, the Confederated Tribes of Warm Springs, and the Nez Perce Tribe. Founded in 1977 to give the tribes a unified voice in salmon management, CRITFC worked with state and federal agencies in regulating the tribal harvest as well as rehabilitating damaged runs and habitat. It appeared to River People that, rather than upholding treaty rights and traditional religion, overeducated bureaucrats were bargaining them away piecemeal. At a Lacey Act briefing in 1986, fishing families blasted the organization for compromising with their enemies. "Our treaty has been abrogated for quite some time," charged Cook's fisherman Lawrence Goudy, "even though the Inter-Tribal Fish Commission has maybe done some good, but have they really went behind the treaty laws and protected them[?]" Lavina Washines, a lifelong river resident and acting member of the Yakama General Council, thought not: "This

Inter-Tribal Fish Commission [that's] sitting in Portland knows more about fishing than I do. They have more authority than I as an elected official to speak on behalf of my rights and it's very disturbing to me. Because they're playing with my religion." Today, says Galen Yallup of the Yakama Nation, some tribal fish and wildlife officials still dread going to meetings on the river because they fear that "only the radicals will show up."[28]

Defenders of the convicted men insisted that they had neither bowed to state regulation nor accepted the system of ceremonial, subsistence, and commercial permits implemented by the tribes. They had stayed true to the "old ways," which were not incompatible with commercial fishing because salmon had always served an economic function as a valuable trade item. River families had to make a living somehow, and it was up to individual fishers to decide how they would dispose of their catch. According to Myra Sohappy, they had suspected all along that their buyers were undercover agents, but David sold fish anyway because friends asked him to and because he had no fear of returning to court. Whatever the case, his offense seemed pitifully small in a year when non-Indian ocean fishers took 129,000 salmon from the same stocks.[29] Tired of shouldering the burden of conservation and the blame for the sorry state of the runs, dissidents repeated the arguments that had underpinned Indian resistance from the start. As Johnny Jackson stated in a 2000 interview:

> I didn't want to see my people going to jail, or pay[ing] for something that they didn't have to, something that we've always had here. Something that the Creator had given us, put here on this earth for us to take care of and use. . . . So when they come and ask me to stop fishing or stop hunting, that's violating my law. The Creator didn't tell me that I had to go and listen to a white man, just because he went and [made] mistakes and depleted the fish.[30]

In the eyes of his supporters, Sohappy was neither an opportunist nor an apostate; he was a martyr for the treaty rights and traditional religion of his people.

Although bitterness over Salmonscam still lingers in some river communities, Mid-Columbia Indian traditionalists and tribal governments have since joined forces to protect and restore the remaining salmon runs. CRITFC offered a natural vehicle for united action by the four treaty tribes. In order to operate on a consensual basis, however, the organization first had to overcome the resentment of tribal fishers as well as their skepticism of scientific resource management. That task fell to Ted Strong, a Yakama with extensive knowledge of computers and finance but little direct experience with fishing. When he became CRITFC's director in 1989, Strong recalled, many of his own tribal members "detested what they felt were unnecessary restrictions upon their right to a free access to fish and fisheries." They not only blamed CRITFC for Salmonscam, they also blamed it for the declining numbers of salmon and the continuing constriction of tribal fishing seasons. "We found ways to try to understand the situation and ease some of the conflict," Strong said a year after retiring in 1999.[31]

> But the Commissioners knew that they would have to go home and face their own tribal membership. And any elected official coming home and saying look, we're only going to get ninety fish this year, have to face tribal members here who will say, "That's why we should never have agreements with the state. The state doesn't do a damn thing to help us. The state isn't there when we're trying to allocate these 390 fish among 17,000 tribal members. They're over there gloating over their scientific restrictions," and so forth.[32]

Convincing them that Western science could supplement spirituality and traditional ecological knowledge thus became one of Strong's core missions: "I really and sincerely believed it was a time of reconciliation . . . a time of reconciling between the deeply held religious and cultural beliefs of Indian peoples and emerging and ubiquitous scientific forums that were being planned and designed, which I also felt were going to take over the Columbia Basin."[33] During his ten-year tenure, CRITFC's expanding technical staff worked to integrate the material and moral dimensions of salmon management. Strong admitted that he initially had a lot to learn about both. Only ten years old when Celilo Falls drowned, he had grown up on the Yakama reservation and attended Bible school instead of Longhouse ceremonies. Although his childhood diet included such traditional fare as fried deer meat and fishback bone soup, his parents farmed and raised cattle rather than trying to wring a livelihood from the depleted runs of the Columbia. College took him even farther from the river and his roots, so he came to CRITFC with business acumen but only limited knowledge of the various salmon stocks the tribes fished. At first, his executive style and bold plans to reorganize the commission antagonized some of its veteran employees. Over the years, though, Strong learned to speak the differing languages of biologists, fish passage specialists, policy analysts, attorneys, and law enforcement officers. He also came to appreciate and participate in the Wáašat religion, partially at the urging of his wife (a Navajo) and partially because it mattered so deeply to the people he represented. This spiritual understanding of the issues helped Strong "set the framework to bring science in. Science is in a larger context—you look at the earth as a kindly mother, generous, bountiful, never forsakes her children. And it is said that her children are the water and the foods. . . . We follow behind them. You can't [just] bring in science because there's no explanation for the spirit of this land. And I didn't bring in science as a replacement. I didn't bring in science to supplant our stories."[34]

Strong was not alone in noting the power of faith to transform and elevate the commitment of CRITFC staff. Douglas Dompier, a non-Indian fish biologist, spent twenty-six years (1979–2005) developing and overseeing fish passage, harvest management, habitat protection, and hatchery programs for the tribes. His recent book, *Fight of the Salmon People: Blending Tribal Tradition with Modern Science to Save Sacred Fish*, chronicles both the history of hatchery production in the Columbia Basin and the deepening admiration he developed for the tribal cause. "As I looked at salmon management through the eyes of the salmon's first caretakers," he writes, "I began to understand the depth and strength of the tribes' culture and their concern for the resource." Each chapter of the book begins with an oral tradition or story that grounds contemporary tribal actions in the indigenous beliefs and customs of Mid-Columbia Indians. Like Strong, though, Dompier recognized that moral suasion alone would not put salmon back in the rivers or sway the agricultural, industrial, and electrical power interests whose practices had pushed wild runs to the brink of extinction. The tribes needed a plan, one informed by traditional values but based on sound scientific data, feasible policy goals, and clear technical recommendations. That plan became known as *Wy-Kan-Ush-Mi Wa-Kish-Wit* ("Spirit of the Salmon"), or the Tribal Restoration Plan (TRP), the Indian alternative to more-timid recovery measures proposed by the state and federal governments.[35]

First issued in 1995 and updated continually, the TRP provides the only basin-wide plan that encompasses the requirements of the treaties, the Endangered Species Act, and the other federal and state laws protecting salmon and their habitat. Unlike competing plans, it also covers Pacific lamprey (eels) and sturgeon, and it goes far beyond mitigation to advocate significant improvements in ecosystem health and changes in hydroelectric power production. The heart of Wy-Kan-Ush-Mi Wa-Kish-Wit is the concept of "grave-to-gravel" management, a life-cycle framework that seeks to shepherd salmon from their natal streams and back again under the best possible conditions. This model, like the spiritual principles that animate it, takes a holistic and adaptive view of the natural systems and cultural modifications that affect salmon survival. "Adaptive management is learning by doing—an approach the tribes have used for thousands of years," explained Yakama tribal chairman Jerry Meninick in 1995. Tribal advocates believe that their plan's blend of faith and reason can restore sanity along with the salmon. As Yakama fish commissioner Wendell Hannigan remarked on the debut of Wy-Kan-Ush-Mi Wa-Kish-Wit, "Our salmon plan is the only vehicle we can use to bring our spiritual and cultural values into the region's restoration efforts."[36]

The TRP's title and Hannigan's words certainly fit the trope of the Ecological Indian, but CRITFC's policy positions are not so easily categorized. Significantly, the tribes and the TRP reject the environmentalist critique of hatchery fish as Frankenstein monsters that will ultimately destroy the genetic purity and health of wild salmon. While CRITFC scientists are very critical of the way hatcheries have been used historically, they place great stock in a technique called supplementation, which combines habitat restoration with hatchery transplants to rebuild naturally spawning runs. Dompier, among others, frankly dismisses the "idealistic dream" of self-sustaining wild runs in a river system transformed by dams. CRITFC conservation biologists see the construct of genetic purity as an impediment to real progress and an excuse to avoid rebuilding salmon runs in the upper basin, where most tribal hatcheries are located. Mid-Columbia Indians would naturally prefer to see hatcheries made redundant and dams removed, but in the meantime they generally support any measure that puts more fish in the rivers. For the same reason, they have backed state proposals to shoot sea lions that gather at Bonneville Dam to feast on migrating salmon. Simultaneously evoking and defying the Ecological Indian stereotype, CRITFC chairperson Fidelia Andy (Yakama) declared in 2008, "There is no nobility in one species squatting in a fish ladder and eating another into extinction. Our Creator gave us the responsibility to protect the balance among all creatures in the ecosystem. Traditionally, we accept responsibility for the survival and prosperity of the resources that surround us."[37]

Tribal fishers and traditionalists are more concerned about the state of the river. They often say that the Columbia is "sick" from pollution, and they worry about its impact on their own health as fish-eating people. Consequently, many have worked to become conversant in the scientific and policy issues that affect their lives. Since his release from prison, Wilbur Slockish Jr. has served on the Bi-State Water Quality Commission and various tribal projects related to salmon recovery. His reasons for doing so remain firmly rooted in traditional spirituality. Like the Yakama chief Owhi, who feared that selling land would anger the Almighty, Slockish believes that he will be held accountable for his ecological actions in this life. When his time comes, he told an interviewer at a meeting of the Hanford Health Effects Subcommittee, he hopes "[to] be able to tell the Creator that I did my best to leave the world as He wanted it. That I did my best to make sure that my children had a place to survive. That my animal resources, that my plant life were here as He placed them. And I did my best to ensure that they were here for future generations."[38]

There is some danger in concluding with such a rhetorical flourish. The eyes of environmentalists become misty, while those of scholars begin to roll. Either reaction obscures our vision of the important part religion has played in Mid-Columbia Indian efforts to protect traditional resources and treaty rights. We need analytical rigor, of course, to avoid reducing Native Americans to stock characters in a morality play written by and for non-Indian audiences. As Shepard Krech has reminded us, "Critics who excoriate the larger society as they absolve Indians of all blame sacrifice evidence that in recent years, Indian people have had a mixed relationship to the environment. They victimize Indians when they strip them of all agency in their lives except when their actions fit the image of the Ecological Indian."[39]

Certainly, the Mid-Columbia Indian example contains evidence of such complexity. Both aboriginal and modern Indian commercial fishing had an impact on salmon populations. Although the demographic catastrophe that started in the 1880s was hardly the tribes' fault, the tension at Celilo Falls during the mid-twentieth century shows that individual Indians were not inherently immune to greed or automatically programmed to respect "tradition." Similarly, later disagreements within tribal communities regarding the actions of dissident fishers reveal that Mid-Columbia Indians have vigorously debated issues of law, policy, and religion among themselves. It is also true that spokesmen such as George Meninick, David Sohappy, and Wilbur Slockish have been savvy in choosing modes of expression that resonate with sympathetic non-Indians. To assume on that basis, however, that their religious rhetoric is somehow insincere does a real disservice to their commitments and their accomplishments.

By taking faith seriously, we come to a fuller understanding of why and how Mid-Columbia Indians have fought so steadfastly to save their five sacred foods. Their investment in these resources and the right to harvest them is more than material and economic, it is cultural and spiritual as well. Wáašat still frames their "logic of engagement" with salmon and other foods, which in turn define what it means to be Indian for many Plateau people today. Recently, the Confederated Tribes of the Umatilla Indian Reservation (CTUIR) developed an entire land management plan specifically dedicated to preserving the five sacred foods. Eric J. Quaempts, the director of the reservation's Natural Resources Department, came up with the idea in 2006 while serving food to tribal members at the annual root feast. "I thought, this is all about the table in front of us and the need to recognize it." Quaempts also holds a degree in wildlife science from Oregon State University, but he and his staff are perfectly comfortable speaking of their work in terms of religion. "When we pray and when we talk," explains education coordinator Wenix Red Elk, "it always is about the foods and the environment and how we are going to protect them." Although their faith has evolved over time, as all religions do, the core principles of Wáašat demand that worshippers honor the five scared foods and the benevolence of the Creator. The challenges posed by resource depletion and state regulation compelled Mid-Columbia Indians to integrate the idea of conservation into their spiritual vocabulary, but the concept was neither alien to nor incompatible with the teachings of the Longhouse. "What it's saying is this is your relationship to the landscape and these foods," explains Eric Quaempts, "and you have to take care of them for them to be sustainable."[40]

Notes

1. Elizabeth Woody, *River of Memory: The Everlasting Columbia* (Seattle: University of Washington Press, 2006), 38.

2. Stephen J. Langdon, "Sustaining a Relationship: Inquiry into the Emergence of a Logic of Engagement with Salmon among the Southern Tlingits," in *Native Americans and the Environment: Perspectives on the Ecological Indian*, ed. Michael E. Harkin and David R. Lewis (Lincoln: University of Nebraska Press, 2007), 238.

3. Malatare quote from Yakama Nation portion of "Our Lives: Contemporary Life and Identities" Exhibition, National Museum of the American Indian, Washington, D.C.

4. Deward E. Walker Jr. and Helen H. Schuster, "Religious Movements," in *Handbook of North American Indians*, vol. 12, ed. Deward E. Walker (Washington, DC: Smithsonian Institution, 1998), 504; Elsie David, interview with Katrine Barber, August 6, 2007, in *Oregon Historical Quarterly* 108, no. 4 (Winter 2007): 653.

5. Walker and Schuster, "Religious Movements," 502–5.

6. Lewis and Clark quoted in Eugene Hunn with James Selam and Family, *Nch'i-Wána, "The Big River": Mid-Columbia Indians and Their Land* (Seattle: University of Washington Press, 1990), 153.

7. Shepard Krech III, "Beyond *The Ecological Indian*," in *Native Americans and the Environment*, 11–13; Hunn, *Nch'i-Wána*, 141; Joseph E. Taylor III, *Making Salmon: An Environmental History of the Northwest Fisheries Crisis* (Seattle: University of Washington Press, 1999), 14.

8. Congress, Senate, Select Committee on Indian Affairs, *Columbia River Fisheries Management: Hearing before the Select Committee on Indian Affairs*, 100th Cong., 2nd sess., April 19, 1988, 49; Haruo Aoki, *Nez Perce Dictionary* (Berkeley: University of California Press, 1994), 707; Lillian A. Ackerman, *A Necessary Balance: Gender and Power Among Indians of the Columbia Plateau* (Norman: University of Oklahoma Press, 2003), 70–71.

9. Walker and Schuster, "Religious Movements," 504; Larry Cebula, *Plateau Indians and the Quest for Spiritual Power, 1700–1850* (Lincoln: University of Nebraska Press, 2003), 81–87. Many contemporary longhouse members resent the implication that Wáašat is influenced by Christianity and insist on truly indigenous origins for their ceremonial practices.

10. Isaac Ingalls Stevens, *A True Copy of the Record of the Official Proceedings at the Council in the Walla Walla Valley*, 1855, ed. Darrell Scott (Fairfield, WA: Ye Galleon Press, 1985), 80–82.

11. Proceedings of the Wasco Council (typescript), MSS 616, Oregon Historical Society (OHS), Portland.

12. Treaty with the Yakima, 1855, in *Indian Affairs: Laws and Treaties*, vol. 2, ed. Charles J. Kappler (Washington, DC: Government Printing Office, 1904), 699; emphasis added.

13. Taylor, *Making Salmon*, 62–64, 144; Francis Seufert, *Wheels of Fortune*, ed. Thomas Vaughan (Portland: Oregon Historical Society, 1980), 12–35.

14. Francis A. Garrett, "An Indian Chief," *Washington Historical Quarterly* 29 (July 1928): 174.

15. Joseph C. Dupris, Kathleen S. Hill, and William H. Rodgers Jr., *The Si'lailo Way: Indians, Salmon and Law on the Columbia River* (Durham, NC: Carolina Academic Press, 2006), 227–28.

16. Ibid., 228–31; Garrett, "An Indian Chief," 299.

17. Garrett, "An Indian Chief," 299.

18. Dupris, Hill, and Rodgers, *The Si'lailo Way*, 232; Fronda Woods, "Who's in Charge of Fishing?," *Oregon Historical Quarterly* (Fall 2005), http://www.historycooperative.org/journals/ohq/106.3/woods.html.

19. Walker and Schuster, "Religious Movements," 504; Johnson J. Meninick to Thor C. Tollefson, June 14, 1974, Box 46, Folder "Yakima 1974," Records of the Washington State Department of Fisheries (WSDF), Washington State Archives, Olympia.

20. Affidavit of Tommy Thompson, in Edward G. Swindell Jr., *Report on Source, Nature, and Extent of the Fishing, Hunting, and Miscellaneous Related Rights of Certain Indian Tribes in Washington and Oregon Territory Together with Affidavits Showing the Location of a Number of Usual and Accustomed Fishing Grounds and Stations* (Los Angeles: Office of Indian Affairs, 1942), 152; George W. Aguilar Sr., *When the River Ran Wild!: Indian Traditions on the Mid-Columbia and the Warm Springs Reservation* (Portland: Oregon Historical Society Press, 2005), 114, 123–26; C. W. Ramsey to Supt. Yakima Indian Reservation, March 12, 1924, Fishing Matters Along the Columbia River (1924), General Correspondence, Yakima Indian Agency, Record Group 75, National Archives and Records Administration-Pacific Alaska Region.

21. C. G. Davis to M. A. Johnson, October 26, 1939, 155–60, Celilo Fish Committee Councils, General Subject Correspondence (GSC), Records of C. G. Davis, Portland Area Office (PAO), RG 75, NARA-PAR; Celilo Fish Committee Minutes, September 4, 1940, Meetings—1940, GSC, Davis, PAO, RG 75, NARA-PAR, 11–12; Carl C. Donaugh to Isaac Albert and the Other Members of the Fish Company, September 13, 1939, 155-E, Correspondence, Celilo Fish—Legal Matters, GSC, Davis, PAO, RG 75, NARA-PAR.

22. Roberta Ulrich, *Empty Nets: Indians, Dams, and the Columbia River* (Corvallis: Oregon State University Press, 1999), 36–40, 108, 112–13; Chief Johnny Jackson, interview by Piper Hackett, March 28, 1999, OrHist 6208, Radical Elders Series, Oregon Historical Society, Portland (Jackson Interview), 41.

23. Ulrich, *Empty Nets*, 125; Charles A. Hobbs, "Indian Hunting and Fishing Rights II," *George Washington Law Review* 37 (July 1969): 1257; Deposition of David Sohappy, May 10, 1976 (Sohappy Deposition), vol. 3, June 17, 1974–March 30, 1978, Civil 68–409, *Sohappy v. Smith*, United States District Court for the District of Oregon (USDC-DO), Records of District Courts of the United States, Record Group 21 (RG 21), NARA-PAR, 1.

24. Ulrich, *Empty Nets*, 127–28; William Dietrich, *Northwest Passage: The Great Columbia River* (New York: Simon and Schuster, 1995), 379–81; Columbia River Defense Project, *In Defense of Che Wana: Fishing Rights on the Columbia River* (Portland, OR: Wheel Press, 1987), 7.

25. Ulrich, *Empty Nets*, 127–28; Wilbur Slockish, personal communication, July 28, 2006; Ted Strong, Interview by Clark Hansen, January 17, 2000, OHS Inv. 2731, Columbia River Dissenters Series, Oregon Historical Society, Portland (Strong Interview), 35.

26. Memorandum in Opposition to Motion for Severance, June 18, 1976, Civil No. 68-409 and No. 68-513, USDC-DO, *Sohappy v. Smith*, RG 21, NARA-PAR, 1-2; Sohappy Deposition, *Sohappy v. Smith*, USDC-DO, RG 21, NARA-PAR, 2; Answer to Motion for Termination of Continuing Jurisdiction and Request for Hearing, May 2, 1978, *Sohappy v. Smith*, vol. 4, USDC-DO, RG 21, NARA-PAR.

27. Dietrich, *Northwest Passage*, 383–85; Robert Clark, *River of the West: Stories from the Columbia* (New York: HarperCollins West, 1995), 361–78; Columbia River Defense Project, *In Defense of Che Wana: Fishing Rights on the Columbia River* (Portland, OR: Wheel Press, 1987), 21–23; Wilbur Slockish Jr., interview by Michael O'Rourke, February 11, 2000, OHS Inv. 2738, Columbia River Dissenters Series, Oregon Historical Society, Portland, 12.

28. Strong Interview, 12–13; Lacey Act Workshop Minutes, November 12, 1986, Personal Files of Carol Craig, Public Information Officer, Yakama Nation Fisheries Resource Management, Toppenish, WA, 46, 49; Galen Yallup, personal communication, July 18, 2006.

29. Clark, *River of the West*, 344–53; Ulrich, *Empty Nets*, 159–63.

30. Jackson Interview, 42.

31. Strong Interview, 12.

32. Ibid., 20.

33. Ibid., 12.

34. Ibid., 1–13, 87.

35. Douglas W. Dompier, *The Fight of the Salmon People: Blending Tribal Tradition with Modern Science to Save Sacred Fish* (Philadelphia, PA: Xlibris Corporation, 2005), 127.

36. "CRITFC Celebrates 25 Years of Protecting Salmon and Tribal Treaty Rights," *Wana Chinook Tymoo* (Summer 2002): 5; "Tribes Release Salmon Restoration Plan," *Wana Chinook Tymoo*, special ed. (1995): 13–17, 8.

37. Dompier, *The Fight of the Salmon People*, 134; "A Century of Loss," *Wana Chinook Tymoo* (Winter 1999): 17; Fidelia Andy, "Sea Lions vs. Salmon: Restore Balance and Common Sense," *Seattle Times*, February 15, 2008.

38. Slockish Interview, 44.

39. Krech, "Beyond *The Ecological Indian*," 216.

40. "Culture and Natural Resources Unite on Umatilla Reservation," *Indian Country Today*, http://www.indiancountry.com/national/ northwest/48620297.html; Richard Cockle, "'First Foods' Guide Tribes' Land Strategy," *(Portland) Oregonian*, March 1, 2009, C1, C4.

CHAPTER 9

Indigenous Spirits

Ancestral Power in a South-Central African Kingdom

David M. Gordon

IN SOUTH-CENTRAL Africa, conquerors, settlers, and indigenes proclaimed that ancestral spirits were responsible for agricultural prosperity and human fertility. These spiritual qualities of indigenous knowledge are often imagined to be timeless tribal religions rather than historically located forms of knowledge that evolved and engaged with changing social and political arrangements. Prior to European colonialism, ancestral powers were discussed (and reified) in oral tradition. Rulers claimed that they were the living incarnations of their ancestors and inherited their powers, or at least held the ability to communicate with them. After European conquest, the imperatives of colonial rule transformed these environmental religions into charters of rule by many of the same rulers, then termed "traditional chiefs."

The indigenous environmental religions of south-central Africa emerged during a pre-European phase of colonialism when Lunda and Luba royals conquered local clan groups. Colonizing elites proclaimed their indigeneity by burying their lineage ancestors in sacred groves and by appropriating older rituals, sacred sites, and stories associated with agricultural and human fertility.[1] The political content of this knowledge was contained in its spiritual form. The Bemba kingdom examined in this chapter is a typical example. Members of a prominent clan claim to have conquered the region in the early eighteenth century. They recognized a system of local knowledge about the environment that was laden with secrets, magic, and witchcraft. It was attributed to the autochthonous inhabitants of the land, referred to by the ethnonym "Bisa," and their leaders, the "owners of the land" (*umwine wa mpanga*). They appropriated this Bisa environmental religion by burying their ancestral heroes in a sacred graveyard termed "Mwalule," from which spiritual power emanated. This Bemba sacred grove attempted to replace local village-based sacred sites previously responsible for human and agricultural prosperity.

In the European colonial period, Bemba environmental knowledge was thoroughly documented by Branislaw Malinowski's renowned student Audrey Richards, who conducted fieldwork and wrote about the Bemba from the 1930s to the 1960s. With much subtlety, her work demonstrated how Bemba knowledge was integrally tied to environmental processes, and especially to productive and reproductive cycles. Her account of Bemba environmental knowledge emphasized its ritual and religious qualities, embodied in the Bemba paramount, referred to by his title, "Chitimukulu," and enacted in rituals associated with his chieftaincy.[2] Richards was a product of functionalist anthropology at its best; she was a thorough scholar and her findings should not be dismissed. After all, Richards spent years in the field. Her functionalist theoretical framework also emphasized the coherence and logic of indigenous forms of knowledge. Yet, in part because of the difficulty of accounting for change in functionalist theory, Richards tied Bemba religion to the then existing structures of power. This not only legitimized Bemba chieftaincy but gave little idea of the deeper history of conflicts that produced this knowledge.[3] The tendency to reify indigenous knowledge, typical of colonial anthropology, was repeated in later accounts that emphasized how knowledge linked the body of kings (or lords or chiefs) with the welfare and fertility of people and land.[4]

In the postcolonial period, the notion of a unified tribal religion has allowed chiefs, a type of postcolonial indigenous activist, to campaign on behalf of their often marginalized communities. They appeal to urban-focused states and even to the international community, often during strategically timed "traditional ceremonies." The chiefs and their entourages associate economic and political marginalization with the erosion of their powers, as enshrined in their indigenous knowledges. In turn, they argue that the state and their urban compatriots should respect indigenous knowledge and indigenous authorities, and thereby reverse processes of marginalization. In such politically heated negotiations, there is little opportunity to reveal local divisions within indigenous knowledge. Instead, environmental religion is presented as evidence of tribal unity.

The rendering of this hegemonic indigenous knowledge is, however, only part of the story. Within Bemba indigenous knowledge there are signs of alternatives to hegemony, reflections of past conflicts rather than an overwhelming consensus that legitimized particular constellations of power and knowledge. Bemba indigenous knowledge was a tool of those who wielded power and of those who resisted power. Instead of the consensus of a tribal dogma, its ideas were often the outcome and reflection of conflict and dissent. The history of Bemba environmental religion reveals the many contested ancestral claims that constitute indigenous knowledge.[5]

In the first section of this chapter, I analyze themes of indigeneity in an oral tradition, the Bemba conquest narrative, which established the religious significance of the Mwalule burial ground and sacred grove. The second section turns to the late nineteenth century, when conquering elites established their religious authority over the environment, a process that was consolidated but also transformed by European colonial administrators who accepted these religious narratives as secular charters of rule.

The Bemba Ancestors

The early modern states of south-central Africa were politico-religious edifices that celebrated the power of the conquerors over the people, the land, and the ancestors of old. The knowledge upon which the governing edifices rested was preserved and disseminated in praises, proverbs, and stories, known by our literate civilization as "oral tradition." Such oral traditions are vibrant forms of knowledge, not factual renditions of the past, but idealized accounts of the relationships between people, the world that sustained them, and the dead.[6] The core ideas of these oral traditions reference frightening, magical, and dangerous pasts; they tell of how this old world was overcome and civilized. The characters in the oral traditions exist in the liminality of human experience and demonstrate that they have access to a world that was beyond the ordinary.[7] While they appear to legitimize certain rulers, they also reflect old struggles over resources and claims of belonging.

By invoking ideas of belonging through references to ancestral spirits, these oral traditions had religious features that resemble the sacred texts of global religions. Central African oral traditions (and indigenous oral traditions in general), however, refer to lineage ancestors and specific local environmental resources. The stories and doctrines of global religions, by contrast, communicate across place and time by focusing on relationships with distant deities. Even while they could be applied to local resources (Christians could pray for rain, for example), such global religious ideas were not integrally tied to local resources. By contrast, sacred oral traditions were characterized by their focus on ancestral heroes and on local resources.

Thus, even while oral traditions across south-central Africa had certain generic qualities, especially in their common symbolism, they were relevant to specific environmental issues and conflicts. This has resulted in numerous similar but unique narratives. In the case of the eastern Lunda to the west of the Bemba polity, for example, the most important narratives share features with the Bemba oral traditions, such as competition between an uncle and a nephew, conflict between matrilineal and patrilineal forms of succession, and the failures of an uncivilized and angry king. Yet the oral traditions of the eastern Lunda address the fishing resources of Lake Mweru and the Luapula River and the fertile lands of the Luapula floodplain. In the eastern Lunda oral tradition, Nachituti, an autochthonous heroine, gave these valuable resources to the conquering king, Mwata Kazembe, after he avenged the killing of her son by Nachituti's jealous brother, Nkuba. By *giving* the land and lakes to the conquering king, the narration emphasizes the agency of the original inhabitants, those who gave the land and lakes away.[8]

The Bemba polity, with its plentiful land and poor soils, had different resource challenges to those of the Luapula Valley. *Chitemene* (a form of slash and burn) agriculture relied on burned tree branches to fertilize the sandy soil before planting the chief crops, millet and sorghum. Bemba political and religious practices had to address the source of agricultural prosperity—the burned tree and the earth. The title of the ruler of the Bemba conquest state, Chitimukulu (The Great Tree) already provides a clue as to how the Bemba conquerors would attempt to do so. The paramount associated himself with a large tree, long considered the most appropriate place to make offerings to ancestral and nature spirits. The way that the tree joined the earth would then form the basic *problématique* of the Bemba oral tradition.

The oral tradition refers to the migration of the royal "Crocodile Clan" (*Bena Ngandu*), from the Luba heartland in the west to the Bemba highlands. We do not know the details of its performance and narration prior to the nineteenth century. If the bare outline of the founding story refers to "historical facts," they probably took place in the early eighteenth century.[9] The first typical sequence of the story establishes the divine origins of the Crocodile Clan through their link with a celestial mother. The joining of sky and earth, a frequently found religious idea on the south-central African plateau, was thereby achieved:

> A lord, Mukulumpe, was hunting in a forest when he met a beautiful woman with large ears, like an elephant. She said that her name was Mumbi Mukasa, she had come from the heaven, and belonged to the Crocodile Clan. Mukulumpe and the woman from heaven, Mumbi Mukasa, married, and had three sons, Nkole, Chiti, Katongo, and one daughter, Chilufya (or Bwalya Chabala)....
>
> The royal sons tried to build a tower to their mother's home in the sky. But it collapsed and killed many people. Their angry father, Mukulumpe, banished their mother to the sky and imprisoned their sister, Chilufya. He blinded Katongo, who managed to send a warning with the talking drum to his brothers, Nkole and Chiti, of a trap set by their father. They fled eastwards, led by a white magician, Luchele Ng'anga. After they crossed the Luapula River, Chiti sent five men to rescue his sister, Chilufya. She joined her brothers, carrying millet seeds in her hair (in some versions, Nkole carried seeds in his hair).[10]

The strife between father and son and the restoration of ties between sisters and brothers is found in many south-central African clan-based oral traditions.[11] Thereby, the story introduces many familiar elements, necessary and convincing fragments and clichés. But the joining of sky and earth and the divine origins of the mother of the Crocodile Clan go beyond a typical clan charter; they establish the principles of sacred king, typical of Luba kingship, which forms the most important claim of the Crocodile Clan royal court.[12] These divine origins then become directed to local agricultural practices, as Chilufya (or Nkole) carries agricultural seeds to the Bemba plateau.

The migrating royals conquered many of the surrounding people and brought their divine rule and civilization. But Chiti would still succumb to local magic when he was seduced by a married woman, Chilumbulu, with her scarifications that resembled the secretive water monitor lizard (*mbulu*):

> Chilumbulu was the wife of a hunter and magician, Mwase. With her attractive scarifications, she seduced Chiti. But Mwase caught them. In their fight over Chilumbulu, Mwase killed Chiti with a poisoned arrow. Nkole avenged the death of his brother, Chiti. He killed Mwase and Chilumbulu and cut up their bodies but carefully preserved Chilumbulu's attractive scarified skin. In future, the skin would be kept as a royal relic, a *babenye*. A virgin would wear the skin of Chilumbulu when it was time to plant the first seeds.[13]

In Chilumbulu's seduction of Chiti, the earth was joined with the tree, and the principle of Bemba agriculture was thereby achieved. Yet this also resulted in death: the Crocodile Clan might have had divine ancestry, but this divinity could not usurp local magic, especially that of women. Thus, while the seeds were brought by the conquering clan, the skin of the autochthone Chilumbulu was needed to make them fertile.[14] In typical Luba stories of the founding of the sacred *mulopwe* kings, the migrating royal symbolically marries the local earth priest, the owner of the land.[15] In the Bemba story, sexual relationships occur, but result in conquest and death, indicating the power of indigeneity, but ultimately affirming the authority of the celestial Crocodile Clan over agricultural rites. Even while they killed the indigenes, the Crocodile Clan royals died at the hands of the indigenes. They conquered *and* succumbed.

> Nkole then searched for a graveyard to bury his brother, Chiti. He found a thick forest, owned by an unmarried women, Chimbala. He purchased the forest from her and requested that she cleanse the burial party. But cleansing could only be performed by a woman after she had had sex with her husband. So her slave Kabotwe had sex with her. Kabotwe (or Chimbala) would then become the caretaker of the graveyard, Mwalule, "Shimwalule" (the father of "Mwalule").
>
> Nkole arranged for the burial of his brother. He carefully preserved the corpse of Chiti by soaking it, drying it in the sun and wrapping it in a cow's hide. His magicians burned the remains of the chief, Mwase and Chilumbulu, so that they could be buried with Chiti. But the smoke from the fire also killed Nkole. They then prepared the body of Nkole in the same way. As the elder brother he was buried above Chiti.[16]

The story of the burial at Mwalule illustrates the acts of negotiation, conflict, and appropriation involved in developing the Bemba polity. The claim that the graveyard, Mwalule, would be cared for by a former "slave" establishes a social hierarchy, but recognizes the sacred significance of indigeneity.

The indigenous sites of memory referred to in the oral tradition became the sacred centers of the Bemba, especially the graveyard, Mwalule, the place where the ancestral kings remained. Chitimukulu's most important relics (*babenye*), such as the skin of Chilumbulu, were kept in a shrine hut at Mwalule. Three elderly women inherited the title the "wives of the relics" (*bamukabenye*); they guarded the relics. About once a month Chitimukulu's chief councilors, the *bakabilo*, came to the Mwalule graveyard to make sure the relics were well kept and to perform ceremonies appropriate to agricultural, hunting, or military affairs.[17] A Crocodile Clan lord, Nkhweto, kept watch over the general vicinity of the graveyard, an area that was known as Chilinda (the place that is watched). But the actual graveyard fell under the control of the autochthone Kabotwe's descendants, the father of the graveyard, Shimwalule.[18]

The emphasis on the power of indigeneity in the stories, sites, and relics associated with Chitimukulu's court traditions and graveyard were not an appropriation by or an imposition of the Crocodile Clan royals.[19] Rather, they were the result of an insistent assertion of local leaders who claimed that they belonged to and owned the land; indeed, such indigenous activists took on titles as "owners of the land" (*umwine wa mpanga*). Through such claims to indigenous ownership, they gained voice in the royal court. They manipulated the oral tradition to make such claims. For example, Shimwalule, the owner of the graveyard, told a different version of the Bemba genesis narrative. He was not a slave of Chimbala, but her lover, and married her upon the request of Nkole. In exchange for the land and for taking care of the graveyard, Chitimukulu was to send a portion of his wealth to Shimwalule.[20]

For such leaders, the recognition of indigenous ownership formed the basic political principle of the Bemba polity. The royal court might choose to underemphasize this indigenous ownership, but Shimwalule insisted on it, reminding the royals of their promises and obligations. Shimwalule, as guardian of the royal graveyard and the sacred center of the Bemba polity, was an especially powerful local agent, for he looked after the living dead. An autochthon was the interface between the living kings and their ancestors; he provided the indigenous authority that catalyzed the sacred kingship. The telling of the oral tradition focused the generic religious principles of south-central African oral traditions on Bemba environmental challenges. It reminded all that prosperity rested on trees and migrating heroes as well as the earth and its owners.

The Making of a Bemba Environment Religion

The ritual, ceremonial, and religious features of Bemba rule expanded and consolidated at the center of the polity as the kingdom engaged with slave traders, attempted a greater degree of centralization, and was threatened by internal fissures and external threats.[21] One of the most powerful and renowned paramounts, Chitimukulu Chitapankwa (d. 1883), was praised as *Mukungula mfuba* (he who sweeps away ancestral shrines), suggesting his attack on or purification of older ancestral shrines and a concomitant enhancement of his own ties to the land.[22] Under Chitimukulu Chitapankwa's reign, the Crocodile Clan insisted that their ancestors ensured the welfare of the land and people. When locusts and wild animals, lions and crocodiles, afflicted Bemba territories, Chitapankwa constructed a shrine to his uncle Bwembya (whom Chitapankwa had deposed) and sent offerings to Shimwalule at the royal graveyard.[23] The Chitimukulu titleholder thereby associated his life, well-being, and that of his ancestral shades to the land. Should he fall ill or fail to perform the appropriate rites, he claimed through story and performance that the land itself would be spoiled: crops would not grow, no rain would fall, and general misfortune would afflict all. Rites of purification, which involved sex with his head wife ("the wife of the land"), ensured the fertility of the land and blessed the most significant tools of agriculture, the ax and the seed. During and after such acts, when the paramount was most closely linked to the land, both good and bad fortune could result.[24] Such rites affirmed and acted out aspects of the original charter, especially the dangerous sexual relations between migrant Chiti and autochthon Chilumbulu. Just before his death, on his last breath, his close elders strangled Chitimukulu to ensure that the land did not "dry up" with the king and that sickness would not spread.[25] A spiritual edifice connected the present and past lives of Chitimukulu to the land.

At the center of the Bemba polity, the hegemonic claims of the Bemba royals were made most successfully. The powers of the royals were enacted and performed in grand royal dances and ceremonies with abundant beer. They were impressive and appealed to many. Consumption, patronage, and the possibilities and promises of wealth became part of these grand gatherings. Chitimukulu was the host, the *mwine lupepo*, the owner of the ceremony, secure in his political authority and demonstrative of his generosity.[26] The ceremony where the living Chitimukulu was absent, his burial, became the most potent illustration of his ties to the welfare of the land. After his death, he was embalmed in the fashion referred to by the oral tradition of Chiti. Only when the royal crop that had been planted since his death was ripe could the king be buried. The close councilors (*bakabilo*) of the king and those who dealt with his death (*bafingo*) then embarked on a journey that lasted up to a week, a type of funeral procession with stops at several sacred sites. The journey itself was dangerous. The pallbearers fought with the embalmers to release the body. A death in such ritual battles signaled good fortune. Slaves, dependents, and the head wives of the dead paramount accompanied the procession. At the Mwalule graveyard, the *bafingo* killed several of them with a blow by a club to the bridge of the nose. If they did not die, the dead paramount had rejected them, "vomited them out" (*mfumu ya muluka*). Several remained as personal slaves of the gravekeepers. The paramount was laid to rest on top of the head wife, another wife supported his head, and another his feet. The burial referenced the oral tradition of Chiti and Nkole. It was a period of great terror and turmoil that was meant to reinforce the ties that the Crocodile Clan ancestors had to the land. Their return to the earth below (*-panshi*), and conversion into ancestors, *imipashi*, claimed to secure the well-being of the kingdom.[27]

At the periphery of the kingdom such claims were not always convincing. Efforts to link the Crocodile Clan to the welfare of the land and people, with distinctive outbursts of ceremony, grandeur, and terror, were contested. By the late nineteenth century the Bemba holder of the title Mwamba extended the reach of Crocodile Clan authority.[28] Challenges to Mwamba's rule were recalled in stories about the powers of Bisa prophets and spirits. In one such story, Mwamba tested the power of the Bisa prophets by challenging them to summon a lion to devour one of his wives while she drew water. She was caught and killed by a lion. An angry Mwamba had the prophets thrown into a bonfire, but they survived and were found sitting in the ashes of the bonfire the following morning. The prophets then summoned lions to chase Mwamba from their land.[29] He fled—but a successor returned a few years later and the conflict-ridden history continued: In 1888, just prior to the European colonial period, Mwamba captured Bisa subjects and sold them to Swahili slave traders.[30] Farther south, a Bisa rebellion exacted the revenge of Chitimukulu, which led to further Bisa subjugation and exile.[31]

The farther from the political center Bemba authority spread, the less convincing the reach of the Crocodile Clan ancestral cult and the greater the profusion of alternative agents who made stronger claims of belonging and indigeneity. Rulers who had only a shallow genealogy of local ancestors could not claim the same ancestral authority over the land as those who had lived at the same place for several generations.[32] In these border territories, many of them only conquered in the late nineteenth century, the Bemba faced invasion by Ngoni warriors and frequent challenges from Bisa subjects. Here the ancestral cult of the Crocodile Clan was less hegemonic and more fractured. The Crocodile Clan rulers could hardly claim that their ancestors were tied to the land. Local claims of indigeneity held greater sway.

Such local claims of indigeinity identified a distant mythical past that belonged to the original "owners of the land," the Batwa.[33] In the borderlands of Bemba authority, people maintained the rites and the secrets of the Batwa in territorial environmental cults termed Ubutwa. According to Plymouth Brethren missionary Dugald Campbell, who described Ubutwa ceremonies in 1914, Ubutwa members spread knowledge about local nature spirits, *ingulu*, which possessed people and made them into either "fathers" or "mothers" of the *ingulu* spirits. They were taught secrets of the land, and learned an esoteric language. During Ubutwa festivals, initiated members constructed temples, drank beer, gave libations, and sang. The association forged cohesive bonds across clan and gender boundaries and promoted "wife-swapping," a form of mutual support during harvesttime, *ubwafwano*.[34] The Ubutwa association presented the most cohesive challenge to the Bemba royal claims to control the agricultural cycles upon which people relied.

Local village-based ancestral rituals prevailed at the outskirts of Bemba royal authority. To the southeast of the Bemba highlands, one villager recalled how he would identify a large tree near the village:

> I would build a shelter under it and put cassava powder as well as sacrifice a chicken or some other animal there to my God. After praying to my God in this way, I could move about safely in the forest and I would be able to kill animals for my meals. No one else was allowed to pray under the tree I had chosen. Each individual, be he a villager, village head or chief, had to possess his own shrine for his particular God.[35]

Another elder reported placing gourds filled with flour under a large tree. If the flour scattered overnight, the ancestors had indicated the unsuitability of the area for cultivation.[36] Often the flour was placed in small spirit huts, *imfuba*, built near trees or the sources of rivers.[37] The missionary and explorer David Livingstone reported that such spirit shrines were scattered across the region.[38] These were individualized and often secret shrines, possessions of village elders and family patriarchs. Among the Mambwe to the north or the Ushi to the south of the Bemba royals, regional shrine priests took charge of local shrines and spread the importance of their sacred relics.[39] Even while the Bemba royals mirrored their sacred rule on this local shrine system, increased its scale, and proclaimed the centrality of their own ancestors to environmental processes, they could not displace it. The local shrines remained an alternative and a challenge to Bemba politico-religious authority.

Europeans and their African mercenaries conquered south-central Africa during the 1890s and early 1900s. Chitimukulu's Bemba kingdom proved resilient, but, increasingly cut off from their Swahili slave-and-ivory-trading allies, they could not arm and defend themselves from the European onslaught. After conquest, the Bemba territory formed part of North-Eastern Rhodesia, later Northern Rhodesia, administered at first by the British South African Company (BSAC) and after 1924 by the Colonial Office directly. Both the BSAC and the Colonial Office invested few resources in the administration of the territory. Single European officers administered vast regions and relied on local African agents, a policy that became formalized as Indirect Rule in the 1930s.

Colonial administrators focused their attention on the most powerful and established political leaders, those whom they reckoned would form the most reliable and effective collaborators in buttressing colonial power. The Bemba under Chitimukulu quickly came to be appreciated as one such reliable kingdom, with Chitimukulu becoming one of three "paramount chiefs" across the vast territory of Northern Rhodesia. (The colonial administration divided rulers into "paramount chiefs," "senior chiefs," "chiefs," "sub-chiefs," and then "headmen," and chiefs' retainers, "kapasus.") Colonial officers claimed that the authority of these chiefs, including the Bemba king and lords, was "traditional," resting on an age-old respect and deference toward the Crocodile Clan royalty.

European colonial support of such powerful leaders changed structures of power and knowledge in the kingdom. When tradition did not coincide with bureaucratic imperatives—or involved too much of a spiritual role—local rulers were eradicated or their duties transformed. The best example of this transformation was the most sacred of Bemba political leaders, the indigene Shimwalule, who looked after the ancestors of the Crocodile Clan at the Mwalule graveyard, the spiritual center of the Bemba polity and the place where the first Chitimukulu and his brother, Nkole, were buried after being killed by the magician Mwase. In precolonial times, after Shimwalule had buried the Chitimukulu, he abdicated in favor of his brother (or sister's son), who would "kill" him, or so it was rumored. Colonial administrators did their best to adapt such rules; at first, for example, they accepted the principle that the position would be succeeded after the burial of a Chitimukulu. Nevertheless, when the first BSAC official, Robert Young, heard that Shimwalule had administered a *mwavi* poison ordeal to eradicate witches in the area, he had him removed from his position and replaced by his rival brother.[40] Still, the pressures to eradicate witches remained and his successor collaborated closely with the Watchtower movement in 1918 to get rid of witches.[41] In 1924, a former Shimwalule, Chandamali, angrily rebuked the Europeans for prohibiting witchfinders from performing their work, and thus for allowing witchcraft and preventing ritual purification, all of which could have led to the death of a government messenger.[42] Shimwalule, desperately trying to shore up his position in the colonial constellation of power, emphasized his political role in precolonial times. "Chitimukulu, Nkula and Mwamba always send me big presents because they know that I am their father," Shimwalule told a burial party in the early 1930s. "If I am doing my work wrong here as Shimwalule the spirits of the dead chiefs will be angry with me and punish me."[43]

With implementation of the formal policy of Indirect Rule in the late 1930s, the position of Shimwalule was thrown into even greater question. The district commissioner, W. V. Brelsford, complained of the tendency of the Shimwalule titleholders to take their "religious duties more seriously than their administrative ones."[44] Brelsford advocated an end to the chieftaincy. "He is an undertaker and a priest rather than a chief," Brelsford complained. He argued that the ritual prohibitions on leaving the Mwalule graveyard prevented Shimwalule from attending district meetings of chiefs, especially those that concerned the institutional development of Indirect Rule, such as the Native Treasury.[45] The provincial commissioner and secretary for Native affairs feared that such changes would interfere in "tribal structure," but was willing to consider the possibility of splitting Shimwalule's position into two, one a permanent chief and one a paid priest.[46]

In 1940, Brelsford discussed the possibility of incorporating Shimwalule's area with the Crocodile Clan Nkhweto chieftaincy.[47] Brelsford went on to publish an account of Shimwalule, where he argued forcefully that "as priest and undertaker he [Shimwalule] cannot be integrated in the present system, so he should relinquish his administrative functions to another and himself retain undimmed his ancient religious prestige."[48] In 1948, the Shimwalule chieftaincy was incorporated into Nkhweto's chieftaincy, an arrangement that satisfied nobody. The reigning Shimwalule refused to recognize Nkhweto's rule, and the new district commissioner, complaining of Nkhweto's insobriety and unreliability, sought to have his entire area incorporated into the more progressive chieftaincy of Nkula.[49] The Mwalule graveyard and surrounding area have remained under Nkhweto's authority up until the present day, however.

Hence European colonialism built on the structure of an older period of Bemba colonialism and transformed it. By and large, European colonialism enabled the conquest rulers of the Crocodile Clan to usurp older autochthonous owners of the land such as Shimwalule, who in the nineteenth century claimed indigeneity through their interventions with the old ancestral spirits and heroes.

All that remained was for the anthropologist, inserted into a colonial world of seemingly powerful and seemingly traditional chiefs, to formalize this arrangement by recording and disseminating a version of Bemba environmental religion that affirmed the religious authority of the Crocodile Clan elite. Most kingdoms of south-central Africa had "their" anthropologist, whether it was Max Gluckman for the Lozi kingdom, Ian Cunnison for the Kazembe kingdom, or Victor Turner for the Lunda. In the case of the Bemba, the numerous publications of Audrey Richards claimed that Bemba religion held Chitimukulu solely responsible for the well-being of the land; his very body, she argued, was tied to the welfare of the agriculture and of reproduction.[50] This hegemonic and inflated view of Chitimukulu's power came to constitute Bemba tribal knowledge. Such a view was not the invention of Richards; it was the outcome of a dialogue between European administrators and scholars and the Bemba rulers who drew selectively on ideas from the period immediately before European rule. From the perspective of these Bemba rulers, the anthropologist was a useful tool in the codification and legitimation of their hegemony. A political narrative was thus turned into a tribal tradition.

Richards was uneasy with this rendition of Bemba knowledge, however, since it was not consistently supported by her field observations. She noticed that not all aspects of Bemba knowledge or religion were directed at or from the chieftaincy. This divergence, according to Richards, was explained by the dual function of Bemba indigenous knowledge, which ritualized individual emotions on the one hand and sacralized the political structure of the tribe on the other.[51] Richards thus viewed the contrast between domestic spiritual forces (such as *ingulu* spirit possession and *imfuba* village shrines) and the public ancestral cult of the Crocodile Clan as a function of the structural tensions between the individual and the community in Bemba society. Her emphasis and fascination were nevertheless on the power embodied in the king, which she deemed far more important than the local shrine system. In her later work, she continued to insist that "all authority came from a single source, from chief to sub-chief to head man. . . . Furthermore the pattern of authority was similar at every level, though each grade of leader was associated with increased territorial, political and supernatural powers."[52]

This chapter has rendered a more historical reading of the treatment of the domestic and indigenous, introducing a struggle not linked to contradictions between tribal structure and individual autonomy, as Richards would have it, but rather to the history of an increasingly marginalized autochthonous underclass, the Bisa, and the assertion of Crocodile Clan royal authority over them. Bemba environmental knowledge appears less as an insular religion than a set of struggles over whose ancestors and which spirits had power over the land and the trees needed for people to flourish.

Conclusions

Struggles between the Crocodile Clan royals and their subjects were played out in battle, assassination, and enslavement. Underlying the physical violence was a conflict over the ownership of the land and the control over agriculture and human fertility through their respective ancestral claims. The Crocodile Clan made every effort to associate their ancestors with the land, to establish their indigeneity. They founded their political *and* spiritual center at the Mwalule graveyard and proclaimed that their ancestors intervened in nature. They appropriated sacred sites, incorporated old stories into their charter, molded their sacred relics from the debris of conquest and the magic of old. Since human and agricultural fertility were political matters, such claims formed an ideology of government. However, the Crocodile Clan's conceptual apparatus of power was not universally accepted. The Crocodile Clan needed to recognize the power and spiritual authority of the autochthones who insisted on the power of their own *ingulu* spirits and local *imfuba* shrines. On the periphery of the kingdom, local shrines and spirits challenged the Crocodile Clan's politico-religious edifice.

In the late nineteenth century, when the Crocodile Clan ruled a centralized kingdom with a monopoly of military force, they attempted to associate the land with their ancestors to an unprecedented degree, ignoring or marginalizing older concepts of indigeneity. This process continued and was strengthened during European colonialism when anthropologists and colonial chiefs molded the intellectual traces of previous struggles over environmental resources into a politically useful tribal knowledge. The hegemonic claims of the Crocodile Clan became a Bemba tribal religion.

This multilayered history of Bemba indigenous knowledge has an ironic end. An ideology of domination, a hegemonic tribal knowledge, in the late precolonial and colonial periods became an oppositional indigenous knowledge in postcolonial times. The most vibrant manifestation of this oppositional Bemba indigenous knowledge occurs at a festival, *Ukusefya pa Ngwena*, which takes place during August or September each year, near the headquarters of Chitimukulu. Attended by prominent Bemba from across the country, many of whom have long left their ancestral homes for the wealth of urban Zambia, together with politicians seeking local political support, the ceremony affirms the political charter of Chitimukulu. It begins with the enactment of Chiti and Nkole's migration to Bembaland, their deaths, and their burial. Then, performances celebrate significant events and happenings in Bemba history. One of the senior Crocodile Clan chiefs gives a speech. In 2000, for example, Chief Mwamba told the audience that the ceremony reminds "us who we are and where we came from. . . . Any Bemba who has not come to this site should consider himself a young boy." The then Zambian Minister without Portfolio (now, the Zambian President), Michael Sata, was the official government representative. He warned the Crocodile Clan chiefs to wait for Chitimukulu's approval before deciding on succession, buttressing the authority of the paramount.[53] In these traditional ceremonies, knowledge is once again mobilized for local political purpose. But it also, perhaps more significantly, brings urban elites back to rural communities and makes claims on the postcolonial state.[54] This reconstituted indigenous knowledge has thus come to speak for the subjects of a forgotten kingdom who are more marginal to the global centers of power than ever before.

Notes

1. A system of sacred governance and belonging also found in other parts of Africa. For example, for East Africa, see Parker M. Shipton, *Mortgaging the Ancestors: Ideologies of Attachment in Africa* (New Haven, CT: Yale University

Press, 2009), 85–108. For West Africa, see Sandra E. Greene, *Sacred Sites and the Colonial Encounter: A History of Meaning and Memory in Ghana* (Bloomington: Indiana University Press, 2002). For a nearby central African example, see the graveyard of the Kazembe kingdom, as discussed in David M. Gordon, "History on the Luapula Retold: Landscape, Memory, and Identity in the Kazembe Kingdom," *Journal of African History* 47, no. 1 (2006): 21–42, esp. 37–40. For a similar central African sacred shrine (but not a graveyard), see J. Matthew Schoffeleers, *River of Blood: The Genesis of a Martyr Cult in Southern Malawi, c. A.D. 1600* (Madison: University of Wisconsin Press, 1992).

2. Audrey I. Richards's most influential book is *Land, Labour and Diet in Northern Rhodesia: An Economic Study of the Bemba Tribe* (London: Oxford University Press, 1939). The functionalist exploration of Bemba kingship rituals is best explicated in Audrey I. Richards, "Keeping the King Divine," *Proceedings of the Royal Anthropological Institute of Great Britain and Ireland* (1968): 23–35.

3. An influential restudy of Richards is Henrietta L. Moore and Megan Vaughan, *Cutting Down Trees: Gender, Nutrition, and Agricultural Change in the Northern Province of Zambia, 1890–1990* (Portsmouth, NH: Heinemann, 1994).

4. Luc de Heusch, *The Drunken King, or, The Origin of the State*, transl. Roy Willis (Bloomington: Indiana University Press, 1982).

5. For a gendered alternative to male Bemba religion, see Hugo F. Hinfelaar, *Bemba-Speaking Women of Zambia in a Century of Religious Change, 1892–1992* (Leiden: Brill, 1994).

6. Jan Vansina, *Oral Tradition as History* (Madison: University of Wisconsin Press, 1985).

7. For south-central Africa, the religious aspects of the oral tradition have been discussed by Maxwell and the cosmogenic and symbolic aspects by Luc de Heusch. I am indebted to both their interpretations. Kevin Maxwell, *Bemba Myth and Ritual: The Impact of Literacy on an Oral Culture* (New York: Peter Lang, 1983), 36–45; de Heusch, *The Drunken King*, 229–45. For the liminal aspects of the oral tradition, see Maxwell, *Bemba Myth and Ritual*, 39.

8. For a complete account of the Nachituti narrative and the politico-religious relationships that it invoked, see David M. Gordon, *Nachituti's Gift: Economy, Society, and Environment in Central Africa* (Madison: University of Wisconsin Press, 2006), 27–61.

9. For an evaluation of the factual basis of the oral tradition and the approximate dating of the founding of Chitimukulu, see Andrew Roberts, *A History of the Bemba: Political Growth and Change in North-Eastern Zambia Before 1900* (London: Longman, 1973), 56–65.

10. A substantially different version omits the story of the tower and instead discusses father-son discord, brought about by a strict father and unruly sons

who refused to clean the royal shrines, in Paul B. Mushindo, *A Short History of the Bemba (As Narrated by a Bemba)* (Lusaka: National Educational Company of Zambia, 1977), 2–4.

11. See, for example, the story of Kimpimpi, in Leon Verbeek, *Le Monde des Esprits au Sud-est du Shaba et au Nord de la Zambia* (Rome: Libreria Ateneo Salesiano, 1990), 89–112.

12. For sacred Luba kingship, see Thomas Reefe, *The Rainbow and the Kings: A History of the Luba Empire to 1891* (Berkeley: University of California Press, 1981).

13. According to Labrecque, the chief's "head wife" danced with Chilumbulu's skin; this is not actually inconsistent, as according to Richards, the "head wife," who performs many ritual acts, is expected to be chaste and past childbearing age. Richards, "Keeping the King Divine," 32. Eduoard Labrecque, *Beliefs and Religious Practices of the Bemba and Neighbouring Tribes,* trans. Patrick Boyd (Chinsali, Zambia: Ilondola Language Center, 1982)

14. Labrecque, *Beliefs and Religious Practices*, 35.

15. For Luba *mulopwe* and earth priests, see Reefe, *Rainbow and Kings*, esp. 46.

16. The above version is based on several accounts, especially: Edouard Labrecque, "La tribu des Babemba 1: Les Origines des Babemba," *Anthropos* 28 (1933): 633–48. Republished in 1968 as Edouard Labrecque, "Les Origines des Babemba de la Rhodésie du Nord (Zambia)" *Annali del Pontificio Museo Missionario Etnologico* 32 (1968): 349-329; Paul B. Mushindo, *A Short History of the Bemba (As Narrated by a Bemba)* (Lusaka: National Educational Company of Zambia, 1977); "Manuscript of Bemba Origins," in Audrey Richards Papers, 1/67, London School of Economics (hereafter cited as LSE).

17. The *babenye* relics were not exclusively located at Mwalule, and were probably relocated to Lubemba through the twentieth century. The traditional residence of *bamukabenye* indicates that they were previously held at Mwalule. Labrecque, *Beliefs and Religious Practices*, 15–16; Brelsford, *Shimwalule*, 212; Richards, *Land, Labour and Diet*, 358–59.

18. The version above is common to Labrecque's and Mushindo's narrations. For an alternative version of the founding of Nkhweto and the meaning of Chilinda, see the transcription of "Tape-recording by Chief Nkweto Mulenga, 17 May 1965," in Roberts, *History of Bemba*, 378–80.

19. As argued by Hinfelaar in *Women and Religious Change*, 19–33.

20. For Shimwalule's details, see Vernon Brelsford, "Shimwalule: A Study of Bemba Chief and Priest, " *African Studies* 1 (1942) 207–23. Further details in Annexure 3 Tour Report 5/1939. "Mwalule and the Shimwalule." SEC 2/751, NAZ.

21. The political process is best covered in Roberts, *History of Bemba*, 125–63. For trade, see pp. 168–214. For "constitutional" changes in Bemba polity after 1860, linked to increase in trade, see Richard Werbner, "Federal Administration, Rank, and Civil Strife Among Bemba Royals and Nobles," *Africa: Journal of the International African Institute* 37, no. 1 (January 1967): 22–49. For general transformations across this region, see David M. Gordon, "The Abolition of the Slave Trade and the Transformation of the South Central African Interior," *William and Mary Quarterly*, Special Edition on Global Consequences of 1807 Abolition. LXVI, no. 4 (October 2009): 915–38. For a comparable intensification of the ritual process in nineteenth-century Dahomey, see Edna G. Bay, *Wives of the Leopard: Gender, Politics, and Culture in the Kingdom of Dahomey* (Charlottesville: University Press of Virginia, 1998), 250–53.

22. Contrary to Andrew Roberts's claim of a growth of "physical, secular" power from the late nineteenth century, Roberts, *History of the Bemba*, 312.

23. Mushindo, *Historical Notes*, 68.

24. Richards, "Keeping the King Divine," 26–30.

25. Ibid., 30. Godfrey and Monica Wilson observed similar rites among the Nyakyusa in southern Tanzania. Richards's data on this practice derives from Godfrey Wilson, who undertook limited fieldwork among the Bemba while studying ChiBemba language in 1938. Letters from Godfrey Wilson to Audrey Richards, November 14, 25, 30, and December 13, 1938, B 4.7, B 880, University of Cape Town, Manuscripts and Archives.

26. Richards, *Land, Labour and Diet*, 361.

27. For precolonial burials, see W. V. Brelsford, *Aspects of Bemba Chieftainship* (Livingstone, Northern Rhodesia: Rhodes-Livingstone Institute, 1944), 26–27; and his "Shimwalule," 219. For burials in the colonial period that did not involve any human killing but referenced many similar rites, see Brelsford, *Aspects of Bemba Chieftainship*, 27–37; District Commissioner's Report on "The Burial Of Chitmukulu IX Mubanga" in SEC 2-307, NAZ; Aaron Mwenya, "The Burial of Chitimukulu Mubanga," *African Affairs* 46, no. 183 (April 1947): 101–4.

28. He thereby challenged the leadership of Chitimukulu Chitankwa's successor, Sampa, as the Bemba paramount. Roberts, *History of Bemba*, 217–29.

29. Mushindo, *Short History*, 53–54.

30. Thomas, *Historical Notes*, 49.

31. Thomas, *Historical Notes*, 43–46; Mushindo, *Short History*, 51–53, 87–88.

32. Richards, "Keeping the King Divine," 26.

33. For comparable appreciation of Batwa indigeneity in West Central Africa, see Kairn A. Klieman, *"The Pygmies Were Our Compass": Bantu and*

Batwa in the History of West Central Africa, Early Times to c. 1900 C.E. (Portsmouth, NH: Heinemann, 2003).

34. Dugald Campbell, "A Few Notes on Butwa: An African Secret Society," *Man* 14, no. 28 (1914): 76–81; Dugald Campbell, *In the Heart of Bantuland: A Record of Twenty-Nine Years' Pioneering in Central Africa* (1922, reprint New York: Negro University Press, 1969), 96–106. Also see Mwelwa C. Musambachime, "The Ubutwa Society in Eastern Shaba and Northeast Zambia to 1920," *International Journal of African Historical Studies* 27, no. 1 (1994): 77–99. Verbeek suggests that Ubutwa might have been an adaptation of Christian doctrines learned from the Portuguese in the Tete region of East Africa during the eighteenth and nineteenth centuries. The best evidence for this is the spread by Ubutwa of the term "Lesa" for God—the term adopted by missionaries—and "Luchele Nganga" for Lesa's son, presumably Jesus. Verbeek, *Le Monde*, 13.

35. Raban Chanda Interview with Maxem Mulinda, Kanswe's Village, March 29, 1974, in Mwelwa Musambachime, edited and annotated, *The Oral History of Mansa, Zambia* (Lusaka: University of Zambia, 1996), 56.

36. Raban Chanda Interview with Lusili Chibuye, April 25, 1974, in *Oral History of Mansa*, 117.

37. Raban Chanda Interview with Timomthy Chila, April 25, 1974, in *Oral History of Mansa*, 110–11.

38. He termed them "tulubi." Livingstone, *Last Journals*, 353

39. For Mambwe and Sikapemba shrine priest, see Macpherson Interview with Henry Siame (Kasumo), Kasumo's Village, Isoka, January 9,1969, box 3, Centre for the Study of Christianity in the Non-Western World, Edinburgh. For the Chishinga and Makumba, see Roy Philpot, "Makumba-the Baushi Tribal God," *Journal of the Royal Anthropological Institute of Great Britain and Ireland* 66 (1936): 189–208, esp. 197; Author Interview with Chelembi Mwewa, Chilembi Village, December 29, 2000; Daniel Yambayamba interview wih Langboy Chakomaulwa, Mabumba Village, April 24, 1974, in Musambachime, ed. and ann. *Oral History of Mansa*, 156.

40. W. V. Brelsford, "Shimwalule: A Study of Bemba Chief and Priest," *African Studies* 1 (1942): 207–23, esp. 211. The original DC's report by Brelsford upon which the above article was based, but with considerable more details, including rumors of European deaths at Mwalule, can be found in Annexure 3 Tour Report 5/1939, SEC 2/751, NAZ.

41. Fields, *Revival and Rebellion*, 161.

42. Based on the Richards papers 1/34, LSE, Megan Vaughan details Chandamali's anger over the death of the messenger, Chanda, in "'Divine Kings': Sex, Death and Anthropology in Inter-War East/Central Africa," *Journal of African History* 49 (2008): 383–401, esp. 395–96.

43. Brelsford, "Shimwalule," 219.

44. Tour Report No. 6. of 1935, NP 1/1/3, NAZ.

45. Annexure 3 Tour Report 5/1939, SEC 2/751, NAZ.

46. PC Comments on Chinsali Tour Report 5/39; TF Standford, Acting Chief Sec. to PC, Kasama, January 12, 1940, SEC 2/731, NAZ.

47. Annexure 2, Tour Report 1/1940, SEC 2/752, NAZ.

48. Brelsford, "Shimwalule," 223. Tour Reports 2–3, 1948, NP 1/1/22, NAZ.

49. Tour Reports 2–3, 1948, NP 1/1/22, NAZ.

50. Richards, "Keeping the King Divine," 23–35. Also see the recent reevaluation by Vaughan, "'Divine Kings.'"

51. Richards, *Land, Labour and Diet*, 359.

52. Richards, "Keeping the King Divine," 32–33.

53. Recorded by Zambia National Broadcoast Corporation Documentary on Ukusefya pa Ngwena, August 19–21, 2000.

54. For a similar ceremony among the nearby eastern Lunda, see David M. Gordon, "The Cultural Politics of a Traditional Ceremony: Mutomboko and the Performance of History on the Luapula," *Comparative Studies in Society and History* 46, no. 1 (2004): 63–83.

CHAPTER 10

Recruiting Nature

Snakes, Serpents, and Social Movements in East Africa and North America

Parker Shipton

SNAKES AND serpents make symbols for expressing hope or dread, and symbols make movements of religious reform and of social and political rebellion. Now and then in eastern Africa, snakes, birds, and other animals have played a role as focal points in uprisings variously peaceful and violent. Considering a few such movements against a background of ones better known from North America and elsewhere, these pages suggest some recurring themes in animal-human and human-human relations. These are not hard-and-fast rules, perhaps, but more fittingly understood as commonalities of a more slippery, winding sort.[1]

Messianic and millenarian movements. Crisis cults and cargo cults. Nativist revivals, ghost dance religions, and apocalyptic uprisings. These are some of the names given to phenomena sometimes classed together under the broader heading of "revitalization movements"—as faiths, as sects, and as continuing historical processes.[2] Commonly associated with autochthony or indigeneity, and with hopes for sweeping change, these entities and processes show endless variety in context and details of expression, and yet some striking similarities, too. The role of prophets and the use of animal symbols, for instance.

Many of the movements are interpretable as responses to contact between human groups or categories with radically different assumptions about the world, and to the social hardship that such contact occasions. They occur where one people has subjugated another or seems to enjoy unshared advantages in life that are hard to justify or explain, and the other found itself impoverished, disempowered, or struck disproportionately with illness or other hardship. Seen as entities fixed in time or place, they can look like individually insignificant gangs or clubs. Seen more as a dynamic process, revitalization movements can seem more like fledgling, transforming churches, or in other cases as nascent movements for political secession and independence. Indeed, some of the world's most popular and enduring religions, and most widespread faith communities, began as local prophetic movements not too unlike ones to be described here.[3] And others have grown into or contributed to broader struggles for independence or sovereignty, with results hard to predict in their times. The young and recurring movements concern themselves with power, wealth, beauty, righteousness, salvation, or more often, a hopeful mix of these. Revitalizations belong to no single discipline.

Nor are they even easy to define. They share, I shall suggest, what philosopher Ludwig Wittgenstein called a "family likeness," constituting in other words what anthropologist Rodney Needham called a "polythetic class."[4] This means that there may be no single feature appearing in all members of the set, nor any member of the set possessing every defining feature . . . but that enough features recur in enough members to make observers perceive connections between the members of the set. Conceived this way, the movements fit into no conceptual box, but maybe better into a sliding category.

This brief, preliminary essay considers a few instances of locally rooted but more eclectically inspired movements in East Africa that may bear comparison with experiences of North American Indian people who have participated in their own movements of long-reaching hope for world reform or radical restoration—ones bearing some resemblance as well to others in Europe, Melanesia, and elsewhere.[5] While confined to no particular era, and to no country, the movements proved more likely to occur in some times and places than in others.[6] Here, then, are some of the main themes that recur: First, an origin in a context of political, economic, and other subjugation and marginalization. Second, a prophet's revelation, with instruction or commandments, direct or indirect. Third, an emphasis on a chosen animal or its kind—and an attempt through these animals to recruit or co-opt some greater power of nature to a cause. An underlying attempt, sometimes unspoken, seems often to be, fourth, the redirection of attention to places and times familiar to the people concerned, and thus a restoration of those people's damaged dignity or collective self-esteem. To these one might add that the image of a feared and reviled creature can also be restored or inverted in the same movements. Revitalization movements, I suggest, are likely to be relocalization and redignification movements too.

Part of a Pattern

The study of prophetic, millenarian, and related movements has fascinated anthropologists and others in the social studies since before Lewis Henry Morgan, in the 1840s, studied the movement and faith called Gai'wiio or the Longhouse religion. This one was begun at the end of the previous century by Handsome Lake, a Seneca prophet, among Iroquois (Hodenosaunee) in western and northern New York and surroundings.[7] It was only one of a long wave of countless protest and revitalization movements among American Indians across the country and continent throughout the nineteenth century and in varied forms into our times.[8] Other well-known examples included the northwest coast "Indian Shaker" movement, which coalesced around a logger of Squaxin origin, John Slocum, or Squ-sach-tum, held to have died and come back to life in 1881; and the "ghost dance" or circle dance movement, which, while drawing on earlier inspirations of like kind, was rekindled by a vision of Jack Wilson or Wovoka in 1889.[9] This one swept the western and midwestern North American plains, and was repressed with measures including the infamous slaughter at Wounded Knee.

Feather dance religions, practiced in diverse ceremonies around and about, are other variants. These and sun dance traditions may seem like dances, musical performances, prayer reunions, healing venues, initiation customs, or religions; they are any and all these things, and moreover they change names as one moves around the country and different features are brought into their names as elements are added and dropped or just selectively emphasized: dream dances, earth lodges, eagle feathers, green corn, and so on. Usually no single name or analytical descriptor captures their essence.

Nor does it do to think of the narratives and celebrations involved as being about distinct species, since a recurring theme in the personal visions and shared stories (and often dance masks, too) is precisely the transformation of a member of one species into one of another, the revelation of an inner animal as a kind of alter ego, or the acquisition of an animal's power by a human. The point is not so much taxonomy or typology as mixture and merger. This is a point easily misconstrued as merely irrational, when it may have its own subtler sorts of reason behind it, not least aesthetic and political.[10]

Few examples of prophetic vision with animals as nature's ostensible messengers to humans, and lenders of power to them, are better known than those of Hehaka Sapa, or Black Elk, an Oglala Lakota (of Sioux) who was reported to have experienced such visions from about the age of nine in the early 1870s. Here it is birds and horses who play the big parts—especially the spotted eagle, who, as the story gets recounted, not only speaks but merges into the visionary himself. The horses seem to partake of, and bestow, the power of lightning, the glory of sunset, and other forces and marvels of nature. Black Elk's visions, transcribed in memoirs only much later, helped establish him as one of the Lakota's most influential "medicine men" (healer-diviners), while he also experienced signal military confrontations with the U.S. Cavalry, including the turning points at Little Big Horn, in his youth in 1876, and in 1890 at the massacre at Wounded Knee.[11] Prophets like these, in troubled times and clashes of cultures, can draw big followings; and this one's influence and renown have extended far beyond American Indians.

American anthropologists since James Mooney have studied up close these hard-to-name, hard-to-describe phenomena carrying many meanings and serving many functions.[12] Meanwhile, "armchair" comparative ethnologists like Edward Tylor and James Frazer helped build the comparative symbolic study of political-religious movements, including some rebellious ones, into the timbers of social anthropology and literary studies in Britain in the late nineteenth and early twentieth centuries. Emile Durkheim, Lucien Lévy-Bruhl, and Max Weber wrote these meanwhile into sociology and anthropology in continental Europe, as these were becoming professionalized disciplines.

Anthropologists' decades-long fascination with totemism, defined and redefined, has also applied itself to these movements, since humans who identified as individuals or groups with particular sorts of animals as their symbols could usually be called totemic in one respect or another.[13] Historians, political scientists, and psychologists have become increasingly interested, too, and more than a few theologians more curious or tolerantly acquiescent. Among the big changes in recent decades has been the increase in attention to female leadership and influence within spiritually inspired movements, an attention by both female and male scholars alike in several disciplines.[14] The change is reflected in continuing work on Africa.

The several African movements to be briefly described in this chapter have found their flashpoints in much the same ways as the North American ghost dance movement, Indian Shaker religion, and Longhouse religion— with individual prophets and their visions or revelations, sometimes inspired by comparable earlier ones, and often disseminated with the help of close accomplices, male or female. The ones to be described here, though, are ones of a more particular sort, one found in any continent. In them a human reports a crucial encounter with an animal or animal-like spirit. It may happen in a home visit or a trip away, or in a dream or trance. The human becoming prophet may be a male or female, young or old, and the encounter may be voluntary or not. But more often than not, it seems, the individual is someone whose background and experience bridge cultures or traditions in some way, for instance someone who went away to school or worked for a period in close contact with a colonizer. The animal or animal spirit may simply converse with the prophet-in-the-making, or in some variants the animal swallows the human and the latter emerges with new learning, wisdom, or ability.[15]

Snakes and Serpents: Nature's Shape-Shifters and Go-Betweens

Among the many kinds of animals available for choosing, some kinds seem to appear more regularly than others to fill the role of messenger of revelation, of guardian spirit, of ally for the prophet and movement, or all three. No animal appears more commonly in such a role than the snake or the bird. Where it is birds and their feathers that seem to appear most often in the North American variants, one sees snakes picked more prominently in East African ones, though both serve some similar roles in each continent. These creatures share some key features that lend them well to the part assigned. They can hide camouflaged in irregular shapes, or dazzle with brilliant colors and designs. Both can shed and renew their covering (snakes their skins, birds their feathers) in a way that eminently suits them to symbolizing death and rebirth, or immortality. Snakes can also symbolize death by constriction or poisoning, though most snake species in fact lack poison. Connoting death comes easily also to some birds: nocturnal raptors like owls, scavengers like vultures or buzzards, including condors; or black omnivorous scavengers like crows and ravens.

Snakes have further features that seem to command particular fascination. They can move in ways hard for most people to understand. They can swallow animals several times their girth. With phallic look and feel (never lost on Freudians), but able in some species (like pythons) to give birth to fifty or more offspring at a time, snakes make consummate symbols of both male and female sexuality, and of human if not also terrestrial fertility. Snakes can move on or under the ground or water, or in trees; and they can be seen to resemble whirlwinds or waterspouts linking surface and sky. Connecting life and death, bridging the sexes, and linking the elements, the snake makes a versatile figure for poetic metaphor, imaginative dreaming, and the expression of human fears and hopes.

Some of this can be well inferred from ancient scripture, as in the book of Genesis with its story of the serpent who tempted Adam and Eve and is made the enemy of humans forever. Or in dramas like Sophocles's *Antigone* or Aeschylus's *Oresteia* trilogy, wherein the snake is used to symbolize human vengefulness, betrayal, and in the latter drama matricidal treachery. But stories like these, showing scorn of snakes, do not fit every culture's template. They misfit many African traditions, in which certain snakes are viewed more ambivalently as dangerous but also potentially beneficial to humans if respected and treated well.[16] Nor do they neatly fit the ambivalences or complexities of serpent cults or faiths elsewhere.[17] Nor, again, do the antiserpent stories fit the agendas of present-day environmentalists or animal-rights advocates concerned with animals as sentient beings, subjects as well as objects of perception, thought, and feeling—a subject reaching beyond our topic, but no less important.

Participants in human social movements involving animal messengers or allies may think of the superhuman power to which these offer access as a diffused, impersonal power; or alternatively as one anthropomorphized as ancestors, other spirits, or a deity. The animal linking earth and sky, life and death, human and divine may be thought able to communicate in language intelligible to the prophet—and maybe to the dead or a deity as well. Co-opting the extra power, through this animal or part-animal, is one of the keys to gaining credibility and adherents. For if a tiny, embattled minority can claim the power of nature or divinity (or some sort of divine nature) on its side, then its members can feel emboldened to take on forces more numerous, or better armed, trained, or organized than themselves. Which is what we shall see some do.

A Decentering Effect

Movements of autochthonous (or "nativistic") rebellion and revitalization seem to occur more commonly—or at least more visibly, in some parts of the world than others. They seem to come to light most often where indigenous political systems don't include centralized political control, permanent hierarchical offices, or large standing armies. And wherever else they have been overrun. Something many parts of Native America and tropical Africa have in common—and much of Melanesia, too—is the ignominy of subjugation since European contact. Nor, for some, was this the first time it had happened. In parts of both Africa and North America, enslavement of captives was common practice before European arrival. This was true, for instance, on the Pacific Northwest coast of America, and in areas of inland eastern Africa that Arab caravans could reach by trade routes from the coast.

Something else that both Native American people and African people south of the Sahara have had in common over the past century and a half, as a result of conquest and colonization, has been a deeply shaken sense of position in the world. Some have had ancestors and elders who once told of humanity as springing with buffalo from caves in the Black Hills (a Lakota conception) or from a giant clamshell in the Pacific Northwest (a Haida story). Others have learned from their grannies in childhood that their forebears once owned all the world's cattle (as many Maasai young have been told). These have all seen their ideal relations with nonhuman animals challenged. People forcibly evicted from their homelands like Native Americans east of the Mississippi in the early 1830s, or Kenyans, Zimbabweans, or South Africans evicted for "white" settler farming later in that century and early in the next, have focused new attention to fixed places on the landscape, such as graves, ancestral homes, forest groves, or the sites of important battles, which become sacred sites, but ones not always accessible. How welcome, to any such people, might be a movement that says in some way about where they happen to live, "Yes, this place *does* matter—and so do we."

The litanies of troubles these movements might address by bringing new hope are too lengthy to rehearse in full. They variously include new diseases for those lacking immunities; racial prejudice and discrimination; linguistic discrimination; diplomatic and legal disadvantage; geographic dislocation and confinement; devastation and replacement of traditional food sources; and economic subjugation including confiscation and job blockage. Land loss (including after individual titling), the collective identity loss it can entail, and alcohol and other intoxicants have also played their parts. The social effects of all these include status and ranking shake-ups, intragroup conflicts, and social fragmentation. Some of these processes can combine in vicious circles, to be overcome only through great ingenuity and resilience, or by unusually successful aid.

One strategy for handling the many hardships of dislocation and decentering, and concentrating that attention, is to focus new attention on a particular animal species—as an emblem of a people, of their past, and of their possibilities for the future. When one such creature perishes, in whatever place, another can sooner or later reappear. The choice suggests that some human minds, and possibly most minds under severe duress, are susceptible to appeal of the kind of symbolism by which these particular animals evoke connections between human and nonhuman powers.[18]

Rebel movements do not always address directly the problems that caused them, if these can even be known. Some may derive in part from adherents' own experience of losing parents, and from the generalized fears and anxieties resulting.[19] Or from individuals' having been grown up in a squeezed place in the birth orders of their families or their childhood cohorts, with elder children having taken already the easy roles of enforcers . . . and needing some sort of rebellion—any sort—as a way out.[20] In East African settings, where it sometimes happens that elder or favored brothers have taken the lion's share of family resources for cattle to marry with, or the money for schooling or migrating to town, joining a rebel gang or church can be about the only way left to procure cattle, instruction, or a ticket of one's own. Factors like adverse climate change mix with human factors like these to raise social tensions all around.[21] Some of the disgruntled or disappointed may direct rebellion at parties they deem outside their societies, others at ones within.[22] Movements of rebellion or liberation can accumulate other etiology, other problems to be rooted out, and other goals, temporal or spiritual. Their pathways of cause and effect have a way of snaking in and out of each other.

The inspirations are not just flights of imagination, though—even if they may arise under duress, involve cognitive simplification, and result in stretched reaching for power or authority. Many of them are practical purification movements, too. They can involve strict codes of behavior for self-restraint, for instance against adultery, partner or kin abuse, or gambling. Some explicitly counter witchcraft or other mystical or occult evils as perceived. Their doctrines can be staunchly pacifist in ends or means, but they can also be ways of mobilizing armies. Some of them rely on mind-altering drugs, for instance in motivating youth to fight; but then again, some are strict temperance movements as well or instead, condemning all alcohol or other substance abuse. Even the ones that missionaries or administrators have so often condemned as demon cults can come to look more benign, or at least morally complex (whether forgivable or just pitiable) from a distance or in hindsight. Not all faiths or traditions that involve respect or reverence for snakes and serpents, anyway, are apocalyptic in vision, or rebellious, subversive, or militant in aim or effect. Some just arise as ways to try to make rain, gain wealth, or heal the sick. In these ways they defy general statements.

Some East African Examples

And yet there are still patterns to be observed. Below are briefly described some African prophetic and spirit-led movements that I think share some salient features with some American Indian movements mentioned above, while taking on some distinctively African forms and expressions. Most of these movements have already been described well and thoroughly enough, in separate bodies of literature, to permit comparisons that can only be started here.

One is the Mumbo movement, traceable at least back to around 1913 in western Kenya, by Lake Victoria (also called Nam Lolwe or Nyanza), near a part of Luo country where I have lived and conducted research. Like many parts of Africa south of the Sahara, this is a region of mixed farming and herding where snakes receive very mixed treatment. Some are feared, reviled, and likely to be beaten or stoned to death on sight (as an excited group of young men once did to a hapless seven-foot cobra who had been found idly reposing one day in a house next to mine). But at the same time others, notably the seldom-seen python, are treated with great respect and even reverence; and so, by extension, are the places in the wild (hilltops, rock formations, ponds) where pythons are thought to live. There are also many old stories about human-python contact. One concerns a python who lured a young girl away from a group of a dozen friends and into his home and gave her the most beautiful belly tattoo of any of the dozen—a tattoo like his own. She returned to tell her envious friends that it was done by "the rope of the jungle" (or of the bush, *thim*).[23] In another Luo story, reminiscent of many others around the continent, the serpent takes on wider powers:

> In Luo history there is . . . the case of Nyang'idi, a python of monstrous proportions, which, in keeping with tradition here and elsewhere, was thought to bring fertility and prosperity to the land. If, however, on its peregrinations through the countryside (where it roamed free and unhindered) it was not duly welcomed, it was apt to wreak vengeance on the culprits by bringing famine to their land. It lived in a small lake, Nam Kanyaboli in Alego location, and slid abroad gaily decked in strings of cowrie shells [another common African symbol of

sexuality and fertility, used sometimes as decoration and sometimes in the past as currency]. When rain was needed on the land, Nyang'idi would stand on the surface of the lake, and, appearing like a great rainbow, would reach up and puncture the skin of heaven.[24]

This is the snake spirit as intermediary, as boundary-breaker. The human who gets tattooed like the snake, and the snake who wears jewelry like a human and is treated like (or as) a guest, seem together almost a calculated attempt to blur distinction between human and animal, just as the last line of the paragraph blurs the boundaries between animal, human, and sky. One thing slides into another.

The Mumbo movement began within a decade of military fighting in the region for "pacification" and the establishment of the first Christian church missions in the area. It happened just after the establishment of district colonial headquarters and within a few years of the first substantial taxes and conscripted labor as the First World War approached. The movement's own origins are traced to Luo prophet Onyango Dunde and his encounter with a creature sometimes said to be a python and sometimes said to be a giant serpent in the form of a waterspout over the lake. Some say the serpent swallowed him—possibly a borrowing from the biblical story of Jonah and the whale—before speaking to him in these alleged words, in various ways pretty typical of such prophetic encounters: "I am the God Mumbo whose two homes are in the Sun and the Lake. I have chosen you to be my mouthpiece. Those whom I personally choose and also those who acknowledge me, will live together in plenty. Their crops will grow of themselves and there will be no need to work . . . but all unbelievers and their families and cattle will die out.

"Christianity is rotten [*mbovu*]," and "Europeans are your enemies," Mumbo instructed him to inform the people of Alego in particular and Africans in general, and he would see to their riddance. "Daily sacrifice—preferably the males—of cattle, sheep, goats, and fowls shall be made to me. More especially do I prefer black bulls. Have no fear of sacrificing and I will cause unlimited black cattle to come to you from the Lango, Maasai, Nandi, and Kipsigis [all names of neighboring ethnic groups whose members sometimes raided Luo cattle]. When this is done, I will provide them with as many more as they want from the lake."[25] Followers smoked cannabis, wore skins, grew their hair long, and refused to bathe. Only a small, unknown minority of the western Kenyan population ever committed to this new faith; but even so, it so perturbed British colonial authorities that they sent the leaders they could catch to jail on the coast. But the movement resurged several times, including unknown numbers of Luo (speakers of a Nilotic tongue) and Gusii (speakers of a "Bantu" tongue), before subsiding in the 1950s.[26] It jumped across periods of time, that is, and across ethnolinguistic boundaries, too.

A second movement to consider is one resembling the Mumbo movement in some ways, but more militant in its organization and execution. This is the Holy Spirit movement of northern Uganda, led by prophet Alice Lakwena from the mid-1980s to the mid-1990s—in a time of severe deprivation and hardship occasioned in part by southern domination of the country, and in part by related civil wars on both sides of the Uganda-Sudan border. In one version of the movement's official narrative, related by Mike Ocan, an Acholi woman named Alice Auma, from Gulu, became possessed by the spirit Lakwena in May 1985 while in Paraa, in a national park. This is where she had gone "to hold court on all creatures on earth." This place may be taken to symbolize not only wilderness, or no-man's-land (*tim*), but arguably foreignness too. The wild animals, the water, and their mountain, proving innocent of the country's bloodshed, were pronounced free of sin.[27] Indeed, after a lamb sacrifice by her father, some of the animals became Alice's and the Holy Spirits' allies in their war against sin and the government of Uganda. Snakes and eagles, along with bees—and rivers, rocks, and mountains too—were among the beings the Holy Spirit movement recruited to its side, while trees and termite mounds were counted as enemies. As for the snakes:

> Snakes had the task of watching over the Holy Spirit soldiers. After the victory over the NRA [the rival National Resistance Army], Lakwena declared that the sinners who still did not want to repent would be punished. If Holy Spirit soldiers encountered snakes, they were not permitted to kill them, but had to say to them: "You are my fellow soldier. Show me respect!" Some snakes were kept in the yard, while others fought actively at the side of the Holy Spirit soldiers. They advanced on the enemy and forced them to leave their cover, thus allowing them to be hit by the Holy Spirit soldiers.[28]

Alas for Alice Lakwena and the Holy Spirits, however, the government army (and the trees, and the termites . . .) ultimately proved too strong for them. Nor did the shea oil butter and ochre used for "bulletproofing," or even the chant of "James Bond! James Bond!" stop the enemy bullets. The

Holy Spirits left alive disbanded without making it to Kampala, and Alice eventually fled to obscurity across the border in Kenya, eventually to die in a refugee camp in northern Kenya in 2007.

But her notorious successor Joseph Kony, head of the rebel Lord's Resistance Army, originally from Acholi country in northern Uganda but roaming and raiding across borders, has claimed to have been possessed by her spirit and others'—and to have taken them over as his, too. Whatever the rights and wrongs involved (and there have been more than a few atrocities committed by government and government-loosed soldiers, too), the recent history of mutual raiding, fighting, forced resettlement, and struggles for readjustment in and around Africa is one of contemporary Africa's grisliest.[29]

All these movements—Mumbo, the Holy Spirits, and the LRA—have involved groups speaking languages deemed Nilotic, particularly Luo (in western Kenya, for Mumbo) and Acholi (in northern Uganda, for the Holy Spirits and LRA). But they have all grown to include members of other ethnic groups and language families too. This is pretty typical of spirit-led resistance movements. They may rely heavily at first on members of a particular kin or ethnic group, but as they expand to include others, they sometimes experience a tension between these kin and ethnic loyalties and the more universalistic doctrines their leaders preach.

Meanwhile, a quieter kind of human snake movement, without such a militant prophet or apocalyptic designs for world reform, has arisen in the Luo country in Kenya in recent decades. This movement has focused on a series of living pythons appearing intermittently, given the name Omieri (or sometimes Omweri), and deemed by some to belong to a line of descent from a nineteenth-century woman ancestor who has changed form. At least one analyst has likened her inconstancy to the vagaries of economic fortunes and the flukiness of "development" in a neoliberal era.[30] Omieri, when welcomed into houses, fed, and otherwise well treated by her human hosts, is thought to bring rain and to be a harbinger of good fortune. This python faith has close counterparts in other farming areas of Africa, for instance in the Fipa country of southern Tanzania, in the Igbo country of southeast Nigeria, and in the Bemba country of Zambia, where pythons are also respected and revered as representing powerful forces that can be put to human good if respected and welcomed.[31] The case of the latest Omieri, the snake who attracted ephemeral press and lucrative tourist attention before she laid her dozens of eggs and made her way away, only added to her local image as representing capricious providence.

A fuller treatment of snake-based faiths in Africa would need also to touch upon such figures as Mami Wata (or Mommy or Mammy Water). She is a western- and central-African temptress water spirit—she could be called a mermaid—who is sometimes depicted as half human, half snake; sometimes as a human surrounded with one or more snakes; sometimes as half human, half fish. In a way like the diabolic "uncle" mine-owning spirit reported by some Bolivian miners as making contracts with them, Mami Wata can reward her followers' prayers with wealth; but she can later extract a heavy price, including human life itself.[32] And like many of the other spiritual figures and movements described above, this one cuts across the lines of ethnolinguistic groups.[33]

Looking Back Across

Whether the movements in Native America that have most closely approximated the African movements noted above—the Mumbo, Holy Spirits, and LRA movements, and the hitherto gentler Omieri faith—have so commonly involved snakes or serpents would be hard to say. It would be easier to claim that they usually involve birds—as in the eagle feather, now such a ubiquitous sign of American Indians and Native life, seen in artistic imagery and in powwows and other gatherings just about everywhere; or the owl feather, such a common symbol of death. Snakes certainly figure in more than a few stories and practices with religious dimensions in Native America, north and south. They appear in forms as long-established as the Mesoamerican plumed serpent depicted in millennia-old sites like Teotihuacan and Tenochtitlan (a polysemic fertility symbol often associated with the deity named Quetzalcoatl); performances as famous as the biennial Hopi snake-antelope ceremonial cycle where, in public portions, rattlers may be picked up in mouths; and representations as mysterious as the fer-de-lance patterns I once observed on subterranean murals painted by anonymous people in Tierradentro, Colombia, where some such snakes still lived around, but where the original intent or significance of the designs remained untraceable.[34] The uses and meanings of these images, stories, and ritual practices are so various, and knowledge of some of the names, objects, practices, and interpretations at the same time so often restricted (even where ceremonies have a tourist face or phase), as to defy easy generalization.

Among North Americans who do not deem themselves Native or American Indian, one sees snakes sometimes used in emblems of subversive, ill-fated military-political organizations like the Symbionese

Liberation Army (SLA) in the early 1970s. Known for kidnapping and co-opting newspaper heiress Patricia Hearst (temporarily renamed "Tania"), this utopian socialist mini-movement used as its insignia a seven-headed cobra. Probably adapted from an ancient Indian and Sri Lankan figure, it was given the meanings of seven virtues, expressed in Swahili terms, by the SLA's African American organizer Donald DeFreeze. Nearly all Americans who knew of the SLA seemed to consider it a band of dangerous outlaws on the radical fringe. But it would be a mistake to think the snake represents only evil to Americans. One finds snakes used in emblems of longer-established "mainstream" organizations like the American Medical Association.[35]

If any general statement is possible about prophetic and messianic movements in both continents that draw upon snake and serpent imagery, it is that they tend to be concerned with the restoration of centrality for places that have been made marginal, and for people who in one way or another have felt deprived of dignity, honor, or respectability. They are also concerned to reweave a world and an experience of it somehow rent asunder, and to do so by whatever imaginative means.

Here, to sum up, are a few features that seem to occur in variously incomplete packages in one case after another—so commonly that where one sees several, one can expect to find some of the others, too.

Preconditions variously include radical intercultural contact, on unequal terms; military defeat; land loss and social shake-up; challenges to ways of attaining manhood or adulthood; new material needs or wants; rising expectations and blocked economic opportunity; and oppressive law. More basically, the partitioning of life into ostensibly separate disciplines or professions like politics, law, and religion, or different "sectors" like health, housing, transport, and trade—in a way that leaves real people, and their real fortunes and feelings, falling between the cracks—can be part of the underlying problem.

There typically unrolls, as seen, a process whereby the prophet, typically an insider-outsider during or after exile or incarceration, and serving as a culture broker, has the encounter with, and/or revelation and commandments from, the animal or part-animal. He or she receives a warning, perhaps expressed poetically or cryptically, that a cataclysm or apocalyptic change is coming. That the living will be sorted into believers and infidels for a selective redemption by a messiah, and/or condemnation. That the dead will reappear to rejoin the living.

The prophet and early disciples bring to believers strict behavioral rules, including many prohibitions and positive injunctions to make oaths, offer sacrifices, and remain strictly loyal to leader(s). They may require them to renounce or even destroy erstwhile kin in the process. Ordinary norms of interaction and conduct (for instance of dress, hair length, washing, diet, or drug use) are inverted. Just as many key formative moments of prophecy involve dream, trance, other altered states, and voice channeling (to some, spirit possession; to others, a form of hysteria), adherents may enter episodically their own such states, amid a call for more general rebellion against an old order. Promises for adherence to the new norms may include unlimited wealth, sexual access or other privilege, and annulment of debts.

As the prophet, disciples, and their messages gain adherents, and the movement turns into an "organization," some of the participants turn to administrators. Members may emulate military ranks, offices, or co-opted status symbols of erstwhile oppressors, as the movement becomes bureaucratized (or in Weberian terms, "routinized").

Meanwhile, outside the movement, fear and panic may lead to harsh repressive measures, from selective token jailing to full-scale military assault. Such repression may be construed by members, in turn, as a test for proving faith and strength. If, however, after any hostilities, aid is eventually delivered to adherents of the movement, adherents and onlookers may construe it as a sign of successful prophecy, of effective leadership of the movement, or of answered prayer and sacrifice.

These, then, are some rudiments of the repertoire in the comparative analysis of revitalizations with animal focus. In an abstract vein, I have suggested that a snakelike rope sorts through these elements, as participants make individual and collective choices at whatever levels of consciousness to bring some elements in—enough to make a pattern recognizable—while usually leaving some out or making some ironic twists.

The aftermath of these sets and series of occurrences, though, can be so various and path-dependent as to defy easy summary once again. Some movements undergo a period of dormancy or of activity "underground." A movement may die out or its followers get exterminated. Or it may grow back, become more official and bureaucratic, and establish a new orthodoxy until some other movement comes along to rebel against it in turn.

In between these extremes lie still other possibilities. Some prophetic movements become co-opted into more-conventional churches. An example is the Northwest Coast Indian Shaker movement mentioned earlier. Its members, if not also doctrines, were largely absorbed into Protestant churches, some of which were affiliated with nationwide and international faith communities.

Where the movements have taken militant forms or involved militant expression, former rebels and other combatants, in order to be reincorporated into their former communities, are commonly expected to undergo ceremonial rites of reconciliation and reintegration. They may, for instance, be asked to drink from the same vessels as their former enemies (an Acholi rite practiced in northern Uganda, for former members of the Lord's Resistance Army). Sometimes, too, they are asked to participate in burning, burying, or otherwise destroying weapons ("bending the spears" in Acholiland; "burying the hatchet" in America; "turning swords to plowshares" elsewhere)—no less a symbolic statement than a practical precaution.

Not all movements that seem dead remain so, as we have seen. Instead, the time passing before memories are actively rekindled, and the reworking of history by selective remembering, always leaves room for debate about whether the movements ought to be connected in continuous narrative or given new names. A series of ghost dance, circle dance, and feather dance movements emerged in Native America as a series of more or less conscious emulations of the ones preceding, despite radical changes in conditions of population, federal subsidies, broken or reframed treaties, and so on. So, too, in East Africa, did Mumbo movements come and go over several decades after British colonization; and so, up to and after independence, have new snakes kept appearing now and again with the name Omieri (or Omweri), right into our own time.

Similarly, in the history of Zimbabwe (the former Southern Rhodesia), a succession of political and military conflagrations have been labeled with the Shona term Chimurenga, roughly meaning revolutionary struggle. The first was directed against British South Africans in the late 1890s. The second was against Rhodesian "whites" in the late 1960s and 1970s, and the third against newer and remaining large landholders and others in the present century. In the naming, the later movements have drawn emotive power semantically by evoking the ones preceding, as well as through narratives about prophets' bones predictedly rising from the dead in renewed struggle. In another time and place, a comparable linguistic ploy has occurred as a nativistic "tea party" like Boston's has found its name co-opted for a movement its costumed crate-tossers might never have dreamed of, as if to reawaken their gallant spirit—or perhaps, in this case, to turn their bones in their graves.

In some cases, a revitalization movement may be a precursor to legal reform, or to even such a radical change as national independence. Consider the 1950s movement called Mau Mau in Kenya, for instance. Even though it was brutally suppressed under British colonial authority, , one of its former organizers and jailed activists, Jomo Kenyatta, became Kenya's first president upon independence in 1963.

Similarly, people in the Dinka, Nuer, and other parts of South Sudan can point to many of their own prophets and prophecies and their local movements—including ones who spiritually drafted nature to their cause through particular species—as leading up to the secession process that culminated in that country's independence from Sudan in mid-2011. Organizers of many other movements with mixed ritual, religious, and political dimensions have dreamed of outcomes like these, whatever they might lead to as history plays out.

Relocalization and Redignification

The choice of local prophets, and of animals as spirit intermediaries and focal points for their messages, serves, I have suggested, to restore the collective self-esteem of marginalized people. It does so in part by reminding them that the time and place where they live can be important, when the media and messages inundating them would all suggest the contrary. Part of what makes foreign centers of power so resented is their inaccessibility to people impoverished, discriminated against, and confined by racial barriers or border patrols. In a sense, turning to the local as a site of reverence makes virtue of necessity.

But it does more than this. In parts of the world where ethnic groups have become confined in one way or another to demarcated territories (as in "native reserves" of former British colonies, or "reservations" of Native America to this day), valorizing a place is valorizing a people, too. Ancestral graves often serve such a focal purpose. They do it in both eastern equatorial Africa and western Native America; and in many parts of both continents, the location and treatment of burial sites and remains has been an issue producing strong feelings, heated legal struggles, and sometimes violence.[36]

For people who have been *removed* from ancestral homes and graves—by economic pressure, military force, or angry mobs engaged in ethnic purging—identifying a local creature as the new center of attention can appeal *all the more*. The revered creature can create, in a sense, a new holy land, one within reach when borders, plane fares, and visa problems make other holy lands inaccessible. Nor is it just the "religious" holy lands afar that can seem so hard to get to. It may be also the centers of fashion and broadcasting, the treasuries of wealth, the citadels of learning and credentialing, that seem out of reach—the holy lands of looser sorts. Snakes and serpents, birds and phoenixes, spread around the benefits, or at least the promise.

The refocus also redistributes attention temporally. It qualifies missionary focus on the long-distant past (the times of Abraham, Jesus, or Muhammad, for instance), refocusing some of the attention to the times of more knowable local figures, including recent ancestors—or just divides the temporal frame of reference. And finally, the movements provide a new focus in a racial sense—in whatever way race may be understood—since new culture heroes are likely to resemble more closely their followers.

Movements that restore the centrality of a place also restore the dignity of a people, and sometimes they do it in a way that restores the dignity of a demeaned animal, too. Snakes make a good candidate for this sort of restoration of image, sliding along the ground and frightening humans and other animals alike as they often do. The animal spirits with snake forms or features are often not wholly animal—talking to and through the prophet to foretell the future and make commandments. These are animals playing human roles, not just animal ones.

Whether stories about talking snakes or birds might help their listeners to appreciate that real-bodied snakes, birds, or dogs might have sentience, consciousness, rights—or all three—remains for now anyone's guess. Listeners young and old may well and easily discern the difference between a real animal's thoughts or feelings and those in a story, film, or cartoon. But revitalizations are a field in which truth and fiction can blur easily—this is what they are about, after all—as hopes and fears color perceptions and interpretations, and as new habits of thought are forged in growing brains and maturing minds. It may well be that stories of talking animals enable us, accustom us, to imagine better the sentience and consciousness of animals around us, even though their thoughts or their feelings may take quite different forms from our own. This is an aspect of the comparative study of cultures, and of animal-human relations, in which much remains to be learned.[37]

Conscripting Nature

The movements described in these pages—classed in a slippery, sliding category—serve their participants not just for *revitalization*, but also for *relocalization* and *redignification*. These are the three Rs of new faiths whose charismatic leaders seek to conscript nature to their side.

Faith in animal contact makes reformers more ambitious, rebels more brazen. Trusting that unseen powers of nature are behind them, some adherents to "crisis cults" attempt uprisings against mighty steep odds. It sometimes seems to be not so much the actual protection itself that matters to a prospective rebel combatant, but rather the *feeling* of protection given by, and by belonging to, something bigger than oneself. This is not a domain of grounded evidence, just as a child's comfort in parental protection is not always so well founded either. In any case, prophetic, millenarian, and apocalyptic movements tend to frighten authorities; and these authorities, once well spooked, tend to overreact. Violence ensues, not uncommonly as one-sided slaughter. In Wounded Knee; in Waco, Texas; or in parts of Acholi country in and around northern Uganda where the killing and suffering have been more sporadic and indirect, history suggests apocalyptic prophecies can self-fulfill.

But "crisis cults" quelled, and insurrections quashed, get taken up again, selectively invoked, given new clothes in later movements. The very kinds of narratives that focus attention on rebirth, reincarnation, or immortality—and on species like snakes and birds that connote these most readily—contribute to the periodic rebirth of the movements that coalesce around the imagery of these animals in the first place.

Notes

1. The participants of the of the 2003 American Anthropological Association conference panel on humans and pythons in Africa, in Chicago, and the 2008 "Indigenous Environments" conference at Bowdoin, deserve thanks for feedback on draft papers, particularly David Gordon for his written comments.

2. The term "revitalization" for such movements comes from Anthony F. C. Wallace, "Revitalization Movements," *American Anthropologist* 58 (1956): 264–81.

3. My use of terms like "movement," "cult," "church," and "religion," where referring to traditions or organizations newer or older, bigger or smaller, more widely accepted or less, is meant to be neutral in value judgment. Such designations often depend partly on perspective.

4. Ludwig Wittgenstein, *Preliminary Studies for the "Philosophical Investigations," Generally Known as the Blue and Brown Books* (Oxford: Blackwell, 1958); Rodney Needham, "Polythetic Classification," *Man* (new series) 10 (1975): 349–67.

5. The choices reflect my own research in East Africa (especially western Kenya) and the Gambia, and briefer periods studying the Northwest Coast and other parts of native North America. But no less of the material presented here comes from written sources.

6. A few of the most influential surveys of the broader kinds of movements and organizations discussed in this essay, with or without animals, include the following. Writings on "charisma" and its "routinization" by Max Weber are anthologized in his *Readings and Commentary on Modernity*, ed. Stephen Kalberg (Malden, MA: Blackwell, 2005). See Ralph Linton, "Nativistic Movements," *American Anthropologist* 45 (1943): 230–40; and Anthony F. C. Wallace, *Revitalizations and Mazeways: Essays on Culture Change*, vol. 1 (Lincoln: University of Nebraska Press, 2003), on the growth of "cults" into "organized religions." Other condensed summaries include Vittorio Lanternari, *The Religions of the Oppressed: A Study of Modern Messianic Cults* (New York: Mentor, 1963), on "religions of the oppressed"; and Weston La Barre, *The Ghost Dance: The Origins of Religion* (New York: Dell, 1972), a psychocultural tome whose title belies its broad geographic coverage and obscures its frequent citing of practitioners' animal inspirations. Arlene Hirschfelder and Paulette Molin, *Encyclopedia of Native American Religions* (New York: Checkmark, 2001), makes reference to many focused in one way or another on animals, most notably birds and their feathers, but also some snakes. For surveys of well-studied Melanesian prophetic and millenarian movements, including scores of "cargo cults," see Peter Lawrence, *Road Belong Cargo: A Study of the Cargo Movement in Southern Madang District, New Guinea* (Manchester, UK: Manchester University Press, 1964); Kenelm Burridge, *New Heaven, New Earth* (Oxford: Blackwell, 1986); and Peter Worsley, *The Trumpet Shall Sound: A Study of "Cargo" Cults in Melanesia*, 2nd ed. (New York: Schocken, 1987). An analysis of contemporary "liberation struggles" around the world (including transnational ones widely feared as terrorist movements) appears in Charles Lindholm and José Pedro Zúquete, *The Struggle for the World: Liberation Movements for the 21st Century* (Stanford, CA: Stanford University Press, 2010), published as this chapter was heading to press.

7. Lewis Henry Morgan, *League of the Ho-Dé-No-Sau-Nee or Iroquois* (Rochester, NY: Sage and Brothers, 1851); Anthony F. C. Wallace, *The Death and Rebirth of the Seneca* (New York: Vintage, 1972).

8. Many are briefly described in Hirschfelder and Molin, *Encyclopedia of Native American Religions*.

9. The northwestern Indian Shaker Church, as it became, is not to be confused with the northeastern and midwestern faith and communities of the United Society of Believers, also called Shaker. See Homer G. Barnett, *Indian Shakers: A Messianic Cult of the Pacific Northwest* (Carbondale: Southern Illinois University Press, 1972).

10. Two bold attempts to theorize this pattern of merging cognition, or thought that overlooks seeming contradictions, were Lucien Lévy-Bruhl's

early work, especially *Les Fonctions Mentales dans les Sociétés Inférieures (1910)*, translated in 1926 as *How Natives Think* (Princeton, NJ: Princeton University Press, 1985); and his *La Mentalité Primitive* (1922), translated as *Primitive Mentality* (New York: Macmillan, 1923). Unfortunately, these books' social-evolutionary idiom, outmoded soon after their writing, make them easy to dismiss as ethnocentric if not racist or imperialist; and the proffered "law of mystical participation" comes across today as too categorical. Even the author later repudiated much of his early work. Most contemporary readers, unsurprisingly, overlook the substantial residual value of his observations, and more important questions, raised about conventions of acceptable perception and reason as these vary across cultures.

11. See John Neihardt, *Black Elk Speaks: Being the Life Story of a Holy Man of the Oglala Sioux* (Lincoln: University of Nebraska Press, 1979, orig. 1932). Black Elk's history has lately undergone some debate and revision.

12. See James Mooney, *The Ghost Dance Religion and Wounded Knee* (New York: Dover, 1896), on that movement.

13. Some of totemism's various assumed meanings, for instance, putative descent from animals, or specific food avoidances or prohibitions, apply unevenly to cases of animal-focused movements discussed herein. For more on the general topic, see Claude Levi-Strauss, *Totemism* (Boston: Beacon, 1971), orig. *Le Totemisme Aujourd'hui*. The term "totem" comes from an Algonquian, perhaps Ojibwe word.

14. Susan Sered's *Priestess, Mother, Sacred Sister* (Oxford: Oxford University Press, 1996) describes female-led movements and religions worldwide, some taken over by males. For published and unpublished literature on Africa tying snakes into feminist concerns, see Ifi Amadiume, *Reinventing Africa: Matriarch, Religion and Culture* (London: Zed, 1997); Nancy Schwartz, "From Freudian Mutations and Christian Diabolization to Africanist and Feminist Herpetology: Some Luo Views on Snakes and Pythons" (paper presented at annual meeting, American Anthropological Association, Chicago, 2003); Sabine Jell-Bahlsen, "The Python as a Religious Symbol in Igbo Cosmology" (paper presented at annual meeting, American Anthropological Association, Chicago, 2003); John Kaoma, "God, Our Ancestors, and the Spirits in Snakes" (unpublished paper, School of Theology, Boston University, 2007); Henry J. Drewal, *Sacred Waters: Arts for Mami Wata and Other Divinities in Africa and the Diaspora* (Bloomington: University of Indiana Press, 2008).

15. Why it is so often just one prophet at first—not two or ten—has never been fully explained. But it can be easier to identify with an individual than with a group. Charisma is sometimes defined as the ability to make every

member of a multitude feel as though personally connected with one. For more on charisma, see Weber, *Readings*; and Charles Lindholm, *Charisma* (Malden, MA: Blackwell, 1993).

16. I thank John Kaoma and Nancy Schwartz for helping me see the importance of this point. While so often and strongly disparaging snakes, ancient Greek and biblical writings yet contain occasional instances of snakes used as symbols of healing, delivery, or redemption.

17. On diverse ways snakes and serpents figure in religion on the Indian subcontinent and elsewhere, see Jyoti Sahi, *The Child and the Serpent: Reflections on Popular Indian Symbols* (London: Routledge); and Balaji Mundkur, *The Cult of the Serpent: An Interdisciplinary Survey of Its Manifestations and Origins* (Albany: State University of New York Press, 1983).

18. A caveat on terminology. Any lexicon for discussing politico-religious movements is slippery, and easy to mistranslate or to misconstrue as morally loaded. From some mouths, "cult" has a venomous ring, implying demon worship or other evil. "Spirit," if translated to non-Indo-European tongues and then retranslated, can come back with any of a number of "shades of meaning," for instance ghost, ancestor, god, devil, demon, elf, goblin, fairy, soul, essence, life force. Or just its puckish cognate, "sprite." Some deem "nature" to include humans, others not; some consider "religion" as encompassing the rest of life, while others treat it as a separate compartment in time, place, or experience. *Millennium* can mean literally a thousand years or just a long time. Other related terms, like "apocalypse," can evoke biblical reference that may or may not be meant. Red herrings abound in this topic.

19. Substitution of spirits and gods for lost or diminished parents by the disillusioned is a central theme of La Barre, *The Ghost Dance*.

20. Frank Sulloway, *Born to Rebel: Birth Order, Family Dynamics, and Creative Lives* (New York: Vintage, 1997).

21. Douglas Johnson, *Nuer Prophets: A History of Prophecy from the Upper Nile in the Nineteenth and Twentieth Centuries* (Oxford: Clarendon, 1994), esp. 37.

22. Burridge, *New Heaven, New Earth*, 9. For Africa, see Elizabeth A. Isichei, *Voices of the Poor in Africa: Moral Economy and the Popular Imagination* (Rochester, NY: University of Rochester Press, 2002), a survey of artful verbal and other imagery variously implicating fellow Africans and foreigners felt to have committed social wrongs.

23. B. Onyango-Ogutu and A. A. Roscoe, *Keep My Words: Luo Oral Literature* (Nairobi: East African Publishing House, 1974), 22.

24. Ibid., 22.

25. "Nyangweso" (pseud.), "Cult of Mumbo in Central and South Kavirondo," *Journal of the East Africa and Uganda Natural History Society* 10, no. 38 (1930): 13–14; Audrey Wipper, *Rural Rebels: A Study of Two Protest Movements in Kenya* (Oxford: Oxford University Press, 1977), 35. The quotations and sacrifices prescribed here are set into broader context in Parker Shipton, *The Nature of Entrustment: Intimacy, Exchange, and the Sacred in Africa* (New Haven, CT: Yale University Press, 2007), chap. 9.

26. Robert Maxon, *Conflict and Accommodation in Western Kenya: The Gusii and the British, 1907–1963* (Rutherford, NJ: Fairleigh Dickinson University Press, 1989); Wipper, *Rural Rebels*, 7; Brett Shadle, "Patronage, Millennialism and the Serpent-God Mumbo in Southwest Kenya, 1912–1934," *Africa* 72, no. 1 (2002): 29–54.

27. Heike Behrend, *Alice Lakwena and the Holy Spirits: War in Northern Uganda, 1986–97* (Athens: Ohio University Press, 1999), 30–31, 64. The book provides much detail on the movement.

28. Ibid., 62–63.

29. Ibid., esp. 59. The chanted "James Bond! James Bond!" is reminiscent of the Maji Maji (water water) rebellion in Tanganyika (now part of Tanzania), when that phrase was supposed to be able to turn enemy bullets to water. See John Iliffe, "The Organization of the Maji Maji Rebellion," *African History* 8, no. 3 (1967): 495–512. See Sverker Finnström, *Living with Bad Surroundings: War, History, and Everyday Moments in Northern Uganda* (Durham, NC: Duke University Press, 2008), 5, 202–4, on Joseph Kony's takeover from Alice Lakena and her putative powers, and on the Acholi and northern Ugandan situation more generally.

30. James Howard Smith, "Snake-Driven Development: Culture, Nature and Religious Conflict in Neoliberal Kenya." *Ethnography* 7, no. 4 (2006): 423–59. Also N. Thomas Häkansson, "Pythons and Politics in Kenya," (paper presented to American Anthropological Association annual meeting, Chicago, 2003), on both the human study and the herpetology.

31. On comparable patterns among Fipa in Tanzania, see Roy Willis, *Man and Beast* (New York: Basic Books, 1974); also in Paul Shepard, *The Others: How Animals Made Us Human* (Washington, DC: Island Press, 1996), 292–95. On Igbo in southeast Nigeria, see Jell-Bahlsen, "The Python as Religious Symbol"; and on Bemba in Zambia, see Kaoma, "God, Our Ancestors."

32. On Bolivian tin miners, the mines' spiritual "owners," and bargains between them, see June Nash, *We Eat the Mines and the Mines Eat Us* (New York: Columbia University Press, 1979); and Michael Taussig, *The Devil and Commodity Fetishism in South America* (Chapel Hill: University of North Carolina Press,1980).

33. A more thorough summary of revitalization movements would also need to take account of churches like the Legio Maria and Roho churches, again in Kenya—spun off from larger Christian churches without such explicit animal focus, and continually redividing, often with female leadership, at least at first. On Legio Maria, see Nancy Schwartz, *World without End: The Movements and Meanings in the History, Narratives, and "Tongue-Speech" of Legio Maria of African Church Mission Among Luo of Kenya* (PhD thesis, Princeton University, 1989). On the Roho (Spirit) Church and offshoots, see Cynthia Hoehler-Fatton, *Women of Fire and Spirit: History, Faith, and Gender in Roho Religion in Western Kenya* (Oxford: Oxford University Press, 1996).

34. Frank Waters's *Book of the Hopi* (New York: Ballantine, 1969) treats in unusual depth Hopi uses of snakes in totemic clanship and in life-renewal ceremonies. Snakes appear scattered around in reference sources like Hirschfelder and Molin's *Encyclopedia of Native American Religions*, along with the more ubiquitous eagles and other birds as noted earlier.

35. See Nathan Williams, "Serpents, Staffs, and the Emblems of Medicine," *Journal of the American Medical Association* 281 (1999): 475.

36. Of course, body burial has not always been universal custom in East Africa or North America. In some parts, exposure for recycling life by scavenging birds or mammals has been more the rule, just as in some Buddhist-dominated areas in Tibet, Nepal, or Bhutan.

37. The late Nancy Schwartz half-seriously compiled the term "ethnozoopsychology" for something like the study of how humans in different language groups, cultures, and societies conceive of, understand, and communicate about the mental capacities and activities (including social ones) of other animals. Ethnozoopsych—by whatever name—is not a new idea; but as a field of dedicated, systematic study, it is still coming to birth.

Part IV

Resource Rights

CHAPTER 11

Marine Tenure of the Makahs

Joshua Reid

TRADITIONAL SCHOLARSHIP on American Indian tenure remains limited to examining the relationship of a particular tribe to its land and related resources. These studies often explore how land is the foundation of tribal identity, explaining that the expansion of settler-colonists across North America resulted in conflict over Indian land. Through a combination of colonial processes, institutional mechanisms, and shifting balances of power, non-Natives dispossessed the former occupants. Most scholarship about current self-determination struggles continues this trend by focusing on land. This terrestrial perspective overlooks those American Indian nations, such as the Makahs of Washington State, who vested—and have continued to vest—marine rather than terrestrial spaces and resources with their most valued tenure rights.

This essay explores the characteristics of Makah marine tenure during the first half of the nineteenth century. These American Indians expressed ownership of nearby ocean waters and resources through indigenous knowledge of their marine environment and through customary practices such as whaling, sealing, and fishing. Additionally, these cultural performances reflected a sentimental connection to the sea and a spiritual dimension of their marine tenure. Based on reciprocity and respect, a Makah spiritual worldview—rooted in the perception that marine creatures such as whales, seals, and fish are people—enabled them both to exploit and to conserve their rich marine resources. Through place-naming, applying indigenous knowledge, and pursuing maritime practices, the Makahs made the sea their country. Becoming increasingly entangled with the non-Native world from the mid-nineteenth century on, they both asserted and reshaped their tenure concepts to retain core Makah values and to respond to challenges. Their current revival of an active whaling practice reflects their efforts at reclaiming the sea.

According to the doctrine of property that predominates in the United States, *tenure* means ownership of land. Understood to be exclusive, ownership gives the owner the right to buy and sell her or his property and to manage the land as she or he sees fit. Colonial empires and settler-colonial nations have used tenure concepts to their advantage in order to dispossess American Indians of lands and terrestrial resources.[1] For example, during the colonial period, expanding empires acknowledged varying degrees of indigenous tenure in order to purchase Indian lands or to seize vast tracts through "just wars." During the treaty era, the United States recognized Indian tenure in order to negotiate for land cessions. Congressional legislation, such as the Dawes Severalty Act (1887), granted ownership rights to individuals, thereby fragmenting tribal holdings and transferring more land out of Indian hands. Like other Western concepts applied to indigenous peoples, tenure has a long history of being used to the advantage of the colonizer.[2] Therefore, when discussing *indigenous tenure*, it is necessary to differentiate it from the version of tenure that predominates in the United States.

In North America, indigenous tenure concepts and protocols varied from one society to the next and over time. For generations, Makahs have embedded their tenure concepts in the marine space around Cape Flattery, the most northwestern point of the continental United States. While Makahs exercised tenure over terrestrial places and objects such as cranberry bogs and stands of timber, tenure rights over marine spaces and resources were among their most valued possessions. Calling themselves *qʷidiččaʔa·tx̌* (pronounced "Kwi-dich-cha-at-h" and meaning "the People of the Cape"), they have rooted their marine tenure rights within the very fabric of what makes them Makahs—their cultural practices and performances related to their marine environment.

Makahs expressed tenure over these waters through their indigenous, local knowledge of this space. For example, during the 1855 negotiations for the Treaty of Neah Bay, Kalchote, the first Makah leader to speak on behalf of his people, connected knowledge to tenure rights. When introducing himself to Governor Isaac Stevens, the head of the U.S. treaty commission in Washington Territory, Kalchote stated, "I know the country all around and therefore I have a right to speak" about Makah ownership of the sea and their fishing rights.[3] As one of the highest-ranking Makah chiefs, Kalchote owned important marine resources, such as some halibut fishing banks just off the coast, and he and his family had fished them for generations. The "country" he and other Makahs described was the ocean around the Cape Flattery villages that provided access to lucrative fishing, whaling, and sealing grounds. Their familiarity with the area transformed this watery void into Makah home waters to which they held title.[4]

Like other societies, the Makahs articulated their ownership and knowledge through place-naming.[5] Many place-names identified fishing locations over which specific families held particular usufruct rights. They called the important halibut banks, located twelve miles off Cape Flattery, *Klushooa*, meaning "place where the water is shallow" or "shoalwater." Makah fishermen named a certain oceanic salmon fishing spot *Slthu-slthu-both*—"fish moving around on top."[6] These names illustrate an understanding of this marine space in terms of its depth, locations for specific resources, and the behavior of certain fish.

Indigenous knowledge of named marine places allowed Makahs to safely navigate their waters. They used both landmarks and seamarks to pinpoint their location. For example, fishermen located fishing spots by referencing features along Vancouver Island and the Olympic Peninsula.[7] Sealers noted the difference between shallower inshore waters and the deeper "blue sea" above the submerged continental shelf.[8] Whaling crews often lost sight of land, staying out at sea for days. In clear weather, they used the polestar to steer by at night. Combinations of regular swell patterns and winds enabled them to fix their approximate location, even in the fogs that regularly concealed the coast. Additionally, experienced mariners used the water's appearance and the set of tide rips to approximate their location when out of sight of land.[9]

Spending substantial time on their waters, Makahs also needed to understand and be able to predict local weather. James Swan, the first Anglo teacher at Neah Bay, described to readers of the *Washington Standard* in 1863 that the Makahs recognized that the clamor of birds and a specific type of swell preceded storms. The swell caused particular noises to emanate from ocean-facing caverns on Cape Flattery. When fishermen and sealers on the water heard these noises, they had just enough time to round the cape and seek safety in Neah Bay before the storm hit.[10] Makah knowledge of navigational markers and weather conditions were expressions of tenure over their home waters.

Knowledge of their marine environment and the species within it allowed Makahs to adapt their gear and techniques to harvest a range of oceanic foods and materials. Like indigenous knowledge, the labor they did in these waters expressed their tenure. Statements from Makah leaders during the 1855 treaty negotiations illustrate that they considered work and ownership as being connected. When speaking of owning the sea, they detailed the importance of maritime labors, such as catching halibut and hunting whales.[11] By mixing their labor with the sea through customary practices such as fishing, sealing, and whaling, Makahs made this stretch of sea their country.

In the late eighteenth and nineteenth centuries, halibut fishing formed the foundation of Makah subsistence labor and provided an important commercial good they traded to other indigenous communities and passing non-Native vessels. During the summers, Makah fishermen worked customary halibut banks in the Strait of Juan de Fuca and the Pacific. Knowledge about the habits of halibut and other species enabled them to exploit this resource heavily. For example, they used curved hooks designed so that the dogfish that infested the halibut banks would not stay on the hook when they struck.[12] Additionally, knowing that *shoo-yoult* (halibut) prefer octopus while *yáh-chah* (dogfish) avoid it, they baited their hooks with octopus.[13] In 1861, Swan estimated that this tribe of 654 individuals annually took more than 1.5 million pounds of fresh halibut during the mid-nineteenth century.[14] By working these named and owned halibut banks, Makah fishermen expressed their tenure over the sea.

A similar combination of labor and indigenous knowledge related to hunting seals demonstrated another expression of Makah marine tenure. Hunters paddled up to forty miles into the Pacific, reaching the hunting grounds at daylight, in order to catch herds of sleeping *kaíth-la-doose* (fur seals). Canoe makers constructed these vessels to ride high in the water so the harpooner could better see his prey, and they scorched the bottoms in order to burn off splinters that might make noisy ripples and wake sleeping seals. After harpooning the seal, they pulled it to the canoe and clubbed it dead. Pelagic sealing entailed a certain amount of manageable danger from biting seals, sharks drawn by bloody hunts, and sudden storms that could blow canoes far out to sea.[15] Indigenous knowledge allowed Makah sealers to minimize these dangers and to hunt this marine resource safely.

Seals provided Makahs with a number of valuable subsistence and commercial products to which they had access due to their marine tenure.

They ate the flesh, rendered the blubber into oil, used the skin for bedding, and employed the bladder to store sea mammal oil.[16] From entire sealskins that they inflated, whalers made floats used when hunting. They often employed thirty to forty of these buoys to tire out harpooned whales, and these prevented the heavy carcass from sinking.[17] In the late 1870s, Makah sealers sold sealskins taken in coastal waters, and they made more than twenty thousand dollars in 1880.[18] A number of individuals used these wages to purchase schooners, which allowed them to take Makah-owned and -crewed vessels into the Bering Sea, where they more than doubled their income from hunting.[19]

Of all their customary practices, whaling best demonstrated how Makahs combined indigenous knowledge with labor to express their marine tenure. Native whalers have relied upon their knowledge of the marine environment to hunt these sea mammals for the last two thousand years. From the early to mid-nineteenth century, most whalers caught one or two annually and up to five in good years. A crew of eight sometimes remained on the ocean for days pursuing *chet-a-pook* (whales) fifty to one hundred miles offshore. Once the whale was dead, a diver sewed shut its mouth to prevent it from sinking. Then the crew towed the whale back to the coast, sometimes taking three days to get it ashore.[20] Staying out for this length of time and paddling across such great distances required Makah whalers to rely upon knowledge of the marine environment and navigational and weather prediction skills.

In 1855, Governor Stevens's treaty commission likely anticipated Makah statements about the importance of their marine tenure because of the high profile of whaling activities. Their whaling skills drew praise from early Anglo-American settlers in Washington Territory.[21] George Gibbs, Governor Stevens's personal secretary during the treaty negotiations, noted that in 1852, Makahs had traded more than thirty thousand gallons of whale oil to passing vessels, and they kept a similar amount for personal consumption and trade with neighboring Indians.[22] Sixty thousand gallons of oil represented approximately twenty-six whales.[23] Acknowledging this fact, Stevens himself told the assembled chiefs, "I know what great whalers you are," and he promised to send them kettles for rendering blubber into oil and barrels for storing this valuable product.[24]

While the Makahs valued the material gains customary practices such as fishing, sealing, and whaling provided, their marine space and the resources within it had an importance more complex than straightforward economic terms conveyed. Unlike most forms of tenure that predominated in the United States during the first half of the nineteenth century, Makah tenure had sentimental—even spiritual—components. By mixing their labor with the sea, they communicated a "bond of belonging."[25] In writing about Hispano loggers' belief that they owned the forests of northern New Mexico, anthropologist Jake Kosek cautions that "sentimental arguments over nature are often considered the antithesis of rational discourse about property rights."[26] Applied to American Indians, scholars mistakenly dismiss these sentiments as stereotypes of the Ecological Indian.[27] For the Makahs, however, their bond with customary marine space has been and continues to be far more complex.

During the nineteenth century, Makahs recognized that tenure entailed both rights and responsibilities. These rights included usufruct rights, and high-ranking leaders decided who else could share the property in question and on what terms.[28] Depending on the property item, ownership rights occasionally included the exclusive right to buy and sell. More important, because Makahs embedded tenure concepts within a larger worldview that recognized "numinous forces" in their environment, they understood that ownership also entailed responsibility.[29] For example, Makahs believed they had a responsibility to maintain a balanced relationship with a community that included the very animals and fish that they harvested. This should not be misconstrued as the Makahs acting like proto-ecologists. Harvesting more than a million pounds of halibut, hunting thousands of seals, and harpooning dozens of whales on an annual basis illustrate that Makahs cannot be stereotyped as Ecological Indians, from a non-Native perspective. But more than anything, this component of their marine tenure differentiates Makah ownership concepts from similar ones that predominated in the nineteenth-century United States.

In order to understand this concept of responsibility as an expression of tenure, we must examine the worldview of the nineteenth-century Makahs. From their perspective, most animals, plants, and prominent landmarks were nonhuman people. Billy Balch, one of Swan's "informants," told him that Makahs believed everything—including trees, animals, birds, and fish—were "formerly Indians who for their bad conduct were transformed into the shapes that now appear."[30] These nonhuman members of their community possessed powers and responded to human actions and events. For example, many blamed the poor salmon and sealing seasons in 1879 on the fact that one of their chiefs had allowed his pregnant wife to eat of the first salmon of the season. This resulted in the deaths of her and her twins and caused salmon to leave the rivers and seals to flee.[31] *Se kar jecta* was an "evil genius" who had transformed into a large rock off the coast south of Cape Flattery. On two separate canoe trips, Swan observed

Makahs throwing offerings of bread, dried halibut, and whale blubber at *Se kar jecta* in order to ensure safe passage.[32] Being responsible holders of marine tenure meant that Makahs at all levels of society needed to maintain proper relationships with the larger community by observing customary practices and protocols.

Expressing tenure responsibilities through protocols permeated marine practices such as whaling. Only the highest-ranking Makahs held the right to hunt whales. Specific titleholders owned these proprietary rights, and they passed them from one generation to the next and kept them within particular lineages. Successful harpooners—captains of whaling crews—had to have more than their own strength; they had to gain supernatural prowess from the numinous powers of the nonhuman community. Before hunting, whaling crews performed specific actions—such as fasting, swimming, bathing, and abstinence—to secure these powers in the form of potent "whale medicine" and to gain the protection of guardian spirits while on the ocean. Only a whaler with strong enough powers could gain the respect of a hunted whale, who, in turn, gave itself to the hunter. Through his whaling success, a harpooner proved that he had received these powers and protection. More important, his success demonstrated that the nonhuman community approved of his ownership of these whaling rights.[33] From the Makah perspective, honoring and propitiating the nonhuman members of the marine community helped to maintain these relationships, a necessary component of their tenure responsibilities.

Additionally, a whaling chief's tenure responsibilities extended into the human community. After welcoming a whale to the village, they butchered it, a process that took an entire day and unsettled the weaker stomachs of some non-Native observers.[34] Butchers observed specific protocols when dividing the meat and blubber. Richest in oil, the hump went to the harpooner. The whaling crew received large strips of blubber and divided the tongue, an organ that contained a large amount of oil. As a whaling chief, the harpooner held a feast to distribute the rest of the blubber and whale meat.[35] This redistribution was not only another way that whalers fulfilled their tenure responsibilities, but it was also how these owners maintained their authority and social status and demonstrated ownership over specific resources.[36]

Makahs also expressed tenure over customary marine space by defending the sea boundaries of their community against non-Makahs. About two hundred years before non-Natives began frequenting the Northwest Coast, the Makahs fought off the Ditidahts, a related people from Vancouver Island.[37] While the oral history about this event details battles over villages on Cape Flattery and Tatoosh Island, the conflict was over controlling the rich marine waters and resources that people could access from these locations. Those who held these villages also owned the offshore waters and resources. As explained earlier, generations of laboring on these waters had developed a bond of belonging to this space. This bond fueled their willingness to fight for their home waters, and violence strengthened their sentimental bond and tenure claims, in turn. Luke Markistun, the Makah who shared this history in 1921, explained it best when he stated that Makahs held title to Neah Bay and Tatoosh Island because they had "shed blood there."[38]

In the final quarter of the eighteenth century, when Europeans and Anglo-Americans began entering Northwest Coast indigenous waters, peoples such as the Makahs defended their marine space from these newcomers. For example, in 1788, Chief Tatoosh confronted the British trader John Meares, the first non-Native to record an interaction with Makahs in their customary waters. Tatoosh made him understand "that we were now within the limits of his government, which extended a considerable way to the Southward."[39] The chief felt that if Meares was going to spend any time in his marine waters and trade with his people, the captain should present him with appropriate gifts. However, the "small present" Meares offered failed to acknowledge Tatoosh's importance. The following day, the chief and a contingent of four hundred warriors circled the *Felice* in a prominent display of Tatoosh's sea power.[40] A veteran of the Royal Navy, Captain Meares recognized sea power when he saw it, and the *Felice* fled Makah waters on the first wind. Two weeks later, Tatoosh's warriors partnered with a related group on Vancouver Island to thwart the British from exploring the Strait of Juan de Fuca.[41]

Nearly seventy years later, Makah leaders asserted the importance of their marine tenure when confronting U.S. treaty negotiators. Territorial governor Isaac Stevens began by explaining his perspective on the proposed treaty, which would transfer Makah land—except that set aside for a reservation—to the United States. In return, the federal government would provide a school, farms, and a physician, among other items. However, Makah leaders appeared to care little for what Stevens offered. Instead, they spoke about the importance of retaining marine tenure. For example, Kalchote stated, "I ought to have the right to fish, and take whales and get food when I like."[42] Moreover, Makah statements also reflected individual ownership to specific marine locations. For example, Keh-tchook of Tatoosh Island explained that his holdings encompassed the island and extended through coastal marine waters fifteen miles away. Most important, these Makahs described the ocean as their homeland. Tse-kaw-wootl stated it clearest: "I want the sea. That is my country." Oral histories record that Tse-kaw-wootl refused to sign the treaty until Governor Stevens accompanied him in a canoe so he could impress this fact upon him.

Makah negotiators used the treaty to protect their marine tenure. For example, article 4 included the fishing rights clause found in the other Stevens treaties of Washington Territory, except this one had been amended to include whaling and sealing rights.[43] Not only had Makah leaders convinced Governor Stevens to alter their treaty—other Stevens treaties remained unchanged—but this was also the only Indian treaty in U.S. history in which an indigenous nation reserved for itself the right to whale. Makahs signed the treaty since, from their perspective, Governor Stevens appeared to understand and acknowledge their tenure claims to customary marine space. They would not have signed the treaty otherwise. Today's Makahs still speak of the treaty as a document in which they "kept the sea" for themselves.[44]

Makahs continued exercising their tenure rights and responsibilities during the post-treaty period. For example, in 1880, Makah sealers planned to prohibit the use of guns by non-Natives hunting in indigenous waters because they feared that this would scare away seals.[45] Most Makah sealers scorned guns, arguing that non-Natives armed with shotguns only secured two in every five they shot.[46] Considering the Makah perspective on respecting the nonhuman people they hunted, a 60 percent loss probably offended their sensibilities.

In 1928, Makah whalers made an extreme decision—they decided to suspend their whaling practice.[47] This decision should be understood within the Makah worldview that included tenure-holders' responsibilities to the nonhuman members of their community. For decades, whalers had noticed the declining number of leviathans. As early as 1866, they had expressed increasing difficulty in securing whales.[48] By the 1920s, Makah whale hunts had become rare. Today's oral histories relate that elders held one final hunt before suspending the practice in order to demonstrate it to their children, some of whom had never witnessed a whale hunt. They expected that their descendants would resume whaling once cetacean populations rebounded.[49]

The foundation of Makah marine tenure—that the sea is their country—has remained constant. Similarly, expressions of their tenure rights and responsibilities have been another element of continuity. Like their ancestors, many Makahs today continue to labor in the ocean, to exploit its resources, and to take steps to protect their waters from harmful practices.[50] Additionally, they continue to see themselves as members of a more expansive community, sentimentally and spiritually connected to other marine species.⁵¹ However, in adapting to changing conditions, Makahs have also reconfigured their tenure concepts from being tied to titleholder lineages to ownership rights held by the tribe.

The 1855 Treaty of Neah Bay set the stage for this shift. Although Makahs used the treaty to secure continued rights to customary waters and practices, the document was still a colonial tool that reflected the predominant European-American assumptions of indigenous societies and how they exercised property rights. Treaties such as this were rooted in the inaccurate premise that Indians only held property in common. These common property notions applied even more specifically to marine spaces.⁵² Throughout the eighteenth and nineteenth centuries, many settler-colonial societies imposed their own versions of sea tenure. During colonial and territorial periods, governments attempted to secure common rights to open-access fisheries, a strategy compatible with the frontier status of coastal waters and efficient for nullifying indigenous marine tenure claims.⁵³ Although Governor Stevens's treaties emphasized extinguishing Native land ownership, they all contained an article about fishing rights, namely sharing these rights "in common with" all citizens of the territory.⁵⁴

During the seventy years following the treaty, Makahs continued to observe marine tenure tied to titleholders and lineages. For example, they continued to limit whaling to the highest ranks. In the 1880s and 1890s, Makahs who purchased schooners were at the top of the social stratum because they had the financial resources to make large capital investments and the kinship connections to crew their vessels. Fishing rights also remained tied to specific lineages. For example, in oral testimony collected in 1941 to determine ancestral fishing locations, Makah elders provided numerous examples of family-owned fisheries. They also explained that they would not fish someone else's grounds without permission.⁵⁵

But this pattern of titleholder and lineage-based marine tenure began changing in the 1920s as Makahs—and other Indian fishermen in Washington—clashed with state officials over fishing rights. From the 1920s through the 1970s, the state's assault on Indian fishing rarified the complex web of family rights into tribal rights. As fish numbers plummeted due to non-Native commercial fishermen, the damming of rivers, and the degradation of salmon spawning grounds, state officials expelled indigenous fishermen—whom they believed held unfair rights due to treaty protections—from customary marine and off-reservation fisheries. Newly reorganized tribal governments, such as the Makah tribal council that incorporated in 1936 under the Indian Reorganization Act, spearheaded tribal efforts at using the courts to protect treaty fishing rights. While individuals played an instrumental role in securing the legal protection of Makah treaty fishing rights, it took the resources of the tribal government to shepherd these cases through the federal courts, a process that took decades.[56] A Makah government with oversight of tribal marine tenure emerged after the twentieth-century fishing rights conflicts.[57]

In 1999, Makah whalers successfully hunted a gray whale, thereby ending the seventy-one-year suspension of this customary practice. This act brought praise from indigenous peoples engaged in cultural struggles and condemnation from certain environmental and animal rights activists and parts of the local community. Additionally, the whale hunt provided critics with an opportunity to vent long-held hostilities against American Indians.[58] The historical and cultural dimensions of Makah marine tenure, however, help us understand that the Makah nation is reasserting its ownership over customary waters through the revival of whaling.

This action should come as no surprise because the Makahs possess a history of vesting their tenure concepts within marine spaces and resources. From their perspective, tenure entails specific rights and, most important, responsibilities for maintaining balanced relationships within a community that includes human and nonhuman people. Through place-naming, Makah created a culturally specific seascape that they could understand through indigenous environmental knowledge. Developed over generations, skills and practices established their tenure over customary marine space and enabled them to maintain their community both economically and spiritually. When confronted by outsiders, threats to their community, and declining sea mammal numbers, they acted to protect their marine space, which they thought of as their country and homeland. Amid this continuity, though, Makah marine tenure shifted from titleholder and lineage-based ownership to tribal ownership as the Makah nation emerged in the latter twentieth century to protect treaty fishing rights. Witnessing the rebounding gray whale population, the Makah nation has decided to reassert tribal marine tenure rights and responsibilities in order to counter today's challenges to their human community.

Notes

1. Stuart Banner, *How the Indians Lost Their Land: Law and Power on the Frontier* (Cambridge: Belknap Press of Harvard University Press, 2005).

2. For a similar argument regarding *sovereignty*, see Taiaiake Alfred, "Sovereignty," in *A Companion to American Indian History*, ed. Philip J. Deloria and Neal Salisbury (Malden, MA: Blackwell, 2002), 460–74.

3. "Ratified Treaty No. 286: Documents Relating to the Negotiation of the Treaty of January 31, 1855, with the Makah Indians," Documents Relating to the Negotiation of Ratified and Unratified Treaties with Various Tribes of Indians, 1801–69 (National Archives Microfilm Publication T494, roll 5), Records of the Bureau of Indian Affairs (BIA), Record Group 75, National Archives, Washington, D.C., 2 (hereafter cited as Treaty Negotiation Notes).

4. For more on the relationships among spaces, cultures, and societies, see Henri Lefebvre, *The Production of Space*, trans. Donald Nicholson-Smith (Malden, MA: Blackwell, 1974); Yi-Fu Tuan, *Space and Place: The Perspective of Experience*, 25th Anniversary Edition (Minneapolis: University of Minnesota Press, 1977). For analysis specific to marine spaces, see John Cordell, ed., *A Sea of Small Boats* (Cambridge: Cultural Survival, 1989).

5. Keith H. Basso, *Wisdom Sits in Places: Landscape and Language Among the Western Apache* (Albuquerque: University of New Mexico Press, 1996); Bernard Nietschmann, "Traditional Sea Territories, Resources and Rights in Torres Strait," in Cordell, *A Sea of Small Boats*, 82–84. The majority of Makah place-names pertain to marine features. See T. T. Waterman, "Geography of the Makah," in Erna Gunther Collection, University of Washington Special Collections (UWSC), Seattle, Washington.

6. James G. Swan, October 7, 1880, Diaries 28 and 29, James G. Swan Papers, UWSC (hereafter cited as Swan Papers); "Exhibit HH: Written Testimony of Nora Barker, Makah Elder & Teacher of Makah History, [August 23, 1977]," Legal Case C85-1606M, *Makah v. U.S.*, Makah Tribal Council Collection (M010), Makah Cultural and Research Center (MCRC), Neah Bay, Washington.

7. "Written Testimony of Norah Barker."

8. "Memorandum—Information Obtained from Robert Lee as to Sealing," December 22, 1938, Seals and Sealskins—Reports, etc. (Original Neah Bay Agency), Decimal File 927.0, Taholah Indian Agency, Taholah, WA, BIA, RG 75, NARA—Pacific Alaska Region (NARA-Seattle), Seattle, Washington (hereafter noted as Robert Lee Info).

9. T. T. Waterman, "The Whaling Equipment of the Makah Indians," *University of Washington Publications in Anthropology* 1, no. 1 (1920): 47.

10. James Swan, "Cape Flattery," *Washington Standard* [(Olympia, W.T.)], June 20, 1863.

11. Treaty Negotiation Notes, 2–3.

12. Peter Eggers, Oral Testimony Collected by Roger Chute, May 29, 1936, MCRC photocopy from original in Ms 15/58, Box 4, Chute Collection, Washington State Historical Society Archives, Tacoma (WSHSA).

13. James G. Swan, folder 191: Bound autograph manuscript journal and memorandum book, 1861–71, box 10, Stenzel Collection, Beinecke Rare Book

and Manuscript Library (Beinecke), Yale University, New Haven, Connecticut (hereafter cited as Manuscript Journal), 76; Eggers, Oral Testimony, WSHSA; James Gilchrist Swan, "The Indians of Cape Flattery, at the Entrance to the Strait of Juan De Fuca, Washington Territory," in *Smithsonian Contributions to Knowledge* (Washington, DC: Smithsonian Institution, 1870), 93–106.

14. Swan, March 16, 1880, Diary 10, Swan Papers; Swan to Miles C. Moore [Governor, Washington Territory], August 30, 1889, "Fishing," Box 1P-1-2, Miles C. Moore Papers, Washington State Archives (WSA), Olympia; Swan, Manuscript Journal, 39–52.

15. This information about pre-schooner sealing is from a variety of sources. Swan, "Fur Seal Industry of Cape Flattery and the Vicinity," [1883?], Stenzel Collection; E. M. Gibson, "No. 64, Annual report of Neah Bay Agency," *Annual Report of the Commissioner of Indian Affairs to the Secretary of the Interior* (ARCIA) (Washington, DC: Government Printing Office, 1873), 306–9; Robert Lee Info; "Pelagic Seal Hunting by Makah & Quilleute Indians," Seals and Sealskins—Reports, etc. (Original Neah Bay Agency), Decimal File 927.0, Taholah Indian Agency, Taholah, WA, BIA, RG 75, NARA-Seattle; "Elliott Anderson: The Last Surviving Member of the Ozette Tribe and Ozette Reservation," MCRC photocopy from original in Ms 15/21, box 2, Chute Collection, WSHSA; Charles Huntington, "Annual Report of Makah Agency," August 25, 1875, ARCIA, 362–64.

16. Bering Sea Tribunal of Arbitration, *Fur Seal Arbitration. Proceedings of the Tribunal of Arbitration, Convened in Paris, Under the Treaty Between the United States . . . and Great Britain, Concluded at Washington, February 29, 1892, for the Determination of Questions Between the Two Governments Concerning the Jurisdictional Rights of the United States in the Waters of Bering Sea* (Washington, DC: Government Printing Office, 1895), 381. See also Robert Lee Info; Swan, "Indian Method of Killing Whales"; Swan, July 6, 1879, Diary 10, Swan Papers.

17. Swan, "The Indians of Cape Flattery," 21; Waterman, "The Whaling Equipment of the Makah Indians," 34–36.

18. Charles Willoughby, "Report of the Makah Agent," August 17, 1880, ARCIA, 155–56.

19. John Keenan, "Report of Neah Bay Agent," August 1, 1896, ARCIA, 313.

20. For archival information on Makah whaling, see Samuel Hancock, *Thirteen Years Residence on the North-West Coast: Containing an Account of Travels and Adventures Among the Indians, Their Manners and Customs, Their Treatment of Prisoners, and Also a Description of the Country* (1860), unpublished typed manuscript version in the Samuel Hancock Papers, UWSC, 139; Swan, Diaries, 1–6, Swan Papers; Samuel Morse, "Report of Neah Bay Agency," August

20, 1897, ARCIA, 291–92; Anderson to Chute, June 19, 1937, MCRC photocopy from original in Ms 15/23, box 6, Chute Collection, WSHSA. Anglo-Americans also described this practice to contemporary audiences, in, for example, Swan, "Indian Method of Killing Whales"; Lucien M. Lewis, "The Whale Hunters of Neah Bay: How on Occasion the Makah Indians Paddle out to Sea in Their Dugout Canoes and Kill 'Chit-up-Puk,'" *Field and Stream*, April 1906 [clipping available at British Columbia Archives, Victoria]. For more recent scholarly discussions of Makah whaling, see Karen Samantha Barton, "'Red Waters': Contesting Marine Space as Indian Place in the U.S. Pacific Northwest" (PhD diss., University of Arizona, 2000), 86; Charlotte Coté, *Spirits of Our Whaling Ancestors: Revitalizing Makah and Nuu-chah-nulth Traditions* (Seattle: University of Washington Press, 2010), 15–41; Ruth Kirk and Richard D. Daugherty, *Hunters of the Whale: An Adventure in Northwest Coast Archaeology* (New York: William Morrow, 1974), 44–50.

21. Michael Simmons, February 3, 1855, quoted in Charles Miles, *Michael T. Simmons* ([Seattle]: V. E. Bower, 1980), 204. One of the translators present at the negotiations for the Treaty of Neah Bay, Simmons later became the territory's first Indian agent. See also Charles J. Russell to Isaac I. Stevens, February 6, 1856, Stevens Papers, Beinecke.

22. George Gibbs, *Indian Tribes of Washington Territory* (Fairfield, WA: Ye Galleon Press, 1972), 35.

23. This statistic is calculated from whaling returns one Makah whaler, Wha-laltl-as sá buy (also known as Swell), told Swan. October 29–November 1, 1859, Diary 2, Swan Papers.

24. Treaty Negotiation Notes, 4. This verbal promise was never kept.

25. Raymond Williams, "Ideas of Nature, in *Problems in Materialism and Culture*, ed. Raymond Williams (London: Verso, 1980), 83. I have adapted his statement where he writes, "We have mixed our labor with the earth, our forces with its forces too deeply to be able to separate each other out." Anthropologist John Cordell calls this "a special fraternity with the sea." Cordell, *A Sea of Small Boats*, 2.

26. Jake Kosek, *Understories: The Political Life of Forests in Northern New Mexico* (Durham, NC: Duke University Press, 2006), 119.

27. Shepard Krech III, *The Ecological Indian: Myth and History* (New York: Norton, 1999).

28. Leland Donald, *Aboriginal Slavery on the Northwest Coast of North America* (Berkeley: University of California Press, 1997), 272–94.

29. Coll Thrush and Ruth S. Ludwin, "Finding Fault: Indigenous Seismology, Colonial Science, and the Rediscovery of Earthquakes and Tsunamis in Cascadia," *American Indian Culture and Research Journal* 31, no. 4 (2007): 6.

30. Swan, December 4, 1863, Manuscript Journal.

31. Swan, March 10, 1879, Diary 25, Swan Papers.

32. Swan, September 24, 1861, Diary 5, Swan Papers; Swan, Manuscript Journal, 63.

33. Swan, April 6, 1866, Diary 9; September 23, 1866, Diary 10; and December 21, 1878, Diary 23, Swan Papers; Swan, January 22, 1865, Manuscript Journal. For more details on these whaling rituals, see Elizabeth Colson, *The Makah Indians: A Study of an Indian Tribe in Modern American Society* (Minneapolis: University of Minnesota Press, 1953), 5–6, 242–51; Coté, *Spirits of Our Whaling Ancestors*, 23–35; Erna Gunther, "Reminiscences of a Whaler's Wife," *Pacific Northwest Quarterly* 33 (1942); Waterman, "The Whaling Equipment of the Makah Indians," 30–46; Peter S. Webster and Campbell River Museum and Archives Society, *As Far as I Know: Reminiscences of an Ahousat Elder* (Campbell River, BC: Campbell River Museum and Archives, 1983).

34. Swan, April 25, 1861, Diary 4, and March 9, 1862, Diary 5, Swan Papers; Swan, "Indian Method of Killing Whales."

35. Waterman, "The Whaling Equipment of the Makah Indians," 45–46; Swan, "The Indians of Cape Flattery," 22–23. For a discussion on the differences between feasts and potlatches, see Eugene Y. Arima, *The West Coast People: The Nootka of Vancouver Island and Cape Flattery* (Victoria: British Columbia Provincial Museum, 1983), 71–82.

36. [Testimony of Joe Sly,] October 15, 1941, "Old Fishing Locations, October 1941," Edward Swindell, Jr. Papers (M005), MCRC.

37. This date is estimated from a genealogical account that separated Makahs of the early 1860s from Deeart, the original "owner" of Neah Bay, by twelve generations. Neah Bay is named after Deeart, who took this village back from Ditidahts. Swan, January 13–14, 1863, Diary 6, Swan Papers.

38. Albert Irvine and Luke Markistun, *How the Makah Obtained Possession of Cape Flattery* (New York: Museum of the American Indian, 1921).

39. John Meares, *Voyages Made in the Years 1788 and 1789, from China to the N. W. Coast of America*, vol. 1 (London: J. Walter, 1791), 247.

40. *Sea power* is defined as "the ability to ensure free movement on the sea for oneself and to inhibit, if need be, a similar capacity in others." Warren Tute and Claire Francis, eds., *The Commanding Sea: Six Voyages of Discovery* (London: Book Club Associates, 1981), 175.

41. Meares, *Voyages Made in the Years 1788 and 1789*, 282–87.

42. Treaty Negotiation Notes, 2.

43. Charles J. Kappler, ed., *Indian Treaties, 1778–1883* (New York: Interland Publishing, 1972), 682.

44. Barton, "'Red Waters,'" 247.

45. Swan, January 24, 1880, Diary 10, Swan Papers.

46. Bering Sea Tribunal of Arbitration, *Fur Seal Arbitration*, 377–87.

47. Cary C. Collins, "Subsistence and Survival: The Makah Indian Reservation, 1855–1933," *Pacific Northwest Quarterly* 87, no. 4 (1996): 183.

48. Swan, April 6, 1866, Diary 9, Swan Papers.

49. Micah McCarty (Makah), pers. comm., summer 2004.

50. Jennifer Sepez, "Political and Social Ecology of Contemporary Makah Subsistence Hunting, Fishing and Shellfish Collecting Practices" (PhD diss., University of Washington, 2001), 18, 198–99, 234–35; Sandi Doughton, "Tapping Tidal Energy: The Wave of the Future," *Seattle Times*, October 7, 2007; Makah Tribe, "Water Quality Standards for Surface Waters," ([Neah Bay, WA]: [Makah Tribe], 2006), 15–20; "Steps Outlined to Avoid or Limit Oil Spills," *Seattle Times*, July 13, 2006; Luis Cabrera, "Makah Plan for Cutter Riles Activists," *Seattle Times*, January 17, 2002.

51. Barton, "'Red Waters,'" 149, 237–38.

52. For a more nuanced explanation of common property concepts, see Bonnie J. McCay, "Sea Tenure and the Culture of the Commoners," in *A Sea of Small Boats*, 203–27.

53. Cordell, *A Sea of Small Boats*, 13.

54. Kappler, *Indian Treaties*, 682.

55. "Old Fishing Locations."

56. The 1974 Boldt Decision upheld Indian fishing rights. *United States v. State of Washington* (384 F. Supp. 312). See also Alvin J. Ziontz, "History of Treaty Fishing Rights in the Northwest," in *Tribal Report to the Presidential Task Force on Treaty Fishing Rights in the Northwest*, ed. Northwest Indian Fisheries Commission (Olympia: The Commission, 1977).

57. Some families contest this shift and the expanded oversight power of the tribal government over marine waters and resources. For example, some Makahs opposed the oversight of the tribal whaling commission over the 1999 hunt. Barton, "'Red Waters,'" 248.

58. Michael Marker, "After the Makah Whale Hunt: Indigenous Knowledge and Limits to Multicultural Discourse," *Urban Education* 41, no. 5 (2006): 485. For an excellent examination of the 1999 hunt and its critics, see Coté, *Spirits of Our Whaling Ancestors*, 115–65.

CHAPTER 12

Reinventing "Traditional" Medicine in Postapartheid South Africa

Karen Flint

IN AUGUST 2004, South Africa officially recognized its "indigenous" medical system and the practice of traditional healers.[1] After years of being criminalized under white minority rule and largely condemned by the biomedical community, South Africa's 350,000 traditional healers—who heal through a combination of local remedies and ancestral interventions—will soon have to obtain a government license to practice.[2] Healers will be restricted from treating fatal diseases such as cancer, HIV, and AIDS, but given their popularity—80 percent of the South African population attends such healers—they are seen by many as a necessary component of health-care delivery and as important agents for educating the populace on the biomedical realities, perils, and prevention of HIV and AIDS. Incorporating traditional healers and medicine into a state medical system that has overwhelmingly preferred the biomedical sciences has not been easy. These two medical cultures not only embrace different ideas about the body and origins of illness, but share a history of commercial and ideological competition as well as different relations to state power. History also shows us that what is considered "indigenous" is constantly in flux, subject to various interactions, knowledge flows, and influence by those in power.

The process of legalization and regulation of traditional medicine has the potential to radically alter our notions of what is or is not traditional medicine. It also presents a number of difficult questions: How will a largely local, unsystematized, nonhierarchical and oral collection of therapies that as of yet is largely unregulated come to be systematized and brought under the regulatory eye of government? Given that governments tend to favor institutional sciences and those who are Western educated and bureaucratically literate, is it possible to rectify the imbalances of power that would enable healers to be meaningfully incorporated in a state-sanctioned system of medical pluralism?[3]

In addition to the challenges of regulating African medicine, healers in the future will have to cope with the growing HIV/AIDS epidemic,[4] an overharvesting of medicinal plants, protecting intellectual property rights, avoiding exploitation for commercial gains, and possibly losing control over the ways in which future generations utilize traditional medicines. Changes in South Africa during the 1990s profoundly altered the stakes of traditional medicine and created new stakeholders that now include pharmaceutical companies, government departments, and university research labs. Bioprospecting of indigenous medicinal plants is now seen as a legitimate and necessary government project. It is promoted not only for its potential health and commercial benefits, but as a means of highlighting the nation's strengths. A former health minister stated: "South Africa is blessed with a rich heritage of medicinal plants that through sustained research and development, could offer a solution to some of the common health problems the world is grappling with."[5]

An integral part of bioprospecting is collecting and collating existing local medical knowledge in a form that is useful and knowable to government, university labs, and pharmaceutical companies. While the collection of medicinal botanical knowledge has roots in the colonial period and the collaboration of healers and scientists is not new, the University of Cape Town's Traditional Medicine Program (TRAMED) began a new type of collaboration in 1994. This program brought in traditional healers during its initial phases, helped them to write articles, produced a *Traditional Healer's Primary Care Book* (1997), promised benefit sharing in the case of successful bioprospecting, and has created an expanding national databank of South Africa's medicinal plants. In addition to helping bridge local and scientific medical knowledges, TRAMED largely shaped the government's agenda regarding the future regulation of traditional medical practitioners and their medicines, and prioritized government funding and research.

A number of factors in the 1990s changed government and scientists' ideas about the importance of African healers and medicinal plants. First, the HIV/AIDS crisis of the 1990s encouraged new collaborative efforts between healers and biomedical practitioners. While such schemes had detractors, evidence of successful collaboration existed.[6] More important, the end of apartheid brought a flush of international funding that sought to support collaboration and HIV/AIDs training for healers.[7] Second, the "legitimacy" of African medicines gained national prominence when Thabo Mbeki assumed the presidency in 1998 and articulated his vision of an "African Renaissance." An important component of which emphasized "Indigenous Knowledge Systems" or IKS—the art, science, technology, practices, and knowledge systems passed down through South Africa's generations. This was a radical break from the apartheid government that had openly disparaged and ignored African medicine and science.[8] Third, traditional healers' associations seeking legalization and licensing of their profession informed government conversations regarding the future of health-care delivery. Fourth, the financial success of the herbal remedy *hoodia* held out hope for both the South African government and its pharmacology labs, who coincidently (or not) have vigorously touted the benefits of IKS ever since.[9] While Medical Research Council funding for TRAMED came earlier, recognizing the commercial potential of South Africa's indigenous cultures and plants has greatly increased government interest, investment, and support. Finally, long-standing environmental concerns moved botanists, government leaders, and healers to consider new options with regard to harvesting and processing of traditional medicinal plants.

This chapter investigates how the transformation of one type of knowledge and power ("indigenous" or "traditional") becomes another (institutional science), and how it can have important repercussions to both knowledge communities. Like Lance van Sittert's earlier discussion for the scientific appropriation of "indigenous" water divining, I seek to understand how these partnerships have been cultivated and/or enforced, and how various stakeholders perceived the benefits or challenges of such interaction. Likewise, how did such collaborative efforts (past and present) not only promote the crossing of boundaries (potentially changing both communities), but simultaneously reinforce divisions between "science" and "indigenous" knowledges? Finally, I ask about the potential for South Africa's indigenous medical knowledges to heal the body politic as well as the corporeal bodies of its citizens. To examine the "reinvention" or reimagining of traditional medicine in the postapartheid period, I begin this chapter by examining the successful bioprospecting of hoodia, which, in addition to introducing local knowledges to the world, also created a new benefit sharing model. I then move to examine the historical means by which such knowledge transfers occur, as well as the incentives and disincentives of more-recent collaboration between government, scientists, universities, and healers. I examine these themes in the creation of TRAMED and its database, which will most likely serve as the basis of a future national pharmacopeia. Following some of the necessary negotiations that eased interaction between these knowledge communities, I conclude with the various implications of this more recent collaboration.

Bioprospecting Traditional Medicines: The Case of Hoodia

In 1996, South African government scientists in the Council for Scientific and Industrial Research (CSIR) isolated and patented compound P57 from the Kalahari's *Hoodia gordonii* plant—an appetite suppressant used by San people in Southern Africa to sustain them during long hunts and times of food scarcity. In 1997, CSIR licensed its patent to the British pharmaceutical company Phytopharm for $21 million, who in turn subleased it for $32 million for commercial development to U.S.-based Pfizer Corporation and then to Unilever, the maker of Slimfast.[10] What was unique and interesting about the hoodia case was the decision by the CSIR to participate in benefit sharing with San communities. Negotiations were prompted when a Pfizer representative in the UK remarked that the San—the original discoverers of this increasingly popular herb—were extinct.[11]

Legally there is little precedent under international laws that would support indigenous people's claims to patent traditional medicine. Existing international patent law as spelled out in the World Trade Organization's Agreement on Trade-Related Aspects of Intellectual Property Rights (TRIPS) (1986–1994 Uruguay Round) prohibits the patenting of whole plants. Instead, patents require new innovations and discoveries. Thus new plant varieties, such as Monsanto's bioengineered crops that resist the weed-killer "Round Up," or discoveries like compound P57, can be patented, whereas the hoodia plant cannot. An integral part of patenting and bioprospecting involves subjecting plants to laboratory testing with the aim of isolating active compounds. Efforts are then generally taken to synthetically reproduce such compounds, not only to reduce the costs of production, but also to create greater chemical stability and quality control. Dependence on laboratory testing thus not only transforms the nature of local knowledges, but makes it very difficult to patent "traditional" knowledges.

As prescribed, international patent law cannot recognize the originators who discovered the use (medicinal or otherwise) of a plant. The inequities of this system, which privilege those with capital and laboratories over those who are knowledge rich but "research" poor, has led a number of researchers to call this process "biopiracy."[12] While moral imperatives for benefit sharing may be missing from international patent law, local patent laws can provide some protection. Yet even these laws presume that patented knowledge is exclusive—to either an individual or a corporate author. This thus raises questions of how to compensate a community such as the San, who also cross national borders, or a smaller number of specialists such as traditional healers for their knowledge, which contributes to the discovery of active compounds like P57. Furthermore, how do such communities even afford the expense of securing an initial patent, or the yearly costs of license renewal, both of which may be beyond their reach? The Convention on Biological Diversity (1992) may provide some protections given that signatories must ensure "the conservation of biological diversity, the sustainable use of its components and the *fair and equitable sharing* of the benefits arising out of the utilization of genetic resources."[13] While such language might implore benefit sharing, it is not prescriptive and thus begs the question of who to compensate (nations, communities, or healers) and how.

In the case of hoodia, the South African San community had received R260,000 from CSIR by 2003, and future royalties were projected as high as R8 to R12 million. In addition, to a percentage of future royalties, the San would participate in growing and cultivating the plant.[14] This last part of the agreement may in fact be the most lucrative, given the world's newfound desire for hoodia and the difficulty in profitably synthesizing P57. Such difficulties, in fact, led Pfizer to drop the project in 2003.[15] This did not dissuade Unilever, however, who paid £6.5 million to conduct further research between 2004 and 2008.[16] Though they also dropped the project and Phytopharm is still looking for a potential partner, contracting of large hoodia farms in Southern Africa has begun and more are anticipated.[17]

While P57 has thus far remained undeveloped,[18] the sale of the patent and a preliminary unpublished study by Phytopharm generated much attention and prompted the sale of hoodia and imitation hoodia by natural-remedy companies worldwide. The increased demand for hoodia led to its being placed on the endangered species list, and its export out of South Africa is now strictly controlled.[19] Nonetheless, this has not stopped poachers from attempting to steal the plant, nor natural-supplement companies from claiming to sell it.[20]

The hoodia example demonstrates that the process by which traditional medicines are transformed and absorbed into the biomedical market is both similar and different to past processes. Bioprospecting means extracting African medicinal plants from both their physical and their social environment, with little acknowledgment of (let alone compensation for) the persons who initially utilized them. In the past, as will be discussed shortly, any acknowledgment that linked African medicinal plants to Africans was generally disparaging. Indeed, it was the process of scientific inquiry in which chemists and pharmacologists extracted African plants that made African *muthi* (medicine), formerly cloaked as superstitious and unscientific, both knowable and valued in the scientific world.[21] Such processes necessitated the crossing of knowledge boundaries, yet also reinforced the differences between these two communities.

While hoodia initially followed this same scenario, changes in South Africa, including its signing of the Convention on Biological Diversity in 1995,[22] along with some strong legal coercion on the part of the San's lawyers, made it impossible to completely dissociate the San from hoodia.[23] More recent South African legislation (2004) seeks to better protect shareholders of "indigenous biological resources" from future bioprospectors.[24] Because hoodia has been largely available through the natural-remedy market rather than as a pharmaceutical, romanticized notions of the San have been used as a marketing ploy. Second, bioprospecting of African medicines, like other traditional medicines around the globe, generally has involved chemical testing of plants for their commercial value and eventual use by nonindigenous populations. Clearly this is the case with hoodia, and it is hard to escape the much remarked upon irony that the San turned to hoodia because they lacked food, whereas obese Americans may use it due to an overabundance.

Finally, it is difficult to determine the impact hoodia's commercial development will have on San communities. While the San have enjoyed greater recognition around the world, with the likes of *60 Minutes*' Leslie Stahl stomping through the Kalahari, what will such attention and monies bring to these communities? As authors Posey and Dutfield ask, will the tenor of relations between local communities and commercial enterprises be one that shows respect for local notions of the environment, or will it create a cycle of dependency?[25] Also, what impact will such benefit sharing schemes have on the ways that government and industry approach the future study and commercialization of local medicinal plants?

Scientific Endeavors: Collecting, Identifying, and Collating Medicinal Plants

The case of hoodia is but one example of a much wider national initiative to test, record, and potentially commercialize the active components of South Africa's medicinal plants. In 1999, CSIR opened a medical plant extraction facility with the help of Phytopharm and Pfizer.[26] Perhaps unsurprisingly, the pharmaceutical industry has been quite supportive of bioprospecting in South Africa, as well as the compiling of a medicinal plant database. Noristan began compiling just such a database in 1974, much of which included plants already within the public domain. The initial collecting, identifying, and collating of native plants, the very foundation of this database, began with the aims of colonial scientific inquiry and commercial exploitation.

While the earliest European travelers and traders to southeastern Africa used indigenous remedies for immediate cures, medical practitioners in the early settlements also looked to local botanicals for their commercial potential and as a means to replace more expensive imported European herbs.[27] By the 1870s, Cape pharmacies stocked their shelves with indigenous herbs and various South African patent medicines that included native plants.[28] The prospecting of local remedies also proved to be a lucrative export business. In the late nineteenth century, such successes led a reviewer of *South African Materia Medica* to conclude: "A wide field and a well-paying one lies open to anyone with sufficient knowledge, business capacity, time and capital to devote to the investigation, cultivation, and exportation of South African drugs."[29] By this time, aloe and buchu, two herbs found in the Cape Colony, were being widely exported back to Europe.[30] While African herbs were sold by both Africans and Europeans, and some were incorporated into Lennons, a local proprietary medicine, or herbal medicines sold in Germany, none reached the pharmaceutical fame of hoodia.

Outside of commercial interests, most Europeans' attention to African plants stemmed from the pursuit of scientific inquiry and Linnaeus classification. The rise of modern science accompanied the rise of European imperialism, which in turn depended upon new scientific research and data generated by new lands and the local knowledge of colonized peoples. Initiated by amateur collectors, botanists, and colonial doctors, interest in African botanicals led such individuals to write, sketch, and send samples of African plants and trees to local and colonial botanical gardens. Such endeavors inevitably meant divorcing African medicine from Africans. The first transformation of indigenous knowledges to botanical and scientific knowledge can be seen with the privilege of these European "discoverers" to designate personal and family names to exotic plants.[31] This was followed by botanists who cataloged and sorted plants into species and genuses at local botanical gardens and those like Kew Gardens.[32] While more general plants may have been "discovered" by Europeans, those with noted medicinal properties initially came to their attention through local populations.

By the late nineteenth and early twentieth centuries, this scientific knowledge was disseminated through scholarly journals, in museum annals, and as books. Consequently, what used to be indigenous knowledge became a part of the public domain that eventually formed the basis of South Africa's medicinal plant database. This notion of public domain is important, as once information has entered the public domain, it can no longer be claimed for patenting purposes. Indeed, the basis of much of the academy's knowledge of South Africa's medicinal plants reflects this earlier conversion of local knowledge to institutional knowledge, with barely a nod to the initial users.[33]

"Our Laboratories Are Our Ancestors": Healers' Incentives for Collaboration

South Africa's traditional healers have sought to convince local and national governments of their legitimacy since the early 1930s. To do so, healers organized themselves into healing associations and made appeals to government administrators in the language and symbols of science and modernism. One early healing association that sought government recognition referenced pharmacologists Watt and Breyer-Brandwijk's work on Southern Africa's medicinal plants (1932), as well as the unequal exchange between Western scientists and indigenous knowledge holders. They observed that "after they [Europeans] have taken it out of the hands of the owners, by saying it is "WITCH CRAFT" . . . [they are] at the same time taking advantage of it."[34] If the scientific labs of white South Africa had tested and recognized the power of traditional medicines, how could they prevent Africans from using them? The need to situate African medicines within the framework of "Western" or academic knowledge was not merely rhetorical. In fact, it is one of the driving forces behind the current collaborative efforts of healers, academic researchers, government departments, and pharmaceuticals, though many healers have remained skeptical of this approach.

Both sentiments were reflected in 1998 by Muzi Mthemjwa, a Durban *sangoma* (diviner) and artist:

Now that the government has changed, they are giving people [healers] the opportunity to change themselves and improve themselves. Now for instance I just buy a grinding machine instead of wasting material like I do when chopping like this. . . . Those who are becoming *sangomas* should go to school to learn mathematics to learn how to mix what with what. Our laboratories are our ancestors, they say "no you've made too much *muthi*, just take some of that out, put more of this stuff and this stuff." But now we cannot rely on our ancestors to prove ourselves, we must have laboratories. We must have people who can purify and test our medicines to see if it is good for selling to other countries. We must have our own laboratories and purifiers to keep pharmaceuticals from taking advantage of us.[35]

This answer highlights a certain tension that existed in 1998 and continues today between modernizing African medicine and legitimizing its existence by rooting it to a precolonial past. Despite the recognition that a healer's medical authority comes from "traditional" or "indigenous" sources such as one's connection to ancestors, the language of science and modernity is used as a metaphor to describe the accuracy of the ancestors. Mthemjwa's comments about the necessity of including mathematics, as well as purifying and testing African medicines in a laboratory, point to a need to establish "traditional" healers' medical authority under a biomedical as well as a local medical model. Mthemjwa's request for a lab seems to signify cutting out a new type of space, both figuratively and literally.

Healers' enthusiasm for modernizing African medicine and legitimating its efficacy within a biomedical model reflects healers' responses to global and local conditions, such as a booming natural-remedy market, bioprospectors from international pharmaceuticals, a government supportive of Indigenous Knowledge Systems, and as of 2004, government recognition of their profession. Current healers, like many of their urban predecessors in the 1930s, are thus trying to figure out ways of balancing what is "traditional" about African medicine while at the same time using biomedical ideas of the body, research, and professionalization to create advantages for themselves.

The government's legal recognition of healers emerged from a largely healer-driven process. Up through the 1980s, a handful of *inyangas* (herbalists) in Natal and Zululand had been the only legally licensed healers in the country. While healers had been actively organizing into regional and national healing associations since the 1930s, the 1980s saw greater efforts to nationalize these organizations.³⁶ Such movements were motivated in part by the need to combat what healers saw as an increase in "charlatanism." Associations thus sought to increase standards of professionalization for their members, and vigorously lobbied for legal recognition. Such efforts only intensified in 1994. Licensing not only would help implement better quality control, but represented government validation of traditional healers. Such validation meant tangible monetary benefits, including reimbursement for medical aid, the ability to bring deadbeat clients to court, and the chance to gain government monies, materials, and support for healer initiatives. The hope of government licensing served as a backdrop to many of the collaborative projects that healers engaged in with government, biomedical practitioners, and academic researchers in the 1990s.

In some cases these collaborative efforts showed immediate benefits to both parties, and in Durban, healers made local gains and steps toward legal recognition on a national level. In 1995, Mr. V. T. Mkize, head of Environmental Health, a subdivision of Durban's department of city health, set up a body composed of department members and heads of local healing associations to assess local healers' needs. Healers complained about the Warwick Junction muthi market and the ways herbs were marketed in both an unsanitary manner and without regard to local customs. For instance, women muthi collectors violated taboos by sleeping at the market to protect their merchandise. From the city's perspective, the muthi market also posed health and safety risks. In response, the city built a new partially covered market that enabled healers to secure their merchandize at night.³⁷ Thus, unlike the early 1990s, when healers and collectors worried about raids by police or the Natal Parks Board (concerned about the illicit gathering of endangered plants and animals), the late 1990s transformed the government into a viable ally. Likewise, the umbrella organization, initiated and mentored in part by Mkize, trumped other regional healing associations in terms of organization and knowledge-testing of healers, thus priming KwaZulu-Natal to become the first province to officially begin licensing healers in 2000. This local council, formed in 1999, had seven regional representatives, which enabled it to acknowledge different ecological and regional knowledge; a model subsequently adopted by the national Traditional Medical Practitioners Council.³⁸

This reinventing of traditional medicine—through legalization and collaboration with biomedicine—has not gone uncontested. The KwaZulu-Natal Traditional Healing Council has debated the legitimacy of processing muthi.³⁹ Likewise, unaffiliated healers express skepticism about such councils, assuming an avaricious leadership rather than one interested in public health. Others argue that licensing will only increase healers' and therefore patients' expenses while adding the burdens of "professionalization" and state regulation. Finally, patients may not be ready for such "reinventions" of traditional medicine, preferring "traditional" medical preparations and presentations over pills, tinctures, or "traditional hospitals." Many healers, on the other hand, have seen collaboration with government and biomedicine as a viable strategy for preserving traditional medicines.

TRAMED and the Making of a National Database

The development of the University of Cape Town's Traditional Medicines Program in 1994 and the various research units and centers that grew around it seemingly represents a radical departure from previous relations between the holders and the recorders of local knowledge. Initially conceived as a national center of information regarding traditional medicines, TRAMED was to serve traditional healers, biomedical practitioners, the Ministry of Health, the pharmaceutical industry, and the scientific community. The aims were to promote the use, documentation, conservation, and scientific validation of these local medicines. A database would then be compiled by pulling together public domain information and include new chemical information as local medicinal plants were tested and analyzed.[40] Such a program had similar draws for healers and the scientific community, as well as unique incentives that appealed to each. Of primary interest to both groups was the preservation of indigenous medical knowledge. Overcultivation and the disappearance of popular medicinal plants in South Africa raised concerns regarding access, cost, and the ability to test plants that might provide future medical cures to a wider international community.[41] Another mutual incentive, as seen in the case of hoodia, was the potential for the commercial development of traditional medicines.

TRAMED was largely the brainchild of Nigel Gericke, a biomedical doctor who had trained in traditional medicine while working in a rural hospital in Gazankulu. These experiences, in combination with a short working stint in Canada, where he saw the Inuit losing their medical knowledge within a generation, prompted him to draw up a proposal for TRAMED. Gericke approached a number of different institutes, universities, and government organizations, all of which told him initially in 1990 and 1991 that they had very little interest in this "ethnic stuff," though the government's Medical Research Council (MRC) told him that they would be interested in a database.[42] Likewise, the ANC government in waiting, whose preliminary national health-care plan was biomedically and primary-care focused, expressed little interest.[43]

Gillian Scott at the National Botanical Institute was one of the few interested individuals, and together she and Gericke convinced the chair of UCT's pharmacology department to house the project if they could secure funding. This chair was Peter Folb, who also headed the MCC (Medical Control Council)—SA's regulatory body of medicines. Folb says he agreed to support the idea because of its potential for research, public safety, regulation, bridging the gap between biomedical and traditional medical practitioners, and developing botanic medicines to address many chronic African diseases. Folb admits that his work at the World Health Organization (WHO) and their drugs program somewhat predisposed him to the idea. TRAMED thus began on a one-year trial basis with funding from the E.U. in 1994, South Africa's first year as a newly democratic country.[44]

After a fairly successful first year, further funding was obtained for the next few from pharmaceutical companies SmithKlineBeecham and South African Druggist. Yet, even then, Dr. Nkosazana Dlamini Zuma, then minister of health, told Folb that traditional medicines were not a high priority.[45] Though this new government was predominantly African, many had been Western educated, spent years in exile in Europe, and tended to view traditional medicine with skepticism. By the late 1990s, however, the same institutions that initially showed little to no interest, to include the MRC, the National Botanical Institute, and University of Western Cape's (UWC) pharmacology department, all became an integral part of the newly formulated South African Traditional Medicines Research Group (SATMERG).

Noristan donated its database to TRAMED, forming the basis of what became the South African Traditional Medicines database, now called TRAMED III. Noristan's database contained a large amount of public domain information as well as the results of in-house testing. This included 46,000 folk-use anecdotes as well as bioactivity assays on 350 medicinal plants.[46] TRAMED aimed to expand the database to make it as comprehensive as possible and to include all vernacular names, treatments, pharmacology, chemistry, and toxicology of each plant. Once in TRAMED's possession, initial efforts focused on updating the public domain information. But new data also came from testing plants for chemical toxicity and pharmacological properties in UCT's own pharmacological labs.

TRAMED initially focused on traditional medicines used for treating two of South Africa's major diseases—TB and malaria—though more recently SATMERG expanded this to include treatments for HIV/AIDS.

After 1997, UWC's school of pharmacy studied and added pharmacological monographs of South Africa's one hundred most commonly used medicinal plants.[47] More recent claims on the MRC website stipulate a desire to increase this number to four thousand species, practically all the medicinal plants currently being used in South Africa.[48] Further data came from testing conducted under the auspices of the MRC, which became not only a major funder of SATMERG but took over responsibility for and ownership of the database. Other data emerged from consultation with traditional healers, who were approached either through healing organizations or by individual students and researchers from UCT's pharmacology lab.

TRAMED and the database had a strong appeal to both the scientific research community and the government, particularly as they envisioned ways to "add value" to this information. Some aims outlined in TRAMED's initial report included "the industrial development of the phytopharmaceutical industry" and becoming an "independent and critical resource for the Ministry of Health in the development of its policies that are aimed at developing the traditional health sector."[49] Others included reorienting UCT's pharmacology department, which is consulted seventy to eighty times a day by biomedical practitioners for clinical cases, to include "clinical work, research, regulation, that ideally would support healers."[50]

Peter Eagles, the new head of the MCC, projected in 2002 that "adding more value to [database information] . . . might mean adding other publications or hard copies, isolating individual activities, selling them to pharmaceutical companies or developing it themselves, helping traditional healers to have more access to better products." The database also would be used to create a national formulary of "safe, effective, 'essential' herbal medicines," which in turn would help guide national policy with respect to regulation, control, and approval for traditional medicines. This goal was pursued within TRAMED's first year as they successfully petitioned the MCC for a "Traditional Medicines Committee" that theoretically would be "supported by a traditional medicines formulary." This subcommittee of the MCC would help determine which plants to regulate and ensure quality control of their production.[51]

The expansion and success of TRAMED/SATMERG, however, was dependent upon collaboration with traditional healers who had less-obvious reasons to support the initiative. Given the apartheid era, when most healers were criminalized under the witchcraft suppression act, harassed by police and park board officials, and faced real and perceived commercial competition with local chemists and natural remedy marketers,[52] healers had good reason for skepticism. Siya Ntutela, then a UCT PhD pharmacology student and TRAMED/SATMERG researcher who worked with healers, noted their reluctance: "Sometimes healers tell you I won't give you the plant I use, because it makes me give food to my family."[53]

Concerns regarding trust and the financial hardship led Gladis Williams, a Coloured healer in Cape Town who worked with TRAMED/SATMERG, to explain, "I mean if we give them [researchers] all what we know, you know, they will do it theirselves and put some more in, something like chemicals to make it a little bit stronger. Then they go to them, the patients, I'm talking about sick people; then we don't get the amount of people that we used to get."[54] Another healer, Philip Kubekeli, in referencing larger issues of intellectual property rights, pointed to *Medicinal Plants of South Africa*,[55] a colorful photo book in its second run that outlines the chemical compounds and indigenous uses of local plants, and claimed that money was being made from healers' knowledge while they saw few tangible benefits.

Likewise, in 1998, a muthi shop owner in KwaZulu-Natal complained about a natural-remedy company that sold pills of African potato for R99 a bottle while he sold the actual herb for R1–2 a piece.[56] In a world where the natural-remedy market itself is worth $30 billion worldwide, and healers possess few of the advantages of government-recognized and -sponsored medicine, nor the clout and capital of international pharmaceuticals, healers seemed acutely aware of their vulnerability for exploitation as their specialized and local knowledge was disseminated to a wider world.

Nonetheless, there were other incentives that made collaboration with TRAMED/SATMERG desirable, and a variety of strategies were used to overcome healers' concerns. This included sending African pharmacology students out to meet healers, inviting healing associations to UCT, publishing the *Traditional Healer's Primary Care Book*, and promises of benefit sharing. A number of individual healers and healing associations responded positively. Ntutela, referencing apartheid's past, stated: "I'm sure during those times people were scared of giving out certain information to the oppressors and exploiters." He then added: "Now, me, I'm black and if I go to a township maybe I'll get a better reception and get told the truth about a plant or so on." Healers' participation seemed related to healers' feelings that they were being recognized and taken seriously by the university. But many healers also saw collaboration as a means to gain government recognition.

Whether or not TRAMED made explicit promises, such expectations played a role in Williams's decision to participate: "The thing is that I was interested [in TRAMED/SATMERG] because the government doesn't want to know us exactly, because we never went to university.... I wanted to know if we could get a chance to work with the medical doctors. So they [the government] refuse us. We don't know nothing. They call us very funny names. We are witch doctors and so on.... Then they [TRAMED/SATMERG] said they will go to them, the government and see if they can get us in." Healers seemed to implicitly believe that government recognition would lead to government aid and other more tangible benefits—such as land to grow muthi, funding for healing centers, and perhaps help in commercializing African medicine—learning how to prepare tablets, and package and sell South African herbs overseas.[57] Given the composition of TRAMED/SATMERG and their influence on the MCC and MRC, this was a fair assumption.

Like healers from KwaZulu-Natal, involved healers were also drawn to the project as a means of preserving indigenous knowledges. Philip Kubekeli, a healing association leader who worked closely with TRAMED/SATMERG, explained:

> I felt it would be very good for us traditional healers ... that we know how good and efficient our herbs are. So we must be sure which part of the herb is good and so on, so we can be sure of some of our indigenous traditional herbs.... I have said a long time ago there must be something written for our future generations, if there is nothing written all our knowledge will just collapse. Truly, look at our children, ... our children don't even know the first principle of our primary health care, ... so I say a database is very good for our future generation.[58]

Again, "modernizing" African medicine through collaboration with universities and government seemed to be one of the driving forces behind healers' collaboration, particularly for the *Traditional Healer's Primary Care Book*, whose 1997 publication showed TRAMED's commitment to meeting traditional healers' needs as well as their own.

Another incentive driving university, government, and healers' participation was the potential for the commercial development of traditional medicines whose profit would theoretically be equitably distributed. While TRAMED's initial report did not mention benefit sharing,[59] SATMERG's later decision to engage in benefit sharing sometimes (intended or not) enticed healer participation. Ntutela explained: "We told them [healers] exactly where we were coming from and what we wanted to do and get out of the study and told them if any commercial development came out, we would work out a system of benefit sharing. So they knew there was a system."[60] Some healers said this was true, while others said benefit sharing was not mentioned. SATMERG tentatively agreed to a 50 percent benefit sharing scheme where money would go back to the community rather than to individuals.[61]

Gilbert Matsabisa, a former graduate of UCT's pharmacology department and head of the Indigenous Knowledge Systems Unit of the Medical Research Council, was charged with determining an equitable scheme for IKS benefit sharing. Matsabisa emphasized that SATMERG would create a benefit trust for which people could then apply for funding for local projects. In 2002, however, he considered a 7 percent incentive for information about medical remedies, followed by time for the public to contest the ownership of this knowledge.[62] The more recently established National Indigenous Knowledge Systems Office (NIKSO) of the Department of Science and Technology, which supports benefit sharing, indicates that legal protections for intellectual property rights are still nonexistent.[63] Such benefit schemes seem rather problematic and possibly divisive, given that IKS are not based on individual knowledge, and there are questions of how healers would even learn about such claims in order to contest them. In essence, benefit sharing for healers contains many of the same problems posed by international patent laws that were mentioned at the beginning of this chapter. Consequently, it is questionable whether healers who use whole plants and combinations thereof would be compensated for successful commercial development of remedies.

Results and Implications of Collaboration

It is not possible to completely discern the results and success of the collaboration between healers, the government, and universities, and it may be several years before the outcomes are fully apparent. Given the university's institutional power and access to government, it is not surprising that much of TRAMED/SATMERG interaction has taken place on biomedical terms or that it will most likely have greater implications for the future practice of traditional medicine than biomedicine. This has been a bone of contention, but has also been seen as another way for healers to gain medical authority in a biomedically oriented state. The reinvention of traditional medicines is also seen by many policy-makers, botanists, and healers as a means to solve some of South Africa's medical woes as well as its ecological, economic, and psychological wounds. The government's plans to regulate traditional medicines and the possible impact this might have on the daily practices of traditional medical practitioners, however, was either unknown or largely ignored by healers interviewed.[64]

The greatest consequence of TRAMED/SATMERG has been the transference of local knowledge into the language of and study of biomedicine. This has opened up various new funding sources as well as opportunities for academic study, commercialization of medicinal plants, and the possibility of future regulation. While this transference is historical in nature, increased resources and a new political climate have sped up the process. These incentives have convinced individual healers and healing associations to participate in this endeavor regardless of other healers' desires or fears. As a result, the academic study of local medicinal plants has opened up a new research field with government and international funding going largely to academic departments and for PhD students, including two from TRAMED who acted as both the former and current head of MRC's Indigenous Knowledge Systems Unit.

With regard to increasing healers' "medical authority," the testing of medicinal plants has shown that the majority do possess pharmacological activity—be it analgesic, anti-inflammatory, antimicrobial, or antiulcer activity. While this points to the efficacy of various indigenous medicines, TRAMED/SATMERG's work has not led to many patents or the development of organic extracts into useful and marketable pharmaceuticals. By 1995, two plants had shown antimalarial activity; by 2002, two chemicals isolated from these plants were patented, and chemical characterizations had been made for a small number of others. Matsabisa, who was responsible for isolating these chemical compounds, was said to have learned of these medicinal plants from his grandmother. Consequently, benefit sharing did not apply, as this herb was common knowledge. Even if research conducted by SATMERG has not thus far been commercially successful, it has succeeded in securing international interest in this research, and encouraged government investment in this field.

Such collaborative efforts also have persuaded a rethinking of how biomedical researchers collect health data and have led researchers to question how one measures the effectiveness of traditional medicines. This included using an expanded diagnostic system, which focused on patient symptoms rather than biomedical terms like TB or malaria. UCT researchers realized, however, that studies of healers' efficacy also needed to include larger cultural questions. Like medical anthropologists who examine the social context in which illness and healing take place, Ntutela stressed the importance of questioning, "How do people use these medicines, and why do they use it the way they do?"

Eliya Madikane, another student and researcher, said that his work with healers made him realize that biomedicine needed "a more holistic approach."[65] Both researchers emphasized that future chemical testing needed to be pursued along with these other issues. Yet with the exception of "the placebo effect," biomedicine's current translation of local medical knowledges and practices leaves little room for understanding culture. There is no recognition of ancestors, or issues concerning pollution or witchcraft, often deemed as underlying causes of certain illnesses. Consequently, the appropriation of local medical knowledge into biomedicine is limited to biomedical understandings and interests, and thus collaboration has in many ways reinforced rather than reduced the differences of these two knowledge communities.

Healers' collaboration with TRAMED/SATMERG has given certain healers in the Cape and heads of provincial traditional healing associations access to important government officials and policy-makers, enabling healers to push their own agendas. These have included more-abstract goals such as establishing medical authority, as well as concrete objectives such as publishing the *Traditional Healer's Primary Health Care* book, gaining government assistance in building local muthi gardens, and establishing a national healers' center in the Cape. Whether or not this particular collaborative project has helped healers to gain a new sense of medical authority, however, remains to be seen. The national licensing of healers most likely would have occurred regardless of TRAMED/SATMERG. Likewise, muthi gardens in places like KwaZulu-Natal emerged from healers collaborating with botanists and the local parks board but without the same transference of medical plant knowledge.

Some problems with collaboration emerged as these two medical communities not only have different ways of knowing, but different ideas of proper social interactions and processes. Healers and the persons they partnered with, be it students or government personnel, often occupied very different niches of society. In addition to class disparities and a different basis of knowledge, the two had different ideas of time consumption—including duration and flexibility. Healers tend to be democratic and more inclusive, whereas government and academics send delegates. Healers were fairly stable and attached to an area and thus there to see a project to its end. Students and government personnel in the new South Africa have rapid upward mobility and thus many disappear quickly. Students are busy, students leave. Different people do things differently; some people have healers sign documents, while others do not. In a new South Africa, things are very much in flux. This can make the possibilities exciting but frustrating when healers are faced with yet another person with new ideas. This seems to have led to some problems of distrust between the two communities.

One healer, commenting on communications between healers and the university, stated, "It was a struggle. . . . Then we go, then there is no answer for us if they accept us or what. . . . The feedback is not all right." Consequently, she concluded, "They don't believe exactly in us." Because the government initially failed to invest energies in the development and professionalization of traditional medicines, healers felt they were not viewed as the equals of biomedical practitioners. Likewise, they were not compensated when they closed their practices or shops to attend meetings that they assumed occurred with biomedical practitioners. Instead, healers complained that the government and TRAMED/SATMERG initially acted as if they were doing them a favor—helping to prove the efficacy of their medicines and making promises of benefit sharing. Yet this attitude may change with the setting up of the Traditional Medicines Council and writing of intellectual property laws to protect indigenous knowledge systems—only time will tell.

Despite these setbacks and points of contention, reinventing traditional medicines was also imagined as a means to heal the nation both physically and metaphorically. In addition, to Mbeki's African Renaissance and touting of IKS, the government began to advocate the use of traditional medicines as a means to treat HIV/AIDS patients. Mbeki's health minister earned the unflattering moniker "Dr. Beetroot Msimang Tshabalala," because she emphasized the importance of good nutrition in lieu of antiretrovirals as a defense against AIDS. She also promoted use of the African potato (*Hypoxis hemerocallidea*)—a traditional medicine shown to boost the immune system.[66]

With regard to healing the body and nation in the time of HIV/AIDS, healers played a largely informal role rather than a formal one initiated by the government. African healers often offered hope and comfort to HIV/AIDS patients particularly, as biomedicine turned away those unable to afford the expensive regiment of antiretrovirals. Between 1999 and 2000, the MRC conducted a study regarding the acceptability and effectiveness of traditional healers as supervisors of tuberculosis treatment. The results indicated that healers provided a number of advantages for care, including accessibility, shorter waits, good patient compliance, and overall care of the patients' well-being. This led the MRC to recommend that health-care authorities "consider integrating traditional healers into other aspects of healthcare including voluntary counseling and testing for HIV and for home-based care for people with AIDS."[67] Later healers were included as one out of fifteen civil society representatives on the National AIDS Council.[68]

Generally, TRAMED and later the South African government approached the incorporation of traditional medicine into national health care by using the 1977 WHO guidelines, which promoted the "rational use" of traditional medicines. This approach, which couples clinical testing with a national formulary, aims to distribute traditional medicine at a low cost to patients. This means ensuring continued access to the most popular traditional medicines, a concern that matches well with environmental aims for maintaining biological diversity. Botanists have been trying to get healers to consider new means of processing herbs. In their rough and unprocessed form, much is wasted as plants lose potency over time and others are lost due to mold and fungus. Processing herbs by grinding them into powder would keep them longer, produce less waste and thus reduce the price of muthi.

Eagles explained that the most popular and effective herbs would be grown on farms, much like hoodia. This would have the impact of creating rural farming jobs, sustaining medicinal plants, creating commerce as herbs were processed, packaged, and sold commercially, and ensuring their availability to the public.[69] Farm growing and processing of medicinal plants potentially means greater accountability and standardization of herbal strength. Standardization also could make herbal remedies safer and certainly easier for the government to test and regulate, though clearly, testing and training of traditional medical practitioners would be required to ensure safety. Indeed, Gericke, working with the legendary healer and author Credo Mutwa, used this model to contract local farmers and began producing and packaging sutherlandia. This included selling ground sutherlandia to two different consumer groups, with substantially different packaging and pricing—ground sutherlandia by the bagful and pills at national drugstores, like Discom and Clicks, through Phyto Nova, a natural-remedy company.

The incentive to commercialize medicinal plants, however, has had certain implications. Oriented toward pharmaceutical research, government and universities lack the financial incentive to study whole herbs, which cannot be patented. This means that whole medicinal plants are unlikely to undergo more rigorous analysis such as human-subject testing. One such example is the herb sutherlandia—historically used by local

Africans and Afrikaners for cancer, flu, depression, ulcers, and arthritis. Because sutherlandia is a full-spectrum herb whose active ingredients are complementary, it cannot be broken down into active components like P57. Consequently, sutherlandia isn't going to make any money for pharmaceuticals, but it also seems to be one of the reasons why it was initially ignored by the government. When applied to AIDS patients, Gericke found that this herb acted as an immune booster and helped persons regain substantial weight.[70] When he wrote the MRC and later the head of the then Department of Arts, Science, and Technology, his requests for a government study of the herb and appeals to grow it on a commercial scale went unheeded. Only when the former prime minister of France, Michel Rocard, wrote to President Mbeki, indicating that the French NGO Afrique Inititatives was examining this herb and encouraged Mbeki to research it, did the MRC gain interest and conduct its own tests.[71]

Conclusions

Historically, it was the process of separating African medicinal plants from African healers and patients that transformed what was deemed superstitious and unscientific as knowable and valuable in the scientific world. Though such processes necessitated the crossing of knowledge boundaries, it also reinforced the boundaries that separated them. Will herbal powders, pills, and extracts divorced from the environment and traditional means of preparation, but administered by traditional healers, resonate in a meaningful way with healers and patients? Can and should healers and patients be convinced to administer and take medicinal herbs in these new forms? From a regulatory perspective, clearly the database and creation of a national formulary will make it easier to control the safety of commercially available herbs. What is unclear are the benefits such a formulary may have for healers, many of whom tend to use raw herbs rather than processed ones.

While it initially seemed that traditional healers would be involved in prescribing such herbs, it isn't clear from MRC's current web page if this is still the thinking or if they would be available at your local market like any other medicine or even if they might be marketed abroad. Either way, few healers I interviewed, including those who worked with TRAMED/SATMERG, anticipated a national formulary or the future of traditional medicine as described by the head of the MCC.

In conclusion, while this chapter helps to answer the first question posed regarding the systemization of traditional medicine, it leaves open the question of how imbalances of power will impact the meaningful incorporation of traditional medicines and healers into a state-sanctioned system of medical pluralism.

Notes

Part of this chapter appeared in the epilogue of Karen E. Flint, *Healing Traditions: African Medicine, Cultural Exchange, and Competition in South Africa, 1820–1948* (Athens: Ohio University Press, 2008). Funding for this research was provided in part by a Junior Faculty Grant from the University of North Carolina, Charlotte.

1. The term "tradition," like "indigenous," is a useful folk category that has been highly problematized by many academics. Consequently, many scholars have preferred different terms to emphasize that healing practices are not static but dynamic and changing. I use the folk term "traditional healers" because it is often used by practitioners themselves and emphasizes the notion of "tradition," an important means of legitimizing such healing practices within public discourse.

2. The law stipulates that "traditional health practices" are based on "traditional philosophy," which is then defined as "indigenous African techniques, principles, theories, ideologies, beliefs, opinions and customs and uses of traditional medicines ... which are generally used in traditional health practice." While such a definition is somewhat circuitous, the terms "traditional" and "indigenous" are assumed as obvious and knowable. Yet these terms mask a complicated history of medical pluralism and more problematically pose the assumption of "indigenous" or traditional medicine. The implementation of the Traditional Health Practitioners Bill, initially introduced and passed by Parliament in 2004, was delayed after a challenge to the Constitutional Court and signed into law only in January 2008. This bill sets up a Traditional Health Practitioners Council, which will be responsible for providing a "regulatory framework to ensure the efficacy, safety and quality of traditional health care services." "Traditional Health Practitioners Act, 2007," *Government Gazette*, January 10, 2008.

3. Clearly South Africa is not the first country to undergo such a transition, but it is an important process to watch. For other countries, see: Murray Last and G. L. Chavunduka, *The Professionalization of African Medicine* (Dover, NH: Manchester University Press, 1986); David Simmons, "Of Markets and Medicines," in *Borders and Healers: Brokering Therapeutic Resources in Southeast Africa*, ed. Tracy J. Luedke and Harry G. West (Bloomington: Indiana University Press: 2006), 65–81; J. Stephan, "Traditional and Alternative Systems of Medicine" in *International Digest of Health Legislation* 36, no. 2 (1985); Charles

Leslie, "Medical Pluralism in World Perspective," *Social Science and Medicine* 14B (1980): 191–95.

4. A series of articles address the AIDS epidemic specifically in Southern Africa, many of which cover new collaborative efforts between traditional healers and biomedicine. See the articles in *African Studies* 61, no. 1 (2002); for an overview, see my epilogue section on "Healing the Nation in the Time of HIV/Aids," in *Healing Traditions*, 187–91.

5. Karen Pretorius, "Institute for Traditional Medicines" April 8, 2004, accessed December 15, 2006,

http://www.southafrica.info/ess_info/sa_glance/health/traditionalmedicine.htm.

6. This included using healers to administrate TB medication at Valley Trust and then under the auspices of the Medical Research Council (MRC). See *HST Update*, no. 37 (October 1998); "Important Role of Traditional Healers in TB Treatment," *MRC News* 32, no. 3 (June 2001); "Turn Left at the Yellow Daisy Bush," *MRC News* 33, no. 1 (February 2002); "Integrating Traditional Healers" *MRC News* 33, no. 2 (April 2002).

7. S. Mgiba et al., "Organizing South African Traditional Healers to Mount Sexually Explicit HIV/Aids Prevention Campaigns." Eighth International Conference on AIDs in Africa, Marrakech, 1993; Edward Green et al., "The Experience of an AIDS Prevention Programme Focused on South African Traditional Healers," *Social Science Medicine* 40 (1995): 505; "Traditional Healers in South Africa—A Crucial Link in Christian Children's Fund HIV/AIDS Work," 2002, accessed August 8, 2008, http://www.christianchildrensfund.org/content.aspx?id=319. This training has also been taken up by local government agencies such as KwaZulu-Natal's Department of Health. Interview with VT Mkize, Environmental Health Officer for Durban's Health Department, Durban, June 2002.

8. South Africa's National Research Foundation began funding IKS in 2000. Gerri Augusto. "Knowing Differently, Innovating Together? An Exploratory Case Study of Trans-Epistemic Interaction in a South African Bioprospecting Program" (PhD diss., George Washington University, 2004), 144.

9. CSIR boasts of *hoodia* on its bioprospecting website, accessed February 15, 2007, http://www.csir.co.za/plsql/ptl0002/PTL0002_PGE057_RESEARCH?DIVISION_NO=1010012&PROGRAM_NO=3410026.

10. M. Sayagnes, "South Africa: Indigenous Group Wins Rights to Its Healing Herbs," www.corpwatch.org/article, accessed September 29, 2005. "It's Prickly and Sour, But This Plant Could Cure Obesity," *Mail and Guardian* (South Africa), January 4, 2003.

11. "The San and CSIR Announce a Benefit-Sharing Agreement for Potential Anti-Obesity Drug," CSIR Media Release from March 24, 2003, accessed

August 8, 2008, http://ntww1.csir.co.az/plsql/pt10002/PTL0002_PGE157_MEDIA_REL?MEDIA_RELEASE; "Bushmen to Win Royalties from Slimming Drug," *Mail and Guardian*, March 27, 2003; "The San and the CSIR Announce a Benefit-Sharing Agreement for Potential Anti-Obesity Drug."

12. Vandana Shiva , *Biopiracy: The Plunder of Nature and Knowledge* (Cambridge, MA: South End Press, 1997).

13. My emphasis, as quoted in Darrell A. Posey and Graham Dutfield, *Beyond Intellectual Property: Toward Traditional Resource Rights for Indigenous Peoples and Local Communities* (Ottawa: International Development Research Center, 1996), 103.

14. A. Barnett, "Fat Windfall for the San" *Mail and Guardian*, April 6, 2002; "Bushmen to Win Royalties from Slimming Drug," *Mail and Guardian*, March 27, 2003; "San Stand to Make Millions off Fat of the Land," *Mail and Guardian,* July 31, 2003; "Protesting Traditional Knowledge: The San and Hoodia," *Bulletin of the World Health Organization* 84, no. 5 (2006). The CSIR signed a similar benefit sharing agreement with WIMSA Nambia that ensured the San N$24 per kilogram of hoodia and sold through the Southern African Hoodia Growers Association. In response to Unilever's 2005 call for commercial production of hoodia, Namibian growers created the Hoodia Growers Association for Namibia to ensure greater profits for local growers. C. Mariental, "Hoodia Growing for Rural Economic Empowerment," *New Era* (Namibia) August 5, 2008.

15. M. Duenwald, "An Appetite Killer for a Killer Appetite? Not Yet," *New York Times*, April 19, 2005; L. Johannes, "Hoodia's Hunger Claims," *Wall Street Journal.* December 13, 2005.

16. "Unilever Gains Exclusive Rights to Phytopharm's Hoodia Extract," *Breaking News on Supplements and Nutrition in Europe.* Accessed December 15, 2004. See *60 Minutes* report at http://www.cbsnews.com/stories/2004/11/18/60minutes/main656458.shtml, accessed December 15, 2006.

17. Nutra Ingredients, accessed December 22, 2010, http://www.nutraingredients.com/Industry/Phytopharm-hints-at-solid-future-for-hoodia.

18. There has been only one unpublished human trial on hoodia conducted by Phytopharm itself. It included only twelve subjects over a three-month period and was not subjected to peer review, leading the scientific community to remain rather skeptical. Tests of ten "hoodia" supplements showed only two brands contained the active compound P57. B. Avula et al., "Determination of the Appetite Suppressant P57 in Hoodia Gordonii Plant Extracts and Dietary Supplements by Liquid Chromatorgraphy/Electrospray Ionization Mass Spectrometry (LC-MSD-TOF) and LC-UV Methods," *Journal of AOAC International* 89, no. 3 (2006): 606–11.

19. Hoodia, which grows only in the Kalahari, is a slow-growing succulent taking decades to mature that must be carefully harvested to maintain sustainability. B. Avula, "Determination of the Appetite Suppressant P57."

20. A farmer was arrested for illegally harvesting two tons of the hoodia plant, said to be worth 2 million rand. S. Kwon Hoo, "Farmer Faces R6 Million Fine After Huge Hoodia Haul," *Diamond Fields Advertiser,* May 25, 2006.

21. A good example is James McCord, "A Zulu Witch Doctor and Medicine Man," *South African Medical Record* 16, no. 8 (1918): 116–22; a more recent example of this in East Africa is Stacey Langwick, "Ethnographies of Medicine," in Leudke and West, *Borders and Healers,* 143–66.

22. Convention of Biological Diversity, accessed February 15, 2007, www.biodiv.org/worl/map.asp?ctr=za.

23. The World Health Organization recognized indigenous medicines as early as 1977, and the more recent 1992 Biodiversity Convention. Lawyers for the San more recently appealed to the Biodiversity Convention to prevent Germany and Switzerland from selling unauthorized hoodia. WHO, "Protecting Traditional Knowledge: The San and Hoodia," *Bulletin of World Health Organization* 84, no.5 (May 2006).

24. The Biodiversity Act required bioprospectors to identify shareholders to include "an indigenous community" whose use or knowledge of the resource is under investigation. An approved benefit sharing agreement that ensures future benefits are paid into a bioprospecting trust fund is then set up. Act No. 10, 2004. "National Environmental Management: Biodiversity Act, 2004," *Government Gazette,* June 7, 2004. Also see E. Koro, "Protecting Indigenous Knowledge Systems," *Mail and Guardian,* August 10, 2005.

25. Posey and Dutfield, *Beyond Intellectual Property,* 50–57.

26. CSIR website home, accessed September 1999, www.csir.co.za/news.html. For an in-depth case study of CSIR, one of the main sites of government bioprospecting, see G. Augusto, "Knowing Differently, Innovating Together?"

27. Andrew Smith, *A Contribution to South African Materia Medica Chiefly from Plants,* 3rd ed. (Cape Town: 1895), 227.

28. Michael Gelfand and Percy W. Laidler, *South Africa: Its Medical History, 1652–1898* (Cape Town: Struick, 1974), 339, 70–72.

29. Anonymous, "A Contribution to South African Materia Medica Chiefly from Plants in Use Among the Natives by Andrew Smith," *South African Medical Journal* 4, no. 1 (1896): 23.

30. Smith, *A Contribution to South African Materia Medica,* 227. Interestingly, these two same herbs, along with devil's claw, African potato, and rooibos tea, remain among the top five South African herbs exported today. Augusto, "Knowing Differently, Innovating Together," 168.

31. P. C. Sutherland (1822–1900) had a number of different plants named after himself, including the well-known Sutherlandia plant. Donald P. McCracken and Patricia A. McCracken, *Natal: The Garden Colony* (Eden Prairie, MN: Frandsen, 1990), 20–34.

32. The late 1890s saw a series of collections written about Natal and Zululand's botanicals. J. Medley Wood, "Native Herbs: Medicinal and Otherwise," *Natal Almanac 1898* (Natal, 1898); Alfred T. Bryant, *Zulu Medicine and Medicine-Men* (Cape Town: Struik, 1966); J. Gerstner, *A Preliminary Checklist of Zulu Names of Plants* (1938). Even the rather skeptical Natal Medical Council collected local indigenous herbs and had them chemically tested in Europe. PAR. NMC, T1, Minutes of the Natal Medical Council, March 11 and June 10, 1898. In the 1920s and 1930s, Professor Watt and Breyer-Brandwijk, two researchers at the University of Witswatersrand, compiled and collected samples of Southern African medical and poisonous plants, writing one of the most comprehensive books on the subject. J. Watt and M. G. Breyer-Brandwijk, *The Medical and Poisonous Plants of Southern and Eastern Africa: Being an Account of the Medical and Other Uses, Chemical Composition, Pharmacological Effects, and Toxicology in Man and Animals* (Edinburgh: 1962).

33. A good work that looks at the exploitative relationship between researcher and subject or colonizer and colonized is: Linda Tuhiwai Smith, *Decolonizing Methodologies* (London: Zed Books, 1999).

34. To Chief Magistrate, Pietermartizburg from President African Dingaka Association, December 18, 1931, Pietermaritizberg Archive Repository (PAR), CNC, 50A.

35. Interview with Mthemjwa, BAT Centre, Durban, September 1998.

36. Annie Devenish, "Negotiating Healing: The Professionalisation of Traditional Healers in Kwazulu-Natal Between 1985 and 2003" (MA thesis, University of Natal Durban, 2003), 85.

37. Interview with V. T. Mkize, Durban 1998, 2002; and Stein Nesvag, "D'Urbanised Tradition: The Restructuring and Development of the *Muthi* Trade in Durban" (master's thesis, University of Natal, Durban, 1999)

38. Interview with Queen Ntuli, Secretary General of KwaZulu-Natal's Traditional Healers Council, KwaMuhle Museum, June 2002. Interview with V. T. Mkize, 2002.

39. A. Devenish, "Negotiating Healing," 85.

40. TRAMED Progress Report: June 1, 1994–May 31, 1995.

41. See "environment" in my epilogue for *Healing Traditions*, 191–92.

42. Interview with Nigel Gericke, July 2002.

43. Traditional healers were mentioned briefly as possible liaisons to help administer a biomedically oriented national health service. *A National Health*

Plan for South Africa, prepared by the ANC with technical support from WHO and UNICEF, May 1994.

44. TRAMED Progress Report.

45. Folb interview, SATMERG, Cape Town, July 2002.

46. TRAMED Progress Report.

47. "South African Traditional Medicines Research Group," accessed November 11, 2006, http://www.sahealthinfo.org/traditionalmeds/aboutuwc.htm.

48. MRC IKS homepage, accessed February 20, 2007, http://www.mrc.ac.za.iks/iksclinical.htm.

49. TRAMED Progress Report.

50. Interview with Peter Folb.

51. According to the TRAMED Progress Report, a traditional medicines formulary was initially requested by the Health Executive of the African National Healers Association, and the Natal Nyangas Association. Interview with Peter Eagles, and TRAMED Progress Report, Appendix 3, "The Registration and Control of Traditional Medicines in South Africa: A Presentation Made to the MCC on Friday, 22 July 1994."

52. See Flint, "Competition, Race, and Professionalization," in *Healing Traditions*, 128–57.

53. Interview with Ntutela and Madikane, SATMERG, Cape Town, July 2002.

54. Interview with G. Williams, Cape Town, August 2002.

55. Ben-Erik Van Wyk, Bosch van Oudtshoorn, and Nigel Gericke, *Medicinal Plants of South Africa* (Queenswood: Briza, 2002).

56. Interview with L. Govender, his muthi shop, December 1998.

57. Interview with G. Williams.

58. Interview with P. Kubekeli, Cape Town, July 2002.

59. TRAMED Progress Report.

60. Interview with Ntutela and Madikane.

61. Interview with Folb.

62. Interview with Gilbert Matsabisa, SATMERG, Cape Town, July 2002.

63. National IKS Office, accessed December 22, 2010, http://nikso.dst.gov.za/.

64. This includes some thirty interviews with healers in the late 1990s, and six leaders of traditional healing associations in 2002.

65. Interview with Siyabulela Ntutela and Eliya Madikane.

66. C. Timberg. "S. Africans Shun a Remedy for AIDS," *Washington Post*, October 21, 2004.

67. South African Medical Research Council Policy Brief, No. 5, December 2001.

68. See SANAC homepage, accessed March 6, 2007, http://www.info.gov.za/issues/hiv/sanac.htm.

69. Ibid.

70. S. Burcher, "Can Traditional Medicine Help Aids?" *ISIS News*. C. Dempster, "Medicinal Plant 'Fights' Aids," *BBC News*, November 30, 2001, accessed August 5, 2008, http:news.bbc.co.uk/1/hi/world/Africa/1683259.stm.

71. Interview with Gericke. Sutherlandia has since successfully passed a Phase 1 clinical trial and is presently undergoing an efficacy trial in HIV-positive volunteers in KwaZulu-Natal under a major four-year grant from the National Center for Complementary and Alternative Medicines, a division of the National Institutes of Health in the US. Correspondence with Nigel Gericke in December 2010.

CHAPTER 13

Dilemmas of "Indigenous Tenure" in South Africa

Traditional Authorities and the Constitutional Challenge to the 2004 Communal Land Rights Act

Derick Fay

THE NOTION of "indigenous tenure" poses challenges in South Africa. Transformations under colonialism and white rule and questions about the compatibility of hereditary leadership and democracy make the identification and legal recognition of indigenous tenure a fraught political question. Successive colonial administrations in South Africa developed a system of property law and private property to apply to cities and "white" areas. In the 13 percent of the country designated for African occupation, though, the state empowered traditional authorities (chiefs and headmen) to allocate and administer land held under so-called "communal" tenure, often transforming local systems and creating new offices and officeholders in the process.

The degree of (dis)continuity between this administrative model and precolonial or "indigenous" tenure has been a subject of considerable debate.[1] This paper does not attempt to resolve these debates, but instead examines their intersection with current legislation and policy in South Africa, and the past and future status of colonial- and apartheid-era models of indigenous tenure that treated land as the domain of chiefs and headmen.

After the country's political transition in 1994, the status of traditional authorities was unclear and contested, even as the constitution required land tenure reform measures in the former "homelands." A decade later, Parliament enacted the Communal Land Rights Act (CLARA), a measure that some observers claimed would entrench the powers over land that traditional authorities had held under colonialism and apartheid. In March 2006, however, four rural communities brought a court case challenging the constitutionality of the CLARA. In October 2009 the North Gauteng High Court ruled it unconstitutional, and the Constitutional Court confirmed this decision in May 2010, leaving the legal status of traditional authorities with respect to land uncertain sixteen years after South Africa's political transition.

Traditional Authorities and Land Prior to 1994

In the decades following conquest and annexation in the late nineteenth century, the state aimed to curtail the powers of chiefs, to prevent any revival of the military power of recently defeated African chiefdoms. Policy aimed "to bypass and weaken the chiefs" through a system of direct rule.[2] Land was legally owned by the South African Native Trust, but administered by headmen, who were directly accountable to district magistrates, leaving chiefs with no official role.

After 1948, the National Party government in South Africa launched its policies of apartheid, leading to the incorporation of chiefs in the state. Segregation was intellectually justified as "separate development," a premise that led officials to grant Africans a measure of autonomy—real or illusory—within an overall system of political and economic domination. One of the first apartheid laws was the Bantu Authorities Act of 1951, which made chiefs central to administration, as heads of Tribal Authorities incorporated into a regional and territorial bureaucracy.[3] The Tribal Authority systems would form the backbone of the ostensibly independent "homelands" that were created from 1963 onward, and existed until the political transition.

While some notable chiefs were active opponents of apartheid, "the implementation of apartheid [saw] the chieftaincy very largely caught up in the machinery of repression and control."[4] Activists critiqued such policies as unwanted "retribalization," while scholars came to understand traditional authority through the lens of the "invention of tradition." Such work typically characterized the roles of chiefs and headmen as manipulated, inflated, and invented by colonial- and apartheid-era officials, and generally argued that traditional authorities should not have a role in land administration.[5]

The African National Congress (ANC) itself contained differences of opinion on the status and future of traditional authorities. Its founders in the early twentieth century had included chiefs, but after the radicalization of the organization from the 1940s, two schools of thought emerged.[6] One favored pragmatic alliances with "progressive" chiefs and headmen, embodied in Chief Albert Luthuli, who was elected as national president of the ANC in 1952.[7] Another rejected collaboration as traditional authorities came to be incorporated more fully into the apartheid regime; as Govan Mbeki wrote, in evolutionary language, "When a people have developed to a stage which discards chieftainship, when their social development contradicts the need for such an institution, then to force it on them is not liberation but enslavement."[8]

Traditional Authorities in the "New South Africa"

With the eventual collapse and displacement of homeland structures after 1990 and the political transition, traditional authorities were in an uncertain position, with many observers expecting them to have no administrative role or powers in an ANC-led government. More than a decade and a half later, traditional authorities' place in land tenure remains hotly contested, but they have inarguably achieved a central place for their interests in state policies for rural areas.

Most observers attribute this rise to the ANC leadership's perception that chiefs can deliver rural votes. Commenting on the passage of CLARA in the weeks before the 2004 elections, Beall, Mkhize, and Vawda ask, "Why, on the eve of achieving its largest electoral victory ever, did the ANC put at risk the principles of democracy for which it fought so hard and which are enshrined in the Constitution, by rushing through legislation that entrenches the power of hereditary and exclusively male traditional authorities? The answer lies in the recognition by the ANC of the electoral influence of chieftaincy."[9]

Recognition of chiefs is not a one-way process, though: traditional authorities have actively lobbied the ANC since the early 1990s, stimulated in part by the prospect of local government redemarcation and spatial development and land reform policies that raised the stakes in struggles over land. The Congress of Traditional Leaders of South Africa (Contralesa) has been particularly effective, under the presidency of ANC member, attorney, and current member of Parliament Phathekile Holomisa.[10] The Zulu nationalist Inkatha Freedom Party (IFP) has also represented the interests of traditional leaders, and has been courted by the ANC in the wake of political violence in KwaZulu-Natal in the early 1990s.[11]

For a decade after the political transition, the status of traditional leaders was unclear and in flux. South Africa's 1993 interim constitution and 1996 constitution avoided any decisive statements on traditional leaders' position with respect to land and local government.[12] The interim constitution provided for provincial Houses of Traditional Leaders that would elect a national Council of Traditional Leaders, but this measure did not survive in the 1996 constitution, which acknowledged traditional leadership in vague terms, but omitted specific measures.[13] "In effect this removed the constitutional mandate and threw the question of the role of traditional leaders back into the political arena," where it remained until the 2006 constitutional challenge to the Communal Land Rights Act of 2004.[14]

Reorganizing Local Government

This uncertain situation was complicated by the placement of Local Government and Land Affairs in separate and largely independent departments in both the 1993 and the 1996 constitutions. Integrating the "homeland" administrations—including traditional authorities—into a unitary South African government required the spatial and institutional reorganization of local government and the fusion of homeland bureaucratic structures with their South African equivalents.[15] Local government structures were subject to several rounds of redemarcation and institutional reorganization.

Traditional authorities opposed efforts to redemarcate local government boundaries, which only took place in 2000.[16] Speaking at a gathering of traditional leaders in late April 1999, Chief M. B. Mzimela, then chair of the National House of Traditional Leaders and the KwaZulu-Natal house, attacked the newly established Demarcation Board and insisted that "no demarcation should happen without the consent of the *inkosi* [chief] concerned."[17] The IFP and Contralesa went on to threaten to boycott the December 2000 local government elections.[18] Redemarcation ultimately proved conservative: the ANC's Regional Policy had aimed to use redemarcation to "de-racialise [the] country,"[19] but demarcation in practice was based upon historically existing boundaries, and generally preserved the administrative divisions that formed traditional authorities' territories under apartheid.[20]

In the meantime, just before the 1999 general elections, chiefs received a doubling of their stipends and allowances,[21] while remaining under the administration of the Chief Directorate of Traditional Affairs—the new name for the apartheid-era Department of Native Affairs. This generous salary increase—widely interpreted as an electoral ploy—was an exception to a general trend of curtailing state expenditure, as 1999 also saw the introduction of neoliberal austerity measures under the policies known as Growth, Employment and Redistribution (GEAR).

GEAR and related neoliberal policies have led Ntsebeza to view the political rise of traditional authorities as, in part, an outcome of policies that have weakened other organs of the state and thereby facilitated the resurgence of traditional authorities. The combination of GEAR's restrictions on state spending and the delays and uncertainty over local government meant that in many areas headmen and chiefs remained the most visible and effective agents on the ground. As one resident of Cala, in the Eastern Cape, put it, local government "rural councillors run in circles. This makes us a laughing stock and divides us. . . . With chiefs and headmen it takes a few days to get what you want, whereas with rural councillors it takes months, and even then you end up not succeeding."[22]

Initial Land Tenure Reforms

In the meantime, the Department of Land Affairs (DLA) was involved in implementing South Africa's ambitious land reform policies, involving land restitution, redistribution, and tenure reform. While tenure reform measures were being debated, legislation in 1996 provided for creation of Communal Property Associations (CPAs) as ownership structures for communities receiving land under land restitution and redistribution policies, with regulations promoting democratic control and preventing gender discrimination. While some of these structures would include traditional authorities among their members, others explicitly aimed to exclude them. At Dwesa-Cwebe, for example, some of the CPA constitutions provide for an *ex officio* role for local headmen,[23] while at Kalkfontein (discussed below), the CPA explicitly aimed to exclude traditional authorities.

The CPA Act drew fire from TAs shortly after its passage; as Chief Mzimela stated regarding the Act in April 1999, "We reject the granting of title deeds in areas under our land . . . and prefer that the land should be registered in the name of the tribal authority."[24] Nevertheless, CPAs were (for the time being) the preferred legal instrument for community land restitution and redistribution, and by 2006, it was estimated that more than one thousand CPAs and similar collective landholding legal entities had been created, holding more than two million hectares of land.[25]

Outside of areas affected by land reform, land in the former homelands continued (at least on paper) to be governed under homeland-era proclamations that maintained the role of headmen and traditional authorities, with vast local variation in the effectiveness of official control,[26] while the DLA developed its land tenure reform policies. Alongside the CPA Act, the DLA developed a Land Rights Bill in the late 1990s that gave no authority to traditional authorities, instead aiming to institute a "rights enquiry" process, which would grant statutory recognition to existing rights and provide for the verification and registration of such rights.[27]

At this point, the DLA was clearly opposed to direct transfer to traditional authorities. A paper by Sipho Sibanda, Director of: Tenure, Department of Land Affairs, at a July 1999 conference on land and agrarian reform, explicitly defended the bill against the charge that it was "anti-traditional authorities."[28] Sibanda cited the Bantu Authorities Act of 1951 as exemplifying "complex and outdated apartheid laws," and emphasized that the new bill would aim "to formally recognise the underlying rights of individuals and groups to much of the land which is nominally state-owned," noting that "if land ownership were vested in chiefs or elected local government and the occupier left with a leasehold interest, the scene would be set for the reproduction of tenure insecurity."[29] His presentation emphasized that the proposed law would allow rights-holders to choose "not to use traditional leaders as the rights holder structure" and would require any rights holder structure to comply with democratic and transparent principles. "It is not anti-chief to require compliance with Constitutional principles," he stated, and added later that "where [chiefs] are popular, they shouldn't be threatened."[30]

Phathekile Holomisa of Contralesa[31] attended the conference and chastised the organizers in a plenary session, complaining that they had done an injustice to traditional leaders by not inviting them, especially given that the agenda included land tenure and local government.[32] In an earlier session, he had spelled out Contralesa's position on tenure, stating that traditional authorities would welcome government recognition and protection of various tenure systems. But, he continued, they opposed suggestions that individuals are land rights holders when they have been granted rights by the community as a whole, and raised concerns about individual alienation of land or default on loans borrowed against land. He also argued that treating land as under the purview of the state departed from local perceptions, stating that "tribal land is tribal land"; "people don't know that the state is the legal owner—they think of it as tribal land."[33]

At the time of the conference, many in attendance expected tenure policy to follow the lines set out in Sibanda's presentation; the main obstacles were expected to be related to capacity, not the claims of traditional leaders. By the time the vastly rewritten bill passed in 2004, however, the interests of traditional leaders were well-represented.

The Rising Stakes in Authority over Land

Other state policies gave an added impetus to traditional authorities' claims over land by effectively increasing the stakes. Policies aimed at addressing the legacies of conquest, segregation, and uneven development created the prospect for traditional authorities both to increase their territorial domain and to increase the value of the land they controlled.

In the past, headmen might have expected occasional payments of livestock, cash, and alcohol in exchange for allocating a residential site or agricultural land.[34] With the Spatial Development Initiative (SDI; a late 1990s strategy explicitly aimed at addressing uneven development by attracting external investment to a number of development "nodes," most situated within the former homelands) and land reform policies, however, traditional authorities have generally welcomed the prospect of being able to provide land to tourism operators, or take over former commercial farms. Throughout the country, much recent writing on traditional authorities concentrates on areas that have been affected by or targeted for investment and development.[35] Even in areas where the added incentive of the SDI was absent, the prospect of acquiring land through land reform programs sparked the interest of traditional authorities.[36]

The Wild Coast SDI, in the former Transkei, illustrates these policies' impact on the politics of land. The proposed SDI node around Mkambati Nature Reserve was subject to a series of claims and counterclaims as chiefs aimed to block the restitution of the reserve to adjoining communities. Farther down the coast, at Coffee Bay, traditional authorities took advantage of the collapse of district administration in the mid-1990s to begin allocating coastal sites to outsiders for vacation homes, leading to uncertainties that deterred SDI investors. At Dwesa-Cwebe, a counterclaim by traditional authorities was eventually abandoned as headmen were incorporated into the Dwesa-Cwebe Land Trust, although discontent has reappeared in recent years.[37] Similar conflicts over traditional authorities' ambitions to enter into contracts with tourism operators appear in several of the communities challenging the CLARA (discussed below).

The Passage of the CLARA

The politics of traditional authority and land took a significant turn with the 2003 Traditional Leadership and Governance Framework Act (TLGFA). The act recognized "traditional councils" as part of local government. These councils would be based on traditional councils where they exist,[38] subject to a transitional provision requiring at least one-third of the members to be women and 40 percent to be democratically elected (TLGFA s.3 and s. 28). The 2004 Communal Land Rights Act went a step further, allowing for giving these traditional councils the authority to allocate and administer land.[39]

The CLARA was subject to last-minute changes. The bill submitted to Parliament in October 2003 was substantially different from prior versions, which had set the maximum representation of traditional authorities on land administration committees at 25 percent. The bill replaced this measure with the provisions for "traditional councils."[40] Public hearings were held within a month of the publication of the bill for comment in October 2003. Land NGOs were instrumental in organizing nearly universal opposition to the proposed measures. Of the thirty-three parties who testified at the hearings, thirty-two were opposed to the bill, with most representing rural communities; the one delegation in favor was that of Contralesa.[41]

In a press statement following the hearings, Phathekile Holomisa of Contralesa denounced the bill's critics, claiming that "detractors of the Bill do not realise that the people themselves will finally be in control," and that "traditional leaders are held accountable by their communities in the same way that the chairperson of an organisation is." Echoing advocates of devolution of government, he argued that CLARA would both "save taxpayers money" and allow "traditional communities" to carry out local government functions "more effectively than a remote municipality that takes decisions without their participation."[42]

Contralesa's voice won out over the weight of opposition testimony. While the speaker of Parliament and the chair of the National Council of Provinces aimed to have the bill subject to provincial consultation, they were unsuccessful; the bill passed Parliament unanimously in February 2004, two months prior to national elections, and was signed into law in July 2004.[43] Shortly after the bill's passage, journalist Allister Sparks asked, "Why is the governing party doing this? There can be only one answer. It is a sweetener to the traditional chiefs and headmen—either in the hope of winning them over in the ANC's bid to gain control of KwaZulu Natal, or, on a more charitable analysis, to prevent them instigating bloodshed during the election campaign."⁴⁴ In any case, "the ANC was correct in its calculations, winning control of KZN provincial government for the first time in 2004."⁴⁵

The Constitutional Challenge to CLARA

Despite being signed into law in July 2004, the CLARA was never put into effect. In March 2006, four communities, Kalkfontein, Makuleke, Makgobistad, and Dixie, supported by the Legal Resources Centre, launched a court challenge to the CLARA and sections of the TLGFA, which would ultimately succeed in the North Gauteng High Court and the Constitutional Court.⁴⁶ The claimants made their constitutional challenge on six grounds.

Two of the grounds for challenge were technical points related to the procedures and structures specified in the South African constitution.⁴⁷ A third argument claimed that the CLARA violates section 25(6) of the constitution, which states that "a person or community whose tenure of land is legally insecure as a result of past racially discriminatory laws or practices is entitled, to the extent provided by an Act of Parliament, either to tenure which is legally secure or to comparable redress." The claimants argued that "community" titling reduces tenure security by undermining property rights and control of land at other levels of social organization (e.g., family, neighborhood, etc.).⁴⁸ Along these lines, a fourth argument noted that the CLARA may violate section 25(6) by rendering insecure tenure under communal property associations created through land reform policies; CLARA would authorize the transfer of CPA property and the restructuring of CPAs, including changing the legal definition of the "community" and allowing traditional councils to take over CPA administration.⁴⁹

Finally, the claimants argued that the CLARA violates equality provisions in the Bill of Rights (section 9) on grounds of race and gender. The CLARA applies only to land in the former African homelands, not land in historically white areas, effectively preserving segregated systems of land administration.⁵⁰ On gender, the TLGFA has a one-third quota for women in traditional councils, but these women may be selected by senior male traditional leaders, and the proportion is well under the proportion (roughly 60 percent) of women in the rural population. Likewise, it fails to recognize "all the relative rights that exist in existing systems of family-based customary land rights, [so that] the 'secondary' use rights held by women will be displaced."⁵¹

In March 2006, the Legal Resources Centre, the communities, and their allies submitted a series of affidavits detailing these arguments to the North Gauteng High Court.[52] The state delayed its response until May 2007,[53] the claimants issued their "replies to the replies" at the end of February 2008, and court hearings were held later that year.

In the meantime, CLARA awaited a presidential proclamation before it would be brought into effect.[54] Nevertheless, the Department of Land Affairs went ahead and published draft regulations in February 2008, providing for creation of land rights boards and land administration committees, offering some clarity on the "land rights enquiry" process, and setting out procedures for recording community rules.[55] In a presentation of the regulations for public comment in April 2008, Sibanda noted the DLA's efforts to build the capacity necessary to implement the act, and expected it to come into effect in 2008, notwithstanding the court challenge.[56]

The Communities Challenging the CLARA

The claimants' arguments against the CLARA emerged in part from communities' experiences with traditional authorities.[57] I review here the arguments of the four communities involved in the constitutional challenge to the CLARA, drawing upon their court affidavits and other available literature.

At Kalkfontein, in Mpumalanga, a group of Africans collectively purchased several farms in 1922. Under the 1913 Land Act, purchases of land by Africans was illegal, so they did not receive title; instead, the land was held in trust by the Native Affairs Department.[58] They managed their land through elected committees, which allocated land and made decisions about such things as infrastructure investment. Their testimony emphasizes the multiethnic (Ndebele, Northern Sotho, and Tswana) character of the community, and describes a system of land tenure grounded in community membership and managed through a community council (*kgotla*).[59] As their testimony before Parliament in the hearings prior to the passage of the CLARA states, "The communities resident at Kalkfontein never had a tribal affiliation, never fell under a chief, and bought their land as co-owners, not in any tribal context."[60]

Their situation changed when the state prepared to make the homeland of KwaNdebele "independent." Nominally still state land, the Kalkfontein territory was designated in 1979 as the territory of "a newly created Ndzundu (Pungutsha) Tribe," with a government-appointed chief and councillors.[61] Immediately afterward, the new chief "settled approximately

1000 outside families on Kalkfontein A without the consent of the co-purchasers or the heirs of the co-purchasers of that farm,"[62] and created a gravel quarry on two of the other farms. Complaints against the new chief led to a commission of enquiry which removed him from office, documenting a "reign of terror, with widespread unlawful detentions, [a] shooting ... and a public flogging,"[63] and replaced him with a new acting chief.

When the new acting chief continued to settle outsiders on Kalkfontein land, the residents organized a legal challenge. They succeeded in receiving a court order in 1992 interdicting the acting chief and homeland administration from taking any action on the land without the consent of the Kalkfontein *kgotla*, and recognizing the rights of ownership of the heirs of the original purchasers, rather than the state.[64] They failed in their efforts to have the court order implemented, leading to a second court case, which would transfer the Kalkfontein farms to a community CPA, excluding the one thousand sites that had been allocated by the chief in Kalkfontein A. This process was halted by a countersuit by the Tribal Authority in 1998, leading to a standoff.

Kalkfrontein residents' opposition to the CLARA thus represents the latest phase in a decades-long struggle against control of their land by traditional authorities, and an attempt to preserve land rights acquired through purchase that predate the policies of apartheid and Bantu authorities. The provisions of the TLGFA automatically recognize the Ndzundzu (Pungutsha) Tribal Authority as a "traditional council"; thus CLARA could place control of the Kalkfontein farms under the tribal authority. This possibility, they argue, threatens their constitutionally guaranteed right to secure tenure (sec. 25[6]), and undermines existing property rights and community control of land, treating their purchased farms as state land, even though it only has such status "on account of prior racially discriminatory practices, which prevented [the] community from [holding land in] its members' own names."[65]

The second claimant represents the Makuleke community: Phahlela Mugakula, "chief of the Makuleke tribe and the elected chairperson of the Executive Committee of the Makuleke Communal Property Association."[66] The Makuleke community does not reject traditional authorities *per se*, but rejects the particular traditional authority who ruled them under apartheid. The territory occupied by the Makuleke is situated in Mpumalanga, adjoining the northern end of Kruger National Park. The Makuleke were removed from the Pafuri Triangle in the 1960s and placed within the boundaries of the Mhinga Tribal Authority, while their land was divided between (1) Kruger National Park, (2) a military-controlled corridor used for border defense against Mozambique, and (3) the homeland of Venda.[67] According to the community's affidavit, "The Mhinga Tribal Authority was complicit in [the Makulekes'] forced removal," as it attempted to subjugate the Makulekes.[68]

At the end of 1995, the Makuleke community succeeded in a land restitution claim, and received the Pafuri Triangle land to be held through an elected Communal Property Association (CPA); since then, they have successfully entered into lease arrangements with ecotourism operators. In his affidavit, Mugakula takes pains to differentiate his roles; he does not claim authority over land as a chief, but as an elected representative of the CPA: "Traditional leaders who genuinely believe that they have an executive role beyond that conferred by the Constitution should, as I did, make themselves available for a democratic election to perform such a leadership function." He goes on to argue that his "powers as a chairman are founded on the [CPA] constitution and not on [his] status as a chief."[69]

As Mugakula tells it, the community does not oppose traditional authorities; they oppose the imposition of the Mhinga Tribal Authority over land that had formerly been under the Makuleke chief (who had never been incorporated into the state-backed tribal authority system). Their opposition springs from the possibility that under the CLARA, "the Mhinga Tribal Authority . . . will be entitled to exercise the rights of a land administration committee for the area concerned, including the land occupied by the Makuleke community."[70] This possibility, Mugakula argues, undermines their security of tenure, in violation of section 25(6) of the constitution.

Makgobistad, in the North West Province, is the third community involved in the challenge to the CLARA. The Makgobistad claimants emphasize that vesting land in traditional authorities undermines control at other levels of social organization. Their challenge focuses on the tribal authority's claim to make unilateral decisions affecting an area called Mayayane, a former cattle post that was converted to agricultural and residential land in the 1940s. The testimony recounts "a [past] communal decision-making process overseen by the chief" and operating "on the basis of consultation and co-operation with the families using and cultivating the land."[71] Since 1997, however, a new chief has designated an unofficial headman to rule Mayayane, who "[has been] allocating outside people residential sites at Mayayane on land which we have inherited and without consulting the people who have established rights at Mayayane."[72]

Their complaint thus turns on the nature of the authority vested in chiefs and headmen: "In terms of custom and precedent at Makgobistad, and in terms of Tswana custom generally, traditional leaders could not make decisions which had the effect of depriving people of rights to arable and residential land without the agreement of the people concerned and without the approval of the community." Emphasizing their history of community control that has been usurped in recent years, they argue that the CLARA "gives . . . traditional councils the power to represent the community as the owner of the land," without requiring downward consultation or accountability.[73] They do not dispute the legitimacy of the tribal authority, or its boundaries; they are voicing their complaints within a discourse of tradition, but calling for legislation that would guarantee a return to consultation between traditional authorities and their "subjects."

Finally, the community of Dixie, adjoining Kruger National Park in Mpumalanga, is challenging the authority of the local tribal authority to enter into contracts affecting Dixie land. Although the farm Dixie is not included in the legal definition of the Mnisi Tribal Authority, the Tribal Authority has asserted its control, and in April 2001, the community was notified that the tribal authority had signed a ninety-nine-year lease with a tourism operator for use of part of Dixie for a tourism lodge, which would have required resettlement of community members.[74]

Community leaders managed to have the contracts canceled, bringing a successful court case in 2002 with the assistance of the Legal Resources Centre. As they explain in their affidavit, "To the extent that our tenure at the farm has been threatened, this has in recent times been as a result of the interventions and activities of the Mnisi Tribal Authority."[75] Their opposition springs from the fear that CLARA may authorize the traditional council to represent them, and undermine an existing community development forum with elected members (including the local headman) that has been responsible for land affairs in the past.[76]

Legal and Social Outcomes of the Court Case

In October 2009, Judge of the High Court A. P. Ledwaba delivered his ruling on the CLARA case. He rejected the technical challenges to the constitutionality of CLARA,[77] but found it unconstitutional on several other grounds, deeming sixteen sections of CLARA unconstitutional in total.[78] He found section 21, providing for traditional councils to serve as land administration committees, unconstitutional because some existing traditional councils have not been democratically elected and may violate gender equality provisions (section 9) of the constitution.[79] He also found section 18 unconstitutional because of the degree of discretion given to the minister of Land Affairs, a point he reiterated specifically in relation to the case of the Kalkfontein and Makuleke communities.[80] Finally, section 39 was deemed unconstitutional, which would have allowed for the application of CLARA to land held under CPAs and other legal structures created through land reform (as in the Makuleke case).[81]

In confirming the unconstitutionality of CLARA, the Constitutional Court ruled in May 2010 that CLARA was unconstitutional on procedural grounds (see note 47), but did not rule on the substantive grounds.[82] In the meantime, the minister of Agriculture and Land Affairs provided an affidavit "in which he stated that CLARA needs to be reviewed" and commented in oral hearings before the Constitutional Court that it would be repealed entirely.[83]

While it was hailed as a victory by the Legal Resources Centre and other activists who were involved in the challenge, the High Court's ruling, the subsequent Constitutional Court ruling, and the minister's announcement have left the state of land tenure in rural areas in a state of legal limbo, sixteen years after South Africa's political transition. While new tenure legislation has been rumored to be part of the commitment to rural development by the administration of President Jacob Zuma, a parliamentary briefing from the Department of Rural Development and Land Reform in September 2010 on the implications of the Constitutional Court's ruling offered no insights into future policy.[84]

From a development perspective (though not necessarily from the perspective of rural smallholders), this means continued *de facto* tenure insecurity with adverse, though indeterminate consequences. As Edward Lahiff remarked with respect to the Eastern Cape, where tenure security contributed to the failure of the Wild Coast SDI, "The true cost . . . of delayed or stalled tenure reform, therefore, is impossible to know, but must be reckoned, not in terms of evictions or feelings of insecurity, but in terms of the investment that never materialised, the development that never happened, the community project that never got off the ground."[85]

"Indigenous tenure," like "indigenous knowledge," "excites and infuriates": chiefly claims to land are compromised by their "relations to conquest and colonial rule," challenged by those whom they would claim as subjects, and—in the latest chapter of a long and ongoing set of struggles—challenged in courts of law, because of conflicts with competing local versions of indigenous tenure and with universalist rights that are seen as threatened by aspects of "tradition."[86] If indigenous tenure in South Africa is a hybrid, as Gordon and Krech argue of indigenous knowledge, it is an unruly hybrid, constituted by diverse actors who pull in many directions at once and appeal to diverse authorities, whether in national politics or single communities, resisting legal codification even as it may complicate aspirations for rural development.

Notes

1. See Ben Cousins, "More Than Socially Embedded: The Distinctive Character of 'Communal Tenure' Regimes in South Africa and Its Implications for Land Policy," *Journal of Agrarian Change* 7, no. 3 (2007): 281–315, for a review; and Elizabeth Colson, "The Impact of the Colonial Period on the Definition of Land Rights," in *Colonialism in Africa, 1870–1960*, vol. 3, *Profiles of Change: African Society and Colonial Rule*, ed. V. Turner (Cambridge: Cambridge University Press, 1971), 193–214, for a classic evaluation.

2. Leslie Bank and Roger Southall, "Traditional Leaders in South Africa's New Democracy," *Journal of Legal Pluralism* 38 (1996): 407–30.

3. Ibid.

4. Ibid.

5. Eric J. Hobsbawn and Terence O. Ranger, *The Invention of Tradition* (Cambridge: Cambridge University Press, 1983); Leroy Vail, "Introduction: Ethnicity in Southern African History," in *The Creation of Tribalism in Southern Africa*, ed. Leroy Vail (Berkeley: University of California Press, 1988), 1–19; Fred Hendricks, *The Pillars of Apartheid: Land Tenure, Rural Planning and the Chieftancy* (Uppsala: Almqvist and Wiksell International, 1990).

6. Lungisile Ntsebeza, *Democracy Compromised: Chiefs and the Politics of the Land in South Africa* (Leiden: Brill, 2005), 258.

7. Bank and Southall, "Traditional Leaders," 414.

8. Govan Mbeki, *South Africa: The Peasants' Revolt* (London: Penguin African Library, 1964), 19.

9. Jo Beall, Sibongiseni Mkhize, and Shahid Vawda, "Emergent Democracy and 'Resurgent' Tradition: Institutions, Chieftaincy and Transition in KwaZulu-Natal," *Journal of Southern African Studies* 31, no. 4 (2005): 755–71. See also Allister Sparks, "Rulers Selling Out the Rural Poor," *Star* February 24, 2004, accessed January 11, 2011, http://www.marxists.org/subject/africa/sparks/sell-out.htm.

10. Bank and Southall, "Traditional Leaders," 415–18. See also Phathekile Holomisa, *According to Tradition* (Somerset West: Essential Books, 2009); and Phathekile Holomisa, *A Double-Edged Sword: A Quest for a Place in the African Sun* (Cape Town: Lotsha, 2007).

11. Ntsebeza, *Democracy Compromised*, 268–72.

12. Barbara Oomen, *Chiefs in South Africa: Law, Power, and Culture in the Postapartheid Era* (London: James Currey, 2005), chap. 2; Heinz Klug, *Constituting Democracy: Law, Globalism and South Africa's Political Reconstruction* (Cambridge: Cambridge University Press, 2000).

13. For a critical account of the constitutional negotiations, see Holomisa, *A Double-Edged Sword* and "Memorandum to the African National Congress," accessed January 11, 2011, http://contralesa.org/communiques.html.

14. Klug, *Constituting Democracy*, 121.

15. See Maano Ramutsindela, "Resilient Geographies: Land, Boundaries and the Consolidation of the Former Bantustans in Post-1994 South Africa," *Geographical Journal* 173 (2007): 43–55. Robin Palmer, Derick Fay, Herman Timmermans, Fonda Lewis, and Johan Viljoen, "Regaining the Forests: Reform and Development from 1994 to 2001," in *From Conflict to Negotiation: Nature-Based Development on South Africa's Wild Coast*, ed. Robin Palmer, Herman Timmermans, and Derick Fay (Pretoria: Human Sciences Research Council, 2002); and Derick Fay, "Property, Subjection and Protected Areas: The Restitution of Dwesa-Cwebe Nature Reserves, South Africa," in *The Rights and Wrongs of Land Restitution:"Restoring What Was Ours,"* ed. Derick Fay and Deborah James (London: Routledge-Cavendish, 2009), examines the institutional complexity that this entailed at Dwesa-Cwebe.

16. Ntsebeza, *Democracy Compromised*, 277–80, 13.

17. Cited in Dudley Moloi, "Royalty Gathers over an Uncertain Future," *Land and Rural Digest* 1, no. 6 (1999): 8–9.

18. Ntsebeza, *Democracy Compromised*, 282–83.

19. Cited in Ramutsindlela, "Resilient Geographies," 49.

20. Ibid.; Oomen, *Chiefs in South Africa*, 37–38; Sarah Mathis, "After Apartheid: Chiefly Authority and the Politics of Land, Community and Development" (PhD thesis, Emory University, Atlanta, 2008), 10–11.

21. Beall et al., "Emergent Democracy," 763–64.

22. Ntsebeza, *Democracy Compromised*, 21–22, 13.

23. Derick Fay, "Kinship and Access to Land in the Eastern Cape: Implications for Land Reform," *Social Dynamics* 31, no. 1 (2005): 182–207.

24. Cited in Dudley Moloi, "Royalty Gathers," 8.

25. Affidavit of Jacobus Pienaar in *Tongoane and Others v Minister for Agriculture and Land Affairs and Others*, case no. 11678/2006, North Gauteng High Court, Pretoria, October 30, 2009, unreported, sec. 31.

26. Sipho Sibanda, "Proposals for the Management of Land Rights in Rural South Africa," in *At the Crossroads: Land and Agrarian Reform in South Africa into the 21st Century*, ed. Ben Cousins (Cape Town: Programme for Land and

Agrarian Studies, University of the Western Cape and National Land Committee, 2000), 306–10.

27. Cousins, "More Than Socially Embedded," 285–86.

28. Sibanda, "Proposals," 309. Quotations are from the published version of Sibanda's paper. I attended the presentation and recorded the same points in my notes.

29. Ibid., 307–9.

30. Fieldnotes, July 27, 1999.

31. Holomisa had also recently been installed as chief of the AmaGebe. Lungile Madywabe, "Not a Traditional Curio," *Land and Rural Digest* 1, no. 6 (1999): 10–12.

32. Fieldnotes, July 28, 1999.

33. Ibid.

34. In remote rural areas, where land allocation is infrequent, such payments would add up to a relatively small sum (see Fay, "Kinship and Access to Land"; and Sarah Mathis, "The Politics of Land Reform: Tenure and Political Authority in Rural Kwazulu-Natal," *Journal of Agrarian Change* 7, no. 1 (2007): 99–120), but in areas of intense demand for land, they could total hundreds of thousands of rand (Affidavit of Stephen Segopotso Tongoane in *Tongoane and Others v Minister for Agriculture and Land Affairs and Others*, case no. 11678/2006, North Gauteng High Court, Pretoria, October 30, 2009, unreported, sec. 51).

35. For example, Thembela Kepe, "Land Restitution and Biodiversity Conservation in South Africa: Analysis of Challenges and the Case of Mkambati, Eastern Cape Province," *Canadian Journal of African Studies* 3, no. 3 (2004): 688–704; Brian H. King, "Developing KaNgwane: Geographies of Segregation and Integration in the New South Africa," *Geographical Journal* 173 (2007): 13–25; Marja Spierenburg, Conrad Steenkamp, and Harry Wels, "Enclosing the Local for the Global Commons: Community Land Rights in the Great Limpopo Transfrontier Conservation Area," *Conservation and Society* 6, no. 1 (2008): 87–97; Beall et al., "Emergent Democracy"; Patrick Sadiki and Maano Ramutsindela, "Peri-Urban Transformation in South Africa: Experiences from Limpopo Province," *GeoJournal* 57, no. 1 (2002): 75–81.

36. For example, Spierenburg et al., "Enclosing the Local"; Scott Drimie, "'Holding' a Rural Crisis: Land Reform and Politics at Impendle State Land, KwaZulu-Natal," in *Transforming Rural and Urban Spaces in South Africa During the 1990s Reform, Restitution, Restructuring*, ed. R. Donaldson and L. Marais (Pretoria: Africa Institute of South Africa, 2002), 101–28; Alistair Fraser, "Land Reform in South Africa and the Colonial Present," *Social and Cultural Geography* 8, no. 6 (2007): 835–51; Deborah James, *Gaining Ground: "Rights*

and Property" in South African Land Reform (London: Routledge-Cavendish, 2007); Mathis, "The Politics of Land Reform"; Charles Chavunduka, "Devolution and the Role of Traditional Leaders in African Land Rights Control: Lessons from South Africa's Experience, 1994–2006" (PhD thesis, University of Wisconsin, Madison, 2007).

37. On Mkambati, see Kepe, "Land Restitution"; on Coffee Bay, see Lungisile Ntsebeza and Eric Buiten, 1998, "Resolution of Land Ownership and Governance Issues in the Tshezi Communal Area (Coffee Bay Cluster)," report prepared for Department of Land Affairs, East London; on Dwesa-Cwebe, see Zolile Ntshona, Mcebisi Kraai, Thembela Kepe, and Paul Saliwa, "From Land Rights to Environmental Entitlements: Community Discontent in the 'Successful' Dwesa-Cwebe Land Claim in South Africa," *Development Southern Africa* 27, no. 3 (2010): 353–61.

38. These include structures entrenched—and in some cases, created—under the apartheid-era Bantu Authorities Act (Ntsebeza, *Democracy Compromised*).

39. Ntsebeza, *Democracy Compromised*, 286–88.

40. Aninka Claassens, *The Communal Land Rights Act and Women: Does the Act Remedy or Entrench Discrimination and the Distortion of the Customary* (Bellville: Programme for Land and Agrarian Studies, School of Government, University of the Western Cape, 2005).

41. Ben Cousins, personal communication.

42. *Mail and Guardian*, "Traditional Leaders Defend Land Rights Bill," November 14, 2003.

43. Claassens, *The Communal Land Rights Act*, 5.

44. Sparks, "Rulers Selling Out the Rural Poor."

45. Beall, "Emergent Democracy," 764.

46. Aninka Claassens and Ben Cousins, *Land, Power, and Custom: Controversies Generated by South Africa's Communal Land Rights Act* (Cape Town: University of Cape Town Press, 2008), which appeared while this chapter was under review, provides a range of perspectives on the challenge and a vast collection of related primary documents.

47. First, the constitution authorizes provincial government to determine traditional authorities' powers, while CLARA was passed using a procedure that did not allow provincial input (Affidavit of Jacobus Pienaar sec. 11-25). Second, beyond the national, provincial, and local tiers specified in the constitution, the CLARA would create "a fourth sphere of government which is not recognised by the constitution." Ben Cousins, "CLRA Challenge and Threats Against Land Rights" (unpublished ms., March 2008, 2).

48. Cousins, "CLRA challenge," 2. This point is carefully grounded in the scholarly literature on tenure, which is cited in affidavits before the court by

Cousins and by Kenyan legal scholar H. W. Okoth-Ogendo; see Cousins 2007 for a review.

49. Ibid.

50. Ibid.; cf. Claassens and Cousins, *Land, Power, and Custom.*

51. Ibid.

52. Renamed the North Gauteng High Court in March 2009.

53. Christelle Terreblanche, "Three Year Old Land Act May Gather More Dust," *Sunday Independent*, November 26, 2006.

54. Cousins, "CLRA challenge," 1.

55. *Government Gazette* 512, no. 30736 (February 8, 2008).

56. Sipho Sibanda, "An Overview of the Regulations for the Implementation of the CLARA," accessed April 10, 2008, http://land.pwv.gov.za/Documents&Publications/Publications/2008/CLaRA%20Presentation%20in%20Durban%207th%20and%208th%20April%202008.ppt.

57. The argument about gender is not prominent in the communities' testimony; Steven Robins and Kees van der Waal, "'Model Tribes' and Iconic Conservationists? The Makuleke Restitution Case in Kruger National Park," *Development and Change* 39, no. 1 (2008): 65–66, note controversies over gender relations in the Makuleke community, suggesting that the Makuleke CPA is no less patriarchal than most traditional authorities.

58. On such purchases, see Harvey M. Feinberg, "Pre-apartheid African Land Ownership and the Implication for the Current Restitution Debate in South Africa," *Historia* 40, no. 2 (1995): 48–63, also cited in Affidavit of Stephen Segopotso Tongoane, sec. 32.

59. Affidavit of Stephen Segopotso Tongoane, sec. 41-42.

60. Kalfontein Community Trust, "Submission to the Portfolio Committee on Agriculture And Land Affairs on the Communal Land Rights Bill," November 10, 2003; Oomen, *Chiefs in South Africa*, 73.

61. Affidavit of Stephen Segopotso Tongoane, sec. 45.2-46.

62. Ibid., sec. 51.

63. Ibid., sec. 63.

64. Ibid., sec. 72.

65. Ibid., sec. 125.1.

66. Affidavit of Phahlela Joas Mugakula in *Tongoane and Others v Minister for Agriculture and Land Affairs and Others*, case no. 11678/2006, North Gauteng High Court, Pretoria, October 30, 2009, unreported.

67. Ibid., sec. 15.

68. Ibid., sec. 17. Robins and Van der Waal, "'Model Tribes,'" 65–66, note government reports drawing on missionary and state ethnography that

support the Mhinga claim, and that the Land Claims Commission refused to rule on the question.

69. Ibid., sec. 89. This perspective is implicitly challenged by Robins and Van der Waal, "'Model Tribes,'" who emphasize continuities between the CPA and the tribal authority.

70. Ibid., sec. 69.

71. Affidavit of Morgan Mogoelelwa in *Tongoane and Others v Minister for Agriculture and Land Affairs and Others*, case no. 11678/2006, North Gauteng High Court, Pretoria, October 30, 2009, unreported, sec. 15-17, 21, 24.

72. Ibid., sec. 29.

73. Ibid., sec. 50.

74. Affidavit of Reckson Ntimane in *Tongoane and Others v Minister for Agriculture and Land Affairs and Others*, case no. 11678/2006, North Gauteng High Court, Pretoria, October 30, 2009, unreported, sec. 16, 20.

75. Ibid., sec. 31.

76. Ibid., sec. 12–14.

77. Judgment in *Tongoane and Others v Minister for Agriculture and Land Affairs and Others*, case no. 11678/2006, North Gauteng High Court, Pretoria, October 30, 2009, unreported, sec. 25 and 56.

78. Ibid., sec. 67(ii).

79. Ibid., sec. 42.

80. Ibid., sec. 48-49, 62-63.

81. Ibid., sec. 67(ii).

82. *Tongoane and Others v Minister for Agriculture and Land Affairs and Others* 2010 (CC) 100/09 sec. 109–10.

83. Ibid., sec. 40.

84. Fieldnotes, September 8, 2010. See also "Communal Lands Right Act: Constitutional Court judgment; Land Rights Management Facility: Departmental briefings," accessed January 13, 2011, http://www.pmg.org.za/report/20100908-department-constitutional-court-judgement-communal-lands-right-act-cl.

85. Edward Lahiff, *Land Reform and Sustainable Livelihoods in South Africa's Eastern Cape Province* (Brighton: Institute of Development Studies, 2003), 39; cf. Cherryl Walker, "The Limits to Land Reform: Rethinking 'The Land Question,'" *Journal of Southern African Studies* 31, no. 4 (2005): 805–24; and Stefan Hofstatter, "Law on Land Reform Struck Down," *Business Day*, November 12, 2009.

86. David Gordon and Shepherd Krech, introduction to this volume.

Selected Bibliography

Akerman, James R. *The Imperial Map: Cartography and the Mastery of Empire.* Chicago: University of Chicago Press, 2007.
Agrawal, Arun. "Dismantling the Divide Between Indigenous and Scientific Knowledge." *Development and Change* 26 (1995): 413–39.
Alfred, Taiaiake. "Sovereignty." In *A Companion to American Indian History,* edited by Philip J. Deloria and Neal Salisbury, 460–74. Malden: Blackwell, 2002.
Asad, Talal. *Formations of the Secular: Christianity, Islam, Modernity.* Stanford, CA: Stanford University Press, 2003.
Banner, Stuart. *How the Indians Lost Their Land: Law and Power on the Frontier.* Cambridge: Belknap Press of Harvard University Press, 2005.
Basso, Keith H. *Wisdom Sits in Places: Landscape and Language among the Western Apache.* Albuquerque: University of New Mexico Press, 1996.
Beinart, William. "Soil Erosion, Conservationism and Ideas About Development: A Southern African Exploration, 1900–1960." *Journal of Southern African Studies* 11 (1984): 52–83.
Beinart, William, and Peter Coates. *Environment and History: The Taming of Nature in the USA and South Africa.* London: Routledge, 1995.
Berkes, Fikret. *Sacred Ecology.* 2nd ed. New York: Routledge, 2008.
Béteille, André. "The Idea of Indigenous People." *Current Anthropology* 39, no. 2 (1998): 187–91.
Botkin, Daniel B. *Discordant Harmonies: A New Ecology for the Twenty-first Century.* New York: Oxford University Press, 1990.
Broster, Joan A. *The Tembu: Their Beadwork, Songs and Dances.* Cape Town: Purnell, 1976.
Burnett, D. Graham. *Masters of All They Surveyed: Explorations, Geography, and a British El Dorado.* Chicago: University of Chicago Press, 2000.

Buruma, Ian, and Avishai Margalit. *Occidentalism: A Short History of Anti-Westernism*. New York: Penguin, 2004.
Carney, Judith A. *Black Rice: The African Origins of Rice Cultivation in the Americas*. Cambridge, MA: Harvard University Press, 2001.
Chanock, Martin. *Law, Custom and Social Order: The Colonial Experience in Malawi and Zambia*. Cambridge: Cambridge University Press, 1985.
Claassens, Aninka, and Ben Cousins. *Land, Power, and Custom: Controversies Generated by South Africa's Communal Land Rights Act*. Cape Town: University of Cape Town Press, 2008.
Colson, Elizabeth. "The Impact of the Colonial Period on the Definition of Land Rights." In *Colonialism in Africa, 1870–1960*. Vol. 3, *Profiles of Change: African Society and Colonial Rule*, edited by Victor Turner, 193–214. Cambridge: Cambridge University Press, 1971.
Comaroff, John L., and Jean Comaroff. *Ethnicity, Inc*. Chicago: University of Chicago Press, 2009.
Cook, Peter A. W. *Social Organisation and Ceremonial Institutions of the Bomvana*. Cape Town: Juta, 1931.
Cooper, Alix. *Inventing the Indigenous: Local Knowledge and Natural History in Early Modern Europe*. Cambridge: Cambridge University Press, 2007.
Coté, Charlotte. *Spirits of Our Whaling Ancestors: Revitalizing Makah and Nuu-chah-nulth Traditions*. Seattle: University of Washington Press, 2010.
Cousins, Ben. "More Than Socially Embedded: The Distinctive Character of 'Communal Tenure' Regimes in South Africa and Its Implications for Land Policy." *Journal of Agrarian Change* 7, no. 3 (2007): 281–315.
Craib, Raymond B. *Cartographic Mexico: A History of State Fixations and Fugitive Landscapes*. Durham, NC: Duke University Press, 2004.
———. "Relocating Cartography." *Postcolonial Studies* 12, no. 4 (2009): 481–90.
Cronon, William. "A Place for Stories: Nature, History, and Narrative." *Journal of American History* 78 (1992): 1347–76.
———. *Changes in the Land: Indians, Colonists, and the Ecology of New England*. New York: Hill & Wang, 1983.
———. *Uncommon Ground: Toward Reinventing Nature*. New York: Norton, 1995.
Crosby, Alfred W. *The Columbian Exchange: Biological and Cultural Consequences of 1492*. Westport, CT: Greenwood, 1972.
Davis, Diana K. "Potential Forests: Degradation Narratives, Science, and Environmental Policy in Protectorate Morocco, 1912–1956." *Environmental History* 10 (2005): 211–38.

———. *Resurrecting the Granary of Rome: Environmental History and French Colonial Expansion in North Africa*. Athens: Ohio University Press, 2007.

de Heusch, Luc. *The Drunken King, or, The Origin of the State*. Translated by Roy Willis. Bloomington: Indiana University Press, 1982.

Donahoe, Brian, Joachim O. Habeck, Agnieszka Halemba, and István Sántha. "Size and Place in the Construction of Indigeneity in the Russian Federation." *Current Anthropology* 49 (2008): 993–1020.

Dove, Michael R. "Indigenous People and Environmental Politics." *Annual Review of Anthropology* 35 (2006): 191–208.

———. "The Life-Cycle of Indigenous Knowledge, and the Case of Natural Rubber Production." In *Indigenous Environmental Knowledge and Its Transformations: Critical Anthropological Perspectives*. Edited by Roy Ellen, Peter Parkes, and Alan Bicker, 209–48. Amsterdam: Harwood Academic Publishers, 2000.

Dove, Michael R., and Carol Carpenter, eds. *Environmental Anthropology: A Historical Reader*. Malden, MA: Blackwell, 2007.

Drewal, Henry J. *Sacred Waters: Arts for Mami Wata and Other Divinities in Africa and the Diaspora*. Bloomington: Indiana University Press, 2008.

Dubow, Saul. *A Commonwealth of Knowledge: Science, Sensibility, and White South Africa, 1820–2000*. New York: Oxford University Press, 2006.

Edgar, Robert R., and Hilary Sapire. *African Apocalypse: The Story of Nontetha Nkwenkwe, a Twentieth-Century South African Prophet*. Athens: Ohio University Press, 2000.

Ellen, Roy, Peter Parkes, and Alan Bicker, eds. *Indigenous Environmental Knowledge and Its Transformations: Critical Anthropological Perspectives*. Amsterdam: Harwood Academic Publishers, 2000.

Flint, Karen E. *Healing Traditions: African Medicine, Cultural Exchange, and Competition in South Africa, 1820–1948*. Athens: Ohio University Press, 2008.

Gadgil, Madhav, Fikret Berkes, and Carl Folke. "Indigenous Knowledge for Biodiversity Conservation." *Ambio* 22 (May 1993): 151–56.

Giles-Vernick, Tamara. *Cutting the Vines of the Past: Environmental Histories of the Central African Rain Forest*. Charlottesville: University of Virginia Press, 2002.

Gluckman, Max. "Zulu Women in Hoe Culture Ritual." *Bantu Studies* 9 (1935): 255–71.

Goody, Jack R. *The Domestication of the Savage Mind*. Cambridge: Cambridge University Press, 1977.

Gordon, David M. "The Cultural Politics of a Traditional Ceremony: Mutomboko and the Performance of History on the Luapula." *Comparative Studies in Society and History* 46, no. 1 (2004): 63–83.

———. "History on the Luapula Retold: Landscape, Memory, and Identity in the Kazembe Kingdom." *Journal of African History* 47, no. 1 (2006): 21–42.

———. *Nachituti's Gift: Economy, Society, and Environment in Central Africa*. Madison: University of Wisconsin Press, 2006.

Greene, Sandra E. *Sacred Sites and the Colonial Encounter: A History of Meaning and Memory in Ghana*. Bloomington: Indiana University Press, 2002.

Grove, Richard H. *Green Imperialism: Colonial Expansion, Tropical Island Edens and the Origins of Environmentalism, 1600–1860*. Cambridge: Cambridge University Press, 1995.

Haley, Brian D., and Larry R. Wilcoxon. "Anthropology and the Making of Chumash Tradition." *Current Anthropology* 38 (1997): 761–94.

Hallowell, A. Irving. "The Backwash of the Frontier: The Impact of the Indian on American Culture." In *The Frontier in Perspective*, edited by Walker D. Wyman and Clifton B. Kroeber, 229–58. Madison: University of Wisconsin Press, 1957.

Hames, Raymond. "The Ecologically Noble Savage Debate." *Annual Review of Anthropology* 36 (2007): 177–90.

Harkin, Michael E., and David R. Lewis, eds. *Native Americans and the Environment: Perspectives on the Ecological Indian*. Lincoln: University of Nebraska Press, 2007.

Harley, J. Brian. *The New Nature of Maps: Essays in the History of Cartography*. Edited by Paul Laxton. Baltimore: Johns Hopkins University Press, 2001.

Harms, Robert W. *Games Against Nature: An Eco-Cultural History of the Nunu of Equatorial Africa*. Cambridge: Cambridge University Press, 1987.

Harries, Patrick. *Butterflies and Barbarians: Swiss Missionaries and Systems of Knowledge in South-East Africa*. Athens: Ohio University Press, 2007.

Hinfelaar, Hugo F. *Bemba-Speaking Women of Zambia in a Century of Religious Change, 1892–1992*. Leiden: Brill, 1994.

Hobsbawm, Eric J., and Terence O. Ranger, eds. *The Invention of Tradition*. Cambridge: Cambridge University Press, 1983.

Hodgson, Dorothy L. "Becoming Indigenous in Africa." *African Studies Review* 52, no. 3 (2009): 1–32.

———. "Introduction: Comparative Perspectives on the Indigenous Rights Movement in Africa and the Americas." *American Anthropologist* 104 (2002): 1037–49.
Hunter, Monica. *Reaction to Conquest: Effects of Contact with Europeans on the Pondo of South Africa.* London: Oxford University Press, 1936.
Ingold, Tim. "Introduction to Culture." In *Companion Encyclopedia of Anthropology*, edited by Tim Ingold, 329–49. New York: Routledge, 1994.
Irvine, Albert, and Luke Markistun. *How the Makah Obtained Possession of Cape Flattery.* New York: Museum of the American Indian, 1921.
Isichei, Elizabeth A. *Voices of the Poor in Africa: Moral Economy and the Popular Imagination.* Rochester, NY: University of Rochester Press, 2002.
Janzen, John M. *Ngoma: Discourses of Healing in Central and Southern Africa.* Berkeley: University of California Press, 1992.
Johannes, Robert E., ed. *Traditional Ecological Knowledge: A Collection of Essays.* Gland, Switzerland: International Union for Conservation of Nature, 1989.
Kelly, Lawrence C. "Anthropology and Anthropologists in the Indian New Deal." *Journal of the History of the Behavioral Sciences* 16 (1980): 6–24.
———. "Anthropology in the Soil Conservation Service." *Agricultural History* 59 (1985): 136–47.
———. *The Assault on Assimilation: John Collier and the Origins of Indian Policy Reform.* Albuquerque: University of New Mexico Press, 1983.
Klieman, Kairn A. *"The Pygmies Were Our Compass": Bantu and Batwa in the History of West Central Africa, Early Times to c. 1900 C.E.* Portsmouth, NH: Heinemann, 2003.
Kosek, Jake. *Understories: The Political Life of Forests in Northern New Mexico.* Durham, NC: Duke University Press, 2006.
Krech, Shepard, III. *The Ecological Indian: Myth and History.* New York: Norton, 1999.
———. *Spirits of the Air: Birds and American Indians in the South.* Athens: University of Georgia Press, 2009.
———. "The State of Ethnohistory." *Annual Review of Anthropology* 20 (1991): 345–75.
———. "Traditional Environmental Knowledge." In *Encyclopedia of World Environmental History*. Vol. 3, edited by Shepard Krech III, John McNeill, and Carolyn Merchant, 1213–16. New York: Routledge, 2004.
Krige, Eileen J. "Girls' Puberty Songs and Their Relation to Fertility, Health, Morality and Religion Among the Zulu." *Africa: Journal of the International African Institute* 38, no. 2 (1968): 173–98.

Kuper, Adam. "The Return of the Native." *Current Anthropology* 44 (2003): 389–402.
La Barre, Weston. *The Ghost Dance: The Origins of Religion*. New York: Dell, 1972.
Lamar, Howard, and Leonard Thompson. *The Frontier in History: North America and Southern Africa Compared*. New Haven, CT: Yale University Press, 1981.
Lanternari, Vittorio. *The Religions of the Oppressed: A Study of Modern Messianic Cults*. New York: Mentor, 1963.
Lewis, Andrew J. "A Democracy of Facts, an Empire of Reason: Swallow Submersion and Natural History in the Early American Republic." *William and Mary Quarterly* 62 (2005): 663–96.
Lewis, G. Malcolm, ed. *Cartographic Encounters: Perspectives on Native American Mapmaking and Map Use*. Chicago: University of Chicago Press, 1989.
Livingston, Julie. *Debility and the Moral Imagination in Botswana*. Bloomington: Indiana University Press, 2005.
Mamdani, Mahmood. *Citizen and Subject: Contemporary Africa and the Legacy of Late Colonialism*. Princeton, NJ: Princeton University Press, 1996.
Marker, Michael. "After the Makah Whale Hunt: Indigenous Knowledge and Limits to Multicultural Discourse." *Urban Education* 41, no. 5 (2006): 482–505.
Mathews, Holly F. "Rootwork: Description of an Ethnomedical System in the American South." *Southern Medical Journal* 80, no. 7 (1987): 885–91.
McCann, James C. *Maize and Grace: Africa's Encounter with a New World Crop, 1500–2000*. Cambridge, MA: Harvard University Press, 2007.
McNamara, Kevin R. "The Feathered Scribe: The Discourses of American Ornithology Before 1800." *William and Mary Quarterly* 47 (1990): 210–34.
McNeill, William H. *Plagues and Peoples*. New York: Anchor Books, 1976.
Merlan, Francesca. "Indigeneity: Global and Local." *Current Anthropology* 50 (2009): 303–33.
Mooney, James. *Myths of the Cherokee*. New York: Dover, 1995.
Moore, Henrietta L., and Megan Vaughan. *Cutting Down Trees: Gender, Nutrition, and Agricultural Change in the Northern Province of Zambia, 1890–1990*. Portsmouth, NH: Heinemann, 1994.
Morris, Brian. *The Power of Animals: An Ethnography*. Oxford: Berg, 1998.
Musselman, Elizabeth Green. "Indigenous Knowledge and Contact Zones: The Case of the Cold Bokkeveld Meterorite, Cape Colony, 1838." *Itinerario* 33 (2009): 31–44.

Nadasdy, Paul. *Hunters and Bureaucrats: Power, Knowledge, and Aboriginal-State Relations in the Southwest Yukon.* Vancouver: University of British Columbia Press, 2003.

Neumann, Roderick P. *Imposing Wilderness: Struggles over Livelihood and Nature Preservation in Africa.* Berkeley: University of California Press, 1998.

Ntsebeza, Lungisile. *Democracy Compromised: Chiefs and the Politics of the Land in South Africa.* Leiden: Brill, 2005.

Offen, Karl H. "Creating Mosquitia: Mapping Amerindian Spatial Practices in Eastern Central America, 1629–1779." *Journal of Historical Geography* 33, no. 2 (2007): 254–82.

Onsman, Andrys. *Defining Indigeneity in the Twenty-First Century: A Case Study of the Free Frisians.* Lewiston, NY: Edwin Mellen Press, 2004.

Oomen, Barbara. *Chiefs in South Africa: Law, Power, and Culture in the Postapartheid Era.* London: James Currey, 2005.

Parman, Donald L. *The Navajos and the New Deal.* New Haven, CT: Yale University Press, 1976.

Pratt, Mary Louise. *Imperial Eyes: Travel Writing and Transculturation.* London: Routledge, 1992.

Richards, Audrey I. "Keeping the King Divine." *Proceedings of the Royal Anthropological Institute of Great Britain and Ireland* (1968): 23–35.

———. *Land, Labour and Diet in Northern Rhodesia: An Economic Study of the Bemba Tribe.* London: Oxford University Press, 1939.

Ritvo, Harriet. *The Platypus and the Mermaid, and Other Figments of the Classifying Imagination.* Cambridge, MA: Harvard University Press, 1997.

Roessel, Ruth, and Broderick H. Johnson. *Navajo Livestock Reduction: A National Disgrace.* Chinle, AZ: Navajo Community College Press, 1974.

Rundstrom, Robert A. "Mapping, Postmodernism, Indigenous People and the Changing Direction of North American Cartography." *Cartographica* 28, no. 2 (Summer 1991): 1–12.

Sanders, Todd. "Rains Gone Bad, Women Gone Mad: Rethinking Gender Rituals of Rebellion and Patriarchy." *Journal of the Royal Anthropological Institute* 6, no. 3 (September 2000): 469–86.

Sanga, Glauco, and Gherardo Ortalli, eds. *Nature Knowledge: Ethnoscience, Cognition, and Utility.* New York: Berghahn Books, 2004.

Schoffeleers, J. Matthew. *River of Blood: The Genesis of a Martyr Cult in Southern Malawi, c. A.D. 1600.* Madison: University of Wisconsin Press, 1992.

Scott, James C. *Seeing Like a State: How Certain Schemes to Improve the Human Condition Have Failed.* New Haven, CT: Yale University Press, 1998.

Sheridan, Michael J. "The Environmental and Social History of African Sacred Groves: A Tanzanian Case Study." *African Studies Review* 52, no 1 (2009): 73–98.

Sheridan, Michael J., and Celia Nyamweru. *African Sacred Groves: Ecological Dynamics and Social Change.* Oxford: James Currey, 2008.

Shipton, Parker M. *Mortgaging the Ancestors: Ideologies of Attachment in Africa.* New Haven, CT: Yale University Press, 2009.

Sillitoe, Paul, ed. *Local Science vs Global Science: Approaches to Indigenous Knowledge in International Development.* New York: Berghahn Books, 2007.

Sleeper-Smith, Susan, ed. *Contesting Knowledge: Museums and Indigenous Perspectives.* Lincoln: University of Nebraska Press, 2009.

Sparke, Matthew. "A Map That Roared and an Original Atlas: Canada, Cartography, and the Narration of Nation." *Annals of the Association of American Geographers* 88 (1998): 463–95.

Spear, Thomas. "Neo-Traditionalism and the Limits of Invention in British Colonial Africa." *Journal of African History* 44, no. 1 (2003): 3–27.

Sturtevant, William C. "Studies in Ethnoscience." *American Anthropologist* 66, no. 3, part 2 (1964): 99–131.

Thomas, Keith. *Man and the Natural World: A History of the Modern Sensibility.* New York: Pantheon Books, 1983.

Thrush, Coll, and Ruth S. Ludwin. "Finding Fault: Indigenous Seismology, Colonial Science, and the Rediscovery of Earthquakes and Tsunamis in Cascadia." *American Indian Culture and Research Journal* 31, no. 4 (2007): 1–24.

Vansina, Jan. *Oral Tradition as History.* Madison: University of Wisconsin Press, 1985.

Vaughan, Megan "'Divine Kings': Sex, Death and Anthropology in Inter-War East/Central Africa." *Journal of African History* 49 (2008): 383–401.

Vogel, Virgil J. *American Indian Medicine.* Norman: University of Oklahoma Press, 1970.

Vogt, Kristiina A., Karen H. Beard, Shira Hammann, Jennifer O'Hara Palmiotto, Daniel J. Vogt, Frederick N. Scatena, and Brooke P. Hecht. "Indigenous Knowledge Informing Management of Tropical Forests: The Link Between Rhythms in Plant Secondary Chemistry and Lunar Cycles." *Ambio* 31 (2002): 485–90.

Walker, Cherryl. "The Limits to Land Reform: Rethinking 'the Land Question.'" *Journal of Southern African Studies* 31, no. 4 (2005): 805–24.

Wallace, Anthony F. C. *Revitalizations and Mazeways: Essays on Culture Change.* Vol. 1. Edited by Robert S. Grumet. Lincoln: University of Nebraska Press, 2003.

Webb, James L. A., Jr. *Humanity's Burden: A Global History of Malaria.* New York: Cambridge University Press, 2008.
Weisiger, Marsha L. *Dreaming of Sheep in Navajo Country.* Seattle: University of Washington Press, 2009.
White, Richard. *The Middle Ground: Indians, Empires, and Republics in the Great Lakes Region, 1650–1815.* Cambridge: Cambridge University Press, 1991.
———. *The Roots of Dependency: Subsistence, Environment, and Social Change Among the Choctaws, Pawnees, and Navajos.* Lincoln: University of Nebraska Press, 1983.
Williams, Raymond. "Ideas of Nature." In *Problems in Materialism and Culture,* edited by Raymond Williams, 67–85. London: Verso, 1980.
Winichakul, Thongchai. *Siam Mapped: A History of the Geo-Body of a Nation.* Honolulu: University of Hawaii Press, 1994.
Worster, Donald. *Nature's Economy: A History of Ecological Ideas.* Cambridge: Cambridge University Press, 1994.

Contributors

David Bernstein, University of Wisconsin-Madison, caseydavidvt@yahoo.com

Derick Fay, University of California, Riverside, derick.fay@ucr.edu

Andrew H. Fisher, College of William and Mary, ahfis2@wm.edu

Karen Flint, University of North Carolina, Charlotte, kflint@uncc.edu

David M. Gordon, Bowdoin College, dgordon@bowdoin.edu

Paul Kelton, University of Kansas, pkelton@ku.edu

Shepard Krech III, Brown University, krech@brown.edu

Joshua Reid, University of Massachusetts, Boston, josh.reid@umb.edu

Parker Shipton, Boston University, shipton@bu.edu

Jacob Tropp, Middlebury College, jtropp@middlebury.edu

James L. A. Webb, Jr., Colby College, jlwebb@colby.edu

Lance van Sittert, University of Cape Town, lance.vanSittert@uct.ac.za

Marsha Weisiger, University of Oregon, weisiger@uoregon.edu

Index

ABCFM (American Board of
    Commissioners for Foreign
    Missions), 161, 162, 163, 165
Acholi, 226–27, 231, 234
Adair, James, 152–53, 154, 167n8
Adanson, Michel, 62
adultery, 153, 223
Aeschylus, 221
African National Congress (ANC), 269–70,
    289, 290, 294–95
African potato, 272, 277, 283n30
African Renaissance, 261, 277
Afrikaners, 14
Agrawal, Arun, 2
*Agricultural Journal of the Cape of Good
    Hope (AJCGH)*, 96, 97, 99, 100, 102,
    103, 104, 106
agriculture
    African, 63, 94–106, 113–23, 196–210, 293,
        298, 300
    Columbia River Basin, 189
    harvesting, 33, 86, 153, 156, 205, 260, 261
    Native American, 29, 33, 39–40, 44
    prosperity in, 17, 196–97, 199
    slash and burn, 199
    See also fertility, human/land; ritual,
        agricultural
ague, 56, 66n11
ague-weed, 58
AIDS, 128n31, 259, 260, 261, 270–71, 277–79
Ainu, 5
*AJCGH (Agricultural Journal of the Cape of
    Good Hope)*, 96, 97, 99, 100, 102, 103,
    104, 106

albatrosses, 87
Albers, Patricia, 34
Albert, Isaac, 182–83
Albert, Thomas, 182–83
alcohol
    as malaria treatment, 58, 60
    as intoxicant, 222, 223, 293. *See also* beer;
        whisky; wine
Alego, 224–25
American Board of Commissioners for
    Foreign Missions (ABCFM), 161, 162,
    163, 165
American centaury, 58
American Medical Association, 229
American wigeon, 72
ancestors
    beliefs of, 173–74, 184, 196–210
    burial of/graveyards of, 12, 196, 197,
        201–4, 207–9, 222, 232
    incarnations of, 196, 221, 227
    indigeneity dependent on, 6
    spirits of, 196–210
Andy, Fidelia, 190
animal rights, 221, 253
animals
    associated with descent, 83
    domestic, 40, 74, 77, 79, 82
    endangered, 268
    human connection to, 175, 216–34,
        248–49
    as prophetic messengers, 86, 216–34
    resources of, 14, 139, 140, 191
    sacrifice of, 205, 225, 226, 230
    spirits of, 167n11, 176, 220, 233

animals (cont'd)
    as symbols, 86, 116, 143, 216–34, 237n16
    See also animism; livestock; totemism;
        specific type of animal
animism, 7, 54, 175
Anna Johanna, 160
anthropologists, 7, 9, 10, 17, 32, 34
    colonial, 197, 208, 210
    on Mid-Columbia Indians, 174, 175, 177
    research of Navajo Reservation land,
        136–37, 143
    on spiritual movements, 217, 218, 219
Antigone (Sophocles), 221
apartheid, 9, 18, 261, 271, 272, 287–92, 297
Army Corps of Engineers, 183
arroyos, 130, 135, 147n22
arsenite of soda, 114
arthritis, 279
aspirin, 59, 67n17
Athena, 86
Auma, Alice, 226–27

Balch, Billy, 248
bald eagle, 74, 75
Baltimore orioles, 75, 76
Banded Rock Boy, 140
bank swallow, 73
Bantu, 3, 226, 297
Bantu Authorities Act, 288, 292
Bangweulu, Lake, 205
Baptists, 165, 170n57
barnacle geese, 87
barn owl, 86, 87
barred owl, 73, 75, 76, 78, 83
Barrow, John, 97, 98
Bartram, William, 75, 76
Basso, Keith, 32
bath, vapor, 59
Batwa, 20n8, 205
Beach, David, 125n9
Beale, Edward, 134–35
Beale Trail, 134
Beall, Jo, 289
bee-martin, 76
beer, 203, 205
bees, 226
Belloni, Robert C., 185
belted kingfishers, 73, 75
Belyea, Barbara, 31, 32, 41–42, 48n11

Bemba, 5, 196–210
Bennett, Hugh Hammond, 132
Bering Sea, 247
Bernstein, David, 8, 13
berries, 173, 179, 180, 244
Béteille, André, 6
biomedicines, 53–65, 259, 261, 264,
    267–69
biopiracy, 263
bioprospecting, 18, 65n2, 260, 261, 262–64,
    265, 283n24
birds
    domesticated, 74, 79, 82, 89n4
    folk beliefs about/perceptions of, 73,
        78–79, 81–89, 248
    as messengers, 116, 219, 220
    naming/classifying of, 8, 13, 69–89
    spirit-birds, 73, 79, 83, 87
    as symbols, 116, 216–34
    See also specific types of birds
Bisa, 5, 197, 204–5, 209
bitterns, 76, 85
blackbirds, 72, 73, 76, 80, 86
black-capped chickadee, 76, 77
blackcaps, 87
black-crowned night herons, 77
black duck, 90n14
Black Elk, 219
Blackhawk Wars, 40
Black Hills, 222
black vultures, 73, 75, 76
bleeding, 60, 161
Blessingway, 138–40, 149n33
blowguns, 81–82
Blue, Sam, 73, 89n4
bluebirds, 74, 75, 78, 83
blue crane, 76
blue darter, 76
blue hawk, 76
blue heron, 76, 78
blue jay, 72
boat-tailed grackle, 75
bobolink, 76
bobwhite, 78
Boilivin, Nicolas, 50n29
Bond, James, 226
boneset, 58
Bonneville Dam, 183, 186, 190
botanical gardens, 65n2, 265, 266

botany, 12, 71
Botkin, Daniel, 143
bowels, 59
brant goose, 72, 76
Brelsford, W. V., 207–8
Breyer-Brandwijk, M. G., 266, 284n32
British South African Company (BSAC), 206, 207
broadbill, 90n14
broad-winged hawks, 73
Brody, Hugh, 32
Broster, Joan A., 119
brown-headed cowbird, 73, 80
Brownlee, W. T., 120
brown thrasher, 73
Bryan, Kirk, 135, 136
(BSAC) British South African Company, 206, 207
buffalo, 33, 222
bullbat, 76
buntings, 76, 83
Bureau of Indian Affairs (BIA), 40, 129, 131–32, 134, 136, 143, 183
butcher birds, 75, 76
buzzards, 75, 82, 220
  See also vultures
Bwembya, 203

Calhoun, Henry, 36
Campbell, Dugald, 205
canaries, 74, 90n6
cancer, 259, 279
cannabis, 225
Cape Flattery, 244, 245, 248–50
cardinal, 72, 74, 76, 83
Carolina chickadee, 75, 76, 77
Carolina parakeet, 72, 75
Carolina wren, 76, 83
carrion crows, 75, 76, 86
cartography. *See* maps/mapping
casinos, 5
castor oil, 84
Catawbas, 70, 73, 78
catbirds, 75, 78
Catholics, 177
cattle, 40, 117
  in Africa, 201, 222, 223, 225, 298
  on Navajo Reservation, 132, 135
  of Mid-Columbia, 175, 179, 180, 188

cedar waxwing, 76
Celilo Falls/Village, Oregon, 173, 177, 179, 182, 183, 188, 191
Celilo Fish Committee (CFC), 182–183
centaury, 58
ceremonies. *See* rituals
Chabala. *See* Chilufya
chaffinch, 86
Chandamali, 207
Changes in the Land (Cronon), 11
Changing Woman, 138–39
chaos, spiritual, 139, 141, 143, 144
chats, 76, 83
chauvinism, scientific and colonial, 14
Cherokees
  bird classifications/naming by, 73, 77, 78, 79–80, 84
  beliefs about disease causes, 60, 65n4
  ginseng use, 57
  magical formulas involving birds, 82–83
  materia medica, 66n11
  smallpox epidemic, 14, 151–65
cherry bird, 76
cherry tree, 58, 66n11
chickadees, 74, 75, 76, 77
Chickasaws, 70, 73, 78, 79
chicken hawks, 74
chickens, 72, 73, 74, 78, 79, 82
  Native names for, 77, 78, 89n4
  sacrifice of, 205
chiefs
  African, 15, 18, 114, 116, 119, 196–98, 201–7
  Cherokee, 160, 164
  colonial, 17
  Iowa, 37, 39, 41
  salmon, 177, 82
  tribal, 15, 18, 114, 116, 119, 196, 197–98, 201–2, 205, 206–7
  Tygh, 178
  Yakama, 178, 180, 191
Chilinda, 202
Chilufya, 200
Chilumbulu, 200–201, 202–3
Chimbala, 201–2
chimney sweep, 76
chimney swift, 76, 83
Chimurenga, 125n9, 231
Chippewa, 38
Chitapankwa. *See* Chitimukulu

Chiti, 200–201, 203, 204, 210
Chitimachas, 87
Chitimukulu, 197, 199, 202, 203–4, 206–8, 210
chough, 86
chloroquine, 64, 65
Choctaws, 70, 78, 87, 88
Christiansborg Castle, 62
chuck-will's-widow, 73, 78
cimicifuga, 59, 67n19
cinchona tree/bark, 54, 58–59, 60, 61, 62, 64
cinchonine, 59
circle dance. *See* ghost dance
Civil War, U.S., 59
civil wars, African, 226
CLARA (Communal Land Rights Act), 287–301
Clark, William, 31, 36, 37–38, 40–41, 176
Clements, Frederic, 133
cobras, 224, 229
Coffee Bay, 293
Collier, John, 132, 136–37
colonialism
  in Africa, 14–15, 116, 196, 208, 210
  conflict/violence in, 14–15, 16
  effect on indigenous knowledges, 2, 3, 7, 9, 13
  European, 14–15, 16, 17
  resources dispossessed during, 18
  threats presented by, 165
colonization
  of Columbia River Basin by Euro-Americans, 177
  conservation knowledge and, 182
  by historians, 48n13
  indigeneity proclaimed by colonizers, 196–97
  indigenous tenure and, 244
  knowledge exchange in, 5, 13, 14, 29, 182, 196–97, 265
  malaria effect on African, 54, 63
  power and control in, 31, 288
  and sense of position in world, 222
  smallpox introduced during European, 152
  in Transkei, 113–23
Colorado Plateau, 129, 130, 133, 135
Colorado River, 133, 134
Columbian Exchange, 53
Columbia River, 173–92
  pollution of, 179, 190–91

Columbia River General Council Fish Commission, 185
Columbia River Inter-Tribal Fish Commission (CRITFC), 186–90
Comaroff, Jean, 10
Comaroff, John, 10
Communal Land Rights Act (CLARA), 287–301
Communal Property Association (CPA), 291–92, 295, 297, 298, 300
condors, 220
Confederate army, 59
Congress of Traditional Leaders of South Africa (Contralesa), 289, 290, 292, 294
conservation, 9, 10, 12–13, 16, 17, 95, 269
  biological, 9, 190, 263
  in fishing, 174, 176–77, 179, 181, 185
  Native American, 129–44, 174, 176–77, 181–82, 187, 192
  soil, 11, 129–44
Convention on Biological Diversity, 263, 264
Cook, Peter A. W., 117
Cook's Landing, 183–86
Cooper's hawks, 73, 76
coot, 80
cormorants, 76
corncrakes, 87
corpse birds/fowl, 86, 87
corvids, 81, 86, 88
Council for Scientific and Industrial Research (CSIR), 262, 263, 265, 282n14
cowbirds, 73, 80
CPA (Communal Property Association), 291–92, 295, 297, 298, 300
Crane, The, 39, 43
cranes, 72, 75, 76, 82
creation, sacred, 139–40, 178
Creeks, 70, 74, 78, 84, 89n4, 90n6
crisis cults, 216, 234
CRITFC (Columbia River Inter-Tribal Fish Commission), 186–90
Crocodile Clan, 199–210
Cronon, William, 11
Crosby, Albert, 166n3
crows, 74, 75, 76, 86, 220
crying bird, 76

CSIR (Council for Scientific and Industrial Research), 262, 263, 265, 282n14
cuckoos, 76, 85, 86
Cunnison, Ian, 208
curlews, 75

dabchick, 90n14
dance masks, 218–19
dances, ritual
  African, 117, 203
  Cherokee, 14, 151–57, 162–63, 165
  dream, 219
  feather dance, 218, 231
  ghost/circle dance, 216, 218, 220, 231
  Sahaptin/Wáašat, 173–74, 175, 178
  sun dance, 218
David, Elsie, 175
Dawes Severalty Act, 244
Dawnee, 159
Dawzizi, 158
DDT, 64
Deeart, 257n37
death
  birds related to, 82, 85, 86, 220
  drowning, 177
  from illness, 63, 64, 65n7, 120, 121, 152, 154, 157, 159, 160, 162, 163
  of king, 204
  snake symbolizing, 220, 221
deer, 33, 173, 180, 188
deerskins, 163
"Deconstructing the Map" (Harley), 30
Deeschii'nii, Fred, 141
DeFreeze, Donald, 229
degradation narratives, 11
Delawares, 77
De Moyen, 35
Department of Land Affairs (DLA), 291–92, 296
depression, 279
Derrida, Jacques, 30
Des Moines River, 38, 44
devil's claw, 283n30
dicky birds, 76, 90n13
didapper, 76, 90n14
Dinés. *See* Navajos
Dinka, 232
dipper, 90n14
diseases. *See* illnesses

Ditidahts, 249–50
diver, 90n14
divorce, 153
Dixie, 295, 299
DLA (Department of Land Affairs), 291–92, 296
dogwood tree/bark, 56–57, 58–59
Dompier, Douglas, 189, 190
Donaugh, Carl, 183
double-crested cormorant, 76
Dove, Michael, 1, 2
doves, 72, 75, 76, 78, 83
  folk beliefs about, 78, 87
Drake, Daniel, 58–59
dream dances, 218
dreams, 220, 221, 230
drought, 98, 120, 122, 130–31, 135–36, 138–41
drugs, mind altering, 223, 225
duck hawk, 90n14
ducks, 72, 73, 75, 76, 81, 83, 86, 89n4, 90n14
duck-vulture, 89n4
Duffy antigen negativity, 56
Dunde, Onyango, 225
dunnock sparrow, 75, 90n14
Durkheim, Emile, 219
Dutch East India Company, 65n2, 97
Dutch Golden Age, 68n26
Dutfield, Graham, 264
Dwesa-Cwebe, 291, 293

eagles, 72, 73, 75, 82, 83, 88, 219
  Cherokee prayers to, 162
  in Creek dictionary, 74
  feathers/claws of, 82, 218, 228
  Holy Spirit movement and, 226
  as king of birds, 86
Eagles, Peter, 271, 278
eastern bluebird, 83
eastern towhee, 72, 77
Ecological Indian, 174, 190, 248
Ecological Indian, The (Krech), 12, 174
ecologists/ecology, 9, 12, 13, 129–44, 174, 248
economists, 10
ecotourism, 10, 298
egrets, 75, 76, 82
Ellen, Roy, 2, 4
English duck, 90n14
Enlightenment, 16
epilepsy, 84

erosion, soil, 129–44
ethnoornithology, indigenous, 69–89
ethnoscience, 70–72
ethnozoopsychology, 239n37
Exodus, 86

faiths. *See* religions
falcons, 70, 71, 72, 73, 83, 85, 90n14
farming. *See* agriculture
fasting, 151, 163, 249
Fay, Derick, 9, 17, 18, 127n21
feasts, 174, 175, 176, 178, 249
    first-food, 175, 176, 184
    salmon, 173, 176
    root, 192
feather dance, 218, 231
Felice, 250
fer-de-lance, 228
fertility
    human/land, 17, 114–19, 153, 196–210, 221, 224–25
    symbols, 117, 119, 221, 228
field lark, 76
Fight of the Salmon People (Dompier), 189
finches, 73, 76, 79, 80, 86
Fingoland, 114, 119–23
Fipa, 227
First World War, 225
Fisher, Andrew, 16
fisheries, 12, 173, 177–88, 252
fish hawk, 76
fishing
    efficient, 176–77
    regulations/rules, 11, 18, 176–79, 182, 184
    overfishing, 179
    salmon, 173–92
    tribal/treaty rights, 18, 173–92, 252
    wasteful, 176–77
fish wheels, 179
Five Civilized Tribes, 79
flickers, 73, 74, 76
Flint, Karen, 5, 17, 18, 95
floods, ancient, 87, 88
flu, 279
fluids, human/vital, 99–100, 102, 103, 138–39, 153, 156
flycatchers, 73, 74, 75, 83
Folb, Peter, 270
foods
    African, 67n20
    Navajo, 139, 142
    respected/sacred, 173, 175, 176, 178, 189, 191–92
    traditional, 180, 222
    See also feasts
Foucault, Michel, 30
foresters/forestry, 10–11, 58, 64, 95, 131, 132, 144
forests, 58, 64
    African, 200, 201, 205, 222
    Navajo Country, 132, 144
    New Mexico, 248
forked tail hawk, 75
Fort Duquesne, 155
Foxes, 35, 37–38, 51–52n42
Frazer, James, 219
Freudians, 220–21
frogs, 88
fungus, 114, 278
fur traders, 176, 177

gadwall, 90n14
Gai'wiio. *See also* Longhouse religion
Gambler Woman, 140–41
Games Against Nature (Harms), 11
gannets, 75, 85, 87
Garrison, Fielding H., 59
geese, 72, 75, 76, 85, 87
George (Cherokee boy), 159
Georgia, 8, 151, 155
Gericke, Nigel, 269–70, 278–79
ghost dance, 216, 218, 220, 231
Gibbs, George, 247
Giddens, Anthony, 30
Giles-Vernick, Tamara, 11, 12
ginseng, 57
Glen Grey Act, 120
globalization, 7, 60
Gluckman, Max, 117–18, 208
goats, 87, 117, 131–32, 138–39, 142, 150n40, 225
goatsuckers, 86, 87, 88, 90n14
Going-to-Water, 153–54, 159–60, 161
golden-crowned kinglet, 73
golden eagle, 82, 86
goldfinches, 73, 79
Goldtooth, Frank, 129–30
Gordon, David M., 5, 12, 16, 300
Gorton, Slade, 186

Goudy, Lawrence, 186
gourd martin, 76
gourds, 82, 206
grackles, 73, 75, 80
grasses, 132, 133, 136, 141
graves/graveyards, 12, 197, 201–9, 222, 231, 232
gray duck, 90n14
gray jay, 91n17
gray plover, 75
greasewood, 134, 141, 142
great blue heron, 76, 78
great crested flycatcher, 83
great horned owl, 73, 74, 76, 83
great savanna crane, 76
grebes, 76, 90n14
green herons, 76, 77
green woodpeckers, 76, 86
Gregory, Herbert, 135, 136
grey heron, 86
griffon vulture, 86
Grove, Richard, 13
grubs, 117
Gullah, 78, 88
gulls, 72, 73, 75, 80, 83, 86, 87
Gulu, 226
Gunrod, 158
guns, 34, 37, 38, 116, 251
Gusii, 226

Hack, John T., 135
Haile, Berard, 137
hairy woodpeckers, 80, 83
halibut, 245, 246, 248, 249
handbells, 177
Handsome Lake, 218
hang-nest, 76
Haraway, Donna, 143
Hard Heart, 37, 51n32
Harley, J. Brian, 30
Harms, Robert, 11
Harris, Carey A., 41
Harris, Holly, 4
Harrison, William Henry, 35
hawks, 72, 73, 74, 75, 76, 83, 90n14
healers, 55
    African, 115, 259–80
    Cherokee, 152, 154, 166
    death of patients and, 152–53, 154
    Lakota, 219

Navajo, 140
    missionaries as, 157–58
Hearst, Patricia, 229
heath hen, 89n4
hedge sparrows, 75, 90n14
Hehaka Sapa. *See* Black Elk
hell-diver, 76
hen hawks, 76
herbalists, 115, 119, 267
herbs, 116
    African, 265–80
    as antimalarials, 58, 60
    European, 265
    medicinal, 62, 158, 159, 271, 279
    processing, 278
    See also hoodia
herns, 75
herons, 73, 75, 76, 77
    artifacts from, 82
    folk beliefs about, 86
Hicks, Charles, 160–61, 164–65
Hicks, William, 164–65
historians, 1, 6, 7, 11, 19, 30, 32, 88, 96, 176, 219
History of Cartography, The (Woodward and Lewis), 30, 32
History of the American Indians, The (Adair), 152
HIV. *See* AIDS
Hobshawn, Eric, 6
hóchxǫ, 139, 141, 144
Hodenosaunee, 218
Holomisa, Phathekile, 289, 292, 294, 303n31
Holy People, 138–39, 140
Holy Spirit movement, 226–27, 228
hoodia, 261–64, 265, 269, 278
Hoodia Growers Association, 282n14
hooting owl, 76
Hopis, 135, 139, 228, 239n34
horses, 97, 130, 132, 134, 140, 179, 219
house sparrow, 74, 76
hózhǫ, 139, 143, 144
Hudson, Charles, 167–68n11
Hughes, Andrew, 40
hummingbirds, 74
Hunn, Eugene, 176
hunting, 11, 12, 33, 70, 138, 178, 187
    ceremonies, 202
    grounds, 33–44, 160

hunting (cont'd)
    wasteful, 176–77
    of whales/seals, 246–53

Igbo, 227
Ihanzus, 118
illnesses, 15, 217
    causes of, 54–55, 60, 70, 120, 158, 176, 259, 276
    in children, 62, 65n7, 114, 119–23
    immunity to, 54, 56, 63, 154, 165n1, 168n15, 277, 279
    natural, 54–55, 60
    protection against, 63, 159, 162
    racism and, 96
    spread of, 14, 34–35, 53, 63–64, 120–22, 151–52, 155–56
    treatment of, 13, 54, 55, 57–64, 159, 161, 275–76. See also healers
    two categories of, 54–55, 60
    virgin-soil epidemics, 34, 154
    wartime, 59
    See also specific illnesses
Indian Doctor's Dispensary, The, 58
Indian Guide to Health, The, 58
Indian hen, 76, 77
Indian pullet, 77
Indian Reorganization Act, 252–53
Indian Shaker, 218, 220, 230, 235n9
Indian Territory, 70, 74
indigenous, defined, 3–7
Indigenous Environments: African and North American Environmental Knowledge and Practices Compared (conference), 2
indigenous knowledges
    characterization/definition of, 7–8, 19
indigenous tenure, 244, 287–301
indigo buntings, 83
Indirect Rule, 9, 15, 206, 207
Indonesia, 85
Ingersoll, Ernest, 85
Inkatha Freedom Party (IFP), 289, 290
insecticides, 63, 64, 114
insects, 60, 71, 143
    See also specific types of insects
Introduction to the History of Medicine, An (Garrison), 59

Inuit, 269
Invention of Tradition, The (Hobshawn and Ranger), 6
Iowas, 13, 27–45
    name variations, 49n16
Iroquois, 218
Isert, Paul E., 62
Itohvnv, 151, 156
Ives, Joseph, 134–35
ivory-billed woodpecker, 83

jackdaws, 75
Jackson, Johnny, 183, 187
Jafta, Dorcas, 118
Jameson Raid, 98
Japan, 5
jaundice, 68n25
jays, 72, 75, 76, 91n17
Jenner, Edward, 165n1
Jerome, Saint, 86
Jesuits, 177
Jesus, 158, 160, 214n34, 233
Jim, Howard, 177
Jim, Robert, 181, 182
Jomon period, 5
joree, 76, 77
Juan de Fuca, Strait of, 246, 250

Kabotwe, 201, 202
Kalahari, 262, 264, 283n19
Kalchote, 244–45, 250
Kalkfontein, 291, 295, 296–97, 300
Kama, 115–16, 118–19
Kansa, 37
Katongo, 200
Kazembe, 199, 208
Keh-tchook, 250
Kelton, Paul, 14
Kenya/Kenyans, 222, 224, 225, 227, 231–32, 239n33
Kenyatta, Jomo, 232
Keokuk, 40, 43
kestrel, 82
Kew Gardens, 266
Kickapoos, 36
kidneys, 59
Kikongo, 78
killdee, 76
killdeer, 73, 76

Kimball, Solon, 137, 143
kingbird, 76
kingfishers, 73, 75, 83
    folk beliefs about, 86, 88
kinglets, 73
Kipsigis, 225
kites, 75
kittiwakes, 87
Klein, William, 185
knowledge, folk, 60, 81, 84, 94, 95–97, 99, 104–6
Kony, Joseph, 227, 238n29
Kosek, Jake, 248
Kosvkvskini, 156, 162
Krech, Shepard, 8, 12, 13, 174, 176, 191, 300
Krige, Eileen, 125n11, 126n14
Kruger National Park, 297–98, 299
Kubekeli, Philip, 272, 273
KwaZulu-Natal (KZN), 268, 272, 273, 276, 286n71, 289, 290, 294–95

Lacey Act, 186
Lahiff, Edward, 300
Lakota, 219, 222
Lakwena, Alice, 226–27
lammergeier, 86
land birds, 71, 72, 73, 75, 81, 84
Langdon, Stephen, 174
Lango, 225
language
    dominant, 105
    of science and modernity, 266, 267
    tribal/Native, 88–89, 160, 176, 184
    universal/communal, 7, 17
larks, 76, 78, 83
laudanum, 159
laughing owl, 76
Lawson, John, 75
least flycatcher, 73
Ledwaba, A. P., 299
Lennons, 265
Le Sueur, Pierre Charles, 33–34
Lévy-Bruhl, Lucien, 219
Lewis, Andrew, 88
Lewis, G. Malcolm, 30, 31, 32, 48n11
Lewis, Meriwether, 31, 176
limpkins, 76, 89n4
Linnaeus, Carolus, 61–62, 81, 265
Little Ateem Island, 182–83

Little Big Horn, 219
little jay, 75
lizard, 200–201
livestock, 115, 117
    pandemic, 96
    payments of, 293
    reduction, 129–44
Livingston, Julie, 128n33
Livingstone, David, 206
locoweed, 142
locusts, 113–23, 124n1, 125n9, 203
loggerhead shrikes, 75, 83
long-eared owl, 82
Longhouse religion, 174–77, 181, 188, 218, 220
longhouses, 173, 175, 184
loons, 72, 85, 90n14
Lord's Resistance Army, 227, 228, 231
Lozi, 208
Luapula River, 199, 200
Luba, 196, 199, 200, 201
Lunda, 196, 199, 208, 215n54
Luo, 224–27
Luthuli, Albert, 289

Maasai, 222, 225
Madikane, Eliya, 276
magic
    African, 60, 67n21, 197, 198, 201, 209
    Cherokee, 82
    Indian, 82, 160
magicians, 200, 201, 207
magpie, 86
Makahs, 12, 243–53
    spiritual worldview of, 244, 248–49
    treaty of 1855, 244–45, 246, 247, 250–52
    weather prediction by, 245–46
Makgobistad, 295, 298–99
Makulekes, 295, 297–98, 300, 305n57
malaria, 13
    in Africa, 61–64, 65n7, 270, 275
    Eastern North America treatment of, 57–60
    introduction in the Americas, 53, 55–56
    miasmatic theory of cause, 60, 61
    treatment of, 53–65
Malatare, Lewis, 175
Malinowski, Branislaw, 197
mallards, 72, 75, 76, 90n14
Mami Wata, 228

maps/mapping
    European, 45
    as form of oppression, 31
    history/historical context of, 27–33
    Native/indigenous, 27–33, 45. *See also* Notchininga's Map
    political power contained within, 30–31
    Ptolemaic, 29, 41
    Renaissance, 32
Markistun, Luke, 250
marriage, 86, 117, 153, 182, 223
    intermarriage, 61, 84, 200
    symbolic, 201
marsh bitern, 76
marsh hawks, 73
marshlands, 60
Martin, Calvin, 48n13
martins, 75, 76, 83, 85
Matsabisa, Gilbert, 274, 275
Mau Mau, 231–32
Mayayane, 298
Mbeki, Govan, 289
Mbeki, Thabo, 261, 277, 279
Mckenney, Thomas, 33
McLoughlin, William, 166n3
McNary Dam, 186
meadowlarks, 76, 83
Meares, John, 250
measles, 53, 121, 162, 163, 164, 166n3
Medicinal Plants of South Africa (Van Wyk, Oudtshoorn, and Gericke), 272
medicine
    African traditional, 259–80
    exchange of knowledge regarding, 13, 53–65
    scientific, 62
    "slave," 67n21
    See also biomedicine; plants, medicinal
medicine men/people, 152–53, 154, 156–57, 160, 162, 166n3, 219
    See also healers
Melanesia, 217, 222, 235n6
Meninick, George, 180–81, 191
Meninick, Jerry, 190
Meninick, Johnson, 181
Menominee, 38
mergansers, 83
mermaid, 228
Methodists, 165, 170n57
métis, 8, 148–49n29

Mhinga Tribal Authority, 297–98
miasmatic theory, 60, 61
Mid-Columbia Indians, 174–83, 187–92
mining, 51–52n42, 63
military, 202
    action/conquest, 34, 43, 62, 210, 219, 225, 230, 231, 232, 288, 297–98
    and map creation, 31, 32
    organizations, 228–29, 230
missionaries, 15, 116
    Cherokee smallpox epidemic and, 151–52, 157–65
Mississippian era, 83
Mississippi kites, 75
Mississippi River, 33–41, 51n32
Missouri River, 33–41, 44, 51n32
Missouris, 34
Mkambati Nature Reserve, 293
Mkhize, Sibongiseni, 289
Mnisi Tribal Authority, 299
mockingbirds, 73, 74, 75, 76
    American Indian naming of, 78, 79
    folk beliefs about, 73, 78, 79
    Mr. Mockingbird, 78, 79
Monsanto, 262
Mooney, James, 57, 66n11, 219
moorhen, 80
Moravians, 151, 157–63
Morgan, Lewis Henry, 218
mortgage bird, 74, 78
mosquitoes, anopheline, 53, 56, 60, 61
    control of, 62, 63
Mother Earth, 175, 189
mourning doves, 72, 75, 76, 83
movements, spiritual
    African, 216–34
    feather dance, 218, 231
    female leadership in, 219, 220
    ghost/circle dance, 216, 218, 220, 231
    Holy Spirit, 226–27, 228
    Indian Shaker, 218, 220, 230, 235n9
    Mumbo, 224–26, 227, 228, 231
    prophetic, 216–34
    rebel, 223
Mpondo, 117, 119
Mpumalanga, 296–97, 299
Mthemjwa, Muzi, 266–67
Mugakula, Phahlela, 297–98
Muhammad, 233

Mukasa, Mumbi, 200
Mukulumpe, 200
Mumbo movement, 224–26, 227, 228, 231
Muscovy duck, 89
museums, 16
Mutwa, Credo, 278
Mwalule, 197, 198, 201–4, 207
Mwamba, 204, 207, 210
Mwase, 201, 207
Mweru, Lake, 199
Mzimela, M. B., 290, 291

Nachituti, 199
Nancy (Cherokee girl), 159–60
Nandi, 225
Narbona, 139
Natal, 99, 267, 268
National Party, 288
National Resistance Army, 226–27
Native Treasury, 207
Navajos
    philosophy of spiritual order vs. disorder, 15, 16, 139–44
    relationships with nature, 138
    reservation, 129–44
    traditional stories, 143
Ndebele, 125n9, 296
Ndzundu, 296–97
Neah Bay, 244–46, 250, 252
Needham, Rodney, 217
Nelson, Ernest, 142
nematodes, 128n31
New Deal, 15, 129–44
New Mexico, 129, 140, 248
Nez Perce, 177, 186
Ng'anga, Luchele, 200, 214n34
Ngoni, 205
Nigeria, 227
night birds, 76, 77, 90n14, 82, 84–85, 86, 87, 220
nighthawk, 76, 90n14
night herons, 77
nightingale, 84–85
nightjar, 87
night raven, 85
Nkhweto, 202, 207–8
Nkole, 200–202, 204, 207, 210
Nkuba, 199
Nkula, 207, 208

Noah, 87
Nobles, Gregory, 31
nocturnal birds. *See* night birds
No Heart's Map. *See* Notchininga's Map
Noristan, 265, 270
North American Indian Doctor, The, 58
northern cardinal, 72, 76, 83
northern flickers, 73, 76
northern mockingbirds, 73, 78, 79
Northern Pacific Railroad, 179
North Gauteng High Court, 288, 295, 296
Notchininga, 29, 41, 43
Notchininga's Map, 13, 27–30, 33, 35, 37, 38, 46n4
    as political tactic, 44–45
    spatial representation of, 41–43
Ntsebeza, Lungisile, 291
Ntutela, Siya, 272, 273–74, 275–76
Nuer, 232
numbers, sacral significance of, 177–78
nuthatches, 73, 80
Nyang'idi, 224–25

oak trees/bark, 58, 59
Ocan, Mike, 226
Occidentalism, 16
octopus, 246
Oglala, 219
oil, sea mammal, 247, 249
Oklahoma, 29, 70, 89
Omahas, 34, 36
Omieri/Omweri, 227, 228, 231
Oneida, 77
ornithologies, 69–89
opium, 57, 60, 68n25, 159
oral tradition
    African, 7, 196, 198–204
    Mid-Columbia Indian, 176–77, 189
orchard orioles, 76
Oresteia (Aeschylus), 221
orioles, 75, 76
Osages, 35, 36, 37
osprey, 72, 73, 76, 82, 86
Otoes, 33, 34
Ottawas, 38
Otterlifter, 159
Owhi, 178, 179, 181, 191
owls, 72, 73, 74, 76, 82–83, 86
    feathers of, 228

owls (cont'd)
   Native names for, 78
   superstitions about, 84, 86, 87, 88, 220
ox-eye, 90

Pafuri Triangle, 297, 298
painted bunting, 76
Painted Desert, 135
painted finch, 76
Pamunkeys, 88
Papua New Guinea, 85
parakeets, 72, 75
parrots, 72, 81
passenger pigeons, 72, 75, 81
passerines, 72, 81
Pawnees, 36, 37
peet weet, 90n14
pelicans, 83
Penobscot, 77
peregrine falcon, 71–72, 90n14
persons, indigenous
   definition of, 3–7
   global encounter between nonindigenous and, 69
   politics of, 8–10
petrels, 81, 86, 87
pewees, 83
Pfizer Corporation, 262, 263, 265
pharmaceuticals, 18, 259–80
pharmacopoeia, official U.S., 59, 64
physic-pots, 152, 154
Phytopharm, 262, 263, 265, 282n18
pied-billed grebe, 76,
pied wagtail, 86
pigeons, 72, 75, 81
pigweed, 142
Pike, Zebulon, 35
pileated woodpeckers, 72, 76, 79, 83
pine siskin, 73
pipits, 90n13
place-naming, 32, 244, 245, 253
plants
   medicinal, 61–62, 142–43, 259–80
   poisonous, 132–33, 142, 284n32
Plymouth Brethren, 205
Poinsett, Joel, 27, 29, 41
poison/poisoning, 60, 67n21, 201, 207
   disease as, 157, 158
   snakes symbolizing, 220

weeds, 132–33, 142
"polythetic class," 217
Potawatomi, 38
plovers, 75, 90n14
Pondoland, 114, 115, 116–17, 119
poor Joe, 78
poplar trees/bark, 58, 59, 67n17
Portland Fish Company, 182–83
Posey, Darrell A., 264
poverty, 10
prairie chickens, 89n4
Prairie du Chien, Wisconsin, 37–39, 41, 43
Pratt, Mary Louise, 13
prayer, 218, 230
   African, 205, 228
   Cherokee, 151, 154, 156, 159, 162, 163, 164
   Christian, 159, 162–63, 199
   Navajo, 140, 143
   Sahaptin, 173
   Umatilla, 192
prophecies/prophets, 122–23
   agricultural, 114
   Bisa, 204
   Wáašat. See Sahaptin
   Xhosa prophet, 123
   See also movements, prophetic
Prosser Dam/Falls, 180–81
Protestants, 157, 177, 230
Provinse, John, 130, 137
Pungutsha, 296–97
purging
   ethnic, 232
   medicinal, 60, 161
purple jackdaws, 75
purple martins, 76, 83
pythons, 220, 224–25, 227

Quaempts, Eric J., 192
quarantine, 121, 151, 156
Quetzalcoatl, 228
quinine, 59, 63, 64

rabbitbrush, 142
racism, 62, 95, 96
railroads, 179
rails, 80, 87, 88
rain birds, 76, 85, 86
raincrow, 76
rain forests, 58

Index | 331

rainmaking, 97
ranchers, 142
rangelands, Navajo, 129–44
Ranger, Terence, 6
raptors, 71, 72, 73, 74, 75, 76, 79, 81, 82, 83, 220
ravens, 74, 75, 83, 87
　folk beliefs about, 85, 86, 220
redbirds, 75, 76
red-breasted nuthatch, 80
red clay, 117
Red Elk, Wenix, 192
red-headed eagles, 74
red-headed woodpeckers, 76, 78, 80, 83
red-shouldered hawks, 73
redstarts, 87
red-tailed hawks, 73, 74, 76
red-winged blackbirds, 72, 73, 76, 80
Reichard, Gladys, 137
Reid, Joshua, 12, 17, 18
religion, 2, 7, 8, 16–17, 32, 82
　African, 15, 102, 123
　Cherokee, 151, 153, 155–56, 157, 165
　Christian, 14, 15, 16, 17, 99, 102, 114, 122–23, 151, 152, 157–65, 174–78, 182, 193n9, 199, 214n34, 225, 239n33
　feather dance, 218, 231
　ghost dance, 216, 218, 220, 231
　global, 199
　Indian Shaker, 218, 220, 230, 235n9
　indigenous/native, 16, 17, 137, 140, 157, 173–92
　Navajo, 137, 140
　Plateau, 176, 177
　Sahaptin/Wáašat, 173–75, 178
　three Rs of new, 233–34
　Yakama, 181
revitalization movements, 216–34
Reynards. *See* Foxes
rheumatism, 59
Rhodes, Cecil, 98
Rhodesia, 63, 206, 231
rice, 67n20
rice bird, 76
Richards, Audrey, 197, 208–9
Richardson, William, 155, 156
ring plover, 90n14
rituals, 228, 232
　agricultural, 114–19, 139–40
　Bemba, 197, 203–4, 207

environmental stewardship, 174
healing, 55, 62, 151–52, 155–56
purification, 154, 207
rain, 118
Wáašat/Sahaptin, 175–77
River People, 184–86
robins, 72, 85, 87, 90n14
Rocard, Michel, 279
Rock River, 35, 38
rooibos tea, 283n30
rooks, 86
roseate spoonbill, 83
Round Up, 262
Rugalema, Gabriel, 128n31
Ruggles, Richard, 31
Russian Federation, 4
rusty blackbird, 80

Sacks, Robert D., 46–47n5
Sacred Dance Religion. *See* Sahaptin
Sacs, 35–45
sagebrush, 133
Sahaptin, 173–75, 178, 184
Said, Edward, 30
salmon, 173–92
Salmonscam, 186, 187–88
San, 3, 18, 262–64
sand dunes, 130, 135
Sanders, Alexander, 161
Sanders, George, 161, 162
Sanders, Todd, 118
sandhill cranes, 72, 76
sandpipers, 80, 90n14
sarsaparilla, 59
Sata, Michael, 210
SATMERG (South African Traditional Medicines Research Group), 270–77, 279
Sauks, 35
scarlet tanagers, 80
scaup, 90n14
Schuster, Helen, 175
Schwartz, Nancy, 239n37
science, Western
　African superstition and, 63
　as ally, 174
　bird name categories, 75, 79, 80, 84
　critiques of, 16
　ecological problems answered by, 143

science, Western (cont'd)
    environmental change and, 11
    folk knowledge overwhelmed by, 84
    oppositions between indigenous
        knowledge and, 2, 19
    plant species, 138
    product of culture, 143
    supplementing spirituality/traditional
        knowledge, 188
scissor-tailed flycatcher, 74
Scott, Gillian, 270
Scott, James C., 8, 10, 131, 148–49n29
screech owl, 73, 74, 78, 82
scripture, 104, 221
scrub jay, 75
SCS (Soil Conservation Service), 129, 132–33,
    134, 135, 136, 137
SDI (Spatial Development Initiative), 293,
    300
sea lions, 190
seals/sealing, 243–48, 251
sea swallow, 90n14
Second World War, 63, 64
segregation, 288, 293
    See also apartheid
semipalmated plover, 90n14
Seneca, 218
serpents. *See* snakes
Seven Drums Religion. *See* Sahaptin
Seven Years' War, 155
sex, 125n11, 153, 201, 203, 230
sexuality, 221, 224–25
shamans, 55, 175
sharp-shinned hawks, 73
sharp winged hawks, 75
sheep, 105, 129–32, 137–43, 150n40, 225
Sheridan, Michael, 12
Shevky, Eshref, 137
shike-poke, 76
Shimwalule, 201, 202–3, 207–8
Shipton, Parker, 8, 16, 17
shirt-tail, 76
shoveler, 90n14
shrikes, 75, 83
shrines, 202–3, 205–6, 209, 211–12n10
Sibanda, Sipho, 292–93, 296
Sibley, George, 37
sickle-cell hemoglobin, 56
Sioux, 33–38, 44, 219

Sillitoe, Paul, 2
Simtustus, 178
siskin, 73
skins
    animal, 33, 163, 220, 225
    sealskins, 247
skulkers, 76
slaves, 3, 8, 60, 69, 70, 78–79, 206, 209, 222,
    289
slave trade, 61, 77, 203, 204
Slockish, Wilbur, 185, 186, 191
Slockish, Wilbur, Jr., 190–91
Slocum, John, 218
smallpox, 53
    African epidemics, 121, 123
    Cherokee epidemic, 14, 151–65
    dance, 14, 151–57, 162–63, 165
    Iowa epidemic, 34, 36
    suicides, 153
Smith, McKee A., 184
SmithKlineBeecham, 270
Smohalla, 184
snakeroot, 67n18
snakes
    bites of, 143
    classification of, 8
    in scripture, 221
    social movements and symbols of, 216–34
    as smallpox cause, 162
snakeweed, 132, 134, 142–43
snipes, 75, 85
Snow, Milton, 134–35
snow goose, 76
Sohappy, David., Jr., 186
Sohappy, David, Sr., 184–87, 191
Sohappy, Myra, 184, 187
Soil Conservation Service (SCS), 129, 132–33,
    134, 135, 136, 137
Soil Erosion Service, 132
songs, ritual
    African, 117–18, 156
    Cherokee, 38, 156
    Navajo, 139–40
    Sahaptin/Wáašat, 173, 178
song sparrow, 80, 91n23
Sophocles, 221
soras, 88
South African Druggist, 270
South African Materia Medica, 265

South African Native Trust, 288
South African Traditional Medicines Research Group (SATMERG), 270–77, 279
South African War, 94, 98, 99, 105
Sparks, Allister, 294–95
sparrow hawk, 72, 76
sparrows, 73, 74, 75, 76, 78, 90n13, 91n23
   Cherokee naming of, 80
   folk beliefs about, 85
Spatial Development Initiative (SDI), 293, 300
Species Plantarum (Linnaeus), 61–62
spirit-birds, 73, 79, 83, 87
spiritual chaos/disorder, 138, 139
spirit of God, 162
spirits
   ancestral, 196–210
   animal, 167n11, 176, 220, 224–25, 227, 228, 233
   evil, 156, 157, 237n18
   fertility brought by, 153, 196
   guardian/tutelary, 175–76, 220, 249
   as illness cause/cure, 54–55, 60, 65n4, 154, 156
   male/female, 156
   nature, 199, 205
   possession by, 209, 230
   See also animism; spirit-birds
spoonbill, 83
spotted eagle, 219
Squaxin, 218
Stahl, Leslie, 264
Stevens, Isaac, 245, 247, 250–51, 252
stories, traditional
   animal, 78–79, 87, 88, 218–24, 228, 233
   biblical, 86, 87, 225
   creation, 138–39
   earth/land, 138, 140–41, 143
   explaining control/threats, 122–23
   See also oral tradition
storks, 75, 82
storm petrels, 86, 87
Strachey, William, 72
Strong, Ted, 188–89
substance abuse, 223
   See also alcohol; cannabis; drugs, mind altering
Sudan, 226, 232
suicide, 153

summer duck, 75
summer tanagers, 75, 80
sun dance, 218
superstition, 63, 101, 140, 151, 182
surf scoter, 72
sutherlandia, 278–79
Swahili, 204, 206, 229
swallows, 73, 75, 90n14
   remedies using, 84
   folk beliefs regarding, 85, 86, 88
swallow-tailed kite, 75
swamp blackbird, 76
Swan, James, 245–46, 248–49
swans, 72, 82, 84, 87
swifts, 75, 76, 83
Symbionese Liberation Army, 228–28

tanagers, 75, 80
Tanzania, 118, 213n25, 227, 238nn29, 31
Tatoosh, Chief, 250
Tatoosh Island, 250
tawny owl, 76, 86
taxation, 31
Taylor, Joseph, 176–77
TB. *See* tuberculosis
teals, 75, 81
Tenochtitlan, 228
tenure, indigenous, 9, 12, 243–53, 287–301
Teotihuacan, 228
TEK (traditional environmental knowledge), 6
terns, 90n14
The Dalles, Oregon, 173, 176, 177, 179
   dam, 173, 182, 183
Thembuland, 114, 115, 116–17, 119
Thompson, Tommy, 177, 182–83
Thonning, Peter, 62, 68n25
Thornthwaite, C. Warren, 135, 136
thoroughwart, 58
thrashers, 73
thrushes, 73, 75
Tierradentro, Colombia, 228
titmouse, 76
tomtits, 75, 76
tongue. *See* languages
Tóp-tut, 180–81
totemism, 17, 219, 236n13, 239n34
tourism, 10
Towessnute, 180–81

towhees, 72, 76, 77
town sparrow, 76
trading post bird, 74
trading posts, 139
traditional environmental knowledge (TEK), 6
Traditional Healer's Primary Care Book (TRAMED), 260, 272, 273, 276
Traditional Leadership and Governance Framework Act (TLGFA), 294, 295, 297
Traditional Medicine Program (TRAMED), 260–62, 269–80
Transkei, 113–23, 293
treaties, 13, 15, 244
    Iowas (1815), 36, 44, 51n32
    Makah (1855), 244–45, 246, 247, 250–53
    Mid-Columbia (1855), 178–91
    Neah Bay, 244–45, 252
    Prairie du Chien (1825; 1830), 37–44, 51n38
    Sacs (1804; 1837), 35, 38, 44
Tropp, Jacob, 14, 15, 130
Tse-kaw-wootl, 250–51
Tswana, 296, 299
tuberculosis, 159, 277, 270, 275
Tuhsiwalliti, 159
tulip tree, 58
turkey-buzzard, 75
turkey cock, 72
turkeys, 72, 73, 75, 79, 81, 82, 83, 89n4
turkey vulture, 73, 89n4
Turner, Victor, 208
turtle doves, 75, 76
Tyghs, 178
Tyger, 158
Tylor, Edward, 219

Ubutwa, 205, 214n34
Uganda, 226–27, 231, 234
ulcers, 275, 279
Umatilla Indian Reservation, 186, 192
Umatilla River, 182
Unilever, 262, 263, 282n14
United Nations, 4
United States Indian Claims Commission, 51n38
University of Cape Town, 260, 269
U.S. Cavalry, 219

vaccines, 14, 151, 163, 164, 165n1
Vai, 78
Vancouver Island, 245, 249–50
Vann Crutchfield, Margaret, 159
van Sittert, Lance, 5, 14, 261
Vawda, Sahid, 289
vireos, 75, 76
virgins, 125n11, 201
vultures, 73, 75, 76, 83, 89n4
    folk beliefs about, 82, 86, 220

Wáašat. *See* Sahaptin
Walker, Deward, 175
Wallahee, Jim, 181
Walla Walla Council, 178, 179–80
warblers, 74, 75, 80, 87, 90nn6, 13
Warm Springs, 173, 186
War of 1812, 51n32
Wasco Council, 178
Waselkov, Gregory, 31
Washats, 16
Washines, Lavina, 186–87
Washington State, 243–53
Watchtower, 207
waterbirds, 72, 73, 75, 81, 83, 84
water divining, 5, 14, 94–106
Watt, J., 266, 284n32
weapons, 82, 31
    See also guns
weather, predicting, 85, 86, 245–46, 247
Webb, James L. A., Jr., 8, 13
Weber, Max, 219, 230
weeds, 58, 132–33, 134, 142, 262
weevils, 128n31
Weisiger, Marsha, 14, 15, 16
whales/whaling, 18, 225, 243–53
whip-poor-wills, 73, 74, 75, 78, 84, 86
whiskey jack, 91n17
whisky, 59
White, John, 72
White, Richard, 13, 166–67n5, 366
white bird, 116
white-breasted nuthatch, 73
White Cloud, 39, 41, 43
white crane, 76
white-throated sparrows, 80
WHO (World Health Organization), 270, 278
whooting owl, 75, 76

wifeswapping, 205
wigeon, 72, 75
Wild Coast SDI, 293, 300
willets, 75
Wilson, Alexander, 84, 88
Wilson, Jack, 218
Wind River, 183
wine, 59, 84
wild cherry tree, 58, 66n11
Williams, Gladis, 272–73
willow trees/bark, 59, 67n17, 85
Winichakul, Thongchai, 46–47n5
Winnebago, 38
winter wrens, 73
witchcraft, 86, 197, 207, 223, 266, 271, 276
witch doctors, 115, 273
witches, 82, 157, 207
Wittgenstein, Ludwig, 217
wives, head, 203, 204
"wives of the relics," 202
Wolf River, 29, 40
women
    council members, 294, 295
    fertility of young women, 114, 119
    muthi collectors, 268
    spiritual movement leaders, 219, 220
    in ritual practices, 117–19, 156–57
Wood, Denis, 48n11
woodcocks, 75
wood ducks, 73, 75, 83
woodpeckers, 70, 72, 74, 75, 76
    in Cherokee magical formulas, 82–83
    Cherokee names for, 79–80
    Chickasaw/Choctaw name for, 78
    Gullah name for, 78
    order distinguished by Linnaeus, 81
    portents of, 86
wood pigeon, 72

Woodward, David, 30
Woody, Elizabeth, 173–74
World Bank, 4, 10
World Health Organization (WHO), 270, 278
World Trade Organization, 262
Wounded Knee, 218, 219, 234
Wovoka, 218
wrens, 73, 75, 76, 83, 86

Yakamas, 175, 178–91
Yakima River, 182
Yakimas. *See* Yakamas
Yallup, Galen, 187
yellow-bellied sapsucker, 80
yellow-billed cuckoo, 76
yellow-breasted chat, 76, 83
yellow-crowned night herons, 77
yellow-hammer, 76
yellow hooded titmouse, 76
yellow poplar, 58
yellow-throated vireos, 76
Young, Robert, 207
Young Wolf, 158

Zambia, 210, 227
Zaujuka, 159
Zeh, William, 131–32
Zeus, 86
Zimbabwe, 125n9, 222, 231
zoology, 12
Zululand, 267
    nationalist Inkatha Freedom Party of, 289
    women/girls of, 117–18, 125n11, 126n14
Zuma, Jacob, 300
Zuma, Nkosazana Dlamini, 270

www.ingramcontent.com/pod-product-compliance
Lightning Source LLC
Chambersburg PA
CBHW031232290426
44109CB00012B/260